THOEMMES PRESS
IDEALISM SERIES

THOEMMES

ALSO AVAILABLE

Current Issues in Idealism
Edited and Introduced by Paul Coates and Daniel D. Hutto
ISBN 1 85506 434 0 : 308pp : Pb : £14.95
ISBN 1 85506 435 9 : 308pp : Hb : £45.00

Perspectives on the Logic and Metaphysics of F. H. Bradley
Edited and Introduced by W. J. Mander
ISBN 1 85506 432 4 : 306pp : Pb : £14.95
ISBN 1 85506 433 2 : 306pp : Hb : £45.00

The Politics of Conscience: T. H. Green and his Age
Melvin Richter
ISBN 1 85506 487 1 : 415pp : 1964 edition : Pb : £14.95
ISBN 1 85506 486 3 : 415pp : 1964 edition : Hb : £45.00

Printed in England by Antony Rowe Ltd

Philosophy after F. H. BRADLEY

A Collection of Essays

by

Leslie Armour
James Bradley
Walter Creery
David Crossley
Philip Dwyer
Phillip Ferreira
Paul D. Forster
Nicholas Griffin

Lorne Maclachlan
Don MacNiven
Lionel Rubinoff
William Sweet
Elizabeth Trott
Michael Walsh
Fred Wilson

Edited with a Preface by
James Bradley
Memorial University of Newfoundland

THOEMMES PRESS

© Thoemmes Press, 1996

Published by
Thoemmes Press
11 Great George Street
Bristol BS1 5RR
England

Philosophy after F. H. Bradley

ISBN 1 85506 485 5 – Paperback
ISBN 1 85506 484 7 – Hardback

British Library Cataloguing-in-Publication Data
A CIP record of this book is available from the British Library

All rights reserved. Except for the quotation of short passages for the purposes of criticism and review, no part of this book may be reproduced or transmitted in any form or by any means, electronic, mechanical, photocopying, recording, without the prior written permission of the publisher.

CONTENTS

List of Abbreviations   vii

Preface by James Bradley   ix

1   F. H. Bradley and Later Idealism: From Disarray to Reconstruction
Leslie Armour   1

2   F. H. Bradley and Bosanquet
William Sweet   31

3   F. H. Bradley and the Canadian Connection
Elizabeth Trott   57

4   F. H. Bradley and C. A. Campbell
Lorne Maclachlan   73

5   Brand Blanshard – A 'Student' of F. H. Bradley
Michael Walsh   91

6   The Autonomy of History: Collingwood's Critique of F. H. Bradley's Copernican Revolution in Historical Knowledge
Lionel Rubinoff   127

7   From Presence to Process: F. H. Bradley and A. N. Whitehead
James Bradley   147

8   Unity, Theory and Practice: F. H. Bradley and Pragmatism
Paul D. Forster   169

Contents

9 F. H. Bradley's Contribution to the Development of Logic
   Nicholas Griffin ... 195

10 F. H. Bradley on Truth and Judgement
   Walter Creery ... 231

11 F. H. Bradley's Impact on Empiricism
   Fred Wilson ... 251

12 F. H. Bradley's Attack on Associationism
   Phillip Ferreira ... 283

13 *Justification and the Foundations of Empirical Knowledge*
   David Crossley ... 307

14 *Bradley, Russell, and Analysis*
   Philip Dwyer ... 331

15 *Bradley and MacIntyre: A Comparison*
   Don MacNiven ... 349

List of Contributors ... 367

LIST OF ABBREVIATIONS

All references in the text to the works of Bradley employ the following abbreviations:

AR	*Appearance and Reality* (Oxford, 1893; 2nd ed., Oxford, 1897).
CE	*Collected Essays* (Oxford, 1935).
ES	*Ethical Studies* (Oxford, 1876; 2nd ed., 1927).
ETR	*Essays on Truth and Reality* (Oxford, 1914).
PL	*Principles of Logic* (Oxford, 1883; 2nd ed., 1922; corrected impression, 1928).

PREFACE

The present collection of essays has arisen out of papers and discussions which were part of a day-long Symposium, with the same title, held at the Canadian Philosophical Association's Annual Meeting, Queen's University, Kingston, Ontario, in May 1991. Since then, new papers have been added and there has been a great deal of discussion and mutual criticism amongst the contributors. Far from representing a set of final conclusions, however, this volume is intended by the contributors to throw open to wider audiences a debate on a particular aspect of twentieth-century Anglo-American philosophy, an aspect which all regard as of considerable importance, historically and conceptually.

There can be little doubt that the time is now ripe for a consideration of the place of F. H. Bradley (1846–1924) in our philosophical tradition. While lip-service is usually paid to his dominating presence in Anglo-American philosophy around the turn of the century, the conventional wisdom has it that he was more or less completely eclipsed by subsequent developments. But this is a version of events which in the last few years has been powerfully challenged[1] – a challenge which the present collections of essays attempts to develop in new directions.

The collection does not pretend to be complete, but to offer the first, reasonably comprehensive accounts of the relations of Bradley's work to other thinkers in his own time and subsequently. His impact and influence on developments in

---

[1] See, for example, Nicholas Griffin, *Russell's Idealist Apprenticeship* (Oxford: Clarendon Press, 1991); Peter Hylton, *Russell, Idealism, and the Emergence of Analytical Philosophy* (Oxford: Clarendon Press, 1990); Don MacNiven, *Bradley's Moral Psychology* (New York: Edwin Mellen Press, 1987); Anthony Manser, *Bradley's Logic* (Oxford: Basil Blackwell, 1985); Anthony Manser and Guy Stock (eds.), *The Philosophy of F. H. Bradley* (Oxford: Clarendon Press, 1984); Peter P. Nicholson, *The Political Philosophy of the British Idealists* (Cambridge University Press, 1990).

idealism, pragmatism, modern logic, empiricism and analytical philosophy are considered, as well as his connections with outstanding individual thinkers such as Collingwood and Whitehead. The collection is not, however, intended only to speak to important features of the history of Anglo-American philosophy in the present century. Central philosophical topics (such as relations, truth, historicity, sensation, and self-realization ethics) are discussed from a variety of perspectives, and it is the aim of the contributors to show that both Bradley's work and the reactions which it generated – critical as well as positive – are of considerable and continuing significance in philosophical debate on these topics. Indeed, the contributors will be satisfied if this collection helps toward dissolving that artificial and distorting division between the history of philosophy and philosophical argument which has often been a feature of academic discussion over the last decades in English-speaking countries.

James Bradley
Memorial University
St John's, Newfoundland, 1996

F. H. BRADLEY AND LATER IDEALISM: FROM DISARRAY TO RECONSTRUCTION

Leslie Armour

1. *Idealism at the Time of Bradley's Death*
Three of the four major figures in the English idealist movement – Bernard Bosanquet, F. H. Bradley, and J. M. E. McTaggart – died in three successive years, Bosanquet in 1923, Bradley in 1924, and McTaggart in 1925. The fourth, Thomas Hill Green, had died in 1882, a full two generations before. Several of the most important of the English-speaking idealists outside England, John and Edward Caird in Scotland, and Josiah Royce and George Holmes Howison in the United States were gone, too, the Cairds before the First World War, Royce and Howison during it. J. H. Muirhead was nearing seventy, and J. A. Smith was over sixty at Bradley's death.[1] Muirhead was, above all, an historian and an editor. As for Smith, a little earlier T. S. Eliot had reported him 'unknown outside Oxford'. H. H. Joachim, a mere stripling in his mid-fifties, was, Eliot said, 'the best philosopher here [at Oxford]',[2] but he was not to be another Bradley. In Canada, John Watson was to live on another fifteen years,[3] and John Macdonald was to go on much longer, but Watson's main

---

[1] In the nature of things, this paper, which is part of a collection of papers devoted to idealism after F. H. Bradley, is about idealism in the English-speaking world, though that reasonably includes philosophy written in English in India. Idealism elsewhere – French and Italian idealism, for instance – are not less important. But they are quite different, and, despite the relations between philosophers like J. A. Smith and R. G. Collingwood and the Italian idealists, they developed separately and in different ways and cannot be dealt with intelligently in the span of a single paper.

[2] See Eliot's letters to William Green, and to Norbert Wiener, *Letters of T. S. Eliot*, ed. Valerie Eliot (London: Faber and Faber, 1988), vol. 1, pp. 65–6.

[3] Watson struggled hard with Bradley's legacy. See Elizabeth Trott's contribution to this volume and chapters 7 and 8 of Leslie Armour and Elizabeth Trott, *The Faces of Reason* (Waterloo: Wilfrid Laurier University Press, 1981).

work was completed, and Macdonald was isolated in Alberta. James Edward Creighton, another Canadian, who became the first president of the American Philosophical Association, died in the same year as Bradley.

Still, idealists had no reason for despair. Three young men, Brand Blanshard, R. G. Collingwood and G. R .G. Mure were beginning to make their marks. Blanshard, more influenced by Bradley than by Royce, and more concerned with trying to rescue reason from its detractors than with metaphysics, was thirty-two when Bradley died. R. G. Collingwood, who was nearly as much historian as philosopher and who was attracted by the Italian philosophers of history,[4] was thirty-five years old. G. R. G. Mure, the most deeply concerned with Hegel himself, had come to Oxford as an undergraduate in 1912 and was a few years younger. In the United States, William Ernest Hocking, an engineer turned philosopher was in mid-career. So was R. F. Alfred Hoernlé, long associated with South Africa, though he was actually a British citizen of German descent and he also taught at Harvard and Newcastle.[5]

But there were serious problems. Bradley was a majestic figure, admired even by his critics, including Russell.[6] His dry wit and gentle self-mockery made him immune from the common charges that idealist philosophy was a mere tinsel wrapping for a waning religion or a vague but convenient intellectual cover for miscellaneous do-gooders who were really acting on their intuitions.

Idealists who followed him had to deal with a philosophy whose central core seemed to admit no development. And they had difficulty occupying the gap he had left in the intellectual life of the moment.

[4] The extent to which Bradley himself contributed to setting Collingwood's agenda is discussed in this volume by Lionel Rubinoff.

[5] Hocking was born in 1873 and lived on to 1966. Hoernlé was born in 1880 and died in 1943. A large number of the lesser figures in the idealist movement were middle-aged at the time of Bradley's death: Edgar Sheffield Brightman, 1884–1953; Mary Wilton Calkins, 1863–1930; May Sinclair, 1863–1946; G. Watts Cunningham, 1881–1968; Ralph Tyler Flewelling, 1871–1960; Albertus C. Knudson, 1873–1953; Joseph Alexander Leighton, 1870–1955; and Alfred Henry Lloyd, 1864–1927. John Elof Boodin, 1869–1950, is also often counted as an idealist.

[6] Bradley and Russell are discussed in this volume by Fred Wilson and Philip Dwyer.

But if Bradley's ineffable Absolute provoked no immediate and satisfactory development, it was partly because he insisted that, though it was a unity of 'the various aspects of experience', its nature was such that the unity itself was essentially 'unknown' (*AR* 414). It may well have been these words which prompted John Watson to say 'nothing is left but the fiction of a reality that we can only define as that which is indefinable'.[7]

The problem with which Bradley presents us has much to do with the general method of argument and exposition which he used in *AR*.[8] He proceeds reductively. Bradley argues that every way of dividing reality fails. It fails because there is no coherent account of relations which permits one to describe the unity on which the diversity depends. That failure, if one analyses Bradley's argument with care, seems to depend on a principle which is always at the centre of Bradley's philosophy: the principle of unity in difference. A relation, that is, holds only if there is some sense in which two terms form a unity and some sense in which they are distinct. Their distinctness can be stated, but their unity cannot be stated clearly without creating an apparent contradiction with the statement of their difference. The unity of all the relations is the Absolute and, in its guise as unity nothing can be said about it. Of course, many things can be said about the ways in which this unity manifests aspects of its nature in various pluralities, and Bradley's philosophy is really about those things which can be said. But all of them in some sense falsify the nature of the Absolute.

It requires an acute mind to discern the reality of Bradley's Absolute and a patient one to live with it. In fact Bradley did suggest that there might well be a positive metaphysical doctrine which would be a kind of dialectical counterpart to the negations he delighted in, and he gave some hints about it. I have discussed these elsewhere, and I shall return to this question later in this paper and suggest, once more, that there

---

[7] John Watson, *The Interpretation of Religious Experience* (Glasgow: Maclehose, 1912), vol. 2, p. 216.

[8] See note 7 above. Bradley's basic argument about relations, put forward in 1893, was not changed in later editions.

4 *Philosophy After F. H. Bradley*

is somewhere to go from Bradley's account of the Absolute.[9] Yet, on the face of it, at the time of Bradley's death, the Bradleyan 'Absolute' did not seem to the young philosophers to be a good subject matter for a research project. Indeed, some thinkers, like John Findlay, have suggested that Bradley's theory of the Absolute was quite inadequate and even that Bradley was an 'amateur' of Absolute theory.[10]

Bradley also occupied a special place because his philosophy, in important ways, looks forward to problems which were to become dominant in the middle and latter parts of this century. *James* Bradley has made a detailed and imposing case for this position, and it is, at any rate, unarguable that Bradley poses hard questions.[11] If, as some of Bradley's readers supposed, the ultimately real cannot be coherently talked about, and, if, as F. H. Bradley argued as well, there is no univocal and finally coherent concept of the self which is trying to talk about the world, then we are on a

---

[9] In his reply to Professor James Ward's critique of *AR*, Bradley says there is a metaphysics which could solve the problem. He speaks first of the principle that the Absolute, 'realized perfectly in no one part of the universe, ... still is realized in every part, and it seems manifest in a scale of degrees, the higher of which comprehends the lower'. Then he says '...the system of metaphysics...which I have not tried to write, would aim at arranging the facts of the world on this principle, the same principle which outside philosophy is unconsciously used to judge of higher and lower' (*CE* 685). (The reply is to James Ward's review of *AR* in *Mind*, vol. 3 ns, no. 10, pp. 232–9.) Bradley even called for a new religion based on a positive metaphysics. In his essay entitled 'God and the Absolute' he says: 'There is...a need, and there is even a certain demand, for a new religion. We want a creed to recognize and justify in due proportion all human interests, and at the same time to supply the intellect with that to which it can hold with confidence' (*ETR* 446). If it exists, Bradley's new creed would have to be founded on the experiences which point up the need for it. He insists that there is an aspect of direct experience involved in such a religion, but he says that this will not be enough. His view in *ETR* is that, although what is needed, in one sense, is '...a religious belief founded otherwise than on metaphysics', we do need 'a metaphysics able in some sense to justify' that creed. He says here, too, that he has not produced that metaphysics, but he adds: 'though the obstacles in its way are certainly great, ...I cannot regard it as impossible' (*ETR* 446–7). The direct experience which is essential seems to be moral experience when one examines Bradley's writings for clues. See my essay in Philip MacEwan (ed.), *Ethics, Metaphysics, and Religion in the Thought of F. H. Bradley* (Queenston: Edwin Mellin, forthcoming).

[10] J. N. Findlay, 'Bradley's Contribution to Absolute-theory', in Anthony Manser and Guy Stock (eds.), *The Philosophy of F. H. Bradley* (Oxford: Clarendon Press, 1984), pp. 269–84.

[11] See James Bradley, 'Process and Historical Crisis in F. H. Bradley's Ethics of Feeling', in *Ethics, Metaphysics, and Religion in the Thought of F. H. Bradley* (see note 9).

path which leads naturally enough through the philosophical worriers about language to the deconstructionists.

But it was also Bradley the man who seemed unlikely to have a philosophical heir. The young T. S. Eliot, fleeing the resolutely forward-looking world of Royce and James, evidently found in Bradley's dark ironies a glimpse of the wasteland.[12] The small riddles of Bradley's life added to the attraction.

He was reputed to be a recluse, but he had at least one close woman friend. His health was said to be bad, though he wrote more than is usually expected of healthy men. And he maintained a shooting gallery above his rooms at Merton. It is reported that he went out shooting cats at night.[13]

The young Brand Blanshard, for whom being reasonable was nearly everything, was written off by T. S. Eliot as 'one who defended with great zeal all the great American fallacies', though we are not told what these were. For one, like Eliot, fleeing America, the fault, one fears, was in Blanshard's stars and not in himself.[14]

Theoretically, the systems of Bosanquet and McTaggart were more easily susceptible of refinement and of development. Bosanquet's Absolute is a kind of systematic unity – a unity which derives its claim on our intelligence precisely because of its power to organize knowledge and life.[15] One could test claims about it, therefore, empirically. One could look at the tendency of these sciences to merge together into a single unified intelligible claim to truth. One could also test

---

[12] But this is not F. H. Bradley's view of himself or his own view of his relation to the pragmatists. Paul D. Forster, in this volume, notices actual affinities between Dewey and Bradley.

[13] All these momentous matters are duly reported in Richard Wollheim's *F. H. Bradley* (Harmondsworth, Middlesex: Penguin Books, 1959).

[14] Blanshard's commitment to reason and to reasonableness is explored in depth in this volume by Michael Walsh.

[15] In fact there are differences between Bradley's and Bosanquet's ethical theories which derive from these differences. See William Sweet's essay in this volume.

them logically by examining the notion of a demonstrably complete and organically unified system of inference.[16]

Two things obviously told against Bosanquet's claims about the Absolute. One was the increasing fragmentation of knowledge itself. The unity of science might remain a pious dream, but it was a simple fact that, since very few practitioners by the end of the first quarter of the twentieth century would want to claim to understand more than a fraction of it, it was becoming increasingly difficult to say how one could show that all the bits of science did or did not fit together.

Everyone still admitted that, if a proposition in biology contradicted one in chemistry, one of them would have to go. The problem was to determine the way in which the pieces fitted together. Different vocabularies, different observational techniques, and different interests characterize the different sciences. There are points of intersection between physics and biology, but who is to say that everything in physics is consistent with everything in biology? Indeed, some biologists have argued forcefully for the notion that there are logically different kinds of laws in the two sciences.[17]

By Bradley's death, problems about the possibility of a system which could embrace the totality of things had already been posed by Russell's paradox. Other problems would shortly emerge from Gödel's proof. Bosanquet had developed a logic which did not really arise from claims about classes and their assembly but rather was developed from conceptual analyses of the ways in which the totality could be expressed. Thus, idealist logicians might have defended themselves against the Russells and Gödels in a number of ways.[18] But Bosanquet's own beginning on this project – directed specifically against Russell – was not seriously pursued at the time

---

[16] This theme runs through all Bosanquet's works, but the essays in *Science and Philosophy*, ed. J. H. Muirhead and R. C. Bosanquet (London: George Allen and Unwin, 1927), illustrate many of its details. Perhaps something of the development of Bosanquet's thought can be gleaned from these essays as well.

[17] See Ernst Mayr, *Toward a New Philosophy of Biology* (Cambridge, Mass.: Harvard University Press, 1988). This debate has been intermittent throughout the century.

[18] See especially Bosanquet, *Logic or the Morphology of Knowledge*, 2 vols., 2nd ed. (Oxford: Clarendon Press, 1911). Bosanquet makes a start on this project, vol. 2, pp. 40–49.

largely because the main interests of idealist philosophers were not in logic.[19] Josiah Royce grasped the point: 'I think it probable that at least some of God's people will in the near future be saved in part by Symbolic Logic', he said.[20] Moreover, he knew logic might prove to be the Achilles' heel of idealism.[21] And, indeed, 'idealist logic' remains a subject of controversy.[22]

The main thrust of Bosanquet's views on science did reemerge nearly two decades later in Errol Harris's *Nature, Mind and Modern Science*, and Harris did indeed, in due course, devote himself to some of the central logical problems which Bosanquet had left unfinished.[23] But by the time Harris turned to logic, the tide had long turned.

McTaggart's deductive system was developed in the form in which we possess it only after he had abandoned dialectical logic. It, too, fell somewhat easy prey to doubts about how logic and language are to be related to reality – doubts, after all, set in train by Bradley himself.

Though McTaggart's *Further Determination of the Absolute* was intended to – and did – respond to some of the weaknesses in Bradley's notion of the Absolute, the massive

---

[19] There are interesting discussions in C. R. Morris, *Idealistic Logic* (1933; reprinted Port Washington, New York: Kennikat Press, 1970). Some issues are explored in Leslie Armour, *Logic and Reality* (Assen: Royal Vangorcum, and New York: Humanities Press, 1972), and others in Errol Harris, *Formal, Transcendental and Dialectical Thinking* (Albany: State University of New York Press, 1987), and H. H. Joachim, *Logical Studies* (Oxford: Clarendon Press, 1948). Most revealing is Peter Hylton, *Russell, Idealism, and the Emergence of Analytic Philosophy* (Oxford: Clarendon Press, 1990), and Anthony Manser, *Bradley's Logic* (Oxford: Clarendon Press, 1983).

[20] Address of 19 October 1903 to the Philosophical Conference at Harvard. Quoted in John Clendenning, *The Life and Thought of Josiah Royce* (Madison: University of Wisconsin Press, 1985), p. 309.

[21] Royce's concern with logic is shown in Daniel S. Robinson (ed.), *Royce's Logical Essays* (Dubuque, Iowa: William C. Brown, 1951). There is more material in the Harvard archives. Royce's concerns are cogently discussed in Bruce Kuklick, *Josiah Royce, An Intellectual Biography* (Indianapolis: Bobbs-Merrill, 1972).

[22] Nicholas Griffin and Walter Creery explore some of the controversies elsewhere in this volume.

[23] Errol Harris, *Nature, Mind, and Modern Science* (London: George Allen and Unwin, 1954). Harris's logical work emerged only in 1987 (see note 19 above).

three-volume study of his system by C. D. Broad led to the belief that his whole system could readily be demolished.[24] No publisher would welcome four volumes on Broad's three volumes devoted to McTaggart's two volumes.

2. Bradley in India

It is interesting, very briefly, to contrast the situation in England and America with the situation in India. Bradley has had a continuous, if never dominant, influence in India. There are many reasons, all of them associated in one way or another with the cultural and political circumstances there, and with the traditions of Indian philosophy.

In a way the Bradleyan Absolute is a model of the official ideal of the British Empire – a unity which manifests itself in an indefinite plurality – and so it provided a vehicle through which Indian philosophers could make contact with the imperial culture without sacrificing their own traditions. And Bradley's philosophy was close enough to the main themes of the Vedantist traditions, so that he could be used as a bridge between modes of thought by Indian philosophers who wanted to show Englishmen that their own traditions had much in them from which Europeans might learn.

But in a very precise way Bradley, in fact, addressed some traditional concerns within Indian philosophy. He could be used by those seeking a middle ground in the ancient controversy between the followers of Sankara and the followers of Ramanuja – between the most Absolute monists and those who wanted to allow a measure of pluralism. When Sarvepalli Radhakrishnan wanted to insist that one need not choose between these traditional positions, he seems to have had in mind something like the distinction which Bradley put forward. In a reply to E. H. Strange, Bradley said that

---

[24] See S. V. Keeling (ed.), *Philosophical Studies by the late J. M. E. McTaggart* (London: Edward Arnold, 1934), pp. 210–72 and, of course, *The Nature of Existence* (Cambridge University Press, 1921, 1927), 2 vols. (vol. 2, ed. C. D. Broad); and C. D. Broad, *Examination of McTaggart's Philosophy*, 3 vols. (Cambridge University Press, 1933–8).

Strange was wrong to infer that, just because the idea of the soul involves inconsistency, the soul does not exist. 'How', he asks, 'could I possibly deny the existence of the soul?' (*CE* 697). And he underlines this in *ETR*. There, he concedes that 'most of us would agree' that the 'contradictory is unreal'. Yet, he says, 'the self-contradictory in some sense exists' (*ETR* 269). The explanation that he gives is that the 'contradiction is erroneous only because it is deficient' (*ETR* 272). In Radhakrishnan's *An Idealist View of Life*, there are echoes of this idea.[25]

Bradley is mentioned in a third of the essays in the first series of *Contemporary Indian Philosophy*, published in 1936 and almost a quarter of those in the second series, published in 1974.[26] Sushil Saxena's 1967 *Studies in the Metaphysics of F. H. Bradley* testifies to the continuing interest in Bradley himself.[27] Most interesting, perhaps, is the fact that the Bradley–Sankara issue continues to fascinate Indian philosophers, as Ganeswar Misra's 1986 and S. P. Dubey's 1987 studies show.[28]

3. *Blanshard, Collingwood and Mure*

In America and England, though, after the First World War, the cultural and political circumstances, if anything, discouraged monistic idealism which had come to seem unduly optimistic and unduly rational. A natural reaction was to turn to philosophical enquiries which questioned the soundness of all claims to knowledge except those of the scientific-technological tradition. To this situation, one natural response was Blanshard's. If one cannot develop the

---

[25] S. Radhakrishnan, *An Idealist View of Life* (London: George Allen and Unwin, 1932; 2nd ed. revised, 1937). There are eight mentions of Bradley. See especially the discussion of experience and unity on pp. 135–6.

[26] *Contemporary Indian Philosophy*, first series, S. Radhakrishnan and J. H. Muirhead (eds.), 1936; second series, Margaret Chatterjee (ed.), 1974 – both published in London by George Allen and Unwin.

[27] Sushil Kumar Saxena, *Studies in the Metaphysics of Bradley* (London: George Allen and Unwin, 1967).

[28] Ganeswar Misra, *Sources of Monism, Bradley and Sankara* (Meerut, India: Anu Books, 1986); and S. P. Dubey, *Idealism, East and West* (Delhi: Bharatiya Vidya Prakashan, 1987).

Bradleyan Absolute and if Bosanquet's project was beginning to appear dubious, there was another possibility. One could look at what Bradley had regarded as the ways in which the Absolute manifested itself, not from the point of view of an ultimate metaphysic but from the perspective of the workings of human reason on experience.

The title of Blanshard's book, *The Nature of Thought*, makes the project clear.[29] One might think this a return to Kant, but Blanshard set himself the task of discovering just how reason and experience work together, and he set out to show that even the concepts of reason and experience themselves require for their explication a theoretical structure in which both are at work. One cannot pit them against one another as if one has a ready-made notion of experience or a ready-made concept of reason. The problems posed by experience and reason arise in this complete context and, if properly posed, can be answered with the resources with which we are provided. Kant is mentioned only three times in Blanshard's two volumes, each time in order to point out how he had laid the foundations for this view even if he did not develop it.[30]

As time went on, Blanshard increasingly wanted to call himself a rationalist – though he was his own kind of rationalist – rather than an idealist. He broke with a central strand of the idealist tradition in denying the unity of facts and values. 'Between the rational as logically necessary and the rational as morally right, there is an abyss of difference', he said.[31]

---

[29] Brand Blanshard, *The Nature of Truth*, 2 vols. (London: George Allen and Unwin, 1939).

[30] *The Nature of Truth* (see note 33), vol. 1, p. 76, where the authority of Kant is adduced for the proposition that 'we do not start below the categories in a region where there is nothing at all but sensation'; p. 79, where it is noted that 'most of Kant's critique is occupied with exhibiting the various relations to be found in the apprehension of a thing as a thing'; and vol. 2, p. 406 where Kant's account of the analytic–synthetic distinction is used to support, again, the interrelation of reason and experience.

[31] Brand Blanshard, *Reason and Analysis* (London: George Allen and Unwin; and La Salle, Ill.: Open Court, 1962), p. 491.

The argument is complex, but, evidently, if reason does not take us through to the Absolute, then the central (if pre-Bradleyan) idealist dream of a single unified body of knowledge which adequately represents reality is lost. If the unity is incomplete, we have lost the Platonic conjunction of goodness and reality.

Collingwood, also, rethought the idealist claims. In *Speculum Mentis*, published in the year of Bradley's death, he carried on, though in a quite different way, Bosanquet's project: the search for the ways in which all the bits of human knowledge might fit together.[32] But Collingwood was seriously concerned with the apparently growing fragmentation of knowledge, and this gave his work a different twist. Bosanquet had seen all knowledge as forming a seamless whole, and he believed that the propositions or judgements which expressed it could all be linked together ultimately on a single level. This level is expressed as philosophy. Thus, he said, 'Philosophy is the connected system of the form or ultimate universal essence of all objects, including, of course, all systems of objects'.[33] Such a programme implies that though various kinds of insight into reality have many different conceptual and linguistic forms, there is a common currency into which they can all be cashed, and cashing them is the business of philosophy.

But in Collingwood's *Speculum Mentis*, art, religion, science, history and philosophy are seen as forming an ascending hierarchy of forms. These forms represent structures of the human mind, and philosophy, the last sentence says, is about 'the self-recognition of mind in its own mirror'.

Again, for all the Hegelian notions which animate *Speculum Mentis*, the book, from the title page to the last sentence, has a Kantian ring about it. But, like Blanshard, Collingwood tended to think that Kant had discovered more than he himself realized. 'The idealistic answer, (as Kant once for all

---

[32] R. G. Collingwood, *Speculum Mentis* (Oxford: Clarendon Press, 1924).

[33] *Science and Philosophy and Other Essays* (see note 11), p. 19. (This essay originally appeared in the *Proceedings of the Aristotelian Society*, vol. 15 ns (1915), pp. 1–21. The quotation therefore represents Bosanquet's view late in his life.)

pointed out)', Collingwood says, 'is that the mind's knowledge of itself is its knowledge of everything else.'[34] The map of the mind is the map of all mind, and therefore the map of all the intelligible objects which can be brought together. There could only be a world hidden from mind if there were something in the world which could not be seen in its own mirror. One could argue (and I think that this was what was in Collingwood's mind in his attacks on 'realism', which are frequently more acerbic than informative) that anyone who supposes that mind has some hidden properties which do not show in the mirror is confusing mind with what it is not, another thing in the world. Before Ryle, Collingwood was well settled into a position which denied that the mind was a kind of hidden machine.

If we cannot get beyond the mind in one sense, it is because we have no need to, but we can, of course, if there is a mind-in-general, get beyond the individual mind. If we cannot have literal realism, we can have intersubjectivity.

But how does mind-in-general show itself in the particular mind? Collingwood says it cannot be conceived of as 'one stupendous whole'. It unites the differences of 'my mind and other people's...as the concrete universal of history unites'.[35]

This needs some explanation. Mind, in any case, is social. The forms which it imposes on things are not simply empty categories, but the result of our shared thoughts. History came to play a decisive role for Collingwood much as it had for Vico: we can understand history because we make it, and because the same thought can be thought, in principle, by any mind.

Whereas in *Speculum Mentis* the fragmentation of knowledge has to do with the scale of the forms of knowledge, in Collingwood's later works, especially the *Essay on Metaphysics*,[36] the historical and social workings of the mind become more important. The limits of the human imagination – in the Coleridgean sense – are expressed at any

---

[34] *Speculum Mentis* (see note 32), p. 299.

[35] ibid.

[36] R. G. Collingwood, *Essay on Metaphysics* (Oxford: Clarendon Press, 1940).

historical moment by a set of absolute presuppositions which colour the ways in which the world is seen. Only a process of historical change can move us from one such sense to another.

Thus, though the absolute mind never wholly faded from sight, the claims of absolute idealism are tempered as Collingwood goes on by an increasing historicism and an increasing concern with the ways in which civilization and knowledge must go together – ending in the dark and difficult *New Leviathan*.[37] It would be wrong to think that Collingwood brought a concern with history which was wholly alien to British idealism. Lionel Rubinoff and others have pointed out the roots of historical concern in Bradley and Bosanquet.[38] But though, for instance, both Bosanquet's political philosophy and his theory of knowledge had an important place for historical knowledge, there is nothing in it which makes historical knowledge crucial and decisive in just the way it becomes for Collingwood. With that importance comes, inevitably, a scaling down of the claims of absolute idealism.

Just as Collingwood was not alone in being interested in history so he was not alone in finding himself in sympathy with the Italian idealists. J. A. Smith carefully delineated his own association with Croce and others.[39] As early as 1920 Smith had read a paper on Gentile to the Aristotelian Society.

G. R. G. Mure, who regarded himself as the most Hegelian of the British idealists, was also the most dedicated to the defence of a traditional absolute idealism, and he is best remembered for his studies of Hegel.[40] But his *Retreat from Truth* is a book from which, I suppose, all of us who continue

---

[37] R. G. Collingwood, *The New Leviathan* (Oxford: Clarendon Press, 1942).

[38] See Lionel Rubinoff's introduction and commentary to F. H. Bradley, *The Presuppositions of Critical History* (Toronto: Dent, 1968), and also his essay in this volume.

[39] *Contemporary British Philosophy*, first and second series, ed. J. H. Muirhead and H. D. Lewis, republished together, 1965, vol. 2 pp. 227–44.

[40] Especially Mure's majestic *Study of Hegel's Logic* (Oxford: Clarendon Press, 1950).

to be suspected of idealism, have at some time or another taken comfort.[41] In this book, toward the end, he outlines yet another strategy for dealing with the difficulties confronted in their different ways by Blanshard and Collingwood. Faced with the question of how the Absolute is to be construed and to be pursued in our world, he says 'Hegel's solution was to contend that to recognize a limit is already to have surpassed it'.[42] This is to say that in confronting all the ways in which we come to our limits, we come to see the nature of what lies on the other side of the limits. Thus we might imagine a series of studies which might examine religion, history, science, and, above all, perhaps, language, and try to show exactly how the limits posed by each of them is a sign of what must lie on the other side. Of course, if we were to do this effectively the idea of the Absolute would begin to take shape in us and the mirror of the mind would begin to reflect the infinite. It would be as if we were gradually to discover the adequate idea of each of us which Spinoza thought was present to God. One would have first to think how this idea might be made intelligible and then to begin the specialized studies.

In fact the germs of some such studies are already present in *Retreat from Truth*, but the rather Spinozistic underpinnings are not examined and the full set of studies did not emerge. Not surprisingly, if my guess about the Spinozistic undertones is correct, Mure says that H. H. Joachim strikes him as a better philosopher than Bradley and Bosanquet, partly, indeed, because of Joachim's interest in Spinoza and partly because he took Hegel more seriously.[43]

---

[41] G. R. G. Mure, *Retreat from Truth* (Oxford: Basil Blackwell, 1958). Interestingly, British philosophy has worked its way around the circle, and this book has recently been translated into Italian by Rita Melillo (as *Fuga dalla verità*, Naples: Loffredo, 1990). Ms. Melillo has also written a study of Mure, *Trà hegelismo e neo-empirismo, Saggio su G. R. G. Mure* (Naples: SEN, 1986).

[42] *Retreat from Truth* (see note 41), p. 245.

[43] *Idealist Epilogue* (Oxford: Clarendon Press, 1978). See, of course, H. H. Joachim, *Spinoza* (Oxford: Clarendon Press, 1901). I share Mure's view of Joachim and his admiration for Joachim's project. See my *Being and Idea* (Hildesheim: Georg Olms, 1992).

All this, of course, ran counter to the main thrust which idealists had to face: the anti-metaphysical turn of the analytical philosophy movement. Eventually, however, that thrust was blunted. But it was not, I think, because idealist arguments – those of Mure or any others – carried the day. More important was the fact that, first the logical positivists, and then the ordinary language philosophers, tended to run head-on into the scientific ideology of our time. The first result of this was a return not to idealist but to materialist metaphysics, and it is only, really, since materialist metaphysics began to run into troubles which even some of its own propounders have realized, that metaphysical idealism has begun to return. True, interest in Hegel returned earlier and for other reasons: but, as has recently been observed, the first revival was not in Hegel's metaphysics or even in anything which could really be called idealism, but in the political concerns of the Frankfurt School, and then in the linguistic and textual interests of various hermeneuticists and deconstructionists.[44]

Recently, perhaps, growing awareness of the complexity of Hegel has been leading to the view that he is more the source of problems than of solutions. The difficulties discussed as far back as Coleridge and developed more fully as British idealism was developed by professional philosophers are not simply to be ignored. Indeed, G. R. G. Mure may yet prove to have offered invaluable clues to the understanding of Hegel himself.

A study of some recent idealist works in English reveals a strong concern with the perceived failings of the analytic philosophers and with the scientific culture. The logical positivists, in insisting that meaning was inextricably tied to empirical verification, inevitably showed scientific laws to be meaningless expressions. Even scientific generalizations appeared to be simply exercises in bad inference. The search for another way of exploring the roots of language led to the still popular notion that meaning is associated with use and that the uses of language are various. On such a view, scien-

---

[44] See, for instance, the preface to Bainard Cowan and Joseph G. Kronick (eds.), *Theorizing American Literature, Hegel, the Sign and History* (Baton Rouge: Louisiana State University Press, 1991).

tific discourse is merely one language game or bundle of language games amongst many. It has no priority over religion unless one thinks that the sociological embeddedness and political power which its games generate can be associated with epistemological priority.

By the middle of the 1950s, exercises in metaphysical materialism, frequently associated with names like scientific realism, began to appear as a natural enough reaction to this situation. If we cannot associate science with a logically dominant epistemology, perhaps we can associate it with a metaphysic. A functioning metaphysical materialism, if it *did* accord with scientific belief, would at least show that the belief that science described reality was coherent.

It is important to notice how Bosanquetian the new metaphysical materialisms which began to develop late in the 1950s were. Bosanquet had not argued that we could show that we had direct knowledge of the Absolute mind, or even that we could reach it by a quick thrust of Bradleyan reductionism, but only that the view of reality most consistent with all our claims to knowledge was a kind of absolute idealism. The claims of the scientific realists and the Bosanquetians were, after all, founded on a view about what it is most consistent to believe. And Bosanquet had the support of at least as many eminent physicists of his own time and of the succeeding two generations as the scientific realists could muster.

4. *Some Recent Idealists: Harris, Foster, Rescher and Sprigge*
Thus one would expect that the revitalization of idealist metaphysics would stem from attempts to show the shortcomings of the new materialism and that it might show Bosanquetian tendencies.

In the darkest days for idealists, the years when logical positivism was fairly strong and when the 'ordinary language' philosophies popular at Oxford were in the ascendency, Errol Harris pursued, as I have suggested, Bosanquet's line. *Nature, Mind and Modern Science* is a book of which Bosanquet himself might have been proud,[45] and, more recently, Harris

---

[45] *Nature, Mind, and Modern Science* (see note 23 above).

has also advanced logical projects which, if not exactly Bosanquetian, surely deal with items on Bosanquet's unfinished agenda. Harris has always been concerned however with the detailed richness of specifically human experience and with the social and political implications of his own metaphysics. Thus though he has defended a very abstract view of the world, a view much like Spinoza's,[46] there is an underlying scepticism in his work about anything which diverges too far from what human beings can immediately grasp. Recently, this tendency has edged him in directions less like those of Bosanquet. His *Reality of Time* advances a doctrine which, unless interpreted very carefully, might not have been much to Bosanquet's taste, the doctrine that 'human self-consciousness is...what must give us our best clue' to the real order of nature, and that we can take the world to be headed toward something like Teilhard de Chardin's 'Omega point'.[47] Harris has developed this theme further in *Cosmos and Anthropos*.[48]

Apart from Harris, though, one can often see a direct connection between the problems of materialist metaphysics and recent idealism, though one can also see ideas like those of Bosanquet at work. Three recent examples – the philosophies of John Foster, Nicholas Rescher and Timothy Sprigge – illustrate the tendencies.

In *The Case for Idealism*, John Foster tried to revive a kind of Berkeleyan phenomenalism, because he thought that the functionalist version of materialism had drawn the opposite of the logical conclusion from the arguments presented – and he also thought that a functionalist analysis of mind would

---

[46] Errol Harris, *Salvation from Despair* (The Hague: Martinus Nijhoff, 1973).

[47] Errol Harris, *The Reality of Time* (Albany, New York: State University of New York Press, 1988), p. 156. The section is headed 'The Clue to Omega'.

[48] Errol Harris, *Cosmos and Anthropos*, subtitled *A Philosophical Interpretation of the Anthropic Principle* (Atlantic Highlands, New Jersey: Humanities Press International, 1991). It has been suggested, indeed, that he takes the anthropic principle – lately canvassed by a number of cosmologists – literally in a way in which the cosmologists do not, and that he draws too much on the specific characterizations of *human* experience.

work better than a materialist analysis.[49] It is surely true that the frustrations produced by the recent materialist arguments (including the defection of Hilary Putnam)[50] are part of the story. Foster's *Case for Idealism* is a defence of reductive phenomenalistic idealism. He sets out to defend the proposition that what we take to be material objects are simply phenomena and that the phenomena are best understood as mentalistic in kind:

> Reductive phenomenalism claims that the physical world is the logical creation of the constraints on human experience... What he [the reductive phenomenalist] claims is that the constraints on their own suffice for the creation of the physical world, irrespective of what (if anything) lies behind them: that if there is an external reality it contributes nothing to the existence of the physical world save what it contributes to the obtaining of the constraints.[51]

His case is essentially based on the thesis of topic neutrality and on an argument for the reversal of the way in which this is usually applied by functionalists in the course of their 'materialist' arguments. The functionalists, that is, claim that when we talk about mental states – whether they be sensations, images, or propositional attitudes – we are not really talking about a kind of thing, but about a kind of function. The functionalist generally regards a sensation as being like a valve lifter. The expression 'valve lifter' names something which performs a function. It might be any kind of thing, so long as it does what it is supposed to do. No particular kind of thing is necessarily named. The expression 'material object', by contrast *does* name a kind of thing. In the eyes of the functionalist, 'sensation' and 'valve lifter' and 'belief' are 'topic neutral' expressions while 'material object' is a 'topic specific' expression. This is to say that, when we are told

---

[49] John Foster, *The Case for Idealism* (London: Routledge & Kegan Paul, 1982). Foster's interest in Berkeley himself is evidenced in *Essays on Berkeley* which he edited together with Howard Robinson (Oxford: Clarendon Press, 1985).

[50] See Putnam's account of his own defection in *Representation and Reality* (Cambridge, Mass.: MIT Press, 1989).

[51] *The Case for Idealism* (see note 49), p. 208.

about sensations or valve lifters or beliefs, we do not know from *their* classifications what kind of thing is being talked about. When we are told about material objects, we do know what kind of thing is being talked about. This supports the belief that 'material object' is an expression denoting not one kind of thing amongst many ontological kinds, but *the* ontological kind.

Foster says:

> Now it seems to me that this way of defending physicalistic realism against the intuitive objection [that it cannot account for such things as propositional attitudes and other apparent mental entities or states] fails. Indeed, it seems to me... it fails catastrophically, since it manages to get everything exactly the wrong way round. It locates topic-neutrality at the very point where our concepts and descriptions are topic-specific, and it locates topic-specificity at the very point where they are topic-neutral.[52]

The major issue, evidently, is topic-neutrality. An expression is 'topic-neutral' if it succeeds in designating something without saying what kind of thing it is where 'kind of thing' denotes some ontological or other status which gives it a place in the classificatory orders of things. Functionalists like to claim that one who talks about valve lifters says nothing about the kinds of things involved. It is not clear to me, however, that there could be mental valves and mental valve lifters and so it is not clear to me that valve lifters could be made of anything whatever.

One might think that a valve is the sort of thing which could exist only in a material context, for a valve is something which, at least potentially, periodically interrupts and periodically permits the flow of something or other. We are dealing here with things which can move from place to place – a liquid or a gas or whatever – and with a flow of something associated with forces which can be impeded by putting some object in their way. But one might think, also, that nothing is a valve unless it has a purpose. Falling rocks may block a

---

[52] *ibid.*, p. 55.

river and so form a lake, only to be worn away in due time by the water in such a way as to restore something like the original river. But we would not call this sequence of events the action of a valve. Valves act and bring about foreseeable results. A valve as we ordinarily speak of it, therefore, may seem to be the sort of thing which requires mind–matter dualism.

The trouble with the phenomenalism with which Foster wants to replace functionalism, or with *any* sort of phenomenalism, is that topic neutrality cannot be found *either* in the way that the materialist functionalists want to find it or in the way that phenomenalists like Foster want to find it.

Notice, however, that this is really a kind of conceptual or logical issue: phenomenalism claims that one interpretation is always and in principle superior to another, that it is always better to take what is presented to the mind as mental rather than as physical, when in fact the expressions mental and physical are intended to distinguish between different classes of what is presented to the mind and obviously do so in so far as, in fact, they serve to make a distinction between kinds of experiences.

Another critique of the failure of the new materialisms derives from Nicholas Rescher's wrestlings with concepts of explanation. His books defend various species of idealism – first a kind of 'conceptual idealism',[53] and then a kind of 'neo-Leibnizian rationalism'.[54] Rescher's later work depends on a complex of logical questions – including his justifications of mathematical physics as plausibly providing access to reality as such.[55] This in turn depends on the ability to deal with the logical issues which I raised at the beginning of this paper. But his 'conceptual idealism' needs to be discussed here.

In *Conceptual Idealism,* Rescher lays out the essence of his position in the chapter entitled 'An Idealist Theory of

---

[53] Nicholas Rescher, *Conceptual Idealism* (Oxford: Basil Blackwell, 1973).

[54] Nicholas Rescher, *The Riddle of Existence, An Essay in Idealistic Metaphysics* (Lanham, Maryland: University Press of America, 1984).

[55] See the concluding section of *The Riddle of Existence* (note 54).

Nature'.[56] In particular, he offers a series of arguments against a standard set of alternative positions identified as Kantian, sceptical, and phenomenalist.[57] Phenomenalists say that objects in themselves are inferred entities. But no [legitimately] inferred entities exist. Therefore phenomenalism is true. Rescher rejects the second premise, basically because what it suggests is that there is no reasonable account of the entities of immediate experience. Earlier in the book, Rescher argues that in fact empirical properties are mind-invoking, and he does this in a way which suggests T. H. Green, claiming that empirical properties of things involve relations and dispositional properties and, indeed, that this is an essential ingredient in scientific reasoning.[58] He argues that to say that something is red, or soft to the touch, or whatever, is to allege (1) that it has some effect on some mind and (2) that it implies a dispositional property – ie. that one has a tendency to respond in a certain way when one is confronted with it.

Rescher claims that though there is a distinction between empirical and theoretical properties, the argument holds equally for both. In short, descriptions of empirical properties also entail inferences.[59]

Kantian idealism, according to Rescher, is predicated on three premises. They are that (1) knowledge of anything 'in itself' depends on knowledge of its proper (non-dispositional) properties; (2) our knowledge of 'natural particulars' (particulars in the natural world) is restricted to products of direct (non-discursive) experience; and (3) all experience and observation can in principle only produce information about dispositional properties of extra-mental realities, never the absolute properties. The importance of the premise about dispositional and non-dispositional properties is that dispositional properties always involve some account of the way in which

---

[56] *Conceptual Idealism* (see note 53), chap. 9, pp. 151–74.

[57] ibid., pp. 163–6.

[58] ibid., pp. 141–5.

[59] This argument is like one in Bosanquet. See *Knowledge and Reality* (London: Swan Sonnenschein, 1892), chap. 6.

things interact with us and therefore seem to create a screen between things and us. Together the three premises seem to lead to the view that we can never have knowledge of things in themselves.

Rescher denies the second premise. We do not simply know the qualities of things, but how they fit together into inferential patterns. Thus, in effect, his argument against phenomenalism carries the day against Kantianism as well – if it succeeds.

The sceptical alternative to idealism attacked by Rescher simply argues that non-dispositional properties of things cannot be known without inference, and inference is always doubtful. But this, again, depends on the claim that inferability is not a natural property of things. The claim throughout *Conceptual Idealism* is that mind is involved in every attempt to know nature, and that this does not lead us to the view that nature is somehow unknowable but to the view that nature is permeated by mind.

Of course, Rescher's account needs to be supplemented by what he calls 'an idealist theory of mind'.[60] What this really amounts to is the claim that, while the properties which belong to the natural world associate the things in it with mind, the properties which belong to mind do not have an analogous relation to the material things in the world. Minds, he says, can be understood on their own terms because they can be viewed *from within*.[61]

This combination of views obviously, however, does not commit him to the position that there are nothing but minds in the world, much less that there is only one ultimate mind, a kind of world soul. His claim is that nature is permeated by minds, but, of course, to be permeated by mind, there must be other things. It is just that they cannot exist independently.

The problem is to distinguish this kind of theory – which suggests that conceptualism should be given an idealistic interpretation – from other kinds of theories which suggest

---

[60] *Conceptual Idealism* (see note 53), chap. 10, pp. 175–94.

[61] *ibid.*, p. 184.

that it should be given a conventionalist interpretation. Rescher argues against standard sceptical and Kantian attempts to give either conventionalist explanations or (in the Kantian case) formalist explanations in terms of the organizing structure of the human mind for this situation, but his argument is chiefly that inferability is a property of events or of the data received and that therefore licensed interpretations can be drawn from the data.

Rescher can hold this combination of views and avoid the conventionalist alternative to his position, I think, if and only if there are not alternative inferences to be drawn from the data of experience and from our conceptual struggles with it. If there is only one system – as Bosanquet thought – then licensed inferences follow from the data. But, if there are alternative and equally legitimate inferences some kind of conventionalism or Kantianism still seems to follow and Rescher has not reached his goal.

It is, in a sense, in the light of this stand-off that Timothy Sprigge begins, though Sprigge, of course, explores traditional moral and humanistic concerns much more fully than Rescher or Foster. These concerns play a role which becomes important by the end of Sprigge's work, though he does not, I would argue, give them the weight which they deserve. His *Vindication of Absolute Idealism*[62] defends an account of ultimate reality which is in many respects Bradleyan, though its ultimate conclusions resemble more closely those found in McTaggart's metaphysical system. (Curiously, McTaggart is mentioned only once.)[63]

Traces of notions which go back to Green and Bosanquet can be found in Sprigge's arguments (though neither Green nor Bosanquet is mentioned by name) and, like McTaggart, Sprigge owes something to Leibniz.[64] His debt to Spinoza is

[62] Timothy Sprigge, *The Vindication of Absolute Idealism* (Edinburgh University Press, 1983).

[63] See J. M. E. McTaggart, *The Nature of Existence*, 2 vols. (Cambridge University Press, 1921, 1927). Sprigge, *The Vindication of Absolute Idealism* (see note 62), mentions McTaggart only on p. 239 and there in a discussion of time which is perhaps not fundamental to the main line of argument.

[64] *The Vindication of Absolute Idealism* (see note 62), especially pp. 183–7 where monadism is discussed.

real and is quite fully acknowledged.[65] He specially acknowledges his relations to Bradley, who is mentioned a number of times.[66]

Here is how Sprigge states his own position:

> The Universe consists of innumerable momentary centres of experience all standing in some relation more or less direct to others. Some of them are so related as to form different phases of the life of a single continuant, others are related in ways which make them phases in the life of different more or less closely interacting continuants. These relations must either be ideal[67] or holistic,[68] for no others are conceivable except as a kind of pragmatic fiction.[69]

He also says:

> The universe, in its true being, is a system of centres of experience in holistic relations to one another within it, which make it, or depend on its being (each is as correct a way of putting it as the other), a concrete whole at least as genuinely individual as anything within it.[70]

Finally, he adds:

> The view that the universe is a unitary experience, timeless, as being neither an element in any larger process nor a con-

---

[65] For example, *ibid.*, p. 157 (where he lays down his overall picture of reality).

[66] In *The Vindication of Absolute Idealism* (see note 62), pp. 110–15 Sprigge lays out his argument that concrete and sentient reality are co-extensive. On pp. 177–80 he deals with the problem of identity; and pp. 276–9 he deals with the question of monism.

[67] In Sprigge's (somewhat idiosyncratic) language, 'ideal' relations are internal relations which hold between properties in virtue of the *nature* of those properties. For instance the relation 'being brighter than' which holds between two coloured patches does so in virtue, he says, of their inherent properties and does so eternally. I think it is the notion of the *nature* of properties and the notion of *eternality* which explain Sprigge's use of the word 'ideal' – *The Vindication of Absolute Idealism* (see note 62), pp. 180–87.

[68] Holistic relations are those which tie entities together in more comprehensive wholes having some ontological significance. See *The Vindication of Absolute Idealism*, pp. 187ff.

[69] Sprigge, *The Vindication of Absolute Idealism* (see note 62), p. 250.

[70] *ibid.*, p. 251.

tinuant existing in successive phases, but temporal within itself, an experience of temporal process as though in a kind of frozen specious present (for such seems the most plausible interpretation of the noumenal nature of the world's temporality) rests on two main conclusions we have reached.[71]

Sprigge's two main conclusions are: first, that noumenal reality is psychical, is composed entirely of what is experienced; and second that all relations are holistic and, indeed, strongly so.[72]

His case comes in two parts. One is concerned with the doctrine which he calls panpsychism, by which he means the doctrine that reality is dominantly psychical.[73] The other is concerned with how the panpsychist unity is expressed through 'holistic relations'.

For his panpsychist doctrine, he gives four arguments – that it is the best and most intelligible answer to the question 'What is the nature of the noumenal reality behind phenomena?';[74] that idealism makes the mind–body relationship more intelligible;[75] that it is best to take one's clues about the noumenal from 'the one good example we have of it...'[76] (the centre of experience which is associated with each of us); and that, finally, nothing is really conceivable outside sentience.[77]

---

[71] ibid., p. 252.

[72] ibid.

[73] Other philosophers, Whitehead, for instance (cf. *Process and Reality*, London: Macmillan, 1929), have been called 'panpsychists' in a different sense. Whitehead merely meant that all real entities have some mental aspect (which he called the 'mental pole', see pp. 40, 48, 130 etc.). His account of this aspect is given in terms of the fact that the ultimate possibilities the world (eternal objects in his system) do not determine the whole of reality, for they are essentially universals, and particulars always have some unique aspect. Whitehead links this notion to the ultimate freedom of particular things and relates it to the 'mental pole' which each such thing must possess.

[74] Sprigge, *The Vindication of Absolute Idealism* (see note 62), pp. 87–96.

[75] ibid., pp. 96–104.

[76] ibid., pp. 105–110.

[77] ibid., pp. 110–40.

Sprigge further believes that there is another kind of relation which is holistic, and that the reality which he addresses is a set of experiences which tend to sum to an intelligible whole. Failing this notion of unity, of course, the basic arguments for panpsychism might well seem weak. Once again the spirit of Bosanquet seems to walk the pages (even though Sprigge once accused Bradley of having 'too much respect' for Bosanquet).[78]

But, basically, Sprigge's kind of idealism, I suspect, breaks down because as soon as one puts some precision on the concept of the Absolute, fitting the Absolute into the world or even into the future of the world becomes impossible. One then tends to take away the hard edges and to leave it meaningless. If this problem is to be overcome, some version of Neoplatonism offers some relief, but I think the whole thing has to be rethought. I think, as I have argued elsewhere, that only goodness can explain the whole. For if we try to explain everything by some thing then it itself needs explanation.[79] Only values have a kind of necessary ontological status without being things, and only goodness, perhaps, could logically be self-explanatory.

5. Rorty's Fantasy and the Future of Idealism

But, however this might be, one can see that, in a sense, Foster, Rescher and Sprigge all struggle with Richard Rorty's philosopher's 'fantasy' – 'a state of consciousness which, *per impossibile*, combines...the best features of inarticulate confrontation with the best features of linguistic formulation'.[80]

---

[78] *ibid.*, p. 285, note 7.

[79] See Leslie Armour, 'Values, God, and the Problem About Why There is Anything at All', *Journal of Speculative Philosophy*, vol. 1 ns, no. 2 (1987), pp. 147–62, and my essay in Philip MacEwan (ed.), *Ethics, Metaphysics, and Religion in the Thought of F. H. Bradley* (see note 9). See also John Leslie, *Value and Existence* (Oxford: Basil Blackwell, 1979).

[80] See the discussion in Mark Okrent's essay 'The Metaphilosophical Consequences of Pragmatism', in Avner Cohen and Marcelo Dascal (eds.), *The Institution of Philosophy, A Discipline in Crisis?* (La Salle, Ill.: Open Court, 1989), p. 177. The quotation is from Rorty's *The Consequences of Pragmatism* (Minneapolis: University of Minnesota Press, 1982), p. 194.

Rorty says that the fantasy can never be realized, and he argues that philosophers either try, unsuccessfully, to create a pseudo-science, or to extend an existing one, or else that they lapse into poetry. He believes that if we knew what we were doing we would leave the solution of serious problems to 'the poets and the engineers'.[81]

But if one is more hopeful than Rorty and if one thinks that the problem is genuine, one is likely to be motivated by the need to relate the world of experience to certain logical conditions which are necessary for knowledge (and for the concepts of truth and error). The conditions usually offered (even lately by defectors from materialism like Hilary Putnam) seem to entail some kind of unified system which is not readily discernible in experience and which doesn't seem to fit in to the world at all.

Very much of the English-speaking idealism we have been talking about is and always has been a reaction to problems posed – and to the way that problems were posed – in the formative phases of British empiricism.[82] And there is a useful clue, I think, to the solution in Locke's posthumously-published *Remarks upon some of Mr. Norris's Books wherein he asserts P. Malebranche's Opinion of seeing all Things in God*.[83] There Locke provides a way of going back to the idea of ideas, so as, if you like, to fulfil Rorty's dream.

He insists that it is true that all knowledge derives (as he kept saying in the *Essay*) from 'ideas', but that ideas are not something in themselves. Yet he finally admits in exasperation that they do have some kind of being. The solution is that what it is to be an idea is to be capable of interpretations. The idea is not something over and above all its interpretations, though it is not exhausted by any one of them either. If, then, one thinks of 'our world' as a set of such interpretations, and of the unified system as what is interpreted, one gets the tension between them without having to get the

---

[81] Rorty in Cohen and Dascal, *The Institution of Philosophy* (see note 80), p. 29.

[82] The essays of Fred Wilson and David Crossley in this volume explore various aspects of the relation between Bradley and the empiricist tradition.

[83] *A Collection of Several Pieces of Mr. John Locke, never before printed or not extant in his Works* (London: J. Bettesworth for R. Franklin, 1720).

unity into the experienced world. To say that there are material objects is to say that there are justified interpretations of the ideas which experience presents which use the concept of material object. To say that there are minds is to say that there are ideas which can be interpreted effectively using such notions. What is interpreted consists of ideas but, if they are exhausted by all their potential interpretations, they are not another kind of thing. Nor does being 'one kind of thing' preclude being another. The 'things' discerned in the world can be admitted to have explanations of one sort which relate them to each other within specific systems. But the world can still be asserted to have another kind of explanation which derives from the fact that ideas have certain structures which permit the explanatory systems which we find. Metaphysics is then the business of exploring *these* structures.

If such a system could be worked out, it would be 'idealism' in the sense that 'ideas' are primary, but not in most of the other usual senses. Bradley would then be relevant to the search for an account of various ways in which experience can be presented as an interpretation of ideas. Indeed, this is a way of carrying out Bradley's own suggestions for a positive metaphysics. It would surely involve G. R. G. Mure's project of seeing just how every interpretation of every idea poses limits, and how in the very act of positing them, one transcends them and thus acquires clues to the final unity.

Yet, in doing so, one would want to resist the temptation to elide two levels of analysis – focusing the ideas and interpreting them. In this way one might avoid the conundrums which arise from the apparent fact that the idea itself cannot be spoken of except through its interpretations.

The natural understanding, then, would be that things are known literally through ideas. Something is a material object if and only if the idea through which it appears is correctly interpreted as a material object. Something is a mind if and only if the idea through which it is known is correctly interpreted as a mind. On such a view one could even ask, as Locke once did, if there might not be thinking matter, and even give his answer, 'Why not?'.[84] For, on this view, all that

[84] *Essay Concerning Human Understanding*, bk 4, chap. 3, ed. Peter Nidditch (Oxford: Clarendon Press, 1975), p. 542.

such an admission amounts to is that we sometimes confront ideas which are correctly interpreted as both thinking things and material objects.

In one sense it is the ideas which are real or which form the primary reality; but that is because everything which is interpreted as being a material object, say, is an interpretation of an idea. But the thing is not both an idea and a material object, but rather an idea which signifies the existence of a material object.

Ultimately this means that ideas are symbols and that we read them much as we read words on paper. A word has various meanings. But it is not something over and above them. An idea has various interpretations, but it, too, is not something over and above those interpretations. A correct interpretation asserts something which really is the case, but it is better, for this purpose, to put it a little differently. To say that there is a motor car in my driveway is to say that certain ideas are correctly interpreted in terms of the presence of a motor car in the driveway.

On such a view the ideas themselves might well form a unified whole, but the range of possible interpretations might well be very great. The pursuit of G. R. G. Mure's programme – a programme which consists in looking at how each division is transcended through the way in which it implies what is beyond it – would provide a technique for distinguishing the search for metaphysical unity from the search for the complex body of useful knowledge which accrues from the specific and detailed interpretations of the ideas. It might still turn out that, as a body of intersubjective interpretation, our scientific knowledge has powerful claims, but such an idealism would not establish the ultimate *superiority* of scientific interpretations but, on the contrary, suggest both their usefulness and their limits.

F. H. BRADLEY AND BERNARD BOSANQUET

William Sweet

Bernard Bosanquet was born two years after F. H. Bradley and died a year earlier, in 1923. Both men came to Oxford in the late 1860s, where they fell under the influence of so-called 'German philosophy', and the similarities in their views led some of their contemporaries to say that the two 'may almost be regarded as a single philosophical personality'.[1] But much of Bosanquet's work appeared only after Bradley had already published on the same, or related, topics,[2] and critics

---

[1] See Rudolf Metz, *Die Philosophischen Stromungen der Gegenwart in Grossbritannien* (Leipzig: Felix Meiner Verlag, 1935). Translated as *A Hundred Years of British Philosophy*, trans. J. W. Harvey, T. E. Jessop, Henry Sturt; ed. J. H. Muirhead (London: Allen and Unwin, 1938), p. 346. According to J. S. MacKenzie, 'Bradley and Bosanquet have almost to be regarded as one person ... Neither is readily intelligible without the other', review of *Ethical Studies*, 2nd ed., in *Mind*, vol. 37 ns (1928), pp. 235–6; cited in Peter P. Nicholson, *The Political Philosophy of the British Idealists* (Cambridge University Press, 1990, p. 243, n. 25). See also Anthony Manser's comment that '[it] has been suggested that there was, at the end of the nineteenth century, a great English philosopher named "Bradley-Bosanquet"', *Bradley's Logic* (Totowa, New Jersey: Barnes and Noble, 1983, p. 198).
  Metz, nevertheless, rejects this opinion. He claims that '[despite] the considerable agreement between them ... Bosanquet's philosophy ... represents an independent re-creation, extension and application of Bradley's doctrine on the part of a genuine thinker who happened to be congenial with him and who scarcely fell below him in ability' (Metz, 1938, p. 346).

[2] *Ethical Studies* was published in 1876, but it was not until 1899 that Bosanquet provided any systematic work on social philosophy (*The Philosophical Theory of the State*) and not until 1918 that he produced a book – in fact, a series of nine essays – on ethics (*Some Suggestions in Ethics*). *Appearance and Reality* (1893) pre-dates Bosanquet's Gifford Lectures, *The Principle of Individuality and Value* and *The Value and Destiny of the Individual*, by twenty years. Finally, even though Bosanquet's essay 'Logic as the Science of Knowledge' (in A. Seth and R. B. Haldane (eds.), *Essays in Philosophical Criticism*, London: Longman, 1883, pp. 67–101) appeared in the same year as the first edition of Bradley's *Principles of Logic*, one of the primary tasks of his *Knowledge and Reality* (1885) and *Logic or the Morphology of Knowledge*, 2 vols. (1888) seems to be to take up, and make more consistent, Bradley's project.

often speak of Bosanquet as simply 'applying [Bradley's world view] and exhibiting its fruitfulness'.[3] Indeed, Bosanquet suggests as much himself. As late as 1920, he wrote that 'since the appearance of *Ethical Studies*... I have recognized [Bradley] as my master; and there is never, I think, any more than a verbal difference or difference of emphasis, between us'.[4] It is no surprise, then, that the standard view of their relationship is that Bosanquet was essentially 'a follower of Bradley'.[5]

Yet one might well ask whether the matter is as simple as the preceding view suggests. According to Rudolf Metz, there existed a 'fruitful exchange of ideas' between the two;[6] Bradley himself acknowledges this.[7] Moreover, while Bradley may have had the more striking personality and the more provocative and vigorous style, according to J. H. Randall it was Bosanquet who was 'the most popular and the most influential of the English idealists'.[8] In fact, in his obituary in

---

[3] Metz, 1938, p. 347.

[4] See his letter to Lello Vivante, 27 March 1920, cited in J. H. Muirhead, *Bernard Bosanquet and His Friends* (London, 1935), esp. pp. 262–3. See also Nicholson, 1990, p. 52.

[5] Arthur Kenyon Rogers, *English and America Philosophy Since 1900: A Critical Survey* (New York: Macmillan, 1923), p. 264. According to François Houang (*Le neo-hegelianisme en angleterre*, Paris: Vrin, 1954), the development of Bosanquet's philosophy corresponds directly to that of Bradley. For example, 'it was the publication in 1893 of Bradley's *Appearance and Reality* that explains the transition in Bosanquet's work from logic to metaphysics' (*op. cit.*, p. 8; see also his *De l'humanisme a l'absolutisme*, Paris: Vrin, 1954, p. 9). See also Emile Bréhier, *Histoire de la philosophie*, vol. 3 (Paris: Presses universitaires de France, 1964) p. 917: 'Le mérite de B. Bosanquet... est surtout de faire ressortir tout ce que l'expérience peut apporter de vérifications à un idéalisme tel que celui de Bradley.'

For a dissenting view, see Jonathan Robinson, 'Bradley and Bosanquet', *Idealistic Studies*, vol. 10 (1980), pp. 1–23. According to Robinson, 'Bradley and Bosanquet disagreed so profoundly over such questions as the nature of reality and the relation of thought to feelings that they ought not to be looked on as representing some common doctrine' (*op. cit.*, p. 2).

[6] Metz, 1938, p. 346.

[7] In a letter dated 11 November 1915, Bradley wrote to Bosanquet that 'there is no one whose opinion weighs with me as yours does, or whose work (amongst the living) I put higher or value more', Muirhead (1935), p. 179. See also Muirhead (1935), p. 315; Nicholson (1990), p. 52 and p. 243, nn. 22, 23, and 24.

[8] J. H. Randall, Jr., 'Idealistic Social Philosophy and Bernard Bosanquet', in *Philosophy and Phenomenological Research*, vol. 26, no. 4 (June 1966), pp. 473–503; reprinted in *The Career of Philosophy*, vol. 3, pp. 97–130, p. 114.

The Times, Bosanquet was described as 'the central figure in British philosophy for a whole generation'.[9] The present study will attempt to address this issue by raising the question of whether Bosanquet's philosophy was 'after Bradley' in any sense other than the chronological.[10] To this end, I propose to examine two areas in which Bradley and Bosanquet are generally believed to have held similar views: ethics and metaphysics.[11] Beginning with ethics, I will argue that several of the frequently cited similarities are only so prima facie. Turning to metaphysics, one will again find some important differences in emphasis, if not in doctrine, in their respective accounts of the self and the Absolute. I shall argue that, in both of these areas, the differences between Bradley and Bosanquet are neither incidental nor accidental, and that they reflect a fundamental divergence concerning the nature and value of the human person. One must, therefore, reject the standard view.

I

While the appearance of Bradley's *Ethical Studies* met with mixed reviews, its influence in late nineteenth-century Anglo-Saxon philosophy was significant. In one of his last essays, Bosanquet writes that '[for] many of us [its] publication ... was

---

[9] Muirhead, 1935, p. 19.

[10] The following titles by Bosanquet are abbreviated in the body of this essay as follows: *The Philosophical Theory of the State*, 4th ed., 1923 (henceforth abbreviated as *PTS*); *Some Suggestions in Ethics*, 1918 (*SS*); 'Do Finite Individuals Possess a Substantive or an Adjectival Mode of Being?: A Symposium', in *Life and Finite Individuality* (ed. H. Wildon Carr), Aristotelian Society Supplementary Volume 1 (1918), pp. 75–194, (*LFI*); *The Principle of Individuality and Value*, 1912 (*PIV*); and *The Value and Destiny of the Individual*, 1913 (*VDI*).

[11] It is in logic that the relation between Bradley and Bosanquet is most often marked (see footnote 2 above), but the influence was not all one-sided and it is frequently conceded (including by Bradley himself) that Bosanquet's logic was not a mere development of Bradley's. For a discussion of issues here, see Houang, *Neo-hegelianisme*, pp. 18–33 and Manser, 1983. While Manser notes Bradley's indebtedness to Bosanquet in logic (particularly on those issues that led to the preparation of the second edition of *PR*), he adds that '[i]n many cases, it seems that Bosanquet did not fully understand Bradley's arguments; at best he gives them a somewhat shallow interpretation' (*op. cit.*, p. 199). It is interesting that there is no record that Bradley himself ever held such a view. Manser holds, however, that 'at a deeper level perhaps neither understood the other's view fully' (1983, p. 198).

an epoch making event'.[12] Indeed, in a recent volume, Peter Nicholson claims that Bradley's book 'served as a manifesto of British Idealism and became part of its foundations' and that, in particular, 'Bosanquet expounded Bradley's moral theory enthusiastically' and 'drew heavily on it'.[13]

That there is some similarity between Bradley and Bosanquet is, of course, not surprising. Both reject utilitarianism and both adopt the Hegelian critique of Kantian ethics as being too formal and incomplete. Both claim, moreover, that the individualist model of the human person which underlies these views is fundamentally inadequate and ignores the essential social dimension in human personality. Both hold that 'morality is coextensive with self realization' (*ES* 224)[14] and see the community as being more than a mere collection of individuals. There is even some evidence that, in the mid 1870s, Bosanquet himself considered preparing a study of moral philosophy – a project which he abandoned at the time of the publication of *Ethical Studies*.[15] Yet despite

---

[12] 'Life and Philosophy', pp. 51–74, in *Contemporary British Philosophy: Personal Statements* (first series), ed. J. H. Muirhead (London: Allen and Unwin, 1924). It is interesting to note that Bradley was invited to contribute to this volume, but refused.

[13] Nicholson, 1990, p. 3; pp. 51–2. Nicholson refers his reader to the references to Bradley in the index of *VDI* and makes some (vague) references to *PTS*, but he does not make the nature and extent of this alleged influence explicit. In fact, many of the references to Bradley in *VDI* concern Bradley's discussion of the nature and presuppositions of utilitarianism and of Kant – but not, interestingly, Bradley's 'positive theory' in Essay VI.

[14] Interestingly, rather than constantly use the notion of 'self realization', Bosanquet instead often employs that of 'self transcendence'. He finds an expression of this in a line from Goethe: 'Stirb und werde' – 'Die to live' (*SS* 161). (See also *VDI* 16–18 on finiteness and self-transcendence.) A paradigmatic case of self-transcendence is that which occurs in love (*VDI* 327), and one should note Bosanquet's view that, in logic, inference is also a kind of 'self-transcendence' (Acton, 1967, p. 349).

Admittedly, Bradley speaks of the moral end as involving transcendence and of the necessity that one 'must die' to one's 'private self [and] ... be made one with the ideal' (*ES* 325). In this context, however, Bosanquet does not mean (as Bradley suggests) that morality must be transcended, but simply that genuine moral activity involves transcending one's private interests. Moreover, the 'dying to oneself' of which Bradley speaks is part of religious (and not, strictly speaking, moral) consciousness.

[15] In a letter to F. H. Peters, dated 13 August 1876, Bosanquet wrote: 'the book I was to write must wait; perhaps forever' (cited in Muirhead, 1935, p. 37). In *Bernard Bosanquet: A Short Account of His Life* (London, 1924), Helen Bosanquet wrote that 'He seems to have contemplated writing a book on Ethics, which was forestalled by Bradley's *Ethical Studies*' (*op. cit.*, p. 34). See also Nicholson, 1990, p. 52 and n. 18, p. 243.

all this, it by no means follows that Bosanquet's later writings in ethics and his work in social and political philosophy are essentially those of a popularizer of Bradley's ideas.[16]

To begin with, Bosanquet's discussion of the nature of morality is neither specifically Bradleyan nor restricts itself to merely applying themes found in Bradley's thought. The notion of self-realization, for example, has its roots in Aristotle[17] – it is found, as well, in the lectures of T. H. Green – and it is to Aristotle that Bosanquet refers in his lengthiest discussion of what is required for the perfection of the individual.[18] Again, Bosanquet's description of moral activity and development is indebted mainly to Green and Rousseau.[19] Here, Bosanquet employs what he calls the general or real will[20] – a notion which he derives from Rousseau and supplements with recent work in psychology; one does not, however, find in Bosanquet's discussion any trace of Bradley's account of the 'ideal self'. At the very least, then, it is not any distinctively Bradleyan view that Bosanquet is proposing.

More to the point, there are striking differences between their respective accounts of the moral life. This, perhaps, is unexpected since, if one thing is obvious to any reader of Bosanquet, it is his frequent appeal to the notion of 'my

---

[16] Interestingly, after *Ethical Studies*, Bradley was to write little more on – and, indeed, to express a distaste for – moral or social philosophy. (See Bradley's letter of 1894, cited in Nicholson, 1990, pp. 52–3.)

[17] Crossley suggests, however, that there are some important differences between the Aristotelian and Bradleyan accounts of self-realization. See David J. Crossley, 'Self Realization as Perfection in Bradley's *Ethical Studies*', in *Idealistic Studies*, vol. 7 (1977), pp. 199–220, p. 201.

[18] 'The perfecting of the soul in Aristotle's *Ethics*', lecture 10, appendix 2 in *PIV*.

[19] *Contrat Social*, I, 7. See Bosanquet, *PTS*, chaps. 4 and 5.

[20] Aside from *PTS*, Bosanquet's major discussion of the general will appears in the following books and articles: 'Les idées politiques de Rousseau', in *Revue de metaphysique et de morale*, vol. 20 (1912), pp. 321–40; 'The Reality of the General Will', *International Journal of Ethics*, vol. 4 (1893–4), pp. 308–21; reprinted in *Aspects of the Social Problem* (London, 1895) and in *Science and Philosophy and Other Essays by the Late Bernard Bosanquet*, ed. J. H. Muirhead and R. C. Bosanquet (London, 1927); 'The Notion of the General Will', *Mind*, vol. 29 ns (1920), pp. 77–81. For a discussion of this, see my 'Bernard Bosanquet and the Development of Rousseau's Idea of the General Will', in *Man and Nature = L'homme et la nature*, vol. 10 (*Individu et collectivites = The Individual and Institutions*), ed. M. Cartwright and W. Kinsley (Edmonton, Alberta: Academic Printing and Publishing, 1991).

station and its duties'.[21] Indeed, even though Green refers to one having 'to fulfil the duties of his station',[22] Bosanquet's use of Bradley's very expression would seem to be clear evidence of the latter's influence. But it is precisely at this point – or so I shall argue – that the two differ markedly.

As most commentators recognize,[23] while Essay V of *Ethical Studies*, 'My Station and its Duties', contains several criticisms of dominant moral theories, it is decidedly not Bradley's final view (see *ES* 190–91).[24] Nicholson points out that one's station 'just prescribes social duties'[25] and Bradley himself argues that, not only is the morality of 'my station' limited in several ways (*ES* 202–206), but 'the self-realization of the whole body... [and] of each member' (*ES* 162–3) includes duties which require us, at times, to go beyond our station. For example, Bradley speaks of the 'production of truth and beauty...as a duty' (*ES* 205) that does not 'directly involve relation to others' (*ES* 205; see also 222ff.). He moves, then, to an 'ideal morality [that] stands on the basis of' this 'common social morality' (*ES* 227). Bradley suggests, in fact, that it may be my duty, as a scientist or as an artist, *not* to

---

[21] See, for example, 'The Kingdom of God on Earth', in *Essays and Addresses* (1889), reprinted in *Science and Philosophy* (1927); 'The Social Good' (in *Some Suggestions in Ethics*, p. 31); and *VDI*.

[22] *Prolegomena to Ethics*, p. 183; see also pp. 313 and 338. It is unclear, however, whether this locution was first employed by Green or Bradley. See Ellen Jacob, 'Bernard Bosanquet: Social and Political Thought', unpublished Ph.D thesis in History (City University of New York, 1986), pp. 84–5. See also Nicholson, 1990, p. 243, n. 14.

[23] Nicholson suggests that this is not so. Of Essay V, 'My Station and its Duties', he says that '[this] part of the book is the most frequently and the most disastrously misread' (Nicholson, 1990, p. 6; see p. 23). But a reading of the major secondary material (Le Chevalier, Wollheim, etc.) shows that there is, in fact, general agreement that Essay V is *not* Bradley's view.

[24] See, for example, James Bradley, 'Process and Historical Crisis in F. H. Bradley's Ethics of Feeling', in P. MacEwan (ed.), *Ethics, Metaphysics and Religion in the Thought of F. H. Bradley* (Queenston: Edwin Mellen, forthcoming) and H. B. Acton, 'Bradley, Francis Herbert', in *The Encyclopedia of Philosophy*, edited by Paul Edwards (New York: The Free Press, 1967), vol. 1, pp. 359–63, p. 359. Interestingly, even after acknowledging that 'my station' is not a 'wholly tenable' point of view (*ES* 190), F. H. Bradley says '[t]here is nothing better than my station and its duties, nor anything higher or more truly beautiful' (*ES* 201).

[25] Nicholson, 1990, p. 32.

fulfil my social service if it leads to 'the detriment of my own moral being' (*ES* 225).[26]

On the whole, however, Bosanquet is satisfied with the morality of 'my station'; he says that 'the main root of individual morals is in social function – my station and its duties' (*SS* 31). Still, he takes care to expand and more clearly define certain of its aspects and, in so doing, addresses some of the problems raised by Bradley.

First, take the idea of 'station'. Bradley never explicitly defines this term, nor does he seem decided about in what entity or in what institution one's 'station' resides. He speaks of stations being part of a 'visible community' (*ES* 204), but it remains unclear whether this 'community' is the nation state or some other social unit (see *ES* 163, n. 1; 173–4; 198; 184–5).[27] Indeed, Bradley gives no explanation at all of why a theory of social duty requires the notion of 'station'.

On this issue, if not more persuasive, Bosanquet is at least less vague. Bradley suggests that, in the morality of 'my station', there is one social order where each individual has one specific place. Bosanquet, however, is aware of the multiplicity of activities and positions a person may have. What Bosanquet means by 'my station', then, is not just one's occupation or vocation, but the set of positions or functions one has in a social order, recognized in social institutions and in law by the state. For example, an adult citizen in a democratic state has the particular 'position' of being a citizen, but this is obviously not the only position she may have – she might be a parent, a spouse, a teacher, a neighbour, and so on. And these 'positions' are not purely arbitrary, for they reflect how that person is recognized within the broader social consciousness (*PTS* 196–7).

Second, consider the question of the nature and origin of one's duties. For Bradley, my duty is 'my will either thought of, or actually, realising the universal' (*ES* 208). Correlative to one's duties are one's rights. Thus, Bradley says that not

---

[26] Compare here Bradley's comment that 'you cannot confine a man to his station and its duties' (*ES* 204).

[27] For a discussion of some of these issues, see Crispin Wright, 'The Moral Organism', in Manser and Stock, 1984, pp. 77–97.

only is it 'false that you can have rights without duties', it is also 'false that you can have duties without rights' (*ES* 213; see 208). He adds, moreover, that just as there are two kinds of duties, so there are two kinds of 'rights': real and ideal. 'The first are the will of the state or society, the second the will of the ideal-social or non-social ideal' (*ES* 208) – ie. rights held apart from one's 'station' (see *ES* 219ff.).

There are, however, several difficulties with this account of one's duties. Some of these are noted by Bradley when he explains why he believes the morality of 'my station' to be inadequate, but there are others as well. For example, Bradley is vague about the role of the state in the existence of rights and is also unclear about its relation to moral principle.[28] If, as Bosanquet holds, Green failed to recognize the full value of the state (*PTS* ix), one might ask whether Bradley did any better. Furthermore, although Bradley refers to rights as corresponding to the individual's station, there is no clear sense of how precisely a person acquires these rights. Similar questions can be raised concerning what Bradley calls 'ideal rights'. From where, exactly, do these rights come, who or what can enforce them, and how can they be binding? It seems plausible to claim that rights and correlative obligations are integral to certain stations. But, independent of social life, how can there be ideal duties and how could these imply, in turn, corresponding general rights?

Bosanquet's version of the morality of 'my station' attempts to avoid these problems. To begin with, he draws a distinction (which Bradley does not) between 'duty' and 'obligation'.[29] Thus, on the one hand, the idea of 'obligation' is tied to those of 'position' and of 'right'. Specifically, it is by virtue of having a position that a person is said to have certain powers or rights. If this power is to be effective, however, other individuals may be required, by law, not to interfere with the exercise of these rights. Alternatively, having a position may require the holder of that position to act in a specific way. Or again, that person may be required

---

[28] See also *AR* 469, n. 1.

[29] Admittedly, Bosanquet does not always make this distinction between duties and obligations. See, for example, his account of conflicts of duty in *SS* 108–109.

to respect the rights – or, better perhaps, 'the functions and positions' – of others (*PTS* 194). In each of these cases, in so far as this requirement is 'enforceable by law' (*PTS* 194), it is an obligation. Still, neither rights nor obligations are fundamental. 'Both', Bosanquet writes, 'are the varied external conditions of "positions" as regarded from different points of view' (*PTS* 195).

Duties, on the other hand, refer to something else. By 'duty', Bosanquet means 'the purpose with a view to which the right is secured' (*PTS* 195). Duty, then, is the moral basis of right, and it is from this that rights and obligations derive their imperative authority. And what does Bosanquet say is one's duty? Self realization: to make 'the best of human capacities' (*PTS* 195).

Given this distinction, along with a more sophisticated account of the state, Bosanquet is able to provide a defence of the morality of 'my station'. First, Bosanquet supplies a means by which one can determine one's duty. Bradley's alternative – 'ideal morality' – allows that a person's duty may be 'to act up to what his light tells him is best' (*ES* 237, see 247). But Bosanquet would presumably respond here that if one fails to distinguish between duty and obligation, and if the discernment of one's duty is left to that individual, there would be nothing to prevent that person's private inclination from masquerading as duty.[30] Consequently, Bosanquet insists that it is in our social life and institutions that we come to know what our duty is. Yet this is not to say that morality is reduced to conformity to the *status quo*. Indeed, one of the 'duties' to which Bosanquet explicitly refers is the 'duty of rebellion' (*PTS* 199).

Again, differentiating between duty and obligation is important for a correct understanding of the nature of rights. Rights are on a par with obligations and, just as obligations are 'demands enforced by law' (*PTS* 194), rights are 'claims which both are and ought to be enforceable by law' (*PTS*

---

[30] Indeed, David Crossley suggests that 'Bradley's own moral theory...is a form of non-hedonistic egoism'. See 'Bradley on the Absolute Right of the State over the Individual', in Guy Lafrance (ed.), *Ethique et droits fondamentaux = Ethics and Basic Rights* (University of Ottawa Press, 1989), pp. 138–44, p. 144, n. 10.

195). There can, therefore, be no 'ideal rights', nor can there be any rights that are not specifically related to a position held by a person. Thus, even if there are non-social duties (eg. of rebellion), Bosanquet would still deny that there could be any corresponding non-social or ideal rights.

Admittedly, the view that one's duty is self-realization, 'the realization of values accepted as supreme for the self' (*SS* 148; see 40, 159, 179), is somewhat vague. Still, what Bosanquet says individuals are called on to do is much more specific. In order to 'respond adequately to the situation' (*SS* 146), they must do nothing less than fulfil the particular *obligations* of their stations. Of course, this does not mean that they *must* not do more. But Bosanquet points out that moral failure usually occurs because individuals do not meet the demands of their stations, not because they do 'only' that much. And lest Bosanquet be accused of proposing too easy a standard, it should be pointed out that even self-sacrifice may be required by one's station.[31]

Yet not only is Bosanquet's account of the morality of 'my station' more complete than the version discussed and rejected by Bradley; it appears to respond to many of the objections that Bradley brought against it. One of these criticisms is that the morality of 'my station' reinforces the *status quo* and makes moral progress impossible (*ES* 204–205). But what does one do, for example, if one's 'social duties' are inconsistent with the moral end? What if, as Bradley notes, 'the community in which he is a member may be in a confused or rotten condition' (*ES* 203)? Both situations are clearly possible since, as Bosanquet himself recognizes, no society or state is 'completely consistent' with what it should be (*PTS* 198).

Bosanquet would reply that, in each case, the question supposes that social life is essentially static, whereas the

---

[31] Compare *ES* 204. Here, Bradley says that one may not '*see* his realization' in sacrificing himself for the community. Bosanquet's point, however, is that a complete understanding of the expression 'Die to live' – that is, of the morality of 'my station' – includes just this. (See n. 14, above.)

increase in knowledge and the intellectual and rational development of human persons in fact points to a different conclusion. As human beings grow and develop, society changes, so that there is a gradual working out of inconsistencies (*PTS* 198). And, as each inconsistency is amended, 'the path is opened to progress by the emergence of another' (*PTS* 198). The morality of 'my station' is essentially dynamic, and Bosanquet suggests that what tensions exist between it and the moral end can largely be addressed and resolved within social life.

Bosanquet believes, then, that while we discover our duty within social life, what society ultimately expects of us is not to preserve existing social arrangements, but for us to become what we have it in ourselves to be. He rejects, as well, any attitude of 'complacency' in moral philosophy: 'It is uncritical and false so far as it accepts any *status quo*, and especially the ease and comfort of any limited section of living beings' (*SS* 175). Bosanquet does not deny, of course, that there could be a conflict between one's duty and one's social obligations. Nevertheless, determining what one's duty is and whether it conflicts with one's obligations depends on social, and not the isolated individual's, consciousness.

One final dissimilarity between Bradley's and Bosanquet's accounts of morality should be noted. While the theory of 'my station' might suggest that one's obligations are determined solely by the society in which one lives, unlike Bradley, Bosanquet is open in principle to the possibility that 'humanity' could serve as the fundamental moral community (*PTS* 305–310).[32] To be sure, Bosanquet admits that there is as yet no basis in common experience for such a community to exist but, in his later work, he allows that institutions like the League of Nations might be seen as reflections of such an 'ethical idea'. A more broadly-based community could, he argues, oblige one to abandon or go beyond the obligations

---

[32] Compare *ES* 205, n. 1; 222, n. 2; 231–2. See also *SS* 77. This question is discussed by Peter P. Nicholson, in 'Philosophical Idealism and International Politics: A Reply to Dr. Savigear', *British Journal of International Studies*, vol. 2 (1976), pp. 76–83. See also my 'Individual Rights, Communitarianism and British Idealism', in Creighton Peden and John K. Roth (eds.), *Rights, Justice and Community* (Lewiston, New York: Edwin Mellen, 1992).

of one's station in a particular society or state.[33] But in saying this, Bosanquet is not (pace Milne)[34] abandoning the morality of 'my station' altogether. He is simply locating the person within a greater whole.

If one grants, then, that Bosanquet's account of the moral life is significantly different from that of Bradley, one may still ask how it is that they came to hold such distinct views. Interestingly, one explanation – perhaps unexpected, given Bosanquet's reputation as a philosopher of the Absolute – concerns the nature and value of the human person, ie. the 'finite self'. That the difference between his and Bradley's ethical thought should involve the notion of 'self' is not, however, entirely surprising. After all, the 'self' is clearly central to any ethics that is defined as 'self-realization' or 'self-transcendence'.

This attention to the human person is evident throughout Bosanquet's work in ethics and politics. The description of morality that he gives, as shown above, emphasizes the moral end as not just the realization of certain values, but one of individual development. Thus, although Bosanquet speaks of self-realization as 'the realisation of all human capacity, without waste or failure' (*PTS* 141), he understands it also to mean the development of talents or capabilities in the individual human person, so that that person can become 'fully what it is able to be' and what it really wants to be (*PTS* 131). In fact, even the former, more general sense of 'self-realization' includes the realization of individuals.

Bosanquet refers to this moral 'end' of both the individual and of the community as 'the rational life' (*PTS* 189), and this life not only reflects, but is based on, the rational character of the human individual. As H. J. Paton says of Kant's 'kingdom of ends', it 'is the framework within which the private ends of ourselves and others ought to be realised'.[35] Such an end

---

[33] A. J. M. Milne suggests that, in this respect, Bosanquet is following Green. See *The Social Philosophy of English Idealism* (London: Allen and Unwin, 1962), p. 262.

[34] Milne, 1962, p. 262.

[35] H. J. Paton, *The Categorical Imperative: A Study in Kant's Moral Philosophy* (New York: Harper Torchbooks, 1967), p. 187.

can be reached, however, only if human beings participate actively in their own realization; if this were not so, there would be no reason for Bosanquet to insist on the importance of moral decision-making. It is precisely through moral activity that human personality is able to develop and, hence, the moral end realized. Of course, one might object that this need not entail that specific individuals have a particular value. All it asserts is that the moral end would be unattainable without human effort. But then, such an obligation ignores that which makes this moral end *imperative* is that it is the realization of the particular individual.

Concern for the human individual can also be seen when Bosanquet underlines the centrality of the individual will for the existence of morality. Its significance is due to more than the fact that 'the moral system' needs 'to particularize itself in a given station and function, ie. in my actions and by my will' (*ES* 180). According to Bosanquet, the moral character or worth of an action is based on the motive – on it being the uncoerced product of an individual's will (*PTS* 156) – not simply on its conduciveness to the moral end.[36] Or again, consider Bosanquet's view of moral development as a process by which persons attempt to live up to, and realize in their lives, what is demanded by the general will. One might infer from this that what counts is just the general will, and that one must entirely 'renounce' the individual will (see *ES* 325). But the general will, Bosanquet holds, is not something merely external to a person. It is an extension of the rational character of the individual self; it is our particular will 'corrected and amended by what we want at all other moments', and more (*PTS* 111). Thus, Bosanquet calls the general will the individual's 'real will', and it is in obeying this 'real will' that, he claims, we are obeying only ourselves (*PTS* 134).

Despite what one might initially believe, it is important to realize that there is no contradiction between the morality of 'my station' and the individual's self-realization. Unlike

---

[36] 'It is...the ground or motive which alone would give [an act] immediate value or durable certainty as an element in the best life' (*PTS* 176). For this reason, Bosanquet holds that the coercive activity of the state must be limited.

Bradley, where the 'end' of ethics ultimately requires transcending not only 'the private self' (*ES* 182), but the moral life (*ES* 314–44), Bosanquet maintains that the 'end' of 'my station' is *my* realization. By holding to this, he believes that he opts for a morality not only in which the individual human person has the greatest chance for success in moral action, but which best contributes to a person's intellectual, material and social development. In short, on Bosanquet's reading of the morality of 'my station', the individual is expanded, not abandoned.

To sum up: like Bradley, Bosanquet identifies self-realization as the moral end, but he puts particular emphasis on the fact that the self which must be realized is the finite self. In fact, Bosanquet says that '[the] aim of politics is to find and realize the individual' (*PTS* lvi) – and it is clear from the context that he is referring here to the individual human person. What each person's will demands and what the nature of the 'self' requires, however, is a process of 'harmonizing and readjusting' to bring this self 'into rational shape' (*PTS* 111). On Bosanquet's view, then, self-realization involves movement towards coherence and consistency in just the same way as the society in which selves live is itself moving towards coherence and consistency. This, in turn, involves individuals doing their duty. Consequently, Bosanquet argues that we find what our duty requires only in social life and that we move towards self-realization only by fulfilling the demands of the various stations that we may have. 'My station and its duties' and individual self-realization are not opposed.

II

Like Bradley, Bosanquet rejected the view that the 'isolated' individual constitutes the principle of value. Indeed, much of what Bosanquet has to say in his metaphysics about the nature and the value of the 'finite self' seems more consistent with Bradley's work than with his own ethics and social philosophy.[37] Nevertheless, there is some reason to believe

---

[37] Andrew Vincent suggests the existence of a similar tension in Hegel. See his 'The Individual in Hegelian Thought', *Idealistic Studies*, vol. 12 (1982), pp 156–68, p. 165.

that the difference between Bradley and Bosanquet concerning the moral life is also reflected in their respective metaphysics, particularly as it concerns the nature of the self and its relation to the Absolute.

Consider, to begin with, the concept of the 'self': an ethic of self-realization or self-transcendence obviously depends on understanding what it is that is to be realized or transcended. The individual self is clearly an important concern of Bosanquet's philosophy,[38] and 'individuality' in all its senses[39] was the theme of his Gifford Lectures. It is no surprise, then, that the notions of 'individual' and 'self' are fundamental, not only for his conceptions of morality and politics, but for his psychology, metaphysics and even his logic.[40]

Admittedly, at first inspection, the accounts given by Bosanquet and Bradley do seem much the same. Like Bradley,[41] Bosanquet rejects a 'false particularisation' of the human self which emphasizes it in its 'aspect of isolation' and 'independently of [its] relation to the end' and to other human beings (*PTS* 189). Nor will Bosanquet accept a view where the individual is seen as an 'atom' – a being distinct from every other being – which 'has so little in him that you cannot imagine it possible to break him into lesser parts' (*PTS* 74). He criticizes this conception of the 'apparently separate human being *wie er geht und steht*' (*PIV* 269; see *VDI* 11), and argues against both the personalist (eg. Pringle-Pattison) and the empiricist (eg. J. S. Mill) views of the 'distinction

---

[38] In *LFI*, Bosanquet distinguishes between the self or soul and 'the finite individual' (*LFI* 100), but such a distinction need not concern the reader here. This distinction is, in any case, quite different from that between the self and 'finite centres of feeling' that one finds in Bradley (*AR* 464–5, n. 1; see also *ETR* 414–21). See Garrett L. Vander Veer, *Bradley's Metaphysics and the Self* (New Haven: Yale University Press, 1970), p. 310.

[39] For a brief summary of some of the senses in which Bosanquet uses this term, see my 'L'individu et les droits de la personne selon Maritain et Bosanquet', in *Études Maritainiennes/Maritain Studies*, no. 6 (June 1990), pp. 141–66, especially pp. 157–8.

[40] In addition to the texts noted above, see also Bosanquet's *Psychology of the Moral Self* (1897).

[41] Recall Bradley's argument that if 'the self has been narrowed to a point which does not change, that point is less than the real self' (*AR* 69).

between finite selves or persons' (*VDI* 46–62). Thus, Bosanquet denies that human individuals could be 'necessarily eternal or everlasting units' (*LFI* 87) or 'differentiations of the absolute' (*LFI* 86; see *PTS* 166).

At times, even the language that Bosanquet employs to describe the nature and value of the finite self seems to be inspired by Bradley. He says that 'the finite world is one with the world of appearance' (*VDI* 15, see n. 1) and that 'the self as we know him in Space and Time...is a figure deformed and diminished' (*PIV* 383) and 'essentially...imperfect and inconsistent with itself' (*PIV* 249). Moreover, in his contribution to a symposium entitled 'Do Finite Individuals Possess a Substantive or an Adjectival Mode of Being?', Bosanquet writes that '[for] what appears as a passage in time, the Absolute has need to express itself through us as very subordinate units...; when its life demands our existence no longer, we yet blend with it as the pervading features or characters, which we were needed for a passing moment to emphasise...' (*LFI* 102). Altogether, these comments seem to point to the human individual as having merely an 'adjectival' mode of being and value.

But it is intriguing that, in the passage just cited, Bosanquet refers to chapter 4 of *Some Suggestions in Ethics*. His point in this chapter is to remind the reader of the value of the contribution of the 'anonymous individual' to the social good, and he repeats this view throughout his work – that individuals characterize the world 'as permanent qualifications' (*LFI* 101). Of course, Bradley would agree that such 'appearances' are 'indispensable' (*AR* 404; 431) for the manifestation of the Absolute. But this is of little comfort to those who wish to retain a special status for the human individual since, for Bradley, *all* degrees of reality – both the self and the non-self – 'are all alike essential and necessary to the Absolute' (*AR* 404). In fact, whatever the place of humanity is, it does not seem particularly important to him; Bradley says, '[where] humanity stands in the scale of being we do not know' (*ETR* 244). But Bosanquet would never ask, as Bradley does, of 'the ideas and wishes of "fellows such as I crawling between heaven and earth", how much do they count in the march or the drift of the Universe?' (*ETR* 243).[42]

Witness, for example, how each attempts to arrive at an adequate concept of the 'self'. While Bradley's approach in *Appearance and Reality* is to 'deconstruct' the individual and to show how various conceptions of the self lead to contradictions,[43] Bosanquet focuses on building the individual up – on 'transmuting or expanding the power of common finite mind' (*PIV* 376). He begins with the finite self and moves to its interconnectedness with other selves and with the environment. But this is not, as Bradley would hold, to confuse the self with the non-self.[44] Rather, it is simply to recognize what is required for the self's most complete expression. For his part, Bosanquet follows the Greek conception of nature as *physis* – dynamism and growth – and, thus, he says that man's 'nature...is in the process of being communicated to him' (*PIV* 259). The finite self, then, has a 'nisus towards absolute unity and self-completion' (*VDI* 4). It is only so far as it falls short of this, Bosanquet suggests, that the individual self is insufficient as an absolute principle (*PIV* 310). According to Bosanquet, then, the difficulty in speaking of the 'reality' of finite consciousness is not (as Bradley would have it) because it is inherently contradictory, but because it is not yet realized.

Again, consider what Bosanquet says about the nature and role of the finite self. He explicitly resists what seems to be a tendency towards 'panpsychism' in Bradley, where nature is seen on the level of consciousness (*PIV* 362; see xxxvi). Such a view not only ignores the 'complementariness of mind and nature' (*PIV* 363), but also excludes 'finite spiritual beings' from a central role – that is, that of mediator between nature and the Absolute (*PIV* 361; 382ff.). For Bosanquet, while the Absolute manifests itself throughout nature, it does so funda-

---

[42] Cited in Vincent, 1982, p. 160.

[43] See *AR* 101 and Richard Wollheim's discussion of 'Bradley's reductionist account of the self', in *F. H. Bradley* (Harmondsworth: Penguin Books, 1959), p. 137.

[44] Recall Bradley's argument that 'feeling' cannot be used to discern or represent the self, because it could not distinguish adequately between the self and the environment and, thus, the extension of the term 'self' would be too broad (*AR* 90–92).

mentally through the self (*PIV* 365),[45] and its privileged manifestation is the work of the human spirit – namely, social life, art and religion.

Of course, Bosanquet often speaks of individuality, not as what is peculiar to an individual human person, but as the 'content of the self' (*VDI* 287). Here he has in mind those 'interests and affections which carry us beyond our formal and exclusive self' (*VDI* 288), and which are present in 'the great achievements of knowledge, of social and super-social morality, of the sense of beauty, and of religion' (*VDI* 378; see *PIV* 270). This corresponds to the more general sense of 'self-realization' referred to in the previous section. In fact, on Bosanquet's view, 'we care for what transcends us, more than for our self' (*VDI* 288), and it is this, and not the finite self, that is fundamentally valuable and most important.

But why, one might ask, is this 'content of the self' so central? To say that it serves as a standard of value does not answer the question, but merely moves it back one step. To say that these characteristics are the 'most coherent' of experiences says something more, but does not explain why they should matter to us. We must add, Bosanquet suggests that they are the product of the logic and the rationality inherent in the finite self – what he calls 'the nisus towards a whole' (*PIV* xx). This kind of argument for the importance of the self is, however, neither explicit nor implied in Bradley.[46]

One further point: when Bosanquet argues that the individual is adjectival and not substantial, he still holds that

---

[45] Thus, Bosanquet says that 'the finite self, then, qua finite, is the centre or awakening of a determinate world' (*PIV* 190; see 382). Andrew Vincent concludes from this that 'the finite mind is the vehicle of the whole. The universe reaches a pitch of comprehensiveness in human consciousness' (Vincent, 1982, p. 159). Similarly, François Houang argues that, for Bosanquet, human spirit in its diverse manifestations is the unique vehicle of the self-revelation of the Absolute. According to Houang, Bosanquet considers 'les esprits humains comme les uniques véhicules de l'auto-révélation de l'Absolu' (Houang, *Neo-hegelianisme*, p. 125).

[46] Arguably, this account of the finite self as mediator between nature and consciousness, and as having a particular importance, is possible because Bosanquet readily adopts the view that the more coherent or inclusive something is, the higher or more real it will be (see *PIV* 270). Bradley, however, does not 'follow' Hegel here. See James Bradley in MacEwan, 1992.

individuals have 'a relative independence' (*LFI* 80), and he takes care to insist – as Bradley does not – that, while finite human beings are 'adjectival', they are not 'mere adjectives' (*LFI* 97). Bosanquet acknowledges that 'it is our nature to be a single self' (*LFI* 92) and that selfhood is not 'a trivial or unreal thing' (*PIV* 289). The difficulty is simply that if 'I set up to be in myself a self centred real' (*LFI* 93), I tend to lose sight of 'the moral and spiritual structure that lies behind the visible scene' (*LFI* 90). For a complete understanding of the self, then, we 'must make at least as much of co-existent as of continuous identity. Otherwise, we unnaturally narrow down the basis of our self' (*LFI* 96).

For Bosanquet, then, the individual self has a unique and important function. Nonetheless, its nature and value cannot be determined independently of its relation to others. The 'perfection of the finite self' (*LFI* 99) occurs through social activity – 'in that distinctive act or service' (*LFI* 170) to the social good. Moreover, it is in this activity that a person has his specific identity. Following what he believes is Plato's view, Bosanquet says that 'every separate mind [is] to be distinguished by uniqueness of function or service within the community' (*VDI* 49). Thus, 'individuality' and personal identity depend on there being something greater than the finite self, and it is in this sense that finite individuality is 'adjectival'. One sees a reflection of this, not only in Bosanquet's politics and ethics, where he discusses the essentially social character of the individual and the relation of individual good to the common good, but even in his logic, where every item of knowledge reveals itself to be part of a larger system. Indeed, this 'inclusion in a completer [*sic*] whole of experience', Bosanquet says, 'is a matter of everyday verification' (*PIV* 373; see 27 and 374).

It is clear then that while there are certainly some important similarities between Bosanquet's and Bradley's accounts of the nature and role of the individual self, there are also significant differences. Nevertheless, one may well ask how Bosanquet's view of the nature of finite individuality squares with his notion of the Absolute, and how this compares to the analysis given by Bradley. It is generally held that Bosanquet's 'absolutism' is the most Bradleyan aspect of his work.[47] According to François Houang, it was the publication of *Appearance and Reality* that put Bosanquet on the road to 'absolutism',[48] and A. J. M. Milne claims that Bosanquet's objective in his Gifford Lectures was 'to reformulate and restate the theory of the Absolute...[to] meet the criticisms which had been made against Bradley's work'.[49] But these assessments overlook some important features of Bosanquet's thought.

Bradley is often taken to emphasize the gap between a self which is fundamentally contradictory and an Absolute in which all contradiction is resolved. Moreover, he does not say just what place the self has in the Absolute, and this Absolute is something which, he maintains, finite mind can never know directly. Now, as neither Bradley nor Bosanquet provides a clear statement of the nature of the Absolute,[50] and since both maintain that those characteristics which reflect the particularity of finite creatures have no permanent place within it, it is no surprise that their views have been seen to be more or less the same. Still, in spite of this apparent agreement, it is interesting that much of what Bosanquet does say about the Absolute concerns its relation to the finite individual. Indeed, understanding this connection is central to understanding Bosanquet's account of both the self and the Absolute.

Bosanquet believes that the theory of the Absolute is entirely consistent with what we take to be the nature and value of the self. He describes the self as characterized by an 'impulse towards unity and coherence' (*PIV* 340), and the Absolute, then, is 'the spiritual organism in which the finite being finds to some extent completeness and satisfaction' (*VDI* 208). By

---

[47] See the references in notes 1 and 5 above. Moreover, in his Gifford Lectures – regarded as the definitive statement of his metaphysical views – Bosanquet acknowledges a great debt to Bradley (eg. especially in Lecture V of *VDI*).

[48] See note 5 above and Houang, *De l'Absolutisme*, p. 9.

[49] Milne, 1962, p. 184.

[50] His most complete account occurs in *PIV*, lecture 10, appendix 1. Here, however, Bosanquet is more interested in attacking certain theories than in saying what the Absolute is.

'the Absolute', Bosanquet does not 'mean simply the social whole or the general will' (*VDI* 208) – though it is in some sense an extension or implication of the principles that lead to society and the general will. Instead, he means 'the whole world of achievements, habits, institutions in which the apparent individual finds some clue to the reality which is the truth of himself' (*VDI* 208). Thus, Bosanquet describes the Absolute as 'our ultimate self' (*PIV* 378) and says, 'if I possessed myself entirely, I should be the Absolute' (*LFI* 85).

It is just this movement to coherence and completeness that was seen to be at work in Bosanquet's analysis of the moral life. While there is no explicit reference to the Absolute in *The Philosophical Theory of the State*, it would seem to be just this that Bosanquet has in mind when he refers to the 'end' both of man and of the State as being 'the rational life' (*PTS* 189). He says, for example, that this life is 'determined by the logic of the [individual's] will' (*PTS* 173; see *SS* 37), and that such an end 'gives effect to the self as a whole, or removes its contradictions and so makes it most fully what it is able to be, or what, by the implied nature of each and all of its wants, it may be said really to want to be' (*PTS* 131). Recall, as well, that Bosanquet identifies this 'end' also with 'the best life' (*PTS* 188). Human beings are essentially minds (*PIV* 381, *PTS* 45), and their 'end' must reflect this. But human minds are not just intelligences; they have emotions, exhibit creativity and spirituality, and more. 'The best life', then, must be a life which 'satisfies the fundamental logic of man's capacities' (*PTS* 169). Indeed, Bosanquet will also describe this 'end' as 'the excellence of souls' (cf. *PTS* xxxvii, xxxix), the complete realization of the individual (cf. *PTS* xv–xvi) and 'the existence and the perfection of human personality' (*PTS* 189). It is precisely this 'realisation of our self which we instinctively demand and desire' that Bosanquet calls, in his Gifford Lectures, 'the eternal reality of the Absolute' (*VDI* 288).

It is significant that Bosanquet's notion of the Absolute can be described as 'the rational life'. Like Hegel, Bosanquet holds that the 'reality' of a thing is a reflection of its rationality, and vice versa, so that it is precisely because the

Absolute is rational that it is also said to be real. By 'rationality' here, what Bosanquet means is simply the elimination of contradiction between, and the increasing coherence in, things. Thus, as one can see in Bosanquet's account of the general will (*PTS* 111; see p. 43 above), the 'finite self' or mind becomes more complete and, therefore, increasingly rational and real, the more it brings into relation both what it knows and wills and the knowledge and will that surrounds it. In this way, the individual self approximates the Absolute, and it is for this reason that the clues to the Absolute are also to be found in the increasing complexity of the relations within and among finite beings.

This view of the Absolute draws two points to our attention. First, it reminds us that, for Bosanquet, the Absolute is the most complex set of relations among finite entities and not, as in Bradley, the absence of all relation. Second, so far as it is continuous with individual rationality, the Absolute is something that can be known. In fact, no matter how wide the gap between the Absolute and the finite individual, it is precisely in the most rational activities – and not (as Bradley would have it) in 'feeling' – that we have access to it (*PIV* 80; 250; *VDI* 312). (By 'the most rational activities' here, Bosanquet has in mind the 'highest of our experiences', such as social morality, art, philosophy and religion.) Bosanquet concludes that whether we are aware of it or not, 'we experience the Absolute better than we experience anything else' (*PIV* 27; see 378).

Bosanquet's description of the self and the Absolute, then, differs from Bradley's in several ways. It is clear that Bosanquet spends more time on the nature of the finite self and is concerned with showing just how many of the average person's intuitions can be accommodated within a non-individualistic metaphysic. His view of the self is also more constructive and 'forward-looking', focusing on relations between it and those features of the world that enable selves to acquire a more concrete and complete individuality. Furthermore, the self is not something that can be felt or known only intuitively, and we know better what the self is when we understand its relations in the world. And

Bosanquet is particularly explicit about the role of the self and about its importance in the Absolute. Indeed, there is even some suggestion that the self has a special degree of reality and, therefore, a special value. Such arguments, however, are not evident in Bradley; in *Appearance and Reality*, the self is just one among many different candidates for the role of ultimate principle.

Given the standard view of Bosanquet's work, one may be apt to overlook this claim that the Absolute is to be identified with, and defended as, the realization of the finite self. For Bosanquet, the Absolute is both the end and, in a sense, the product of the 'logic' or 'nisus' to totality present in rational mind. One consequence of this is that the distinction between the finite self and the Absolute is not an unbridgeable gap. In fact, Bosanquet holds that the Absolute is especially evident in our highest experiences and that it is expressed in everything and present all around us. Unlike Bradley, then, Bosanquet gives more attention and emphasis to the nature, value and role of the finite self and to its compatibility with the Absolute.

If one is to grant that the relation between Bradley and Bosanquet is not as close as has been generally maintained, one may still wonder how to account for the differences noted above. Admittedly, no definitive answer presents itself, but it may be, in part, that there are important dissimilarities in the empirical basis from which each began.[51] Bosanquet brought a wide range of practical experience to his philosophical work. While Bradley spent his adult life almost entirely at Merton College, Bosanquet moved back and forth between the academic world and public affairs, teaching at Oxford (1871–81) and at the University of St Andrews (1903–1908), but also working in the 1880s and 1890s with the Charity Organisation Society, the London Ethical Society and, later, the London School of Ethics and Social Philosophy. This involvement in social assistance and education not only convinced him of the importance of individual effort in the

---

[51] Both Bradley and Bosanquet saw their work as expressing the 'plain man's' view, even if it was not what the 'plain man' explicitly believed. The matter of its 'empirical' dimension, however, cannot be dealt with here.

development of autonomy and character; it also confirmed his view of the social dimension of the individual person. It is in one's 'service to the whole' that one is 'realized', but it is also precisely in this service that the whole depends on the human individual.

Another relevant factor is that Bosanquet came rather late to Absolute theory. His Gifford Lectures – the first complete statement of his metaphysics – were given when he was already sixty-three, and he no doubt saw the Absolute as providing an explanatory background in terms of which the data he had long acquired in his public service might now be explained. Of course, one can find traces of so-called 'absolutism' throughout Bosanquet's writings, but his concern with individuality is evident from his earliest work in logic. His description of the individual as having an inherent tendency to totality, the identification of the 'real' with the 'rational', and the definition of 'the rational' as the most comprehensive and coherent, suggests that the best account of the finite human person requires that it be understood as having a place – though a distinctive and unique place – within a larger system. Arguably, then, it was through his efforts to understand the nature of individuality, rather than an a priori attachment to absolutism, that Bosanquet came to a theory of the Absolute.

III

What this study has attempted to defend is the view that, even though Bosanquet and Bradley share certain insights into ethics and metaphysics, their positions diverge significantly. Specifically, I have suggested that a fundamental reason for this divergence concerns the status of the finite self. Unlike Bradley, Bosanquet was interested in not losing sight of this in his theory of ultimate reality – which was reflected in his insistence on the moral philosophy of 'my station' over Bradley's 'ideal morality', his frequent references to the finite self as an essential element in metaphysics, his view of the Absolute as the realization, and not the extinction, of the finite self and, of course, in his work in social welfare and education. There is good reason to hold, then, that the humanist tendencies noted by François Houang in Bosanquet's early work continue through his 'middle period' and on into his later studies in metaphysics. In fact, there seems to be some ground for saying with Charles Le Chevalier[52] that Bosanquet is, even if not much less of an absolutist, at least more of a humanist than generally thought.

How are we to understand the relation between Bradley and Bosanquet? The fact that Bosanquet often cites Bradley does not by itself constitute any conclusive proof that he 'follows Bradley'. Such references are generally illustrative rather than employed to prove a particular point – for example, Bosanquet makes almost as many references to Green in the Gifford Lectures as he does to Bradley. Again, Houang's view, that the development of Bosanquet's philosophy corresponds directly to the influence of Bradley,[53] ignores that much of what Bosanquet says in 1889 on the role of the individual in society is very much the same as what he said in 1923, in the fourth edition of *The Philosophical Theory of the State*.

This being said, it is clear that Bosanquet considered Bradley's work in metaphysics and ethics to have been momentous. But this admiration was, surely, influenced by the fact that what Bradley was doing and the way in which he did it, more or less reflected Bosanquet's own interests and approach. Thus, even though much of Bosanquet's published philosophical work came 'after' similar work in Bradley, and even if he was to some degree influenced by it, it does not follow that Bosanquet merely 'followed Bradley'. It is worth noting that, despite the similarity in education, interest and outlook, the two men were not friends, and the existing correspondence between them exhibits a strong formality.[54]

---

[52] According to Charles Le Chevalier, 'à son insu peut-être Bosanquet fut avant tout un moraliste' and his metaphysics 'se nourrit d'un continu moral', *Ethique et idealisme: Le courant neo-hegelien en angleterre* (Paris: Vrin, 1963), p. 14.

[53] Houang, *Neo-hegelianisme*, p. 8. See note 5 above.

[54] See G. R. G. Mure, 'Francis Herbert Bradley', in *Les études philosophiques*, vol. 15 (1960), p. 76 and Muirhead (1935), *passim*.

Perhaps, then, the most accurate statement of the relationship between the two is that which Bosanquet himself gave after the publication of *Appearance and Reality* that Bradley was 'only "telling him his own dream"'.[55] But for one to be told his own dream, it is clear that he must have already dreamt it.

---

[55] Muirhead, 1935, p. 26.

BRADLEY AND THE CANADIAN CONNECTION

Elizabeth Trott

Imagine, if you will, a crackling cold morning, minus 20°C, and snow drifts high enough to all but obliterate a small wooden shelter from view, save for its stalwart steeple. Imagine crowded inside a handful of friends and strangers so bundled in heavy woollens as to make their faces barely visible, huddled together on wooden benches, their feet on sacks of hot potatoes and rocks brought in from the buggies and cutters outside, all hoping the sermon will be short and that the rocks won't cool to freezing before the trip home.

Imagine a certain restlessness. There is only *one* building to gather in and only *one* pastor to hear. The *other* church building can't be started till the spring break-up because the barge with lumber is frozen in twenty miles up stream. The *other* pastor, having been kicked by his horse is twenty miles downstream waiting for his broken leg to heal. Shoulder to shoulder, Catholics, Protestants, and a miscellany of others wait for guidance and comfort, while each curses his or her luck at having to sit beside infidels, fools (who are muttering Latin and crossing themselves) and the unenlightened (who think hard work *alone* will bring salvation).

And now imagine a young man armed only with a Bible and a sheaf of lecture notes, his fingers half frozen from trying to clear a path and get the door open before his parishioners arrived, wondering what to say.

It isn't a scene that John Watson (1847–1939), Canada's most eminent philosopher, ever faced himself. But during the early part of his career in Canada (Watson taught at Queen's University in Kingston, Ontario from 1872–1924) many of his students, as circuit preachers or small-town ministers, would face such situations and Watson could not have been ignorant of the problems they were going to confront. Watson and his English-Canadian colleagues needed to develop principles of metaphysics and ethics which would provide ground for common understanding of diverse perceptions and shared experience in a newly developing country. The multiple faiths and intuitions of settlers would be inadequate tools for reconciling conflicting perceptions and contradictory modes of determining truths about reality. There had to be a common reality that people shared or there would be no hope of settling disputes. And for such a reality to be recognized as common, the sharing process, whereby knowledge was formulated and expressed, had to be part of that reality. Furthermore, God, or the Absolute, or the ultimate reality could not be separate from or stand in opposition to that reality, let alone wear too many different coats, lest the attempt to find common ground for first principles be thwarted by beliefs that acted as road blocks to communication.

The seclusion afforded to reclusive Oxford dons which enabled them to speculate about the world was nowhere in evidence in Canada. It was not uncommon for professors to be carrying a teaching load of twenty or so hours a week, to be teaching more than one subject, carrying substantial administrative duties and writing papers and books (not to mention helping to raise several children). One's daily habits and experiences were very much rooted in the developing country. Philosophers travelled to church basements and private homes to give lectures; they conducted public debates in newspapers, acted as school inspectors, rabble rousers, and community servants.[1] Sense needed to be made of the unimaginable conflicts and contradictions of a world where nature was a far cry from Wordsworthian reflections, and God had no favourites, no elite, no select few. If the same God was overseeing the tough little sparrows that did survive a Canadian winter, as well as the English swallows that

[1] For a fuller account of philosophers in Canada see Leslie Armour and Elizabeth Trott, *The Faces of Reason: An Essay on Philosophy and Culture in English Canada, 1850–1950* (Waterloo: Wilfred Laurier Press, 1981), 516pp.

wintered in the Mediterranean, some new way of explaining (and making accessible to ornery and ordinary people) this ultimate ground of existence had to be found.

Watson's concept of the Absolute was intended to provide that explanation. Hopefully it would translate into a few urgent words that would reach everybody who had made it to church that day, and in having achieved *just that* probably felt they had done enough to appease whomever thought that the road to salvation was partially paved with frozen outhouses.

The first step in finding common ground was understanding contradictions and learning from them, not being defeated and isolated by them. Bradley, in Canada, was not going to be very helpful.

By the time *Appearance and Reality* appeared in 1893, Watson had published more than thirty articles and four books. He would go on to publish over a hundred more articles and five more books, two of which were the published Gifford Lectures, *The Interpretation of Religious Experience*.[2] Little of the fanfare which surrounded the publication of *AR* spread to Canada. For Watson, it was one more book amongst several idealist works appearing at the turn of the century.

Watson did not ignore Bradley, however. In fact he filled several ledgers with his lecture notes and commentary on Bradley. Some criticisms occur in *The Interpretation of Religious Experience*, Part Second Constructive (pp. 214–16), and there is a brief discussion of Bradley on the feeling life (immediate experience) in *An Outline of Philosophy*. Further references exist in several articles.[3] Watson never published

---

[2] John Watson, *The Interpretation of Religious Experience*, Part First Historical, Part Second Constructive (Glasgow: J. Maclehose and Sons, 1910–12).

[3] John Watson, *An Outline of Philosophy* (Glasgow: J. Maclehose and Sons, 1908), pp. 450–59. Watson challenges Bradley's discussion of feeling as containing the very distinctions in his description for which feeling or immediate experience is intended to be the ground, or given. Bradley's references to quality, quantity and tone assume, according to Watson, an already developed consciousness:

> It would almost seem as if Mr. Bradley regarded the feeling being as already containing, preformed within itself, the whole articulated world which is present for the rational consciousness. (p. 459)

a major response devoted to Bradley alone. One reason may be that, during the flurry of excitement surrounding the book, Watson was formulating his own vision of metaphysics, having lived in his new home, Canada, for twenty years. Yet Bradley's work probably spurred Watson on in developing his speculative metaphysics, so detailed were his lecture notes and attempts to dispense with Bradley's contradictions.

Watson's main critical analysis of the recent spate of works covers T. H. Green, F. H. Bradley and J. Royce and is to be found in an unpublished speech entitled 'Recent Metaphysical Speculation'.[4] The contrast between who Watson thinks is on the right track in idealism, and who is not can be illustrated by briefly reviewing Watson's comments on Green, and then turning to Bradley.

Watson viewed the rash of Absolutist theories as a continuation of what he understood to be the problem confronted by both Kant and Hegel – the need to explain the principles of experience, in conjunction with the need to sustain beliefs in God, freedom and immortality. With the separation of Church and State, religion and science, individual and community, metaphysics faced the crisis of either banishing God to the realms of the unknowable, or dispensing with the concept as unnecessary for an explanation of experience, or finding a way of reconciling these seemingly conflicting concepts.

Watson's response suggests that Bradley is on the verge of contradiction. For Watson, the feeling stage of consciousness is but vague awareness. Distinctions of perception arise developmentally. Such distinctions cannot be used to analyse the lowest form of consciousness, for which there are not objects, perceptions, concepts of whole, or parts. To expound on feeling, as Bradley has done, is to put the cart before the horse.

See also 'The Absolute and the Time-Process', *Philosophical Review*, vol. 4 (1895), pp. 353–70, 486–505; 'Pragmatism and Idealism', *Queen's Quarterly*, vol. 21 (1914), pp. 465–72; 'Conflict of Absolutism and Realism', *Philosophical Review*, vol. 33 (1924), pp. 229–44; 'The Conflict of Idealism and Realism, A Symposium held in Glasgow University in the Year of our Lord One Thousand Nine Hundred and Seven', *Queen's Quarterly*, vol. 31 (1924), pp. 343–64; vol. 32 (1924), pp. 14–24, pp. 104–18.

[4] Unpublished speech, 'Recent Metaphysical Speculation', Queen's University Archives, John Watson Papers 1064 a, box 6, lecture 62.

There were several avenues for tackling this problem: the foundation of ethical claims, the ontology of existence, the source and validation of knowledge and truth claims. Though in pursuing one, one could hardly avoid the others. Differences did emerge amongst philosophers as to starting points and priorities.

Green opted to start his assault on the legacy of metaphysical dualisms left by Kant in challenging the currently popular trends of sensationalism and hedonism (Mill and Spencer).

Watson is somewhat sympathetic to T. H. Green as a lone battler against 'sensationalism and hedonism'. The thesis which Green sought to prove, and which according to Watson he did prove, was that a disconnected series of sensations cannot explain the simplest form of knowledge, just as a disconnected series of feelings is no explanation for intelligent action. Watson describes Green's argument as a 'reductio ad absurdum' of sensationalism. Knowledge consisting only of atomic sensations and feelings excludes any explanation of the workings of the mind. Watson comments:

> But with the exclusion of such workmanship or relations, there is no knowledge, since the minimum [condition] of knowledge is the consciousness of objects which do not pass away with the moment, but involve permanence of some kind.[5]

Green, he notes, proposes that the relating activity of thought is an essential part of knowledge and the condition for all of this is the unity and identity of the subject. Watson thought this to be Green's main contribution to metaphysics. He did not think Green fully developed his thesis to account for our conception of the world, because of his interests in ethics and politics and because the current philosophical trends of Green's time were quite opposed to a revised Hegelianism. Watson saw in Green a first step towards a unified theory of ultimate reality, but an incomplete one.

---

[5] *ibid.*

Green's Absolute, 'complete self-consciousness', was still unknowable to the individual.

> The defect, if defect it is, which besets Green's doctrine seems to me to lie...in his denial that of the Absolute we can be said to have 'knowledge' in the sense in which we have knowledge of ourselves. Now, it does not seem to me that Green can consistently affirm that the Absolute is an Eternal self-consciousness, and at the same time maintain that knowledge of the Absolute is impossible.[6]

Watson suspects that Green has failed to overcome the phenomena-noumena distinction that Watson is anxious to dissolve. There must be a way of making the idea of the Absolute accessible to intelligible beings, or the gaps between individuals of various intuitions and faiths cannot be bridged. Watson supports the idea that the world is spiritual but points out that that does not mean the world is identical to the Absolute. Rather it is the Absolute as it exists for itself. By this Watson means that the world is knowable. The Absolute is consciousness, or the rational order of experience. The Absolute mind is differentiated into the elements of the world system. Our experience is experience of those elements, progressively understood as our knowledge develops.

> Just as experience is nothing apart from its content, or its content [is nothing] apart from experience, so the world and the Absolute are distinguishable but inseparable aspects of a single Unity.[7]

Watson notes that one may call this pantheism but insists that he is not advocating the abolition of the *distinction* of subject and object. He thinks Green failed to extend the necessary connection between them to include the world as the object of the Absolute, the Absolute as viewed by itself. Absolute mind will know the infinitude of differences in reality, differences united by their comprehensibility. Various conceptions of the universe, mechanical or teleological, are not final.

---

[6] *ibid.*

[7] *ibid.*

They are some of the ways in which the world can exist as an object of knowledge for Absolute consciousness. They are manifestations of universal reason at work. Without our grasp of such a principle 'we must be prepared to admit that what we call knowledge is a fiction'.[8] Understood in this way, we cannot but have knowledge of the Absolute, as we know the conditions of our own experience. Our known world will not be identical to the world as it exists for the Absolute, for our knowledge is in process. Watson identifies with Green on this point. He simply wants to extend Green's argument to its logical conclusion:

> for as Green rightly insists, our knowledge is in process and as such it cannot be a complete knowledge of the Absolute. This is of course true, and hence we must distinguish between what we know and the ideal of complete knowledge which is never for us realized. What we must hold is, not that we have a complete knowledge of the world – which would be a complete knowledge of the Absolute – but such a knowledge as reveals to us the essential nature of the world and therefore of the Absolute.[9]

In whatever sense we know the essential nature of the world, Watson continues, in the same sense we know the nature of the Absolute. If these essential natures are different how can we make any claim at all about the Absolute? How can we even think about ultimate reality if we are unable to know it? What is there to think?

Certainly Watson thinks Green is on the right track and has merely failed to extend his metaphysics as rigorously as his initiative warranted. But Watson's tone is less the warmhearted supporter and more the didactic admonisher when he turns to Bradley. Here is someone clearly to be kept *out* of the frost-covered pulpit.

If Green was one step forward, Bradley was two steps backward. Yet he serves as an excellent foil for the promotion of Watson's own views.

---

[8] John Watson, *The Interpretation of Religious Experience*, Part Second Constructive, p. 218.

[9] See footnote 4.

Watson has alerted his audience to the trouble ahead by suggesting in his introduction to Green that Green's focus on the relating activity of thought 'has been strangely misunderstood to mean that knowledge consists *merely* of relations...'[10] and he offers no modified apology for suggesting error in Bradley, as he did for Green. With characteristic Scottish bluntness and sly understatement, Watson responds:

> I am not so presumptuous as to attempt a refutation of Mr. Bradley in a small part of a single paper: all that I shall attempt to do is to point out what seems to me a fundamental defect in his method.[11]

This defect was Bradley's whole attempt to apply the logical relations of identity and contradiction to experience, or, as Watson said, 'the attempt to deny and affirm the reality of appearance in the same breath'.[12] Watson, once he has dealt with the impasse of contradictions, will extend his criticism to illustrate the major flaw in Bradley's conclusions: that we can know and yet not know the Absolute.

Watson focuses on Bradley's well known claim: that appearances are contradictory.[13] According to Bradley these contradictions stem from the inadequacy of our concepts of objects and the relations between these concepts. No matter what relations we appeal to in attempting to account for our experience of objects, others are required in order to locate those objects in a larger whole.

---

[10] *ibid.*

[11] *ibid.*

[12] *ibid.*

[13] *ibid.* Watson summarized Bradley's major departure from Green as follows:

> To Green it seemed manifest that the presupposition of all experience is the unity of self-consciousness. Mr. Bradley denies that such a unity is demonstrable, and therefore he seeks to determine the nature of the Absolute in an independent way. His method is to start from the 'absolute criterion' that 'ultimate reality is such that is does not contradict itself'. (*ibid.*)

Further expansion of Bradley on contradictions can be found in this volume. See James Bradley, 'From Absolute Idealism to Transcendental Cosmology: Bradley and Whitehead'.

Watson works out his objections over many pages of lecture notes. What follows is a truncated summary of one or two major points of focus.

Watson's first concern is Bradley's application of the principle of contradiction. Bradley has argued that because appearances generate self-contradictory conceptions, they cannot give us knowledge of reality, which must be, he concludes, self-consistent.[14] Watson wonders why Bradley thinks that this observation reveals any positive knowledge. In his notes on chapter 13 of *AR*, Watson claims that the principle of self-consistency gives no positive content. His example concerns mechanical causation. Nothing, he points out, can be both mechanically caused, and self-determined. The principle of self-consistency will not tell us which predicate is true of an object under consideration. We must ask which predicate is an adequate determination of reality, consistent with the ultimate explanation of all that is. 'Does the conception of mechanical causation explain the total facts of experience?'[15] Knowledge, Watson assures us, requires an intelligent subject, and mechanical causation does not explain an intelligent subject, only the world viewed as a mechanism. Contradiction lies not in any kind of self-contradiction in the concept, but in the inadequacy of a particular concept to serve as a determination of the whole. 'Contradiction arises only when a limited way of determining Reality is taken as ultimate.'[16] For example, if we were to try to determine the whole by mechanical causation, that category does not adequately explain self-consciousness.

---

[14] Garrett L. Vander Veer, argues in his book, *Bradley's Metaphysics and the Self* (New Haven: Yale University Press, 1970), that Bradley is not referring to the law of contradiction as such, in his discussion of contradictions. He is suggesting that thought is unsatisfied with the association of differences in things, or as Vander Veer adds in a footnote (p. 40), the 'is' of predication. Thought seeks a necessary connection and is perpetually pursuing the 'why' of association. We seem only, in the pursuit of wider grounds of conjunction of subject and predicate, to continue to affirm their association as if it were explanatory and this act of thought (an affirmation is not an explanation) 'is precisely what it means to contradict oneself' (p. 42).

[15] Loose, typed lecture notes, 1904–1905, found in Queen's Archives, John Watson, 1064 a, box 2.

[16] *ibid.*

What Watson urges is that contradiction does not signal to us failure to grasp truth or the real; it signals that there may be more than one way of conceiving experience. Each way will contribute to our understanding of what is. In every conception there will be an awareness of not only the content of the idea, but also awareness of what is excluded from that conception. For example, I may see railway tracks as converging but as I travel along them, as I *experience* railway tracks in time, I gain other ways of conceiving of them. It is not so much that my senses deceive me and only give me appearances, rather my senses reveal one conception of railway tracks, a visual one, and that must be included with a mathematical one involving parallel lines as I grow to know what railway tracks are. My reason enables me to accommodate these seemingly contradictory conceptions as features of knowledge. To know ultimate reality, according to Watson, would be to have complete knowledge of all possible conceptions of experience and things.

Watson's ultimate concern is that Bradley's Absolute has no content, and is but an empty piece of logic. Dissolving all contradictions gives one nothing to think about. Watson's own proposals were intended to thwart the abyss signalled in such claims as 'The bewildering mass of phenomenal diversity must hence somehow be at unity and self-consistent; for it cannot be elsewhere than in reality, and reality excludes discord'.[17] Watson responds that Bradley's Absolute is 'self-consistent only in the sense of not being self-contradictory; but the absence of self-contradiction is due to the absence of all content: nothing cannot contradict itself'.[18]

This radical defect, the attempt to use a logical device to undermine the legitimacy of experience, rankled Watson for the next twenty years. His own response to the defect was to argue for necessary connection between knowledge and reality. A criterion of logic will be part of the principles of knowledge, which in turn will be part of ultimate reality. The law of contradiction does not isolate the knower from the

---

[17] AR 123.

[18] See footnote 4.

known; it is merely one way in which reality is knowable, as determinate and differentiable. If knowledge and thought have any status at all, it is surely *as part* of what exists.

> Philosophical criticism... does not apply the logical principle of contradiction (which can determine nothing as to the nature of reality), ... it brings to light the presupposition of any theory of reality... that, in claiming to make an affirmation about the nature of reality, we are presupposing that it is knowable.[19]

If knowledge is possible, the conditions of its possibility must be part of what is ultimately real. Thus Watson will argue (painstakingly and at great length working through all of Bradley's chapters), 'Ultimate reality is such that it does not contradict the possibility of knowledge'.[20]

Watson was quick off the mark to give his criticisms focus. *Appearance and Reality* appeared in 1893. In the July issue (1895) of *The Philosophical Review* he published 'The Absolute and The Time-Process'. His introduction suggests a paper on science and religion. Although he discusses both Hegel and McTaggart the crux of the paper is devoted to arguing that Bradley's remarks on judgement and time are misleading. By challenging Bradley's categories of content and existence, 'that and what' (see *AR* chap. 16), judgement and predication, Watson proposes an Absolute, the nature of which can be understood, even though never completely known. Judgement doesn't separate components of our experience; it unites and alters what is already intelligible.

> When the scientific man affirms that light is due to the vibration of an aether, he does not separate the 'content' already involved in the conception of the luminous object, and then predicate this 'content' of the subject; what he does is to determine the already qualified subject by a totally new 'content' which it did not previously possess, and in this determination of the subject the judgement consists.[21]

---

[19] Notes on chapter 13, Queen's Archives, John Watson Papers 1064 a, lecture 9.

[20] ibid.

[21] John Watson, 'The Absolute and the Time-Process', *Philosophical Review*, vol. 4, no. 4 (July 1895), p. 358.

Such new determinations occur over time and for that reason we can never know all there is to know of reality. This defect, he reminds us 'is not in the character of thought, as distinguished from feeling or intuition, but in the very nature of man as a being in whom knowledge is a never-ending process':[22]

> reality is not for us stationary, but grows in content as thought, which is the faculty of unifying the distinguishable elements of reality, [and] develops in the process by which those elements are more fully distinguished and unified.[23]

The Absolute is not self-complete *apart* from time or *perfect* in any unknown way as Bradley suggests. Bradley's absolute reality 'is a trans-relational unity which simply surpasses the divided nature of all experience... It simply has nothing to do with time, for time is a relation.'[24] For Watson time is a postulate that makes sense of motion, change, permanence, indeed the conditions of science. Knowledge is gained through process, through our experience of the order of events and things as cumulative and successive differences. Yet man is also 'capable of transcending in idea all limits of space and time, and grasping the principle from which all that is has proceeded. If man were not thus capable of transcending the limits of his finite existence, he would never become conscious of his finitude.'[25] Thus experience reveals to us the principle of reason in reality; it does not deceive us with appearances. Finite, dependent interrelated beings are understood to be such because we can conceive of a self-determining principle.

> The consciousness of the finite presupposes the consciousness of the infinite... The very fact that the time-process is never complete compels us to refer it to a principle which is complete.[26]

---

[22] *ibid.*, p. 360.

[23] *ibid.*

[24] Leslie Armour and Elizabeth Trott, *op. cit.*, p. 278.

[25] John Watson, *The Interpretation of Religious Experience*, Part Second Constructive, p. 216.

[26] John Watson, 'The Absolute and the Time-Process', p. 368. See footnote 21.

Contradiction and contraries help to develop the knowable, not propose the unknowable, or unthinkable abstraction. Subject and object are united in the Absolute, not eliminated.

Watson continued his defence of the knowable nature of reality in part 2 of 'The Absolute and the Time-Process' in the September issue of the same year. Watson now boldly states his thesis in the opening paragraph:

> The ideal is the only real of which we can have any knowledge; in other words, reality is constituted for us in the continuous process by which it is determined as a thought reality. Judgement we must conceive, not as broken up into separate judgements, but as a single living self-conscious process, in which the real constitution of the world is revealed in its differentiation and integration.[27]

In part 2 Watson's targets are Kant and Bradley. Bradley now suffers from yet another 'misconception' about time. Images of presented time will of course generate contradictions with the character of time. Watson suggests Bradley thinks of time's character as a kind of abstract reality, 'as if there might be a number of different realities'.[28] Watson counters that the thought of time 'is the idea of distinguishable elements in the continuous, each element being itself continuous. Time is always the same thought of continuous succession',[29] and moments cannot be understood except in relation to the whole of reality which experience tells us is continually

---

[27] John Watson, 'The Absolute and the Time-Process, Part II', *Philosophical Review*, vol. 4, no. 5 (September 1895), p. 486.

[28] ibid., p. 495. Watson did not share Bradley's beliefs about degrees of truth and reality. Knowledge, its conditions and conceptions, was of reality, a single unity of differences.

The idealistic view, that only for a thinking or universalizing subject is there any 'cosmos of experience', is not dependent upon the Kantian assumption that sense supplied a mere 'manifold'; on the contrary, it denies that, in our thinking experience, there is any mere 'manifold', maintaining that, when the sensitive life has become an object of knowledge, it has been transformed by being determined as a knowable aspect of the one world which exists only in the medium of thought. See John Watson, *An Outline of Philosophy*, p. 450.

[29] John Watson, 'The Absolute and the Time-Process Part II', p. 494.

changing. Time is not separable from these states, as Bradley suggests, but rather is an idea which reveals the nature of existence as continuous and contiguous.

'To think time is to be beyond it, because the thought of time as continuous succession contains all that it involves.'[30] Thought brings to clear consciousness what is involved in perception. But our minds can transcend the limit. Watson's point is that even though thought, as part of reality, changes, it is not *limited by* the thought of successive change (or time). (For example, presupposing causal succession is a condition of our perception of reality as ordered in our finite experience.) Watson does not make Bradley's mistake of using the metaphors of 'in' and 'out' of time, or 'beyond' time to suggest some new ontology. Rather to transcend the limit of time is to conceive not of actual determinate ordered events in succession, but of a world of all possible events – 'the universal possibility of events'.[31]

Throughout the rest of his career Watson continued to use the logic of contradiction as a tool for building knowledge, not as a device for demonstrating its shabbiness. The Gifford Lectures, the culmination of his metaphysical work, spell out his own version of Speculative Idealism. The Absolute is knowable, but not completely, because experienced reality is forever changing.

---

[30] ibid., p. 496.

[31] ibid., p. 497. Watson's articles did not go unnoticed by Bradley who addressed them briefly in the explanatory notes of the second edition of *AR* 554–5. Ultimately Bradley is seeking a middle position between time as apparently self-contradictory and time as it relates to the Absolute. Watson says there are no terms more fundamental to time than it being characterized as a continuous succession of real events. Time for Watson is real. Our conception of the world of all possible events does not invalidate time. It merely means the Absolute continuously reveals itself through our coherent lives in communities. In response to Watson, Bradley reiterates his own position about time's contradictory nature. But it rests primarily on a rejection of Watson's theory of the self.

> The many selves seem (we know) to themselves to be a succession of events, past, present, and future...these successive individuals are an appearance, necessary to the Absolute, but still an appearance, self-inconsistent, mixing truth with falsehood, and – if and so far as you offer it by itself as the truth – then not the truth but a *mere* appearance. (AR 555)

Watson sought in all his writings to overcome the metaphysics of dualism, to bridge the gap between appearance and reality, phenomena and noumena, science and religion. Such dualities would only foster exclusivity and isolation. There was enough isolation in Canada. Only a common capacity to reason about the differences between selves, and existences as parts of a common reality would unite people despite apparent insurmountable perceptions. The urgency of his concerns about Bradley are evidenced by Watson's sudden shift of focus towards the end of his article on time. Watson turns to selves. Selves, he reminds us, only develop in a world of other selves.

> The first consciousness of exclusive or adverse relations to others must be supplemented by the conception of man as essentially spirit, that is, as a being whose true self is found in what is not self. Man is therefore not adequately conceived as an exclusive self, but only as a self whose true nature is to transcend his exclusiveness and to find himself in what seems at first to be opposed to him. In other words, man is essentially self-separative: he must go out of his apparently self-centred life in order to find himself in a truer and richer life.[32]

What at first seemed opposed to someone could very well be another self. Understanding contradictions meant that this other-than-one's-own self was part of reality, part of that which could be known, and one's capacity to conceive of and then unite differences in new ways both enabled one to develop one's own self (and knowledge) and gain further understanding of one's place in the scheme of things. Besides, if one could not conceive of differences as real and not appearances, as necessary to increase knowledge and understanding, one might never find reason to help a Catholic build a barn, or shelter a Protestant in a storm, or share a plough-team with a stranger who spoke a language never heard.

---

[32] *ibid*, p. 505. Bradley's concept of the self as a moral concept is further discussed in this volume by William Sweet, 'F. H. Bradley and Bernard Bosanquet'.

For Watson, Bradley's idealism was the opposition which required a reasonable response. Watson's conception of reason as a tool of interpretation could be carried into those little churches. Sense could be made out of apparent contradictions, for they revealed new perspectives and enabled new judgements to be developed. Reason didn't just reveal opposition but enabled us to develop knowledge and new concepts in which oppositions could be accommodated. God or the Absolute was not punishing, or selective; God was the idea of all possible events, things, ideas, and change in harmonious co-existence, united, not dissolved. The rationality of the world and its intelligibility was the only hope for self-realization. Subservience to some mystical, transcendent, inaccessible Being, provided no formula for solving problems and understanding new perspectives.

Many of Watson's students fanned out across the country as preachers and teachers. A good number joined the civil service. The seeds of tolerance, respect, cooperation and innovative problem-solving spread far and wide. The contradictions of isolated communities had to be overcome, if only for an hour or so in the cold, little church. At least during the sermon, the conception of uniting all possible contradictions could be contemplated as a possibility. To experience harmony even briefly was to confirm its real possibility.

But even though thoughts were not limited by time they still had to make sense of experienced time. When the young preacher and his stalwart flock heard the jangling harnesses of anxious horses, and out of the one window saw new grey clouds appear, no one had any doubt as to what those sounds and that appearance meant. Rush the last prayers, acknowledge the hymn but don't sing it, forget the announcements and head for home. Those were real storm clouds on the horizon and not a soul in the little church had the slightest doubt that God knew that too.

F. H. BRADLEY AND C. A. CAMPBELL

Lorne Maclachlan

1. *Introduction*

C. A. Campbell was Professor of Philosophy at Bangor, North Wales from 1932 to 1938 and Professor of Logic and Rhetoric at the University of Glasgow from 1938 to 1961. He is most widely known today as a defender of free will, and his work makes frequent appearances as a champion on the libertarian side in anthologies prepared for the student.[1] But what Campbell himself took to be his main contribution to philosophy – his discussion and development of the supra-rationalism of F. H. Bradley – has almost completely disappeared from view.

Campbell expounded the metaphysics of supra- rationalism in his early book *Scepticism and Construction*.[2] His views on this matter remained essentially unchanged throughout his life. Although the invitation to give the Gifford Lectures at the University of St Andrews[3] provided an excellent opportunity to change his position, if he were so minded, the views expressed in these lectures do not represent any essential shift in his central thesis. In explaining the theory, it is therefore appropriate to focus on the earlier work.

---

[1] To give but two examples, 'Is "Free Will" a Pseudo-problem?' (from *Mind*, 1951) appears in *A Modern Introduction to Philosophy*, edited by Paul Edwards and Arthur Pap, 3rd ed. (New York, 1973), pp. 67–82; and 'Free Will Rules Out Determinism' (from lecture 9, 'Has the Self "Free Will"?', *On Selfhood and Godhood* (London and New York, 1957)) appears in *The Problems of Philosophy*, edited by William P. Alston and Richard B. Brandt, 3rd ed. (Boston, 1978), pp. 414–28.

[2] London, 1931. Future references to this work will be abbreviated to *SC*, followed by page number, and will be incorporated into the main text.

[3] 1953–4 and 1954–5, published in a revised and expanded version as *On Selfhood and Godhood* (London and New York, 1957). Future references to this work will be abbreviated to *OSAG*.

The defence of free will has, on the face of it, no natural tie to the doctrine of supra-rationalism; but, as we shall see, the two topics are by no means unconnected. The freedom of the will which Campbell is anxious to defend is 'the freedom to decide between genuinely open alternatives', which is 'the freedom presupposed by moral responsibility' (*OSAG* 166). This is the freedom with which agents naturally suppose that they are endowed when faced with a choice among various possibilities. The problem of free will is generated by theoretical systems which claim that this sense of freedom must be an illusion.

The most influential of such systems, of course, is mechanistic determinism, according to which everything which happens, including so-called human acts of choice, is necessarily determined by its antecedents in accordance with a causal law. This is not, however, the only form of determinism which challenges the instinctive belief in the freedom of the will. Historically, there is also the view that everything is predestined by God, promulgated by John Calvin and others. The form of determinism by which Campbell himself was most closely troubled was yet a third form – the form universally adopted in the idealist school in which he had been raised. Campbell recounts the 'ill-concealed scorn' of his teacher, Sir Henry Jones, 'or ignoble natures [like Campbell himself] which still hankered after a free will in the old "vulgar" sense' (*OSAG* 165). Nor was Bradley any comfort, writing in a note to *Appearance and Reality* on page 435: 'Considered either theoretically or practically, "Free Will" is, in short, a mere lingering chimera. Certainly, no writer, who respects himself, can be called on any longer to treat it seriously.'

An idealist theory in which everything is connected with everything else in a rational system can have no place for acts of free will, such as Campbell envisages. Such acts would constitute a 'break in the rational continuity of things' (*SC* 116). There can be no genuinely open possibilities in an idealist system where everything is determined by everything else.[4] Thus, Campbell was faced with a choice of either

---

[4] Such a system was vigorously defended by Campbell's American contemporary, Brand Blanshard. See the discussion in this volume by Michael Walsh.

breaking with the idealism in which he had been nurtured, or else abandoning his belief in the freedom of the will. It was in this predicament that Bradley, although himself no friend of free will, offered a ray of hope; for Bradley had also broken with the thoroughgoing idealism which insisted that the real is the rational and that truth or thought is identical with reality.

One general problem facing the defender of free will is the need to concede that the act of free choice is in some sense inexplicable. As Campbell says: 'free will is *ex hypothesi* the sort of thing of which the request for an *explanation* is absurd' (*OSAG* 175). This would appear to put the libertarian at something of a disadvantage as compared with his determinist opponent, who does have an explanation. The determinist explains the choice by the factors which determined the decision to go this way rather than that. Of course, we do not always know what these factors are, so that our ignorance of causes may generate an illusion of freedom (as Spinoza would agree). But there are other times, even when the agent is, as we say, 'struggling with himself or herself', when we can predict the outcome, because we have a fair idea of the factors which will determine what is done. And even when the factors responsible for the choice have not been identified, the theory of determinism prescribes that such factors must be present.

It is to Bradley that Campbell turns to defuse the force of this argument; for the implication of Bradley's basic position is that no explanation of human choice offered by determinists can ever satisfy the intellect.

2. Bradley's Epistemological Scepticism

Campbell presents what he takes to be Bradley's central argument in the second and third sections of the first chapter of *Scepticism and Construction*. He relies primarily on the important Note A: 'Contradiction and the Contrary' in the appendix to the second edition of *Appearance and Reality*.

The fundamental assumption is that the goal of philosophy is 'a view of the general nature of reality which will satisfy the intellect' (*SC* 5). This looks innocuous, if not particularly helpful; but it suggests the question 'What in general *would* satisfy the intellect?' One thing is clear, at any rate: we know what will *not* satisfy the intellect. 'The intellect will accept as genuinely expressing reality no content which contradicts itself' (*SC* 7). This is the easy bit: it is generally agreed that the Law of Contradiction constitutes a negative criterion of truth – a *conditio sine qua non*. The hard bit is to specify what more is required to satisfy the intellect over and above bare self-consistency. Bradley evades completely this second difficult question. The question becomes inoperative, since no act of thought can pass even the first, minimal test: in the last analysis, no act of thought can avoid self-contradiction.

The argument begins with the logical nature of the unit of thought – the act of judgement. The act of judgement involves a combination of differences which is no mere association of ideas.[5] The union of differences must depend on a sufficient ground which justifies the combination. Now, there is, indeed, a principle which will justify the combination of elements in judgement – the Law of Identity. Any expression of the form 'A is A' is completely warranted by the Law of Identity and proof against any charge of self-contradiction. The trouble is that any such expression contains no genuine differences and is an empty tautology. No one could be more severe on tautologies than Bradley himself. 'A bare tautology is not even so much as a poor truth or a thin truth. It is not a truth in any way, in any sense, or at all' (*AR* 562).

Thus, if an act of thought identifies elements which are, in fact, identical, the act is entirely empty. On the other hand, if an act of thought identifies elements which are, in fact, different, we have a standing self-contradiction. 'A is A' is mere tautology; but 'A is B', which amounts to 'A is not -A' is contradiction.

But this is surely to go too far too fast. 'No one really supposes that thinking, in uniting differences A and B, pronounces them to be *identical*' (*SC* 8). This kind of talk is likely to attract the charge which Bertrand Russell levels against Hegel – 'confusing the *is* of predication... with the *is*

---

[5] See the discussion in this volume (by Phillip Ferreira) of Bradley's attack on Associationism.

of identity'.[6] Surely there is a way of uniting differences in thought which does not involve the inconsistent attempt to identify them! This brings us to the nub of the issue. Any such way of uniting differences in thought requires a ground which will satisfy the intellect. Bradley claims that no such ground can be produced.

Bradley, in fact, goes on to make the further claim that if he is right, reason, lacking the necessary ground of connection and distinction, will attempt, against reason, to identify the differences in a point and will commit suicide in an act of self-contradiction. I am tempted to dismiss this further claim as a rhetorical flourish, designed to spread consternation, but not supported by hard argument. Why, after all, should the intellect, just because it can produce no satisfactory ground of connection for the combination of the elements in judgement, allow itself to be stampeded into affirming that connection which it must know to be the least satisfactory of all – the sheer identification of differences? Perhaps we should back away from the paradoxical thesis that all judgements are self-contradictory, and content ourselves with the more modest claim that all judgements are intellectually unsatisfactory?

Does Bradley establish even the more modest proposal that thought can produce no satisfactory ground for its transitions? He points out, and I agree, that it is not enough to posit a mere psychological movement from one mental state to another. 'Thought demands to go *proprio motu*, or, what is the same thing, with a ground and reason' (*AR* 562). Bradley's claim is that thought can neither produce the required ground from its own internal resources, nor can it accept it from outside. The first alternative is the one supported by orthodox idealism: the second alternative is supported by nearly everyone else.

Most philosophers, when asked about the ground which justifies the connection of elements in an ordinary empirical judgement would point to the actual world which the

---

[6] *Our Knowledge of the External World* (London, 1914), p. 48n. This charge is also levelled against Bradley in this volume by Michael Walsh, p. 111.

judgement tries to describe. In the judgement, 'This cat is black', the connection between subject and predicate is to be justified by reference to an actual creature living in a world beyond the judgement. Bradley himself seemed to subscribe to the position of sanity when he was writing the *Principles of Logic*. 'Judgement proper is the act which refers an ideal content...to a reality beyond the act' (*PL* 10). What, then, is the problem? The problem is that thought cannot accept as ultimately satisfactory a ground which is merely given from outside. 'To pass from A to B, if the ground remains external, is for thought to pass with no ground at all' (*AR* 562–3).

One reason why Bradley and Campbell are so unimpressed by the offer of an external ground is that they have a vision of the kind of internal ground favoured by objective idealists where

> the diversities were complementary aspects of a process of connection and distinction, the process not being external to the elements or again a foreign compulsion of the intellect, but itself the intellect's own *proprius motus*... And the Whole would be a self-evident analysis and synthesis of the intellect itself by itself. Synthesis here has ceased to be mere synthesis and has become self-completion, and analysis, no longer mere analysis, is self-explication.
> (*AR* 568)

No one supposed, of course, that the finite intellect of man could attain to such an apotheosis. This is a vision of Absolute Spirit – of the structure of that ultimate reality within which finite spirit finds its place. Bradley, however, is not able to share this vision of absolute idealism. For him, 'unable to verify a solution of this kind, connections in the end must remain in part mere syntheses, the putting together of differences external to one another and to that which couples them' (*AR* 569). In this rejection of absolute idealism, Bradley is fully supported by Campbell. The fully intelligible system which can be accepted as an expression of and identical with reality is a goal which is unattainable even in principle. Through the processes of thought, we make progress in coming to understand the world we live in. We do not have to accept observed correlations as mere brute facts: we can offer explanations, perhaps by identifying some factor which mediates the connection, perhaps by formulating a general law which governs the process. But neither style of explanation provides anything remotely like the goal of idealism, which is 'a system of differences wherein perfect mutual implication reigns' (SC 19). Factor B which mediates the connection between A and C must itself be intelligibly connected to A and connected to C; and the scientific laws which we use to predict and explain the phenomena all contain an unintelligible and ineradicable element of facticity. In the Law of Gravity, for instance, why does the gravitational constant have the exact value it does?

We cannot use this meagre basis to extrapolate to a state in which thought through satisfying its own demands has become identical with reality. The very nature of thought as we enjoy it precludes any such consummation. 'Inherent in the very nature of the process is a reference beyond itself which raises fresh problems on the basis of temporary solutions' (SC 19). For both Bradley and Campbell, the Real is not the Rational: the Real is the Supra-rational. 'Reality in its true character must be pronounced to be disparate from each and every thought product' (SC 19).[7]

3. The Supra-rational in Bradley and Campbell

Although Bradley and Campbell are agreed that the Absolute is not to be construed as a purely intellectual system, at this point their paths begin to diverge. Bradley's position is not true idealism, if by this is meant the doctrine that the Absolute is Thought and nothing but Thought. But he certainly defends the cognate view that the Absolute is Experience and nothing but Experience. His quarrel with orthodox idealism is that with its emphasis on the intellectual, it does not do justice to other sides of our nature. For although the Absolute is Experience, 'It is not one-sided experience, as mere volition or mere thought; but it is a whole superior to and embracing

---

[7] This represents a major parting of the ways between Bradley and Campbell, on the one side, and Bosanquet and Blanshard, on the other side. See the discussion in this volume of Blanshard (by Michael Walsh) and Bosanquet (by William Sweet).

all incomplete forms of life' (*AR* 241–2). The Absolute is not just a harmony of thought, but a harmony which incorporates and transforms all aspects of our being.

What Bradley is getting at can be clearly understood only in terms of his concept of immediate experience. In immediate experience, which is below the level of thought, we have that unity in difference which thought demands for its own satisfaction and which it must posit in the Absolute. Not that immediate experience is a primitive phase of psychical life which evaporates when discursive consciousness comes upon the scene. Rather, it is an enduring feature *within* which discursive consciousness has developed. The development takes place through a loosening of content from existence which is the essence of ideality. '*Feeling* reality as one, we yet find ourselves confronted in *thought* with a many' (*SC* 50). But the unity of feeling no longer satisfies, because it has been transcended by the act of thought. Nor can thought by itself, as we have seen, supply the unity in difference which it demands. 'Thus, there arises in us the conception of that which answers to the demand for theoretical satisfaction as being a unity which has the same *kind* of immediacy as that which we experience in feeling, but which is *supra*-relational, not *sub*- or *non*-relational' (*SC* 50). Moreover, since this immediate experience obviously contains more than mere thought, this unity which transcends thought must also incorporate all other aspects of immediate experience.

Campbell has a more austere conception of the suprarational, and rejects Bradley's contention that the Absolute must be conceived as experience. Bradley's argument is that we cannot conceive of any form of existence apart from experience: 'to be real, or even barely to exist, must be to fall within sentience' (*AR* 144). To affirm an Absolute Reality, then, is to affirm an Absolute Experience. Campbell challenges the leap of faith which this conclusion involves. 'It may very well be that while everything which finite mind, with its deficient equipment, can regard as "fact" is charged with the character of "experience", *the* fact, genuine Reality, is not' (*SC* 47).

Campbell also attacks Bradley's suggestion that the unity-in-difference, which is found in immediate experience, may be used as a clue to the higher unity-in-difference, which must be posited in the Absolute. His objection is that even if immediate experience or feeling is in itself a unity, this is not the same as a feeling *of* unity. 'The whole point of the analogy is that in immediate feeling we are directly aware of a many as a one' (*SC* 52). But to be aware of anything implies a distinction between the awareness and that of which it is aware. With this distinction, a relational consciousness is already at work.

Campbell, then, is working with a highly formal concept of the Absolute. It cannot be conceived as thought: 'there is a fundamental difference in kind, such as renders thought-products and Reality strictly incommensurable... we must have for Reality differences united in a certain way, and we actually have in thought-products differences united in quite another way' (*SC* 20). Nor can the Absolute be conceived, with Bradley, even as experience.

4. *Degrees of Truth and Reality*
Campbell's scepticism about the supposed character of the Absolute (whether conceived as the apotheosis of thought, as in orthodox Hegelianism, or as the self-completion of experience, as Bradley believes) has one important corollary to which we must now turn. This is the rejection of the celebrated doctrine of degrees of truth and reality.

Bradley lays down for thought conditions of satisfaction which thought as such can never satisfy. This means that no judgement is ever quite true. But does it follow that all judgements are equally unsatisfactory? This Bradley cannot allow. He gives the following comparison. 'Suppose that for a certain purpose I want a stick exactly one yard long, am I wrong when I condemn both one inch and thirty-five inches, and any possible sum of inches up to thirty-six, as equally and alike coming short?' (*AR* 557). From one point of view, it is not wrong. Either the stick will do the job or it will not and a miss is as good as a mile. From another point of view, it is a mistake to make no distinctions, since there are degrees of failure. 'In the imperfect', writes Bradley, 'there is already more or less of a quality or character, the self-same character which, if all defect were removed, would attain to and itself would be perfection' (AR 557). Thus, even if we grant, to use a slogan quoted by Campbell, that 'Only the whole truth can be wholly true' (SC 22), this does not exclude *partial* truths which may differ in degree. The ideal is a completely harmonious and self-contained system with no loose ends trailing to the outside. All we can ever achieve are partial systems of thought which require a transcendence of their own content. But such limited systems of thought, although partially false are also partially true. 'The partial *truth* of every judgement lies in the fact that every judgement is, in however inchoate a fashion, the exhibition of a unity in difference, and attains in some measure to the systematic coherence which is the character of Reality' (SC 22).

Campbell attacks the doctrine of degrees of truth for reasons which he takes to be necessarily implicit in Bradley's own supra-rationalism:

> For it is of the essence of Bradley's position to hold that differences are united in Reality in a manner intrinsically different from the mode of union which is characteristic of, and inseparable from, the finite intellect; and that of this ultimate mode of union the intellect can know nothing. How then can it be possible to grade thought-products according to the degree in which they manifest the nature of this unknown and unknowable Reality? (SC 31)

In the case of the stick one yard long, we have a clear conception of the standard to be attained, and hence we can assess the varying degrees in which shorter sticks fail to meet this standard. But we have no conception at all of the standard in ultimate reality to which our thought-products are supposed to approximate in their different degrees.

Campbell believes that if Bradley had been conscious of this implication of his supra-rationalism, and had campaigned vigorously against the doctrine of degrees of truth, he would have been perceived as a critic rather than a member of the idealist school – 'a brother whose occasional backslidings are indeed to be deplored, but whose heart is in the right place' (SC 35). My own view is that Bradley's heart was in what idealists would consider the right place. When he talks about the transmutation that thought must undergo in order to become fully adequate to reality, he explains that about this we are ignorant 'in detail'. This suggests that we do understand how 'in principle' the finite is to be supplemented and rearranged in the absolute system. No idealists would claim any more than this: no idealists would claim that they understood in detail the workings of Absolute Spirit.

Whatever may be the truth about Bradley, it is clear that Campbell has made a decisive break with the idealist position. He has produced a critique of idealism from inside the tradition itself, using ammunition provided by Bradley. The philosophical world has not, indeed, shown much interest in this exercise, for historical reasons which are not difficult to understand. Surviving idealists had more to worry about in the form of other, more vicious criticisms coming from other quarters, whereas non-idealists were not prepared to take seriously the idealist-style discourse within which Campbell's criticisms were developed.

5. *Noumenal and Phenomenal Truth*

Campbell makes an important distinction in reply to the objection that we know, at least, that Reality is self-consistent, so that judgements may be graded in accordance with their degree of self-consistency. Campbell dismisses this as a mere play on words, which exploits the ambiguity of the term. The true self-consistency, which applies to the Absolute, and which lies beyond any relational arrangement, also lies beyond our comprehension. This differs, and must differ, from any criterion of self-consistency which we may use in grading actual judgements. We have, then, pure self-consistency, which Campbell calls the 'noumenal' ideal. We also have 'empirical' self-consistency 'which is the criterion and positive guide in our actual intellectual operations' (SC 32). This is the 'phenomenal' ideal. 'The contradiction in Bradley's doctrine of "Degrees" is that he uses the *second* form to apportion degrees of the *first*' (SC 32).

The doctrine of degrees of truth was designed to avoid the equal condemnation of all judgements which fail to measure up to the strict criterion of the intellectually satisfactory (which means all products of finite intellect!). The difference in status between the judgement that the cat is on the mat, when it is, and the judgement that the cat is on the table, when it is not, is construed as a difference in degree of truth – as a difference in the degree to which the judgement approaches that Absolute Truth which is the complete system of Reality. However implausible this may seem, when one eschews generalities and considers specific cases, it is at least an attempt to make distinctions among the class of failures. But if all our cognitive attempts fail to satisfy the intellect, not just in degree, but in their essential nature, what are we to make of the distinction between truth and falsehood, which is a necessary presupposition of judgement, and without which the life of the mind would lose all meaning? Since ultimate or noumenal truth cannot serve as a criterion, what account can we give of the phenomenal truth at which alone the intellect can significantly aim?

To the correspondence theory of truth the idealist objection is that such a theory makes sense only at the level where there is a distinction between thought or judgement and the reality beyond thought with which thought is concerned. Since truth which is the goal of thought involves transcending this dichotomy, there is no way in which truth can consist in some relation between the two components. Truth is the identity of thought and reality. Campbell, however, has neutralized this idea of noumenal truth by arguing that it can have no bearing on the kind of truth with which we are familiar. This truth necessarily emerges in a situation in which there is a distinction between thought and the 'other' over against thought. Thus, 'we do have to recognise in "Correspondence" a meaning which is ultimate for positive, concrete thinking' (*SC* 86). Campbell agrees with Joachim that 'so long as the duality [between thought and reality] is maintained, *some* form of the correspondence notion is the only possible theory of truth'.[8]

The objection from the side of absolute idealism is not, of course, the only problem for a correspondence theory of

---

[8] *The Nature of Truth* (Oxford, 1906), p. 119.

truth, as Campbell himself recognizes. Moreover, to agree that some form of the correspondence theory must be correct is not the same as working out a specific form which is in fact defensible. One move which Campbell makes to clarify the theory reveals his idealist affiliations. He accepts completely Bradley's distinction between logical and psychological ideas, and argues that it is the logical idea or ideal content which is taken to correspond to reality. To suppose that it is the psychological idea or mental state which corresponds to the reality beyond the mind is to make the theory 'clearly nonsensical' (*SC* 90). Campbell's suggestion is not, indeed, entirely clear to me, but it is some sort of advance to replace the nonsensical with the obscure.

A second qualification insisted on by Campbell is that although correspondence with reality is the very meaning of truth, this correspondence cannot be used as a viable test of truth. We may sometimes think that we can check our judgements against the facts. I predict that there will be a thunderstorm tomorrow, and when tomorrow comes, my prediction is confirmed by the facts. But what happens, according to Campbell, is that a judgement I make one day is confirmed by another judgement I make the following day. What I conceive as 'facts', I conceive only through the medium of judgement.

If Campbell rejects correspondence as the test of truth, it looks as if he must agree with the idealist thesis that coherence is the test of truth, even if he continues to maintain that coherence is not the *essence* of truth. Campbell certainly allows that coherence is *a* test of truth. We can and do test the truth of a judgement 'by its capacity for harmonizing with all the other judgements which we make about reality' (*SC* 97). But for Campbell, coherence is not the *sole* test of truth. It is also necessary to have our system of judgements pegged down to reality at various points. This is possible because the judgements which report our own subjective sensations are intellectually incorrigible and exempt from the Coherence test of Truth. Judgements about the objective world all involve an element of interpretation which is subject to correction as knowledge develops. For example, our common sense beliefs about the physical world are continually replaced through the growth of science, and more primitive scientific beliefs are replaced by more sophisticated theories. But our reflex judgements about our own beliefs, feelings, etc., which are guaranteed by self-awareness, are not subject to this kind of modification. If I judge that I am in pain, nothing will convince me that I am in error.

The notion that there are at the human level such intellectually incorrigible judgements would not and could not be accepted by the thoroughgoing idealist. Thus, if Campbell is right, this constitutes a valid criticism of orthodox idealism. I say 'If Campbell is right', because I cannot automatically endorse the sort of foundationalism which he espouses, given the serious challenges which have been made in recent years, coming from quarters not obviously contaminated by idealist metaphysics. Campbell also wants to argue against idealism that the fundamental assumptions of Euclidean geometry are intellectually incorrigible (*SC* 108–12), and here he is on even shakier ground.

6. *The Freedom of the Will*

Among the judgements which Campbell believes to be intellectually incorrigible is the judgement that the will is free. This may seem a strange candidate for special status, given the procession of philosophers throughout history who have endeavoured to correct precisely this judgement. But the fact that a judgement is intellectually incorrigible does not debar philosophers from arguing about whether it is incorrigible or not. It is widely believed that the judgement 'I am in pain' is intellectually incorrigible. Suppose that this is right. This still does not make it either illegitimate or irresponsible for philosophers to seek out arguments to challenge the widespread belief. To say that a judgement is incorrigible is to say that it is directly apprehended, and that there is no evidence which can count against it. The freedom of the will is directly apprehended. It is 'what Sidgwick has called "the immediate affirmation of consciousness in the moment of deliberate action"' (*SC* 113). Whether or not this immediate affirmation can be subverted by other considerations is what the fight is about, but if Campbell is right, the freedom of the will indeed satisfies his criteria of the intellectually incorrigible.

Campbell calls these intellectually incorrigible judgements 'final phenomenal truths', so that the freedom of the will is a final phenomenal truth. This is an ironic twist, given the important influence of Kant on Campbell's thought. For Kant, the final phenomenal truth is necessary determination. We posit the freedom of the will, only because it is a necessary condition of the categorical imperative. This posit must take place at the noumenal level, where we have a rational will which is responsive to the unconditioned demands made by the moral law. The domain of phenomena has been surrendered to determinism, and it is only through the recognition that these are phenomena that we can distinguish a possible domain of things in themselves, in which we can place the free will required by the claims of duty.

Campbell denies that we can posit the freedom of the will as a noumenal truth. Noumenal truth must satisfy the intellect, and no judgement to the effect that a person has made a free choice from among open possibilities is intellectually satisfactory. This is, in a sense, to go with the flow, since a traditional objection to the libertarian theory is that the posited acts of free choice are unintelligible. But Campbell's cunning move defuses this objection, since he is able to argue that in this respect acts of free choice are no better and no worse than anything else. No judgement can present a fact which is fully intelligible to the intellect. This uncompromising position dissipates the supposed advantage of determinism that it can provide an explanation of human behaviour. Even if one can find a general law under which one can subsume the sequence of the antecedent state and the act of choice, the connection of the elements in the general law is not intelligibly mediated, as both Campbell and Bradley are agreed. Thus, 'the same reasons which compel us to say that "freedom" (as man must conceive it) is illusory, compel us also to say that "determination" (as man must conceive it) is illusory' (SC 118).

If we move down to the level of phenomenal truth, Campbell would claim that it is free will and not determinism which has the better of the argument. Just as, without the corroboration of anything else, I am able to judge that I am in pain, when I am, so also I am able to judge without corroboration that I have made an effortful choice, when I do. These are final phenomenal truths which are intellectually incorrigible. They are not required to conform to other judgements: other judgements must conform to them. Any judgement which would stipulate causal factors determining what appears to the agent as a free choice will necessarily belong to the category of judgements which are intellectually corrigible: we have interpretative supplementation through the use of a system of thought – an interpretation which is liable to qualification or even reversal when a wider system is brought into play.

To sum up, Campbell's distinction between noumenal truth and final phenomenal truth gives him great support in his defence of free will. The doctrine of noumenal truth allows him to destroy the claim that the determinists have an explanation of action, whereas the idea of final phenomenal truth gives a special status to our immediate consciousness of freedom.

7. *The Supra-rational*

I have already said that Campbell has a very austere concept of the supra-rational and have explained his criticisms of Bradley's much richer notion. Indeed, the concept of the supra-rational has become so austere that it is getting dangerously close to the Kantian concept of the Thing-in-Itself. The transition from Kant to Hegel involves the repudiation of the unknowable noumenal reality behind the phenomena. It looks as if Campbell is bringing it back.

If Campbell's Absolute is a Thing-in-Itself, it inherits all the problems associated with that notion. How does Campbell propose to deal with them? Campbell is a metaphysical sceptic, more so even than Bradley, as he admits when he talks of himself as 'out-Heroding Herod' (*SC* 45). But his scepticism consists, not in denying the Absolute and Unconditioned Reality, but in rejecting anything anyone tries to say about it. The Absolute is not Thought: it is not Experience: it is neither free nor determined, and so on. But if a thing is deprived of all its possible characters, how can it continue to exist? How can what is totally faceless make a meaningful appearance in discourse? We have something like Schelling's Absolute, which Hegel destroyed with the epigram 'a night in which all cows are black' (SC 2).

Campbell, however, is unrepentant. His move is to associate himself with the religious consciousness of 'the whole vast army of mystics' (SC 3). For the mystic, there is exactly the same problem about the representation of God. One might say, even, that the concept of God is the concept of the Absolute in theological dress. Campbell would agree with Nicholas Berdyaev that 'There are no rational and conceptual categories, nor any categories of affirmative theology, which can express the final truth about the divine, for they are all relative to this world and to the natural man and are adapted to their limitations'.[9] Both Campbell and Berdyaev were profoundly influenced by the work of Rudolf Otto, and in *On Selfhood and Godhood* (lecture 16) Campbell examines the views expressed by Otto, whom he considers 'the most illuminating religious thinker of modern times' (OSAG 327). Campbell comes down in favour of Supra-rational Theism which he defines as follows:

> a Theism which proclaims that the Nature of God is in principle incapable of being conceived in terms of rational concepts in their literal significance, but that certain of these concepts are validly applicable to God when understood not as literal portrayals, but as appropriate symbols, of the Divine Nature. (OSAG 345)

Thus, for the metaphysician, the reality beyond thought – the Supra-rational Absolute – need not be treated as a complete blank. It is possible to represent it symbolically, but one must be conscious all the time that the symbols used do not apply to the Absolute in a literal fashion.

This is a difficult doctrine, with many ramifications, and I do not propose to explore it further at this point. Suffice to say that with the help of material from Otto and the concept of the symbolic, Campbell is coming back from the extreme

---

[9] *Freedom and the Spirit*, translated by Oliver Fielding Clarke (London, 1935), p. 64.

of scepticism and may be ending up in a position not all that different in spirit from the position reached by Bradley in *Appearance and Reality*. It is not clear that Bradley would insist that everything he says about the Absolute is to be taken with total literalness.

BRAND BLANSHARD – A 'STUDENT' OF BRADLEY

Michael Walsh

It does seem odd to refer to anyone as a 'student' of Bradley, for it is well known that Bradley had no students in the conventional sense of that word. His life fellowship at Merton College did not require that he give lectures or tutor students, and Bradley did neither. Further, owing to ill health, he was extremely reclusive, rarely being seen by students, or his colleagues for that matter.[1]

Nonetheless, there are a few individuals who could make a claim, at least in a limited sense, to being 'students' of Bradley. Brand Blanshard (1892–1987) is one such person. His claim would rest not only on his personal contact with Bradley, but, more importantly, upon the philosophical legacy which he received from Bradley's work and which he advanced in his own distinctive way.

A few biographical highlights will help to explain how a young man from rural Michigan fell under Bradley's sway. In his junior year at the University of Michigan, Blanshard won a Rhodes Scholarship, and enrolled at Merton College in the Fall of 1913. For him Oxford was 'like Mecca to a Moslem' (1980a, p. 1).[2] At this time, Blanshard's greatest influences

---

[1] This is the standard image of Bradley. A. E. Taylor suggests that the picture is extreme.

> It is...true that, owing to the serious physical trouble which beset him all through life..., Bradley had to be careful of draughts and chills, and this naturally prevented him from going out much into Oxford 'society'. But he was neither naturally unsociable nor difficult of access. At the time of my own residence in Merton [ie. 1891–6] it was his habit, unless actually out of health, to dine daily in Hall or in Common Room, and there he was accessible enough to all the numerous guests who were constantly frequenting the College. (Taylor, 1925, p. 3)

[2] References without another author's name refer to Blanshard's writings. See my Bibliography.

at Oxford were Harold Joachim and Bradley. Joachim because he became Blanshard's tutor and because he first set Blanshard the task of reading Bradley, and Bradley because his work and presence at Merton cast a spell on the aspiring young philosopher. While Joachim was the severe though gentle critic who guided Blanshard's work, it was Bradley who then and later became his inspiration.[3] 'There are readers of the present day who may feel that the veneration I felt for Bradley was itself a little absurd. I make no apologies for it. Bradley was easily first not only in Oxford philosophy but among all the British philosophers of his time' (1980a, p. 25).[4]

Despite Bradley's reclusiveness, Blanshard decided that he must seek him out before leaving Oxford. His written request for an interview was successful, and he twice met with Bradley in the Summer Term of 1920[5] in order to discuss *The Principles of Logic*.[6] The marks left on Blanshard by this contact and his study of Bradley's work proved indelible. Of his various Oxford teachers, it is Bradley to whom he always

---

[3] 'It was probably Bradley more than any other who helped me to find my vein... Though I cannot claim to have mastered his system, I was greatly impressed and influenced by it' (1974a, p. 20).

[4] 'It is hard to convey to anyone in the eighties what Bradley was to the Oxford of the early twenties. He dominated the philosophical scene. There were other voices of weight – Joseph, Joachim, Prichard, Ross, Collingwood. But Bradley was the Mahatma' (1984b, p. 8).

[5] Blanshard's stay at Oxford was interrupted by World War I. Prior to the US's entry into the War, he served with the British YMCA in India and elsewhere; after the US's entry, he did a short stint in France, largely as an educator. However, between these episodes (ie. from 1917–18) he completed an MA at Columbia University. Notably, while at Columbia he taught a seminar on Bradley's philosophy.

[6] In his *Journal of Philosophy* 'Memoir' of Bradley, Blanshard says he was surprised to receive a friendly reception:

> I had heard much of how formidable he was; what I found, on the contrary, was a rare courtesy and cordiality... [I]n spite of age and illness he was a splendid figure to look at, powerfully built and erect as a military man... In his conversation any one who knew his writing would have found something familiar. There were the same conciseness and clarity, the same impatience with anything obscure, the same unwillingness to express himself at all until he could do so with decision.
> (1925, p. 7)

For a fuller account of these meetings see Blanshard, 1984b, pp. 7–8.

returns, particularly the 'Spinozistic' Bradley, whose philosophy satisfied for Blanshard aspects of a 'religious' need which he then and later felt.[7]

Blanshard was impressed not only by Bradley's philosophy, but also by his intellectual integrity, his gifts as a dialectician, and his consummate skill as a literary artist,[8] all of which traits Blanshard sought to embody in his own philosophical career. And, despite the fact that Bradley claimed limited originality,[9] Blanshard believed that to everything he touched he brought a new freshness and genius. 'His product is so finished, and its parts so closely articulated as to make this plain – that any ore he had got from others had been so smelted and refined in the processes of his thought as to be virtually a new thing in the world' (1925, p. 15).

---

[7] Blanshard writes further in this regard:

> No doubt Bradley's strong appeal to me had something to do with the religious root that sustained much idealist thinking... He said in the preface to *Appearance* that for some men philosophy was a means of experiencing Deity, and that probably no one who did not feel this had ever greatly cared for metaphysics. Here, as in much else, he was sealed of the tribe of Spinoza. The work of analysis was important for him, and he had spent much of his life at it; but without an ulterior interest that was essentially religious, such brainwork would not have supported itself; it would have been for him a vine cut at the root... Bradley regarded philosophy as the intellectual means of adjusting oneself to the universe, of trying to see things steadily and whole; and for him such a search was both speculative and religious. (1980a, p. 26)

This 'religious root' of late nineteenth-century idealism has been much noted and criticized; however, one should not forget that the genesis of an idea or theory has nothing to do with its truth.

[8] 'He was the outstanding stylist of the school that included such widely differing masters as John Caird and A. E. Taylor. Here was a case in which the style was the man' (1984b, p. 13). For a full assessment of the positive *and negative* aspects of that style, see Blanshard, 1984b, pp. 13–14.

[9] For an example, see the 'Preface' to the second edition of the *Logic*:

> It is not that in this book or elsewhere I lay a claim to original discovery. In these pages there is perhaps no result which I do not owe, and where, if my memory served me better, I could acknowledge my debt. But when a man has studied, however little, the great philosophers, and felt the distance between himself and them, I hardly understand how, except on compulsion, he can be ready to enter on claims and counterclaims between himself and his fellows. And all I care to say for myself is that, if I had succeeded in owing more, I might then perhaps have gained more of a claim to be original. (*PL* vii–viii)

What, then, are some aspects of the legacy which Blanshard inherited? He shares Bradley's bold conception of the task of philosophy. He has the same central presupposition regarding the fundamental nature of reality. And, like Bradley, he believes that metaphysics seeks a special object of knowledge which would uniquely satisfy the intellect. He shares with Bradley the view that truth is best understood as a characteristic of propositional sets – ie. their degree of coherence and comprehensiveness. He and Bradley both believe in internal relations, but differ fundamentally as to the reality of relations. Blanshard's ethical theory is an ethics of self-realization, but he develops it along different lines than those Bradley takes. And although Blanshard believes in the Absolute, at least in some sense, he does not accept that one can apply moral predicates to nature. These are some of the important points of doctrine on which their paths meet and sometimes diverge.

Before discussing these, however, something should be said regarding similarities in philosophical intent and method. Blanshard persistently reiterates the view that philosophy is 'a peculiarly determined effort to press the question Why?' (eg. 1974a, p. 22). That is to say, the philosopher wishes to know *why* something is the case rather than being otherwise. Blanshard clearly does not believe that probing the nature of reality is the restricted province of the 'non-philosophical' sciences, or that philosophy's task is to clear up the conceptual confusions attendant to the 'scientific enterprise'. This emphasis placed on the quest for intelligibility or understanding of reality is the key to explaining his philosophy, and in this respect, at least, he believed that he was close to Bradley:

> The main thing I owe to Bradley was his conception of what philosophy was seeking to do. This borrowed stone became the head and corner of my philosophy. When I came to write a book on *The Nature of Thought*, and tried to make clear to myself what reflective thinking was attempting to do, the only answer that seemed plausible was that it was seeking understanding, that under-standing was explanation to oneself, and that explanation lay in placing

something in a context of relations that rendered it intelligible. This is probably the cardinal idea of my philosophy.
(1974, pp. 20–21)

For Blanshard, then, his task is to determine what will satisfy this powerful and unique drive in human nature – ie. the quest for understanding – and he finds that this task can only be completed when what has been puzzled about is placed in a context which makes it intelligible. This context is a *system* of relations which renders its terms intelligible, in the sense that they are now seen to be *necessary*. That is to say, it is judged that the things or states of affairs in question could not be otherwise than they are.[10]

We are, of course, left with the question whether we have reason to believe that thought's demand for systematic intelligibility is satisfied by its object – ie. does reality possess such systematicity? Blanshard maintains this is a 'natural assumption', although it cannot be proved.

Next, there is the issue of method. It is often remarked that Bradley's writings, despite his disavowals (eg. *AR* xi), are highly, if not excessively, polemical. He was an especially acute and punishing critic. Blanshard's writing shares these traits, though to a more moderate degree. However, despite his usually more tolerant tone, Blanshard's way is also the *via negativa*.[11] It is characteristic of his method that he advances

---

[10] On these points, Blanshard writes:

> My conception of philosophy, then, involves three theses: (1) that the theoretical impulse at the root of philosophy is a distinct drive in human nature, (2) that the end of this drive is to order things in an intelligible system of relations, and (3) that as our understanding advances, there is a closer approximation of the system within to the system without [1974a, p. 25] ... the attempt of thought is to discover what independently exists, what must be there already as a condition of the discovery... Such inquiry finally rests, I think, only when it reaches necessity and the question Why? cannot intelligibly be asked again. The postulate of philosophy is thus that its central question is answerable and its search for understanding legitimate, in short that the world set for its dissection is intelligible. My view that the Absolute is a logically articulated but not a morally perfect whole thus accords with the natural assumptions of our activity in these two realms. (1974a, p. 44)

[11] For his part, Bradley is well aware of the negative cast of his thought. For instance in the 'Preface' to *Appearance and Reality* he writes: 'My book ... will be satisfied to

positions only after forcefully refuting alternative theories which are generally accepted as correct answers to the questions under consideration. 'My views on any subject seem to advance only by negations; I try one theory after another and reach a stable view only after zigzagging my way along between alternative theories till I arrive at one that survives the criticisms made of the others' (1980a, p. 180). However, despite a similar emphasis on rendering the positions of others into unintelligibility, Blanshard is less dogmatic in his conclusions than Bradley. Indeed, of Bradley's 'overweening self-confidence' Blanshard writes:

> Is there anyone else who, at the end of a long and controversial book, could write like this? 'With regard to the main character of that Absolute our position is briefly this. We hold that our conclusion is certain, and that to doubt it logically is impossible. There is no other view, there is no other idea beyond the view here put forward. It is impossible rationally even to entertain the question of another possibility.' (1984b, p. 14; the reference is to *AR* 459)

Blanshard continues, 'In philosophy no one is entitled to this tone' (*ibid.*). And one finds no similar intellectual arrogance in his own work. Indeed, it would be inappropriate to insist that his conclusions are dogmatic certainties, for Blanshard's philosophy implies a commitment to fallibilism – ie. the view that no actual proposition is immune from error or the necessity of reformulation. While this commitment is rarely explicit within his work, it is nonetheless implied by his notion of truth in terms of an *ideal* goal of thought, rather than an actual outcome. However, this leaves Blanshard with the task of explaining a certain residual tension in his philosophy which arises from holding this position as well as the view that there are certain rationalistic principles of knowledge that cannot be denied except under pain of contradiction. Be that

---

be negative, so long as that word implies an attitude of active questioning. The chief need of English philosophy is, I think, a sceptical study of first principles. By scepticism...I understand...an attempt to become aware of and to doubt all preconceptions' (p. x). He believed that his 'English' predecessors, in particular, the Scottish common-sense school and then Mill and his followers, had failed to be sufficiently sceptical.

as it may, the important point is that both philosophers see themselves on the last line of defense of true philosophy. What Blanshard says of Bradley's attacks on his predecessors is true of Blanshard himself – he saw empiricism as 'a huge and hydra-headed monster, sprawled quite across the countryside and everywhere inviting attack' (1925, p. 11). In such a situation one does not concern oneself too much with the sensitivities of the opposition – one takes no prisoners.

What both men defend, in large part, are the fundamental principles of Rationalism. Susanne Langer has remarked that:

> Every philosopher has his tradition. His thought has developed amid certain problems, certain basic alternatives of opinion, that embody the key concepts which dominate his time and his environment and which will always be reflected, positively or by negation, in his own work. They are the forms of thought he has inherited, wherein he naturally thinks, or from which his maturer conceptions depart. (Langer, 1949, p. 381)

Blanshard's tradition is that of classical philosophical rationalism. However, the concepts and problems which dominate his time – the philosophical agenda, so to speak – are determined by the philosophical response to rationalism. That is to say, they are the claims of late nineteenth and early twentieth-century radical empiricism. Just as Bradley reacts to Hamilton and Mill, so Blanshard responds to behaviourism, pragmatism, logical positivism, and central aspects of the 'analytic revolution' – all of which he sees as challenging the legitimacy of 'reason' as a source of knowledge about reality and morality. Like Bradley's, his philosophy has a genuine freshness, but it too remains, in important respects, a defense of the 'old dispensation'. Indeed, for a mid twentieth-century philosopher, there is, as noted, an unusual clarity and surprising confidence about philosophy's role: 'Philosophy is a persistent raising of the question Why? Taken at its loftiest, it is the attempt to understand the world. Philosophy is a continual effort to render the world intelligible' (1980b, pp. 211–12). Perhaps it seems more striking in Blanshard, than in Bradley, to see such a deeply felt belief in reality's ultimate intelligibility; however, this contrast with their respective contemporaries is only more intense in Blanshard's case because Bradley's victories are part of a war which was apparently lost.

Reason is the human capacity which makes our quest for intelligibility rational: 'Philosophy is the persistent attempt to understand the nature of things by the exercise of reason' (1980a, p. 96). However, Blanshard does not mean simply 'thinking reasonably', for the most fundamental products of reason's work are not inductive generalizations but rational insights and deductions. He characterizes rationalism as:

> the philosophical view that regards reason as the chief source and test of knowledge. Holding that reality itself has an inherently logical structure, the Rationalist asserts that a class of truths exists that the intellect can grasp directly. There are, according to the Rationalists, certain rational principles – especially in logic and mathematics, and even in ethics and metaphysics – that are so fundamental that to deny them is to fall into contradiction. (1974, p. 527b)

He goes on to contrast this with 'Empiricism' which he asserts holds that *all* knowledge both comes from and must be ultimately tested by sense experience. In contrast, 'Rationalism holds reason to be a faculty that can lay hold of truths beyond the reach of sense perception, both in certainty and generality' (*ibid.*). What is it that Rationalism maintains can be gained through a priori, or rational, insight – ie. a direct apprehension by the intellect as distinct from sense experience?

> What the intellectual faculty apprehends is objects that transcend sense experience – universals and their relations. [Universals] cannot be seen, heard, or felt [but] man can plainly think about them and about their relations. Such a priori knowledge is both necessary (ie. it cannot be conceived as otherwise) and universal, in the sense that it admits of no exceptions. (1974, p. 528a–b)

But Rationalism, according to Blanshard, involves metaphysical as well as epistemological commitments; for instance, the 'belief that the world is a rationally ordered whole, the parts of which are linked by logical necessity and the structure of which is therefore intelligible' (1974, p. 528a). The rationalist's beliefs may range from (a) the belief that '*a & ~a* cannot coexist' holds for the real world and not merely for sentences, to (b) the belief that 'facts' involve a positive coherence, ie. that 'they are so bound up with each other that none could be different without all being different' (*ibid.*). Blanshard also holds that causal relationships exhibit a necessity which is logical in character – ie. that if a causal law were fully and precisely stated it would reveal a connection in which the cause would be seen to necessitate its effect. This being so, all the facts and events in the world would have to compose a single rational and intelligible order or system. This entails a denial of the contingency of the world – a radical determinacy. Indeed, Blanshard defines 'reason' as 'the power and function of grasping necessary connections' (1962, p. 382).

Blanshard's attack on empiricism does not entail the rejection of a role for empirical investigation in understanding the world; rather, his target is empiricism's claim to be the sole source of knowledge. He would endorse Bradley's remark that, 'On sensation and feeling I am sure that we depend for the *material* of our knowledge. Our intelligence cannot construct the world of perceptions and feelings, and it depends on what is given – to so much I assent' (*ETR* 203, my italics). Allowance must be made for experience in the whole which is the Absolute. Indeed, at least for Bradley, the Absolute, in some sense, *is* experience, while, for Blanshard, there exists a genuine continuity between scientific and philosophical enterprise.[12]

---

[12] Blanshard, at least, could have written *much* of the following remark by the arch-empiricist Quine:

> I think of philosophy as concerned with our knowledge of the world and the nature of the world. I think of philosophy as attempting to round out 'the system of the world', as Newton put it. There have been philosophers who thought of philosophy as somehow separate from science, and as providing a firm basis on which to build science, but this I consider an empty dream ... I think of philosophy as being continuous with science, even as a part of science ... Philosophy lies at the abstract and theoretical end of science ... Philosophy is abstract through being very general ... Philosophy seeks the broad outlines of the whole system of the world.
> (Quine, 1978, pp. 170–71)

Bradley's eventual outlook is deeply sceptical with respect to our being able to lay bare the nature of reality.[13] He believes that discursive thought is inescapably inadequate, as it deals with the realm of appearance – ie. a world fraught with contradictions and antinomies – and moves in the sphere of relations. Although Bradley's Absolute is everything that is the case – the totality of appearances – it is not a mere congeries of appearances, but this totality understood as forming a significant or substantial whole. But awareness of this truth is not the result of a generalization from experience of particulars. Bradley's belief in the Absolute and his characterization of it depend as much on a deeply felt 'mysticism', or better 'fideism', as they do on rational thought and argument. Ultimately, he relies upon an insight into the character of the Absolute which is based on his intuition or insight into the nature of immediate experience or feeling. In contrast, Blanshard is less inclined to delimit the *theoretical* power of human reason. For him, although the ultimate goal of thought – systematic understanding of reality – is accepted as the only end or purpose of theoretical thinking, it remains just that, a *goal*, not an actual or possible outcome. However, despite this important difference, each philosopher is similarly concerned to defend the capacities of reason by undermining the pretensions of empiricism.

In this regard, Blanshard notes that while T. H. Green had ably criticized empiricism, it was

> Bradley who picked up Green's sword, which he wielded with incomparable address. He had learned from Green and Hegel that experience is more than a chaos of sensations, and that thinking is not a mere drifting along a line of associations; that experience is on the contrary shot through with necessary connections and that thought at its best is a movement under rational constraint.
>
> (1980a, p. 25)[14]

---

[13] Cf. this assessment of Bradley's position by a sympathetic and closely aligned philosophical contemporary: '"The Absolute", when all is said, remained in his view a transcendent mystery; it never became, as it tends to become in the hands of some "Idealists", transparent. The cloud of "unknowing" between ourselves and It was always there' (Taylor, 1925, p. 12).

[14] See Blanshard, 1925, pp. 10–12 for his assessment of the specifics of Bradley's attack on empiricism.

There can be no question that Blanshard sees himself as a wielder of the same sword, even if a less original and able champion than Bradley. His chief works, *The Nature of Thought*, and the trilogy, *Reason and Analysis*, *Reason and Goodness* and *Reason and Belief*, are sustained attempts to refute the claims of empiricism and to legitimize those of rationalism. In particular, Blanshard sees the conflict with empiricism in terms of its insistence that *all* knowledge is ultimately founded upon and tested by sense experience.

In contrast, both Bradley and Blanshard hold that it is possible to acquire knowledge, through the use of reason, which is superior to what is obtained through the senses. Bradley, in particular, is highly suspicious of the 'knowledge' provided by sensation. Discursive thought is founded upon a 'common sense' way of seeing things and their qualities – ie. seeing them as distinct independent objects and properties gathered together in a complex of external relations. While such thinking may be adequate for practical life[15] it does not make known the true nature of reality, which is one seamless web, not an aggregate of disparate particulars.[16] Such thought is inevitably relational, whereas reality is one, or One. For Bradley, the relational is simply false, and he states at the end of a key chapter on relations that once this is seen, all the other arguments against appearance are largely superfluous.[17] As we will see, this is one area in which Blanshard

---

[15] As W. H. Walsh aptly puts it: 'What this comes to is that there is no conflict between Bradley and common sense, only between Bradley and common sense *philosophy*, which is by no means the same thing and whose credentials are by no means so obviously impeccable' (Walsh, 1964, p. 435).

[16] On this point, Blanshard similarly writes: 'The notion that the world is a gigantic ragbag of loose ends, in which nothing is connected intelligibly with anything else, will not stand even a cursory examination. The world as we know it is shot through and through with lines of necessity' (1964, p. 442).

[17] 'The conclusion to which I am brought is that a relational way of thought – any one that moves by the machinery of terms and relations – must give appearance, and not truth. It is a makeshift, a device, a mere practical compromise, most necessary, but in the end most indefensible' (*AR* 28). 'The reader who has followed and has grasped the principle of this chapter, will have little need to spend his time upon those which succeed it. He will have seen that our experience, where relational, is not true; and he will have condemned, almost without a hearing, the great mass of phenomena' (*ibid.*, 29).

and Bradley part company, for Blanshard insists upon the reality of relations. In spite of this difference, for both, 'sense givenness' is rejected as the foundation of knowledge of ultimate reality, not only because it cannot give such knowledge directly, but also because sensible qualities themselves cannot be understood except by the use of rational principles.

Blanshard's rationalism is also necessitarian. At its starkest, necessitarianism is the view that there are no contingent true propositions. Anything that is the case *must* be so. Nothing simply 'happens', or 'might have been otherwise'. He would agree with what Spinoza writes in the metaphysical appendix to his exposition of Descartes: 'For if men understood clearly the whole order of Nature, they would find all things just as necessary as are all those treated in Mathematics. Yet because this is beyond human knowledge, we judge certain things to be possible, but not necessary' (Spinoza, vol. 1, p. 332). In particular, for Blanshard, the relation between cause and effect is not contingent. Given sufficient knowledge we could deduce an effect from a prior knowledge of its cause. An important rationalist principle which is based on such an understanding of reality is the Principle of Sufficient Reason – that nothing happens without a sufficient reason why it should be so, rather than otherwise. That is to say, for any positive truth there is some sufficient reason for it, something which *makes* it true, although in most cases we do not know this reason. What is insisted upon is the *theoretical* possibility of such knowledge.

Indeed, Blanshard often refers to his own work as 'neo-Spinozism', and he maintains this trait is present in Bradley. 'Bradley richly fertilized my budding rationalism with his own neo-Spinozism' (1980a, p. 126). What Blanshard recognized in both Spinoza and Bradley was a 'view of the world as an intelligible whole, set as a puzzle for unravelment by human reason' (1980a, p. 125). Together with the belief that thought is purposive, this is perhaps the most important common point in Blanshard's and Bradley's thinking – ie. their monistic position as to the underlying character of reality. The metaphysics of both rests on this *presupposition* that reality is an intelligible whole. That it is a presupposition, and not the result of proof, Bradley admits. 'I have assumed that the object of metaphysics is to find a general view which will satisfy the intellect and I have assumed that whatever succeeds in doing this is real and true, and that whatever fails is neither. This is a doctrine which, so far as I can see, can neither be proved nor questioned' (*AR* 491).[18] Blanshard agrees that there is no way to *prove* that the laws of logic hold for the world, for such a proof would have to employ the very same laws, ie. assume their validity. But, he insists, because we cannot think without laws such as that of Contradiction, we have an entitlement to assume their truthfulness. In respect to reality we must accept a 'Postulate of Rationality', ie. the supposition that the theoretic system reflects the world as it is.

What needs emphasis in the previous quotation from Bradley is the reference to 'satisfaction'. Elsewhere he writes: 'If there is to be philosophy its proper business is to satisfy the intellect' (*ETR* 221). Bradley asks, what will satisfy the intellect? His answer is, not the disjointed world of everyday experience, or, as he more often says, appearance. The intellect cannot rest in the presence of contradiction, and appearance is fraught with it. Blanshard writes similarly:

> That the world is an intelligible system rather than a congeries of accidents seems to me rather a postulate of inquiry than a conclusion decisively made out. One may say, if one wishes, that it is a matter of faith. But that suggests that the postulate is dispensable or arbitrary, and it is clearly not. Thought is an unavoidable human enterprise; if it is to succeed, the question Why? which it continually raises must be answerable; to assume that it is answerable is to assume only what is necessary unless the enterprise is expected in advance to be a failure... One is not running gullibly beyond the evidence; one is assuming

---

[18] Cf. further: 'Philosophy demands, and in the end rests on, what may fairly be termed faith. It has, we may say, to presuppose its conclusion in order to prove it. It tacitly assumes something in general to be true in order to carry this general truth out in detail' (*ETR* 15).

at each step of the journey that there is solid ground ahead and that this will hold for each subsequent step.

(1974a, p. 25)

This is connected to another point, for Blanshard also learned from Spinoza, Bradley, Joachim, and others, that thought is purposive in character:

> It was the position of all these men that there is a *conatus* or drive in human nature that demands for its satisfaction an understanding of the world, a vision of the whole, in which the nature and place of each thing is to be understood only by seeing its place in an all-inclusive order. Philosophy is the systematic attempt at the apprehension of that order.
>
> (1980a, p. 126)

Spinoza's *conatus* is a drive towards 'adequate ideas', in other words, a comprehensive view of reality which is so ordered internally as to satisfy our logical sensibilities. In short, by seeing that things *must* be as they are, thought is satisfied, at least for the moment, and comes to rest. Thought thus moves under rational constraints towards the apprehension of order. The associationist and behavioural traditions in psychology, in contrast, did not 'take seriously the contention of Spinoza and Bradley that thought had an end of its own, namely rational insight or understanding, and that this end could direct and control the process' (*ibid.*). The empiricists, whom Bradley attacks, held that thinking is merely a matter of relating ideas or images on the basis of past associations. On the contrary, Bradley insists that thought is concerned with universals which are connected necessarily.

Both Bradley and Blanshard maintain variants of the coherence theory of truth.[19] Their contention is that truth

---

[19] In an otherwise excellent article (Candlish, 1989), Stewart Candlish insists that Bradley did not hold a coherence theory of truth, because he *only* held that coherence was its test or criterion and not its *nature* – which, so Candlish argues, he held is the *identity* of truth, knowledge, and reality. Leaving the correctness of this reading aside, surely it distorts what one must hold in order to count as a 'coherence theorist'. For example, perhaps the best known recent monograph on the theory is Rescher's *The Coherence Theory of Truth* (1973). Rescher considers himself a coherence theorist, and yet argues only for a criterial theory, indeed, rejecting coherence as truth's nature. (He later significantly modified his position to accept that '*ideal* coherence'

must be understood in the context of satisfying a want of our nature. The answer to the question, 'What can be the criterion of truth?' must be given in the context of satisfaction. 'What in the end is the criterion? The criterion of truth, I should say, as of everything else, is in the end the satisfaction of a want of our nature. Truth to my mind is a satisfaction of a special kind' (*ETR* 219–20). For both, the true must be coherent and comprehensive (characteristics of the Absolute or reality), for this is what reason or intellect demands. 'Truth is an ideal expression of the Universe, at once coherent and comprehensive. It must not conflict with itself, and there must be no suggestion which fails to fall inside it. Perfect truth in short must realize the idea of a systematic whole. And such a whole [possesses] essentially the two characters of coherence and comprehensiveness' (*ETR* 223). Only if reality were seen in this way, could it satisfy the intellect's quest for intelligibility or understanding.

Their theories of truth are built upon a shared presupposition as to the nature of reality – that it is such that it does not contradict itself. In considering what could be a positive criterion for knowledge of reality, Bradley writes that there is an answer: 'Ultimate reality is such that it does not contradict itself; here is an absolute criterion. And it is proved absolute by the fact that, either in endeavouring to deny it, or even in attempting to doubt it, we tacitly assume its validity' (*AR* 120). For both men, this criterion provides a sure point of contact which makes the claim to knowledge reasonable – ie. it is a necessary condition of propositional sets that they be coherent in order that they state what is the case. Similarly, it is a necessary condition of such sets that they be comprehensive, because only in this way could they capture the all-inclusiveness of the Absolute. For Blanshard, truth lies

---

was the nature of truth. See 'Truth as Ideal Coherence' in his *Forbidden Knowledge*, Dordrecht, 1987.) Two other prominent 'coherence theorists', Keith Lehrer and Lawrence BonJour, maintain criterial theories only. BonJour, for example, insists that the nature of truth is correspondence.

Indeed, in a sympathetic discussion of Candlish's article (Baldwin, 1991), Baldwin so much as says that the 'identity theory' promulgated by Candlish amounts to no more than the redundancy theory – which has been considered by some as a variant correspondence theory which tries to do its work on the criterial side without the necessity of inventing 'facts' for the purpose.

in system, and above all in that perfect type of system in which each component implies and is implied by every other. We shall speak sometimes as if the aim of thought were understanding, and this also is true; the two aims are equivalent to each other. To know the truth about anything is, so far, to apprehend it in a system of relations that makes it intelligible, and this is what we mean by understanding it. (1939, vol. 1, p. 78)

This connection between truth and understanding lies at the root of Blanshard's coherence theory of truth. It is because Blanshard believes that we can only have understanding when we possess contextual knowledge of something – an awareness of *necessary* connections – that he identifies truth with coherence, and that he sees therein the only possible means of determining truthfulness:

Thought aims at understanding, and to understand anything means...to grasp it as necessitated within a system of knowledge... The end that thought is seeking, the only end that would satisfy it wholly, because the only end that would bring complete understanding, is a system such that nothing remained outside and nothing was contingent within. (1939, vol. 2, p. 304)[20]

Of course, truth understood as the coherent and comprehensive remains an 'ideal', for discursive thought cannot achieve such a goal. We cannot combine the particularities of discursive thought with the abstractness necessary to encompass Bradley's Absolute, and we must recognize, if only as a practical matter, our finitude. But nonetheless, just as certain elements of appearance can be more real than

---

[20] Blanshard explains this point more fully in replying to Rescher:

The upshot of this...was what seemed to me a clear insight that thought from the beginning was a drive toward understanding, and that this drive could in the end be satisfied by one thing only. This was the achievement of a system of thought in which the question Why? had been pressed through to the end in all directions. Such a system would be at once all-comprehensive and so related internally that nothing unintelligible remained. In short, thought was a distinctive drive in human nature in which from the very beginning the end of a coherent system was immanently at work and became clearer in conception and firmer in its guidance as the development progressed. (1980c, p. 591)

others because they more fully or adequately disclose the Absolute or reality, so certain propositions or combinations of propositions can be more true or false – ie. can have a greater degree of truth or falsity.

The doctrine of degrees of truth is connected both with truth recognized as an 'ideal' and with the notion of comprehensiveness. The all-inclusiveness of the Absolute requires that error, at least in some sense, be contained in the Absolute. If complete truth is identified with the Absolute, partial truths are diluted aspects of this complete truth – ie. errors. Error is thus a matter of degree rather than absoluteness.

For both Blanshard and Bradley the acceptance of coherence as the test of truth is the result not simply of their positive metaphysical beliefs, but the consequence of the apparent failure of alternative theories to withstand criticism. Indeed, Blanshard goes further, arguing that when our beliefs are put under pressure, we always use coherence as the *ultimate* court of appeal or test of truth. Even when we think that we are applying other tests, such as 'correspondence with fact', we often resort to coherence without being aware of it. For instance, some criterial accounts of correspondence depend upon the required verification being accomplished by what is 'given' in sensory experience – ie. putative 'brute facts'. But even here, we will ultimately resort to coherence to justify the assertion of truthfulness.

For this reason, as soon as we attempt to say *what* is given, we find ourselves thrown back upon coherence anyhow. '[Brute facts] are illusion. There are no such things. The "facts" that were to support our system are themselves relative to the system. In short, the coherence of judgements within a system is our test, and our only test, of any truth or fact whatever' (1939, vol. 2, pp. 214–15).

That is, we find that our 'brute facts' are themselves judgements, which must be compared with others before these 'facts' are admitted as being decisive.

Earlier, I noted that both men believe in the internality of relations – ie. that a relation cannot be changed or removed without affecting the terms themselves between which that relation holds. This position has been aptly characterized by

Wollheim when commenting upon Bradley's insistence

> that we must cease thinking of the world as consisting entirely of objects that possess certain properties, that stand in certain relations to other objects, but that could possess other properties, could be differently related to other objects, and yet be the same; we must not think, for instance, that the bird before us, brown, sitting on the bough, could be black and flying across the sky, and yet be the same bird.
>
> All the relations in which an object stands are rooted in its nature as firmly as triangularity is rooted in the nature of the triangle. (Wollheim, 1956, pp. 21-2)

On this view, there is a sense in which we cannot refer to anything without referring to everything, or effect a change in anything without changing everything. For Bradley, this has the consequence that when we think in the common-sense relational manner, that is, in terms of isolated independent objects whose relations to one another are not internal, we distort reality. We make distinctions in thought where none exist in reality. And we fail in thought to see the implications of change. Consequently, because discursive thought depends on non-internal relations, and uses concepts such as Space, Time, Causality, and Change, which are inherently relational, then it cannot be anything but illusory.[21]

Blanshard has independent arguments for internal relations. The first is the 'argument from difference': for any two things there is a relation of difference (ie. that something which makes them not the same thing). But if that relation is removed they would be the same thing – neither would be

---

[21] Cf. Bradley's final writing on this subject, the unfinished article 'Relations':

> If 'relation' is not used merely as a vague term for any sort of connexion or union of that which is both one and many, but is employed in a stricter and more limited sense, then to me relations do not in the end as such possess truth or reality. Experience, so far as in a proper sense relational, I take to be in no sense either primary or ultimate... any relational view involves self-contradiction in its essence. (CE 630)
>
> I have shown in the first place that relational experience has to fall back on a non-relational form of unity, and is therefore not ultimate... Nothing to myself is real ultimately but that super-relational unity of the One and Many, which is at once the consummation and the pre-condition of all and everything. (CE 650)

what it is at present. This is true of any two differing things in the universe.[22] And the second is the 'argument from common causal connection': take two seemingly unconnected events, such as your going to church last Sunday and President Bush's last State of the Union Address – it can be shown that these seemingly unconnected events are inextricably causally related:

> In what possible way could the latter depend on the former? The explanation is in outline simple enough. It consists, first, in showing that your going to church is the effect of a line of necessary causes extending into the past indefinitely. You went to church, let us say, because you were taught to do so in youth; you were taught because your parents were Lutherans; they were Lutherans because their great-great-grandparents were anti-papal non-conformists who fled from the England of James II to escape persecution; they chose America because they had heard of it as a land of freedom from reports of Captain Smith; Smith made his voyages because Columbus preceded him and reported on what he found. To make this causal account complete we should have to fill in millions of details, but that is a matter of practical rather than theoretical difficulty. Now if argument from the denial of the consequent is valid, [ie. *Modus Tollens*: p then q, $\sim q$, therefore $\sim p$] the denial of any of these steps would commit us to the denial of the entire preceding series of steps, provided, of course, that each is the necessary cause of its successor. It follows that James's persecution, Smith's voyage and Columbus's discovery could not have taken place as they did if you had not gone to church. Having ascended this ladder of causation, we then come down. If these steps had not taken place, then the radiating lines of causation that issued from each of them would also have been different. That

---

[22] The argument derives from Hegel's *Science of Logic*, vol. 1, bk 1, sect. 1, chap. 2, sect. B(b), and latterly McTaggart's *A Commentary on Hegel's Logic*, pp. 29–30. See Blanshard, 1967 for a summary of his arguments for internal relations. An earlier, fuller account is given in chaps. 31 and 32 of *The Nature of Thought* (ie. Blanshard, 1939).

implies that the later world would have been different, and vastly different, though just how and where, it is impossible to say. In a world as different as one would be in which all these causal chains were different, would [President Bush] be President at all? It is surely doubtful, and still more doubtful whether his [State of the Union Address] would have occurred just when and where it did. And if one cared to ascend still further the chain of causation, to follow it back to the discovery of fire, or the emergence of the first mutant that could be called human, or the formation of the sun, could any limit be set to the change in the existing world? (1967, pp. 231–2)

Blanshard grants that both are mind-spinning arguments but, to the end, he believed that the many attacks on each argument had missed their mark.[23]

Despite their agreement on the nature of relations, however, Blanshard disagrees fundamentally with Bradley as to their reality. Blanshard notes that Bradley's position is that all the 'separate facts' of experience are but elements in one seamless experience, in which the contradictions of common sense are transcended. 'In such an experience the realm of things and relations resolves itself into a single undivided immediacy, an immediacy which contains all the salvageable remnants of ordinary experience, but blended into a whole as immediate as that from which the long ascent began' (1984a, p. 214). Even so, what *is* wrong with relations? Blanshard restates Bradley's arguments as follows:

1. To say that 'A is related to B' raises these issues:
   (a) The relation 'R' is not an adjective of A or B, nor of both taken together.
   (b) It 'links' A and B but is distinct from each.
   (c) But how is A related to R, or B to R?
   (d) Does it not take a further relation, R^1 to relate A to R,

---

[23] Blanshard's position is not that *all* relations are internal, but that *some* are, which had been denied by his opponents, and which is all that is needed to make his case. Cf. 1962, pp. 475ff.

and a further R^2 to relate to R^1, and so on, ad infinitum? Now if both A and B are connected with R by chains that have no end, then they are not connected at all... To say that they are intelligibly related is self-contradiction.

(1984a, p. 215)

Blanshard thinks the argument is invalid because Bradley has been misled by a metaphor. 'He is thinking of a relation as if it were another term, as if A-R-B were three beads on a string, and then the relation of R to A or B will present the same problem as that of A to B. But R is not the same sort of being as its terms. It is neither a thing nor a quality. It is a relation, and the business of a relation is to relate' (*ibid.*).

2. Bradley also argues (1893, p. 26) that one cannot have relations without qualities, but that qualities are the sort of item that cannot be joined.

However, Blanshard contends the argument depends upon drawing non-existent distinctions between qualities.

3. Bradley offers another argument (1893, p. 17), which confuses the 'is' of identity with the 'is' of predication, with the result that he seems to hold that all judgements are ones of identity.

But when I say, 'That cube is white', of a lump of sugar, I am not identifying a shape with a colour. Here we are not asserting identity, but saying that white belongs to the cube, ie. predicating. There is nothing unintelligible or contradictory about such a relation.

Blanshard agrees with Broad[24] that Bradley was not really moved by such poor arguments, but rather by his fundamental position as to the nature of reality – ie. that a plurality of related things or qualities is incoherent:

> The true consideration is rather that terms and relations alike are abstractions from an underlying unity, and one has no right to assume that these elements, when dissected out from this unity, remain what they were within it.

---

[24] In *The Examination of McTaggart's Philosophy*, vol. 1, pp. 86–98 (Cambridge, 1933).

'Everywhere in the end a relation appears as a necessary but a self-contradictory translation of a non-relational or super-relational unity'.
(1984a, p. 219; the quotation is from *AR* 309, n. 1)

But, Blanshard argues, the mere fact that our intelligence is active in constructing our experience does not give us good reasons for holding that all the things around us are unreal. Bradley is relying here not so much on argument, but on his intuition into the character of immediate experience; deriving, by analogy, the assertion that the finite things and events around us must possess the putative unity of immediate experience – ie. that they must be non-relational. Blanshard's view of reality is also monistic, but his monism is not of this kind – it does not deny the possibility of a plurality of real things uniting relationally in one system, world, or universe.

What Blanshard is rejecting, in part, is Bradley's idealism (ie. that whatever is, is experience) in favour of a form of realism.[25] 'There was a universe long before sentience emerged from it, a universe that will persist long after consciousness has had its day. For Bradley to build the universe itself out of one of its own transient products [ie. human experience] was arbitrary and question-begging' (1984a, p. 220). In contrast, Blanshard believes we simply can't get along without relations:

1. As the Law of Contradiction is itself a relation, it would be thrown out with everything else. The same could be said of consistency and of coherence.

2. Thought must bear a relation to its object to be truthful or to be knowledge. Blanshard believes this relationship is teleological in that the object of thought (viz. complete understanding of reality) is the controlling end of thought.

3. One might argue, as Wittgenstein did, that thought (in this instance, relations) is thrown down once we have reached the top of the ladder – that its weaknesses are in this way left behind. But, 'If you ask us to accept your conclusion because

---

[25] I do not wish to contend that Bradley's idealism is simply the subjective idealism of Berkeley; for one thing, he seems to have argued that the very notion of a self requires, or makes no sense without, something other than the self.

it has been reached on a series of solid rungs, you cannot also expect us to accept it once you dismiss them as worm-eaten. If they are sound, you cannot expect us to jettison as worthless what has carried you safely through' (*ibid.*, p. 224).

4. Lastly, 'Bradley faces a dilemma. Either he admits phenomena as such into the Absolute or not. If he does, he is admitting what, by his own insistence, is unreal and illusory, and thus has an Absolute no longer. If he does not admit them, his Absolute is not all-comprehensive and dies of privation' (*ibid.*, p. 226).

Blanshard concludes: 'My own choice is to preserve the ladder [ie. discursive thought and logical reasoning] and forfeit the empyrean to which it is supposed to lead [ie. the Absolute mystically conceived]... The things and relations of common life may be illusions but illusions exist; they are not mere nothings. A place must be found for them in the Absolute, and it cannot be done' (*ibid.*, pp. 224, 226).

Both Bradley and Blanshard argue for ethical theories based on self-realization. For Bradley, the end of morality is self-realization, in particular the realization of the good will. In asserting this, he rejects the emphasis on pleasure that is implicit in the hedonistic calculus underlying classical utilitarianism. That is to say, the Principle of Utility or the Greatest Happiness Principle holds that actions are right if they tend to promote the greatest happiness, wrong if they tend to cause its opposite. Happiness is understood in terms of pleasure and the absence of pain. Actions are judged by their consequences in respect to increasing pleasure and minimizing pain. Thus, the utilitarian deduces that the aim of the moral life is the 'greatest happiness of the greatest number'. Bradley criticizes this central dependence on pleasure for its excessive sensationalism, just as he similarly criticizes Kant's emphasis on 'duty for duty's sake' for its excessive rationalism. If the emphasis is on *my* pleasure, then this can give no rule of life; if on the pleasure of *all*, then this is an illusory abstraction. For Bradley, ethics must be tied to the actual experience of the moral agent in the world. That world is one of a community which has shaped the agent and in which his or her actions have their objects. The moral law is not an abstraction (as in Kant or the Utilitarians) but attains concreteness because it arises from the experiences and traditions of the community of moral agents. The good will which must be realized is a universal will (the moral law being an instance of a 'concrete universal') or the will of a social organism. Consequently, as Bradley says in his famous essay 'My Station and Its Duties': 'To be moral, I must will my station and its duties; that is, I will to particularize the moral system truly in a given case; and the other side to this act is, that the moral system wills to particularize itself in a given station and functions, ie. in my actions and by my will. In other words, my moral self is not simply mine' (*ES* 180).

Blanshard's ethics of self-realization is more Aristotelian than Bradleyan in its emphases, both for the critical role it gives to pleasure and for its emphasis on the intellectual rather than the social virtues. In Aristotle, the Good is happiness, well-being, or, more precisely, 'the best life' (*eudaimonia*). Such a life is the supreme end of all endeavour. Every being attains happiness only by fulfilling its own nature. In the case of humanity, the activity peculiar to its nature is reason, for man is *the* rational animal. Virtue for humans, therefore, is that state of mind by which they are most capable of practising rational activity. But the fruit of this activity is satisfaction or pleasure. In daily life, ethical virtue arises from training the will to act according to right reason or insight, ie. to follow practical reason or wisdom (*phronesis*). Humans thus gain the self-control through which they do what is *known* to be right. In particular, their rational insight finds the mean between the unreasonable extremes to which natural impulse leads. Aristotle's ethics does have its social component, because moral excellence always arises in the context of the community or State. However, the purpose of the state is itself to facilitate the fulfilment of its citizens. This it can accomplish by effecting their ethical training and by providing the required conditions for their achieving the best life, eg. by establishing conditions of good order or peace. In this way, humans are lead from a rude state of nature to one of ethical and intellectual culture; that is to say, they live the life which is appropriate to human nature. But, here the ethical foundation is not the state *per se*, as one *might* contend it is in Green or Bradley, but the nature *per se* of humanity.

For Blanshard, goodness, ie. intrinsic goodness, always will be found to have two characteristics: (a) the fulfilment of a drive of human nature, and (b) an element of pleasure or satisfaction in such fulfilment. 'To say of an experience that it is intrinsically good means, then, two things: first, that it satisfies; and second, that it fulfils. Pleasure without fulfilment, as Aristotle saw, is hardly possible. Fulfilment without pleasure, as Mill saw, is valueless' (1954, p. 110). Blanshard believes that moral judgements are true or false and he sees in Aristotle's naturalism the clue as to how to account for this: 'Aristotle's insight [was] that the great goods of human nature lay in the fulfillment of its needs' (1980a, p. 166). Moore would have said that this is an instance of the 'naturalistic fallacy' – ie. confusing the natural conditions of goodness with goodness itself – but Blanshard disagrees, finding 'in the fulfillment of human nature and the satisfaction that accompanied it the very essence of goodness' (*ibid.*).

Blanshard maintains that Aristotle's naturalism provides a proper foundation for ethics because it helps us to avoid philosophical errors which result from inattention to the actual actions of moral agents. Most significantly, by examining such actions we find that 'goodness' is not a single unvarying property, but is as differing as the needs and impulses of humankind. 'Value is so fundamental in human life that its true character can be seen only against the background of human nature... I am convinced that if we find certain things good, it is not merely *because* they fulfil needs; such fulfillment enters into the very meaning of goodness' (1961a, pp. 292–3).

And pleasure, in the sense of satisfaction, is part of the notion of fulfilment. Blanshard's argument, summarized in *Reason and Goodness* (1961a, pp. 290–314), is substantially as follows:

1. Conscious processes are goal-seeking. Consciousness does not simply meander, but is carried along by seekings and strivings. 'Mind just *is*... a set of activities directed to ends' (*ibid.*, p. 309).

2. Desire springs from and is limited by the experience of satisfaction. Past impulses and satisfactions provide the foundation of future desires, with intellect and imagination refashioning prior experience.

3. Our *ideas* of what is desirable grow out of what is desired. What is prized is what has satisfied upon reflection; but, 'nothing is good for us if we can take no satisfaction in it' (*ibid.*, pp. 297–8). However, while satisfaction is a necessary condition of goodness, it is not a sufficient condition.

4. What makes something desirable or satisfactory is not exhausted by the *fact* that it is desired or satisfies, for the pleasure derived from satisfaction of a desire cannot be divorced from the object of desire. We cannot distinguish the enjoyment of music from what is enjoyed, viz. the music, because together they make an experiential whole. What we seek is something that provides fulfilment – ie. the achievement of the end which impulse is seeking – and because it fulfils it satisfies.

5. Impulses transformed into desires by thought (ie. 'impulse-desires') define our major goods. Eg. the aesthetic satisfies differently than the intellectual – each demands a different content – and thus their differing objects are both good, viz. a good called 'beauty' and a good called 'knowledge'. More exactly, they are each forms of goodness, 'which consists jointly in the fulfilment of impulse-desire by the content it demands and the attendant satisfaction. *A* good is what *is* thus satisfactory. *The* good is what would be satisfactory in the end' (*ibid.*, p. 302).

6. The process of realizing the good is governed by its goal – the good. That is to say, an end, or good, may direct the process of its realization. An inability to antecedently specify that end does not mean that the process is purposeless, for often a purpose 'only defines itself in the course of its realization' (*ibid.*, p. 304).

7. Hence, the good or desirable always outruns the desired. Much that may be a proper object of desire may not yet be consciously desired. Our seekings grow in clarity and positivity as we approach the fully-developed satisfiable impulse-desire.

8. The *good* is 'the most comprehensive possible fulfilment and satisfaction of impulse-desire... one that takes account not only of this or that desire, but of desires generally, and not only of this or that man's desires, but of all men's' (*ibid.*, p. 311).

Reason again plays a central role in Blanshard's ethics, for the search for intelligibility, which we generally associate with the life of reason, is itself an instance of desire – an instance of the moulding of perhaps our highest good. It is reason that converts impulse into desire, providing it with the idea of its own completion. 'It is thus absurd to say that reason and goodness are extraneous to each other. So far as thought enters into desire, it is the architect of the good' (1961a, p. 347).[26]

Aristotle is right – all men, *by nature*, do desire to know. Indeed, this is what uniquely defines their humanness. That such desire is only minimally present in some men and women is simply evidence of a failure to fulfil their nature, for 'to be moral is in the end to be natural and reasonable and sane' (1954, p. 112). Our happiness depends upon satisfaction of the desire for understanding, for this particular satisfaction uniquely fulfils our nature.[27]

Possession of a rationalistic temperament is merely the actualization of such a desire. 'If there is anything in my philosophy that I should hope might last, it is the quite

---

[26] Regarding the relationship between *thought* and *desire*, Blanshard writes:

> These impulses are the raw material of the good life, just as sensation is the raw material of knowledge. Without them there would be no goods. Food and drink would not be good if there were no hunger or thirst to satisfy, nor Maxwell's equations if no one cared about knowing them... When thought supervenes upon impulse, it transmutes it into desire by supplying it with conscious ends. Our goods, from that point on, lie in the fulfilment not of bare impulses, but of desires into whose nature thought has entered once for all, with its own demands for consistency, integration and expansion. It is one of the merits of T. H. Green's great book on ethics to have driven this truth home. Thought and desire are different, he agrees, but so intimately bound up together that thought is impossible without desire, and desire without thought. To think is to desire, because it is to seek the answer to a question... On the other hand, to desire is to go beyond impulse to the thought of what would fulfil it... Thought and desire are means to the same general end, the removal of a maladjustment between idea and fact. (1961a, p. 347)

[27] Blanshard cites (1961a, pp. 313–14) with approval the following account by A. E. Taylor, another 'student' of Bradley, of what Plato and Aristotle mean by eudaimonia:

unoriginal but none the less important thesis that the rational life is at once the worthiest of lives and the most valuable' (1980a, p. 97).

In this way, Blanshard's rationalism is 'more than the name of a favored theory; it stands for the way of life I most admire. I do not conceive of reason as exhausted in exercises in logic and mathematics. It is the organ of choice among values, and therefore the ultimate compass of practical life also' (1980a, pp. 123–4). Of course, not only philosophical rationalists exemplify the rational temperament.[28]

Further, a true rational temper must not be confused with a narrow 'intellectualism' which finds no place for feeling. 'Depth of feeling and strength of impulse are essential to the richest life. The type of man I place highest is the man of strong feelings and impulses whose reflective nature is in control, whose beliefs are seen in the light of their implications and whose decisions are made in the light of their consequences' (1981, pp. 13–14). However, in assessing ultimate values Blanshard insists, like Aristotle, that reasonableness is

> eudaimonia, for both of them, is not primarily getting something which I desire; it is living the kind of life which I have been constructed to live, doing the 'work of man', and if we want to know what life rather than any other should be pronounced eudaimon, we have to begin by asking what is the 'work' which man, and only man, in virtue of his very constitution can do. It is true, no doubt, that Plato holds that all of us also do desire eudaimonia, if only most of us were not as unaware as we are of the real nature of our most deep-seated desires. But the very reason why we all have this insuperable *desiderium naturale* for a certain kind of life is that it is the life we have been constructed by God or by Nature to lead. We are unhappy, without clearly knowing why, so long as we are living any other kind of life, for the same reasons that a fish is unhappy out of water. The true way to discover what it is that we really want out of life is to know what kind of life we have been sent into the world to lead. We do not lead that life as a 'means' to the 'enjoyable results' of doing so, any more than the fish lives in the water, or the bird in the air as a means to the pleasure of such a life; we enjoy the pleasure (as the tenth book of the *Nicomachean Ethics* explains) because we are living the kind of life for which we were made. (Taylor, 1939, p. 280)

[28] On this point, Blanshard writes:

> In philosophy I find myself crossing battle lines in pursuit of my admirations. Fortunately the rational temper is not confined to rationalists. Locke and Hume, Mill and Sidgwick are not of my speculative camp, but they exhibit the spirit in which I think philosophy should be pursued. 'The love of truth', said Locke, 'is the principal part of human perfection in this world, and the seed plot of all other virtues.' That is a sweeping and indeed astonishing statement to make. But is it not true? (1980a, p. 125)

itself the highest of virtues. Late in life, and in a popular forum, he writes in this regard:

> In the sixty years since I began teaching philosophy, three questions have cropped up incessantly. The first is: Why study philosophy at all? The second is: What is the end we ought to pursue in education? The third is: Among the virtues that make a good citizen, a good person, a good life, which is the most important? And it grows clearer to me that the answers to all these questions, different as they are, are the same. Why study philosophy? To reach truth, of course. But when you consider for how many centuries philosophers have been pursuing the truth, and how widely they still differ, what are your chances of capturing that truth? Not high, one must agree. Is the study therefore wasted? Not at all. For if you pursue the truth seriously, and fail to get it, as you may, you come out with a mind invaluably honed and whetted, and that in itself is prize enough. What is the end of education? Not knowledge, or skill, or financial security, good as these are, but something far rarer, the habitually reasonable mind. What is the most valuable of the virtues? It is that in us which makes us most likely to be right in thought and act, and that seems to be the use of one's reason. Indeed, I am inclined to think that to be right is always to be reasonable and to be reasonable is to be right. So all three answers are the same. What we seem to need above all is the rational temper, the habitual attempt, at least, to be reasonable. So my text is a beatitude that Matthew somehow missed: Blessed are the reasonable. (1982, p. 15)

There is another important ethical position on which Blanshard disagrees with Bradley. Bradley insists that the Absolute, or reality conceived as a single self-differentiating system, is also *good*, in some ultimate sense of that term. This is so, because our wants must find satisfaction in the Absolute – ie. what is supremely real must also be supremely valuable. However, it is not just a matter of reality being the way that we wish it to be – ie. of having a character which provides us with pleasure. Rather, goodness must be a property of any true Absolute:

> If the Absolute is to be theoretically harmonious, its elements must not collide... Since reality is harmonious, the struggle of diverse elements, sensations or ideas... must be precluded. But, if idea must not clash with sensation, then there cannot in the Absolute be unsatisfied desire or any practical unrest. For in these there is clearly an ideal element not concordant with presentation but struggling against it. (*AR* 137)

Blanshard disagrees with such a position. In stark contrast, he believes that there always remains a gap between knowledge and value. For Blanshard, value only arises in the context of human experience. That is, while the 'object known need not be confined to our experience of it; the value of an object *is* so confined' (1974a, p. 43). While truth requires an object to which thought conforms, this is not the case for goodness:

> My idea of the Absolute is thus arrived at by a different road from that of Bradley, Bosanquet, or Royce. In their thought, the various demands of our nature, moral and aesthetic as well as intellectual, are somehow already realized in the Absolute. It is a postulate of my own thought that the intellectual ideal is so realized, and a postulate of my ethics that the moral ideal is not. (1974a, p. 44)

Here is another case in which Blanshard may be closer to Spinoza than to Bradley. While Bradley insists that what is supremely real must also be supremely valuable, Spinoza, on one popular way of reading him, holds that while 'infinite substance' may be 'perfect', because it is complete and self-contained, 'God or nature [is] neither good nor bad, neither beautiful nor ugly, neither admirable nor the reverse' (Walsh, 1964, p. 431).[29] The terms 'good' and 'bad' do not express the nature of things in themselves, but *for us* – in other words as we judge them in reference to an ideal. Similarly,

---

[29] This reading of Spinoza is also that of Joachim, Blanshard's teacher, but it has been criticized. See, for example, John Leslie, *Value and Existence*, pp. 212f. (Oxford, 1979).

while Blanshard's metaphysics culminates in an Absolute, 'that is, upon the universe as the ultimate and inclusive system of things' (1980a, p. 182), he does not believe that this Absolute should be identified with the good. This is because he holds that goodness is properly ascribed to the fulfilment and satisfaction of conscious desire, and he sees no way of ascribing mentality to the universe. Nor does ultimate reality seem morally good, as the universe can hardly be said to make ethical choices or to want to do its duty. Indeed, for reality there is no 'other' to whom it can do its duty.[30] Nor does Blanshard think that we have good grounds for describing reality as being good 'as a whole', in either the sense that the amount of good is greater than the amount of evil, or that evil is merely apparent and would be seen as good in a fuller context of understanding. First, there is no way of determining the balance of good and evil; and second, we have little, if any, evidence for the notion that perceived evil will on further reflection turn out to be necessary to the good. Indeed, Blanshard believes that both theologians and many philosophers have been inadequately impressed with the problem of evil.[31]

Among such philosophers he would place Bradley, who asserts that evil, as such, does not exist in the Absolute *per se*,

---

[30] It might be argued that this ignores the possibility of having 'duties to self'. But even this won't do, for on a strictly monistic view such 'selves' are included within the Absolute.

[31] On this point, Blanshard writes:

> The treatment of evil by theology seems to me an intellectual disgrace. The question at issue is a straightforward one: how are the actual amount and distribution of evil to be reconciled with the government of the world by a God who is in our sense good? So straightforward a question deserves a straightforward answer, and it seems to me that only one such answer makes sense, namely that the two sides can *not* be reconciled. Many attempts at reconciliation have been made: evil was introduced by man's free will, and became general through inherited original sin; it is offered to test us or to educate us or to strengthen us; it is really an illusion, and if seen in perspective would vanish away; it represents some inexplicable impotencies... in the divine power; and so on, and on, and on. These theories break down so promptly and notoriously that theologians commonly give up and fall back on faith to justify a belief that eludes support by evidence.
> (1974b, p. 546)

which transcends morality in this sense.

Blanshard learned much from Bradley. There is no other contemporary philosopher for whom he had greater regard, though his respect did not prevent an independence of mind. He saw, as most philosophers since Bradley's death have failed to see, the importance of his work – indeed, for many years he was nearly alone in being his champion. He proved prescient in his faith that ultimately the value of Bradley's work would be more widely recognized. These points are all captured in this comment which he made while gently chiding Wollheim for one aspect of his book on Bradley:

> Mr. Wollheim cannot resist the temptation to do a little amateur 'depth psychology' on his distinguished subject and to find in his acceptance of an Absolute a means of dealing with a deep-seated anxiety. It may be true. If so, we could do with more people who see visions and feel insecure. Bradley's warmest admirers must admit that he was an uneven thinker, with curious blind spots (as for mathematics), and with certain prejudices (against Mill and Sidgwick, for example) that are hard to share. But he is a dangerous man for 'minute philosophers' to write about, for by so doing, they will send students back to him, and that is always a perilous thing to do. For Bradley, with all his defects, was a philosopher in the grand manner, and there breathes through his writing the vitality – the fire, force, and gusto – of a mind intensely alive. (1961b, pp. 373–4)

Blanshard may have rejected too much of Bradley to be considered by many a 'Bradleyan', but the spirit of his work remains close to Bradley's. Although he failed to accept completely Bradley's attack on 'appearance' or his characterization of the Absolute, he had his own sympathetic understanding of how the philosophic enterprise led to a monistic view of reality. One of Bradley's favourite philosophers, Schopenhauer, asserted that 'whoever would have an understanding of any single thing in the world, clear and exhaustive to the ultimate ground, would also have to have a complete understanding of everything else in the world' (Schopenhauer, p. 41). Blanshard's *epistemic* monism reflects such a belief:

[The philosophic enterprise] is to start anywhere or with anything and keep pressing the question, Why? The question can be answered only in terms of a necessitating context. One explains X by A, B, and C, given which X has to be what it is. But can one stop with A, B, C? No; the question must be renewed with each of them, and thus the circle of determinants grows larger. Can one fix its circumference anywhere? Certainly not with present knowledge; the circle started by the pebble dropped in the ocean, or by the flower in the crannied wall, moves out beyond the horizon. As one follows it further, one becomes convinced, with Bradley and Spinoza, that the same would be true wherever one dropped the stone, indeed that every point on every circle is a point of intersection between many lines of connection, causal and necessary, and that the world is a vast network of such explanatory lines. There is no reason to think that any thing or any event falls outside this network, or that the disappearance of pebble or flower would not be registered in the remotest star. It is this infinite web-work of connections, visible throughout to the eye of intelligence, even if for the most part unseen, that constitutes for me the Absolute. (1984a, p. 225)[32]

---

[32] I would like to thank my wife, Virginia, and my friend, John Leslie, for their assistance in removing certain infelicities in an earlier draft. Responsibility for those that remain, as well as for errors of fact or interpretation, should not be laid at their doorstep.

BIBLIOGRAPHY

Baldwin, Thomas (1991). 'The Identity Theory of Truth', *Mind*, vol. 100, pp. 35–52.

Blanshard, Brand (1925). 'Francis Herbert Bradley', *Journal of Philosophy*, vol. 22, pp. 5–15.

————, (1939). *The Nature of Thought*, 2 vols. (London: George Allen & Unwin Ltd).

————, (1954). 'The Impasse in Ethics – And A Way Out', Howison Lecture for 1954 (Berkeley: University of California Press, 1955).

————, (1961a). *Reason and Goodness* (London: George Allen & Unwin Ltd).

————, (1961b). Review of *F. H. Bradley*, by Richard Wollheim, in *Philosophy*, vol. 32, pp. 372–4.

————, (1962). *Reason and Analysis* (London: George Allen & Unwin Ltd).

————, (1967). 'Internal Relations and Their Importance to Philosophy', *Review of Metaphysics*, vol. 21, 227–36.

————, (1974). 'Rationalism', in *Encyclopedia Britannica*, 15th ed., vol. 15, pp. 527–32 (Chicago: Encyclopedia Britannica, Inc.).

———, (1974a). 'Rationalism In Ethics and Religion', in Peter A. Bertocci (ed.), *Mid-Twentieth Century American Philosophy: Personal Statements*, pp. 20–46 (New York: Humanities Press).

———, (1974b). *Reason and Belief* (London: George Allen & Unwin Ltd).

———, (1980a). 'Autobiography of Brand Blanshard', in Schilpp (1980), pp. 1–185.

———, (1980b). 'Reply to Sterling M. McMurrin's: Blanshard's Conception of the Nature and Function of Philosophy', in Schilpp (1980), pp. 211–19.

———, (1980c). 'Reply to Nicholas Rescher: Blanshard and the Coherence Theory of Truth', in Schilpp (1980), pp. 589–600.

———, (1981). 'The Rationalist Outlook', in *Philosophers on Their Own Work*, vol. 8, pp. 5–26 (Berne: Peter Lang).

———, (1982). 'On the Difficulties of Being Reasonable', in *Swarthmore College Bulletin*, vol. 79, January, pp. 15–18.

———, (1984a). 'Bradley on Relations', in A. Manser and G. Stock (eds.), *The Philosophy of F. H. Bradley*, pp. 211–26 (Oxford: Clarendon Press).

———, (1984b). 'Bradley: Some Memories and Impressions'. Originally read *in absentia* at Southern Illinois University on 26 April 1984. Published in Richard Ingardia, *Bradley: A Research Bibliography*, pp. 7–16 (Bowling Green: Philosophy Documentation Center, 1991).

Candlish, Stewart (1989). 'The Truth About F. H. Bradley', *Mind*, vol. 98, pp. 331–48.

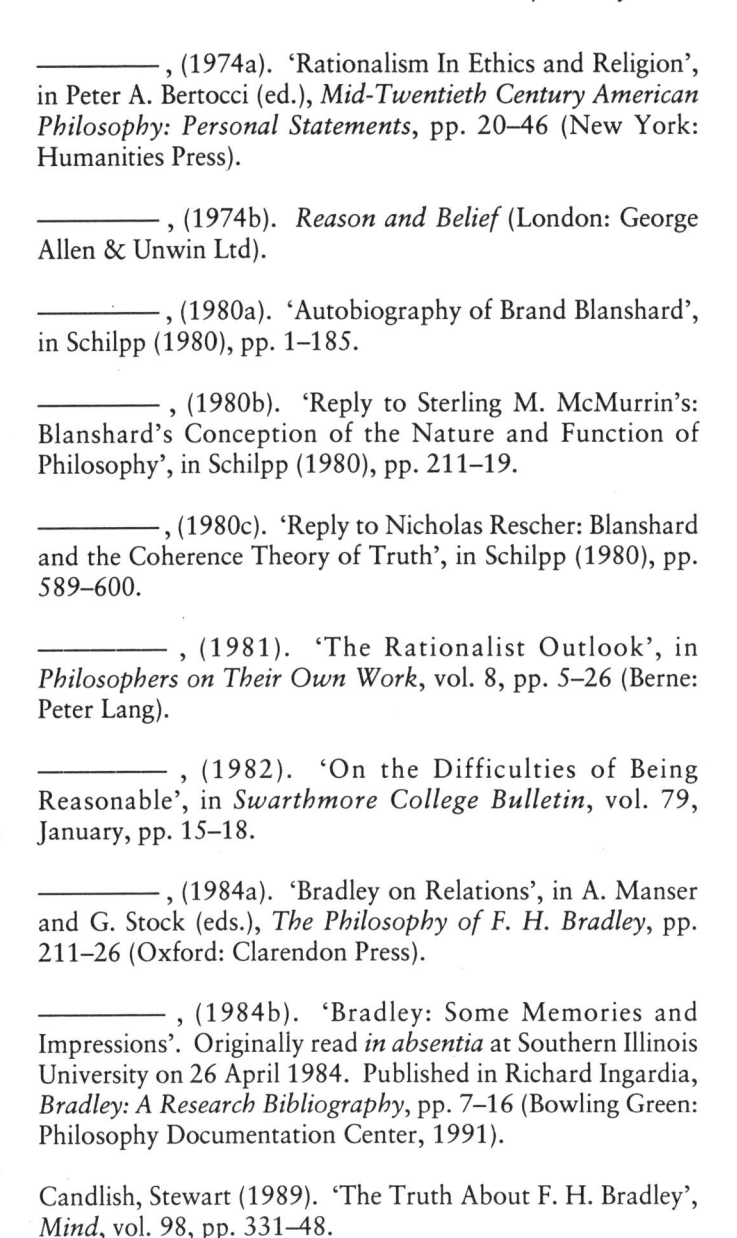

Langer, Susanne K. (1949). 'On Cassirer's Theory of Language and Myth', in Paul A. Schilpp (ed.), *The Philosophy of Ernst Cassirer*, pp. 379–400 (Evanston, Illinois: The Library of Living Philosophers).

Quine, W. V. O. (1978). 'Interview', in Bryan Magee (ed.), *Men of Ideas: Some Creators of Contemporary Philosophy*, pp. 168–79 (London: British Broadcasting Corporation).

Schilpp, Paul Arthur (ed.) (1980). *The Philosophy of Brand Blanshard* (La Salle, Illinois: Open Court).

Schopenhauer, Arthur (1965). *On the Basis of Morality*, trans. E. F. J. Payne (Indianapolis: Bobbs-Merrill Company).

Spinoza (1985). *The Collected Works of Spinoza*, ed. and trans. Edwin Curley (Princeton University Press).

Taylor, A. E. (1925). 'F. H. Bradley', *Mind*, vol. 34, pp. 1–12.

——————, (1939). 'The Right and the Good', *Mind*, vol. 48, pp. 273–301.

Walsh, W. H. (1964). 'F. H. Bradley', in D. J. O'Connor (ed.), *A Critical History of Western Philosophy*, pp. 426–36 (New York: Free Press of Glencoe).

Wollheim, Richard (1956). 'F. H. Bradley', in A. J. Ayer et al., *The Revolution in Philosophy*, pp. 12–25 (London: Macmillan & Co. Ltd).

THE AUTONOMY OF HISTORY:
COLLINGWOOD'S CRITIQUE OF
F. H. BRADLEY'S COPERNICAN REVOLUTION
IN HISTORICAL KNOWLEDGE

Lionel Rubinoff

F. H Bradley's very first publication was an essay entitled 'The Presuppositions of Critical History', written and published in 1874. Of this essay R. G. Collingwood wrote: 'Bradley's essay, inconclusive though it is, remains memorable for the fact that in it the Copernican revolution in the theory of historical knowledge has been in principle accomplished' (*IH* 240).[1]

The foundation of this revolution, according to Collingwood, lies in the recognition that, contrary to the common-sense, realist view of history, historical truth does not consist in the historian's beliefs conforming to the statements of his authorities or witnesses, but is rather the outcome of a judgement in which the evidence is measured by the historian's own standards; standards which, while lying within the consciousness of the historian, are nevertheless embodiments of objective truth. With Bradley history thus becomes critical, and the criterion of criticism is none other than the historian himself, the historian's own experience of the world in which he lives. It is the critical historian who must now assume the responsibility for deciding whether the

---

[1] All references to Collingwood are to the following editions: *An Autobiography* (Oxford University Press, 1939), hereinafter *A*; *The Idea of History* (London: Oxford University Press, 1946), hereinafter *IH*; *An Essay on Philosophical Method* (London: Oxford University Press, 1933), hereinafter *EPM*; *Speculum Mentis* (Oxford: Clarendon Press, 1924), hereinafter *SM*. References to Bradley are to *The Presuppositions of Critical History*, ed. L. Rubinoff and Don Mills (J. M. Dent & Sons, Canada and Chicago, Quadrangle Press, 1968), hereinafter *PCH*. Reprinted from *Collected Essays*, vol. 1 (Oxford: Clarendon Press, 1935).

persons whose testimony he is using as evidence were, on this or that occasion, judging correctly or incorrectly. It is the historian's own experience, and the knowledge derived therefrom, that enables the historian to decide what kinds of things can or cannot happen. This is the canon by which he criticizes testimony (*IH* 137).

At the same time that Bradley places the criterion of historical judgement within the historian's own experience he acknowledges that this experience is necessarily constrained by the fact that since as a general rule every person is the 'child of his time' the historian's judgement is therefore shaped by the times in which he lives. Bradley thus applies to the historian precisely the same constraints which, according to Hegel, necessarily apply to the philosopher. To repeat the well known passage from the Preface to the *Philosophy of Right*.

> To comprehend what is, this is the task of philosophy, because what is, is reason. Whatever happens, every individual is the child of his time; so philosophy too is its own time apprehended in thoughts. It is just as absurd to fancy that a philosophy can transcend its contemporary world as to fancy that an individual can overleap his own age, jump over Rhodes.[2]

For Bradley, not only philosophers but historians together with their witnesses – whose testimony provides the basis for historical analysis – are products of their times. As such, their minds and experiences will undoubtedly be shaped by that which bears *most* the stamp of the respective ages in which they live: a consideration which led Bradley to the conclusion that 'The historian as he is, is the real criterion; the ideal criterion...is the historian as he ought to be. And the historian who is true to the present *is* the historian as he ought to be' (*PCH* 78).

Bradley's Copernican revolution thus consists in recognizing the historicity of both the testimony of the witnesses (ie. the evidence) and the point of view of the historian. In the final analysis what counts as acceptable testimony or evidence,

---

[2] Translated by T. M. Knox (Oxford: Clarendon Press, 1942), p. 11.

as well as historical truth itself concerning 'what is the case', depends upon the historian's inference; a process which is mediated by the historian's present standpoint; a standpoint which includes a number of what Bradley calls 'prejudications', or 'presuppositions'. In Bradley's own words:

> there is no single history which is not so based, which does not derive its individual character from the particular standpoint of the author. There is no such thing as a history without a prejudication; the real distinction is between the writer who has his prejudications without knowing what they are, and whose prejudications it may be, are false, and the writer who consciously orders and creates from the known foundation of that which for him is the truth.
>
> (PCH 96)

According to Bradley, then, the historical narrative is not simply a set of descriptive propositions purporting to represent the past as it was. It consists rather of a coherent unity of critical inferential judgements in which it is the historian who decides precisely what picture of the past is supported by the evidence. Coherence rather than correspondence with the statements of witnesses is what counts. On this account of what is involved in constructing historical explanations the chief task for philosophy of history is to investigate the nature and sources of the historian's presuppositions, which, given the historicity of the historian's own critical standpoint, is itself a quasi-historical activity. It may thus truly be argued that Bradley's essay was the first attempt in the English language to construct something like a critique of historical judgement: an enterprise which may be compared with the accomplishments of Bradley's contemporaries, Johan Gustav Droysen and Wilhelm Dilthey, with whose works Bradley himself was unfamiliar at the time of writing his essay.[3]

---

[3] In a footnote to the Preface of his essay Bradley mentions his discovery, for the first time, of Droysen's *Grundriss der Historik* (p. 78) but only after having completed his own essay. The comparison between Bradley and the German historicists is thus entirely coincidental – although all three of these thinkers owe a debt to their common ancestry in Kant and Hegel. Any differences that may separate Bradley from his German contemporaries are no doubt due to the influence on Bradley of the English empiricist tradition of Hume and J. S. Mill.

For Bradley, as for Dilthey, the most fundamental of the conditions of the possibility of historical understanding is the principle of the uniformity and universality of human nature. This principle, Bradley argues, must be presupposed as the condition upon which all historical inferences depend for their justification, but which as a presupposition cannot itself be justified (*PCH* 96–7) – and for precisely the same reasons that had already been explained by Hume. Also like Hume, Bradley does not see any inconsistency between the uniformity of human nature principle and the concept of liberty or freedom-of-the will. Indeed, Bradley argues, 'If the freedom of the will is to mean that the actions of men are subject to no law [ie. uncaused], then the possibility of history, I think, must be allowed to disappear, and the past to become a matter of almost uncertainty. For if we are precluded from counting on human nature, our hold upon tradition is gone, and with it well nigh our only basis for historical judgement' (*PCH* 99).

In Bradley's account of the role of the principle of the uniformity of human nature in historiography historical understanding is often achieved by pursuing analogies between the historian's experience and that of the agents or witnesses whose testimony is being critically evaluated. In effect what happens is that, based on the available testimony or evidence, the historian internalizes the experience of the agent or witness and then passes critical judgement on its possibility, reliability and authenticity (*PCH* 105).[4] The real challenge arises, as it did for both Dilthey and Collingwood, when the historian is confronted with reports of past experiences for which there is no analogy in the historian's own immediate experience. Bradley presents this as the problem of 'unanalogous testimony' (*PCH* 113–14). Not all such testimony can be authenticated by understanding. It is only when the historian's own human nature is potentially capable of incorporating unanalogous experiences that any kind of

---

[4] Bradley speaks here of possessing ourselves of the consciousness of others, of assuming the identity of their standpoints with our own (*PCH* 105), and of 'identification of consciousness' (106) – all of which is reminiscent of Dilthey's 'transposition of the self'.

meaningful historical understanding is possible. Bradley's example of a successful encounter with an alien experience is the 'messmeric phenomenon'. Here is a phenomenon or experience which, alien though it is for the historian trying to comprehend it, may yet be described in testimony capable of evoking analogous experiences within the historian, thus producing the necessary identification of consciousness by means of which the historian is able to conclude that such a phenomenon as hypnotism is possible (*PCH* 105). Needless to say, the success of this identification of consciousness depends upon the reported experience being consistent with the known laws of nature and hence within the limits of reasonableness.

Precisely the same point was made by Dilthey when he writes, with regard to the attempt to understand the religiosity of Martin Luther:

> The course of every person's life is a process of continuous determination in which the possibilities inherent in him are narrowed down. The crystallization of his nature always determines his further development... But understanding lays open for him a wide range of possibilities that are not present in the determination of his actual life. For me as for most people today, the possibility of experiencing religious states of mind in my personal existence is sharply circumscribed. However, when I go through the letters and writings of Luther, the accounts of his contemporaries, the records of the religious conferences and councils, and the reports of his official contacts, I encounter a religious phenomenon of such eruptive power, of such energy, in which the issue is one of life or death, that it lies beyond the experiential possibilities of a person of our time.

Yet, Dilthey writes, notwithstanding the inherent difficulty of the task:

> I can re-live (*nacherleben*) all of this... And thereby this process opens up for us a religious world in Luther and his contemporaries in the early Reformation that enlarges our horizon by including possibilities that are available to us only in this way. Thus man, who is determined from

within, can experience many other existences in imagination. Although he is limited by his circumstances, foreign beauties of the world and regions of life that he could never reach himself are laid open to him. To put it in general terms, man, bound and determined by the reality of life, is made free not only by art – which has often been pointed out – but also by the understanding of things historical.[5]

In Bradley's example of the messmeric phenomenon he finds that it is possible for him to achieve the necessary identification of consciousness for judging whether such an experience is possible, thereby extending his own limited experience. Where no such identification of consciousness is possible, however, no meaningful expansion of experience is possible either. To the question, 'What determines whether or not an identification of consciousness is possible?', Bradley's answer, as we have already noted, invokes the principle of the uniformity of nature. In all such cases, he argues, we are guided by our human nature or inherent sense of rationality which is universally distributed throughout all mankind.

It is this inherent sense of rationality or common sense that allows us to accept some testimony and reject others – such as, for example, those reports of miracles which have provoked so much consternation among biblical scholars. It was the same common sense that enabled Bradley to determine that the person whom he believed he had seen on the day following that person's death was not an apparition (which would have been genuinely miraculous) nor an hallucination, but simply a case of mistaken identity. Of all the possible hypotheses by means of which this experience might be explained, the hypothesis of mistaken judgement proves to be the most credible, because only this hypothesis remains consistent with the known laws of nature according to which, neither do the dead arise nor do hallucinations occur without cause (*PCH* 95).

With respect to such reports it was Bradley's view that even though the witness were to be convinced that he had experi-

---

[5] *Gesammelte Schriften*, vol. 7, *Fortsetzung*, pp. 215–16.

enced a genuine miracle, common sense, guided by an understanding of the known laws of nature, would rule out any possibility of authenticating such an experience. Or, to put it in slightly different terms, no historian who is true to the present could reasonably accept such testimony, because to the extent that he is genuinely true to his present he can comprehend the world only from within the framework of the paradigm of rationality that defines that particular world. Unlike Collingwood, Bradley did not entertain the prospect that paradigm shifts might occur on precisely those occasions when human thought encounters situations for which there are no precedents, and for which traditional modes of rationality are no longer adequate as vehicles of understanding.

Bradley's discussion of these examples revives arguments that had already been proposed by Hume in his celebrated essay on miracles. But although they serve the purpose of illustrating how on some occasions the conception of the uniformity of nature rescues us from affirming the incredible, they do not do justice to the full substance of Bradley's accomplishments in this essay – particularly with respect to its influence on R. G. Collingwood. For Collingwood what really stands out in Bradley's essay as deserving of praise is his attempt, on the one hand, to establish history as a genuine science, a science based on inferences from well substantiated evidence whose conclusions are falsifiable, and his determination, on the other hand, to preserve the autonomy of history by establishing a clear-cut distinction between the natural and the historical sciences. The former, the founding of history as a science, is accomplished by locating the conditions or presuppositions of historical understanding in the socially and historically conditioned point of view and universal human nature of the historian. Historical science is thus founded on the principle – paradoxical as it may seem – that what counts as history depends upon the particular standpoint of the historian (*PCH* 94), which is historically relative, and the 'common experience of reasonable beings' (*PCH* 94), which is universal. This is the first step in Bradley's Copernican revolution.

The second step, the characterization of history as an autonomous discipline, is accomplished by drawing a clear-cut distinction between human nature and nature proper, or, between human conduct, the subject-matter of history, and natural processes, the subject-matter of the natural sciences. The interest of the natural sciences, writes Bradley, is 'the permanent amid change', while the objects of history are 'the changes of the permanent'; 'facts to the one are illustrations, to the other are embodiments; the individuals of the one are limited to be abstracted, of the other are incorporated to be realized' (*PCH* 112). This is an obvious and clear reference to the distinction between the abstract and the concrete universal. Abstract universals transcend their exemplifications, thus giving rise to a logic of genus and species. Concrete universals are identical with their exemplifications and may thus be said to be embodied in them. The abstract universal exists outside of time while the concrete universal is imminent in or inseparable from the temporal process. It was with regard to precisely this distinction that R. G. Collingwood was later to declare in *Speculum Mentis* (1924), with respect to the distinction between natural science and history, that while the abstract universal is the subject matter of science, 'the concrete universal is the daily bread of every historian, and the logic of history is the logic of the concrete universal' (*SM* 221; cf. also *EPM* 160).

History is also to be distinguished from science, according to Bradley, by the emphasis in history on the personal, an emphasis which was picked up and further developed by Collingwood. History is not only knowledge of the past but self-knowledge and self-discovery. Thus Bradley declares, in various places throughout *The Presuppositions of Critical History*:

> the interest which gives birth to historical testimony is a human interest, an interest in the particular realization. Our common nature, which is personal in us all, feels in each one of us 'that nothing human is alien to ourselves'. Our interest in the past is our feeling of oneness with it, is our interest in our own progression; and because this human nature to exist must be individual, the object of

historical record is the world of human individuality, and the course of its development in time [112]...the interest of history is...the exhibition of the oneness of humanity in all its stages and under all its varieties; it is ourselves that we seek in the perished [114] ...The remembrance of our childhood and our youth is the sweetest of pleasures, for it gives us the feeling of ourselves, as the self of ourself and yet as another [115].

In these passages Bradley takes an important step in the direction of defining history as self-knowledge, a direction which when developed by Collingwood led eventually to the conception of history as self-making. In Collingwood's words:

Knowing yourself means knowing, first, what it is to be a man; secondly, knowing what it is to be the kind of man you are; and thirdly, knowing what it means to be the man *you* are and nobody else is. Knowing yourself means knowing what you can do; and nobody knows what he can do until he tries. The only clue to what man can do is what man has done. The value of history, then, is that it teaches us what man has done and thus what man is. (*IH* 110)

What is even more important, Collingwood argues:

If the human mind comes to understand itself better, it comes to operate in new and different ways.... (*IH* 85)
The historical process is a process in which man creates for himself this or that kind of human nature by recreating in his own thought the past to which he is heir. (*IH* 226)

And it is in this sense, Collingwood concludes, that history may be regarded as 'a school of political wisdom' (*A* 96ff.), bringing to moral and political life a 'trained eye for the situation in which one has to act' (*A* 100).

But while Bradley warmly embraces the possibility that historical understanding (particularly when it extends to novel experiences without precedent) can enlarge or enhance the experience of the historian, thus leading to a kind of self-making through self-knowledge, he was considerably less adventurous than was Collingwood in recognizing the possibility of there being more *radical* forms of human self-making, not to speak of radical paradigm shifts.[6] This is due chiefly to the fact that Bradley's view sets more precise limits on what is knowable than does Collingwood's. For, as Collingwood himself often complained, while Bradley recognized that human nature develops progressively throughout history, this progress was constrained by the principle of the uniformity of nature, which for Bradley was the ultimate organon of historical science and was ironically conceived even by Bradley himself as an abstract rather than concrete universal.

In Collingwood's view, then, Bradley was prevented by his own presuppositions from taking the final step from self-knowledge to radical self-making, thus completing the Copernican revolution in historiography that he had initiated. He was defeated, first of all, by his positivistic belief that the historian's capacity for understanding was constrained and limited by certain abstractly conceived universal characteristics of human nature, which, while they accounted for the understanding of change, did not themselves change. In the second place, his attempt to found a genuine science of history was frustrated by his belief that the past is entirely a matter of *inference* and never *directly* knowable.

Since, according to Bradley, knowledge of the past is a product of our judgement which in turn is constrained by our human nature, it follows that there can never be any understanding of those pasts which are so alien that they cannot be recognized as akin to ourselves (*PCH* 115). As a result, 'where we encounter an alien element which we cannot recognize as akin to ourselves...the hope and purpose which inspired us dies, and the endeavour [to understand the past] is thwarted' (115). The past as such 'perishes as it arises. It dies and can never be recalled. It cannot repeat itself, and we are powerless to repeat it' (117). Knowledge of the past, in other words, is determined by an already formed human nature which, while it can certainly be enriched, can never, in

---

[6] Indeed, as Leslie Armour points out in his contribution to this collection, for no British philosopher of the Idealist tradition was historical knowledge 'crucial and decisive in just the way it becomes for Collingwood'. See 'F. H. Bradley and Later Idealism'.

any truly meaningful sense, be radically transformed.

Finally, since so far as the past can be known at all, it can be known only as the product of an inference and never as it really was, it follows, Bradley confesses, that we can never be certain in our judgements. History is at best merely probable. Historical facts, once ascertained, can never be proven theoretically by methods independent of those by means of which they have been arrived at (*PCH* 113–14). Here, according to Collingwood, are the sceptical implications of Bradley's affection for the tradition of Hume; an influence due chiefly to Bradley's uncritical acceptance of the positivistically conceived principle of the uniformity of nature.

Like Bradley, Collingwood argues that although the mind and human nature of every historian is shaped by the times in which he lives, there is nevertheless a universal human nature that makes it possible for one age to understand another. Collingwood also shared with Bradley the conviction that the understanding of history is an important source of self-understanding. But whereas Bradley's conception of human nature and the universal principles by means of which it is determined sets limits to what is both possible and therefore understandable, for Collingwood there are virtually no limits to what can be understood; providing, of course, that what presents itself for understanding is an expression of rationality. Which is to say that Collingwood's conception of what sorts of things are possible is much broader than Bradley's.

Collingwood argued further that the self-understanding achieved by history is a condition of all other knowledge (*IH* 205). This marks an important difference in outlook between Collingwood and Bradley. In keeping with the tradition of Hume and J. S. Mill, Bradley conceived the 'scientific method' along the lines of the methods of the natural sciences. He was, to this extent, a positivist for whom the natural sciences provided the paradigm of rationality against which all other modes of rationality are to be measured. The historical method thus becomes a mere species of the universal method of science whose generic essence is determined by what is in fact only one of its species, namely, the species known as natural science now elevated to the rank of a universal. Without recognizing the category mistake involved in this equation Bradley held this view of the scientific method together with the belief, as we have already noted, that there was an essential difference between the historical processes and those of nature. *A Parte Objecti*, nature is the permanent amid change; history, the changes of the permanent; natural events are mere illustrations, while historical events are embodiments (*PCH* 112). It was left for Collingwood to expose the inconsistency of these positions concerning the methodology and ontology of history, and to articulate a conception of method more in keeping with the ontological distinction between nature and history to which both Collingwood and Bradley were committed. Collingwood argued that not only does the difference between nature and history conceived *a parte objecti* imply differences *a parte subjecti* at the level of method, but rather than the methods of the natural sciences defining the essence of the scientific method per se, it is actually the methods of history which make possible the understanding of and hence progress of science.

With this conclusion we encounter the full force of the Copernican revolution, broadly understood. Kant took the first step when he argued that neither mathematics nor science could be accounted for except through an understanding of the human mind. Bradley extended this insight to historiography, but fell backwards into positivism by embracing the enlightenment theory of human nature, which even Kant still held.

Against this doctrine Collingwood advanced the doctrine of the historicity of mind and human nature. In so doing he was simply working out the full implications of Bradley's conception of historical events as embodiments rather than as mere examples or instances of universals. With Collingwood human nature remains universal, but as a genuine concrete universal its generic essence shapes itself and progresses through the differences and variations which comprise its embodiments in history. Differences and variations arise at the point at which new challenges and problems present themselves for solution requiring new and unprecedented forms of action, which in turn produce variations in human nature itself. What for previous generations might have seemed either inconceivable, or at best a mere possibility without any real prospect of actualization, now takes its place on the stage of history as actuality. And because each present moment of the concrete universal incorporates or encapsulates all of its previous (past) moments, the understanding of its own past, no matter how remote, is always in principle possible.

This possibility exists whenever the study of the evidence revives the encapsulated residue which lies latent in the historian's own human nature – a point which is stressed throughout Collingwood's unpublished manuscript on folklore and magic, written between 1936 and 1937 at the same time that he was working on *The Principles of History*.

> As the child, with his infantile fears and passions is contained within the adult man, but contained there as a transcended element which reasserts itself only when the balance of adult life breaks down into neurosis, so the primitive life of the savage is contained within the life of civilized peoples who achieve and maintain their civilization precisely by solving the psychological problems which it presents, but which the mere savage cannot solve... Since we can understand what goes on in the Savage's mind only in so far as we can experience the same in our own, we must find our clue in emotions to whose reality we can testify in our own persons ... Magical practice has its base in the emotions which are universally human and can be found in and among ourselves.[7]

For Collingwood, then, the understanding of the past is possible because the historian's human nature, in which lies the universal, a priori conditions of understanding, has developed dialectically from the past. The conditions of understanding are thus products of the same historical process

---

[7] Unpublished Folklore MS (1936–7), chap. III, p. 2, chap. IV, 'Magic', p. 2. Cited by Jan van Der Dussen, *History as a Science: The Philosophy of R. G. Collingwood* (The Hague: Martinus Nijhoff, 1981), p. 187.

which is the object of understanding and not simply presuppositions or universal laws transcending as well as determining it.

In Bradley's positivistic, covering-law model of explanation, history and human nature are shaped by a fixed set of universal laws which are not themselves affected by the changes which are understood to embody them. According to the method implied by this model the laws of human nature, once ascertained by means of inductive logic, can then be applied to the evaluation and understanding of new facts which resemble the facts from which the laws themselves were originally derived. For Collingwood, however, the universal characteristics of human nature arise in the very course of that nature expressing itself through individual actions, including the act of understanding itself. The history of human nature is thus the history of a self-making process in which man makes himself, as it were, by coming to know himself (see IH 85, 226, quoted above p. 135).

Implied by this conception of historical self-making is a method which begins with the study of individual actions having both an inner thought side as well as an outer behavioural dimension. The outer dimension of the event – what is observed to have happened, eg. Caesar's assassination on the steps of the Senate chamber – is explained by rethinking the thought of the agents whose actions comprise the event. By rethinking the thought side of the event the historian discovers its universal dimension: eg. the pursuit of power for its own sake, or the redressing of grievances for the sake of either revenge or justice. Unlike Bradley, however, the generic essences of Collingwood's universals do not transcend but are rather identical with their variable elements, from which it follows that qua universals they undergo substantial and unpredictable changes and can therefore be comprehended only through a study of those changes.

If, for example, we are dealing with the history of power, each chapter in this history, as represented by the actions of exemplary individual agents – Caesar, Henry VIII, Napoleon, and so on – represents an incremental change in the very essence of the meaning of power, just as in the history of music, each composer represents an incremental change in or redefinition of the meaning of the very idea of music. Viewed this way, the science of history, whether its subject matter be political behaviour or music or whatever, can never yield definitive conclusions. The conclusions of history, together with the principles of its method, can never be anything more than an inventory of the wealth achieved by the human mind at a certain stage in its development, and as such is bound to be superseded by new conclusions and principles whose content and meaning cannot be understood until they have been worked out and articulated.

> in history... no achievement is final. The evidence available for solving any given problem changes with every change of historical method and with every variation in the competence of historians. The principles by which this evidence is interpreted change too; since the interpreting of evidence is a task to which a man must bring everything he knows: historical knowledge, knowledge of nature and man, mathematical knowledge, philosophical knowledge; and not knowledge only, but mental habits and possessions of every kind: and none of these is unchanging. Because of these changes, which never cease, however slow they may appear to observers who take a short view, every new generation, not content with giving new answers to old questions, must revive the questions themselves; and – since historical thought is a river into which none can step twice – even a single historian, working at a single subject for a certain length of time, finds when he tries to reopen an old question that the question has changed. This is not an argument for historical scepticism. It is only the discovery of a second dimension of historical thought, the history of history: the discovery that the historian himself, together with the here-and-now which forms the total body of evidence available to him, is a part of the process he is studying, has its own place in that process, and can see it only from the point which at this moment he occupies within it. (*IH* 248)

It is only by thus recognizing the historicity of human nature and the a priori principles of historiography that full justice can be done for Bradley's Copernican revolution which, as he himself argued, is founded first, on the recognition that the historian who is the child of his time is the criterion of history and secondly, on a distinction between nature and history. Nature is conceived as the permanent amidst change, history as the changes of the permanent; changes which for Bradley are to be conceived as embodiments rather than mere instances.

When carefully dissected by Collingwood, Bradley's position amounts to a declaration that the best that historians can expect to achieve in their attempt to reconstruct the past is an affirmation of the claim that what the testimony alleges is within the realm of *possibility*. The *actuality* of such allegations, however, can be established with only relative degrees of probability. The historian is able to determine what is possible on the basis of his own knowledge of human nature. However, Collingwood complains, this knowledge is conceived in the typical empiricist and positivistic manner as based on induction from observed facts on the principle that the future will resemble the past and the unknown the known (*IH* 139). The result is that the criterion which the historian brings with him is the historian as scientist, whose conception of human nature will not allow for facts deemed to be inconsistent with the known laws of that nature. If therefore the historian were to encounter anything which was inconsistent with the known laws of nature, the actual occurrence of these alleged facts is so improbable that no possible testimony could convince him of them; an implication which appears to ignore Bradley's own recognition of the important difference between human and physical nature.

Collingwood's solution to this impasse is to correct Bradley's conception of the criterion or a priori of historical judgement. In Collingwood's critical appropriation of Bradley's thought the science of human nature is assimilated to history and the principle of the uniformity of nature is historicized. Rather than the historian qua scientist it is the historian qua historian that rightly qualifies as the canon of historical judgement. In short, it is only by actually practising historical thought that historians learn to think historically. Accordingly, the canon of historical judgement is never ready-made but lies within the historian's a priori imagination, which is itself the product of historical thinking. The criterion of history, in other words, is both a product as well as a presupposition of historical thinking, subject to change and dialectical development. What is more, the past ceases to be merely what can be inferred from testimony that has been evaluated in terms of the known laws of human nature – a collection of known facts whose resemblance to the actual past is at best a matter of probability – and becomes instead the product of imaginative rethinking.

Thus, while Collingwood praises Bradley for holding that to accept testimony means making the thought of the witness one's own thought by re-enacting that thought in one's own mind, he criticizes Bradley for stopping short of taking the next step and recognizing that the historian re-enacts in his own mind not only the thought of the witness but the thought of the agent whose action the witness reports (*IH* 138). If, Collingwood argues, history can be conceived as the re-enactment of the thought of the agent, then, he concludes, the historian's knowledge can be regarded as consisting not simply of inferences concerning the credibility of testimony, but of judgements about the past itself; the real, actual, historical past as it comes to life once again within the historian's critical imagination. The known past and the actual past are one and the same, and even though, for Collingwood, it is the responsibility of each generation to rewrite the past, with the result that our picture of the past changes, these changes, because they are the expressions of a concrete rather than an abstract universal, can both exhibit genuine novelty and yet retain the past as it actually was. The historian's past, in other words, is not simply an imagined or constructed but a real past.

In summary, then, Bradley's mistake, according to Collingwood, lies in his conception of the relation between the historian's criterion and that to which he applies it. His view is that the historian brings to his work a ready-made body of experience by which he judges the statements contained in his authorities. But because this body of experience is conceived as ready-made, it cannot be modified by the historian's own work as an historian. In other words, as Bradley conceives it, the historian's criterion, the a priori of historical judgement, pre-exists or transcends the actual process of historical reconstruction, and is not, therefore, historical in its own right.

For Collingwood it is only by historicizing the canon or criterion of history that historical science can lay claim to genuine autonomy with respect to both the methods and subject matter of history. On Bradley's view, the subject-matter of history, human conduct, is inadvertently and paradoxically assimilated to the very same physical nature from which he expressly tried to separate it. It was Collingwood's purpose to rescue the autonomy of history and overcome Bradley's paradox by conceiving the historical process as essentially the life of mind, which, unlike nature proper, creates itself by knowing itself. Indeed, Collingwood argues, such a view is actually closer to the metaphysical doctrines of *Appearance and Reality* than the positivistic account of the essay on the *Presuppositions of Critical History*. The fundamental thesis of *Appearance and Reality*, after all, is that reality is not something other than its appearances, hidden behind them, but is these appearances themselves, forming a whole of which we can say that it forms a single system consisting of experience and that all of our experiences form part of it. A reality so defined, Collingwood argues, 'can only be the life of mind itself, that is history' (*IH* 141).

But not only is the reality or subject-matter of history the life of mind; it is the life of a mind which makes itself by knowing itself. Such a process, Collingwood will argue, is only possible by thinking historically in accordance with methods uniquely suited to the task. For Collingwood, these methods are scientific in the sense that they consist of rules of inference from evidence to verifiable conclusions; but unlike the conclusions of natural science, historical judgements not only describe but re-enact the 'facts' to which the evidence points. These facts consist not simply of events to be described – Caesar crossing the Rubicon, Napoleon's invasion of Russia, etc. – but of events together with the reasons, motives and intentions of the agents whose behaviour or conduct is being described. And as historical facts their relationship to the past is not one of mere resemblance or correspondence, but of identity.

History, in other words, is the history of thought, a reality which can become an object of knowledge only by being rethought in the mind of the historian. It is because history involves rethinking that Collingwood is able to regard the historical process as the sphere of human self-making and historical knowledge as the chief catalyst of that process. It is this conception of history as a rethinking of the thought of the past in the mind of the historian which stands out as the distinctive contribution of Collingwood to the critique of historical judgement. But by Collingwood's own admission, the foundations for such a critique were first laid down by F. H. Bradley, of whose thought it can truly be said, to repeat once again Collingwood's tribute, that 'in it the Copernican revolution in the theory of historical knowledge has been in principle accomplished'.

FROM PRESENCE TO PROCESS: BRADLEY AND WHITEHEAD

James Bradley

It is obvious that the title of Whitehead's major work explicitly refers to that of Bradley's: Bradley's *Appearance and Reality: A Metaphysical Essay* (1893) becomes Whitehead's *Process and Reality: An Essay in Cosmology* (1929).[1] But while the importance of Bradley's thought for Whitehead is now well established,[2] what needs further attention is the larger significance of their relation. For inscribed in these differences of title is nothing less than a transformation in the nature of metaphysical analysis – a transformation in which neither the role of Bradley's work nor the nature of Whitehead's achievement has yet been properly appreciated. To analyse some of the main connections between these two thinkers is to see both in a way quite different from conventional accounts.

I

Bradley and Whitehead are both engaged in metaphysical analysis in the sense that what unites them is that both

---

[1] The following texts and abbreviations will be used for those of Whitehead's works referred to: *UA – A Treatise on Universal Algebra* (Cambridge University Press, 1898); *AE – The Aims of Education and Other Essays* (1932; 2nd ed., 1950, London: Ernest Benn); *RM – Religion in the Making* (Cambridge University Press, 1926); *FR – The Function of Reason* (Princeton University Press, 1929); *PR – Process and Reality: An Essay in Cosmology* (1929; corrected ed., New York: The Free Press, 1978); *AI – Adventures of Ideas* (New York: The Free Press, 1967); *MT – Modes of Thought* (New York: The Free Press, 1968); *ESP – Essays in Science and Philosophy* (New York: Philosophical Library, 1947). The abbrevations are followed by page numbers.

[2] See Leemon B. McHenry, *Whitehead and Bradley: A Comparative Analysis* (Albany, New York: State University of New York Press, 1992).

maintain a metaphysical or positive theory of being or existence. That is to say, in contrast to empiricist-oriented accounts of being or existence, they do not regard being or existence merely as (in one form or another) an underivable 'given,' about which nothing else can be said. Rather, they maintain that being or existence has a specific or 'positive' (*AR* 215) nature of its own which is describable (cf. *PR* 20), although statements about the positive nature of existence cannot be treated as having the status of qualities or attributes or predicates in any usual sense. In this context, the best way to understand both the unusual character of Bradley's absolutism and its historical role in relation to Whitehead's thought is in terms of the close relation between two distinctive features of Bradley's work – the concept of philosophical method and the theory of immediate experience or 'feeling.'

Too often Bradley's work is seen as a typical piece of Victoriana, a curio eccentrically and over-confidently cast in the 'high priori' style of an alien rationalism. In other words, his account of the nature of philosophical inquiry is commonly held to be intellectualist in character; ie. to rest on some form of the principle of non-contradiction, or, more usually, on a purely logical analysis of the concept of relations. Bradley's own ironic protests on the issue go unnoticed: 'There is an idea', he says, 'that we start...with certain axioms, and from these reason downwards. This idea to my mind is baseless' (*ETR* 311).

In his *Principles of Logic* Bradley characterizes all theoretical inquiry as a matter of what he calls 'ideal experiment', the elaboration, as he puts it, of 'working hypotheses' (cf. *PL* 340, 720).[3] That position is more fully developed in *Essays on Truth and Reality* where, in response to critics such as Russell, Bradley says that the 'method' he employs is not axiomatic but 'experimental' (*ETR* 311; cf. 289, 291): 'we experiment ideally on the nature of things' (*ETR* 314).

---

[3] See Don MacNiven, *Bradley's Moral Psychology* (New York & Queenston: Edwin Mellen Press, 1987), chapter 1.

The starting point of philosophical inquiry for Bradley is not any kind of metaphysical presupposition but what he calls 'a principle of action'; namely, the search for what he terms 'intellectual satisfaction' (*ETR* 26). In seeking intellectual satisfaction, Bradley holds that 'philosophy...in the end rests on what may fairly be termed faith' (*ETR* 15). That is to say, philosophical inquiry presupposes that intellectual satisfaction can be achieved. As he describes his approach in *Appearance and Reality*: 'I have assumed that the object of metaphysics is to find a general view which will satisfy the intellect, and I have assumed that whatever succeeds in doing this is real and true, and whatever fails is neither' (*AR* 491). In other words, the assumption of inquiry is that it is the world which we are trying to understand, and that in some sense this world is intelligible (cf. *ES* 73).

Bradley says two things about the nature of this faith or assumption. First, he remarks that it 'can neither be proved nor questioned' (*AR* 491). Secondly, he points out: 'But as to what will satisfy I have of course no knowledge in advance...the way and means are to be discovered only by trial and rejection. The method is clearly experimental' (*ETR* 311).

These remarks make quite clear that we are not here being provided with an 'intellectualist' criterion of reality. In all respects open-ended, the principle of satisfaction – the search for intelligible order of some kind (cf. *ES* 209) – does not embody a metaphysical premise of any kind, but is offered as nothing else than a procedural rule to which any participant in philosophical inquiry subscribes. Everything clearly depends on how Bradley goes on to determine the content of the concepts of 'satisfaction' and 'reality.'

The central text for Bradley's account of the nature and relation of the concepts of 'satisfaction' and 'reality' is chapter 13 of *Appearance and Reality*. Here it emerges that it is the 'non-contradictory' or 'consistent' which satisfies the intellect as true and real. But as Bradley now observes: 'The question is solely as to the meaning to be given to consistency' (*AR* 123; cf. 506; *PL* 165 n. 9, 145–6; *ETR* 315).

The real problems begin at this point. For Bradley is clearly maintaining both that non-contradiction or consistency cannot be understood in metaphysics as a merely formal criterion – either in the sense that it is absolutely independent of any subject-matter or in the sense that it is relatively independent of any subject-matter – and that it cannot be understood as a report of linguistic usage, a convention with no reference to the world. As a result, it is usually claimed that Bradley's theory of non-contradiction is rationalist in nature – that, like Bosanquet or Joachim, he maintains the law of non-contradiction, as an absolute necessity of thought, to be also an apprehension of necessity in the being of things.

But what has always been overlooked here is the way in which Bradley derives the nature of 'inconsistency' in chapter 13. For having stated there the unavoidability of taking the principle of consistency (in some indeterminate sense) as the criterion of the real (in some indeterminate sense), he then goes on to show that the consistent or the real could not be plural in nature, ie. that it could not be a collection of independent or externally related reals. And why not? Both because 'a mode of togetherness such as we can verify in feeling' – which Bradley defines as non-relational in character –'destroys the independence of the reals', and also because 'Relations... are unmeaning except within and on the basis of a substantial whole [of feeling]' (*AR* 125; cf. *ETR* 313–14).

For Bradley, therefore, it is feeling or immediate experience which defines the metaphysical account of contradiction. The contradictory is that which fails to include the non-relational unity or substantial whole of feeling. In Bradley, non-contradiction is not a matter of some *a priori* demand of the intellect, but is a demand of the object as experienced in non-relational feeling (cf. *AR* 504; *ETR* 313–14).

II

The concept of non-relational feeling has more than one important role in Bradley's work. Besides defining the nature of intellectual satisfaction – a topic which will be further considered below – non-relational feeling also provides Bradley with an account of the pre-cognitive content of our system of beliefs in terms of an adverbial theory of sensory acquaintance, as David Crossley shows elsewhere in this volume.[4] Two further roles should also be briefly explained.

In the first place, the concept of non-relational feeling means for Bradley that there is no such thing as direct knowledge of immediate experience. This is what puts him among the idealists: all knowledge is held to be a matter of ideal or relational activity, and consequently any identifiable term or quality is what he calls an 'ideal construction', ie. all identifiability or particularity is a matter of the ideal or relational differentiation of non-relational feeling. It is thus hardly surprising that, like the idealists, Bradley prefers the doctrine of internal, to that of external, relations. Neither an axiom which he takes for granted, nor the result of some metaphysically presuppositionless analysis of the nature of concepts, the doctrine of internal relations is for him a consequence of the claim that, as ideal products, terms are nothing apart from their relational differentiation.[5]

In the second place, however, unlike other idealists such as Bosanquet, Bradley does not regard non-relational feeling as a privative concept. That is to say, as his use of the term 'substantial whole of feeling' suggests, he does not regard feeling as the merely indeterminate starting point of thought which as such is assimilable in the process of cognition. Rather, Bradley maintains the irreducibility of the distinction between thought and sensation, concept and object. This is not, however, held to be a matter of some distinction between knowing subject and object of knowledge, nor of any surd-like particulars. It is instead a matter of the difference between the non-relational unity of feeling and the relational form of thought.

For unlike other idealists Bradley maintains that thought is inadequate to the nature of things on account of the fact that the non-relational unity of feeling, *as such*, cannot be ideally

---

[4] Besides this volume, see his important paper, 'The Multiple Contents of Immediacy', *F. H. Bradley Centenary Essays* (Oxford: Clarendon Press, 1995).

[5] See *AR* chapter 3; on which, my article 'Relations, intelligibilite et non-contradiction dans la metaphysique du sentir de F. H. Bradley: une reinterpretation', part 1, *Archives de philosophie*, vol. 54 (1991), pp. 529–51.

or relationally comprehended or 'reconstituted' (*ETR* 231). On this analysis, even internal relations are regarded as contradictory in that, as relations, they necessarily fail to provide an intelligible or satisfactory account of the connectedness of things as experienced in the non-relational unity of feeling (cf. *ETR* 190).[6] Thus, in contrast to the rationalist idealisms of Bosanquet or Joachim or Blanshard, the realm of ideality or relations is graphically described by Bradley as a tragic realm of 'endless', 'hopeless' 'process' (*AR* 28, 157). This is his realm of 'appearance', or contradiction, in which relational thought fruitlessly searches to render intelligible or to reunite ideally the connectedness of things as experienced in the non-relational unity of feeling. He therefore argues that the feeling-based principle of non-contradiction or intellectual satisfaction can be met only if we 'postulate a higher form of unity' (*ETR* 190) which includes both the unity of feeling and the differentiations of relationality. Such a non-contradictory, supra-rational unity is of course Bradley's Absolute: the real is understood as eternally and completely present, and defined as the perfect infinite, the all-inclusive, self-subsistent unity of all things. The search for an intelligible account of the non-relational unity of feeling ironically takes reflection beyond both thought and feeling.

III

This brief summary of some of the roles of non-relational feeling in Bradley's work indicates that it is the main premise and driving principle of his thought. Its larger significance remains to be considered.

It is already evident that Bradley's non-relational feeling is an account of the nature of sensory acquaintance. Feeling is non-cognitive, a matter of the sensory apprehension of a plurality of features or 'felt mass' (*AR* 155) without

---

[6] For a more complete analysis of Bradley's feeling-based critique of relations, see my article, *ibid*.

distinction of subject and object. Sensory apprehension is thus a non-relational state in the sense that there is no distinction between feeler and felt, between what he calls the 'finite centre' of experience and the experience; there is only the experience of their unity.

But that is not all Bradley means by non-relational feeling. For the non-relational feeling-whole is held to be the permanent ground or 'present foundation' (*ETR* 159–60) of all ideal construction or differentiation. It is this peculiar metaphysical status accorded to non-relational feeling which makes it much more than an account of sensory experience. There are at least four points to be considered here.

1. In the first place, defined as the ground of all differentiation, the concept of non-relational feeling means that Bradley's metaphysics has the character of a theory of affirmative or 'positive' 'being' (*AR* 215). That is to say, Bradley denies both that negation is based on opposition or privation – the abstract negation of the empiricist tradition – and that negation is equivalent to affirmation – which in his view is Hegel's position.[7] In contrast, under the slogan 'no ideas float' (cf. *ETR* chapter 3), Bradley maintains that all negation has its basis in the 'positive' diversities of feeling (*PL* 122, 150, 410, 662ff.). Where all ideal content belongs to the real, for all ideal content is a differentiation of the real as it is experienced in feeling, it makes as little sense to call Bradley a metaphysical idealist as it does to call him a metaphysical realist (cf. *AR* 485) – *as will emerge even more clearly in the next point.*

2. In the second place, as the 'foundation' or 'vital condition' of the objective world (*ETR* 159–60, 161, 176), which is neither subjective nor objective but the condition which makes such distinctions possible, non-relational feeling has the status of a logical ground of possibility in the strong transcendental sense of that term.

---

[7] On Bradley's view of Hegel on negation, see my *Archives* article, cited in footnote 5, especially p. 548.

That is to say, firstly, there is nothing in the objective world which the concept of non-relational feeling as logical ground denotes, nor to which it refers, nor which corresponds to it, for it is an account of the conditions of denotation, reference and correspondence.[8] Secondly, there is therefore nothing 'out there' in the world which makes statements about permanent feeling determinately true or false, either independently of, or in terms of, our capacity for knowledge. Thirdly, there is nothing in the objective world which stands to permanent feeling in any relation of resemblance or actualization; ie. permanent feeling does not stand to anything in any the causal or productive relations in terms of which the connection of the possible to the actual has usually been understood.

In its role as transcendental principle Bradley endows permanent feeling with structural complexity. To be sure, in order to express this structural complexity, relational concepts have to be employed. Hence, as Bradley emphasizes, any description of permanent feeling is analogical; ie. that which is non-relational in nature can only be analysed on analogy with the relational order (*ETR* 177, 196, 411). But this is of course strictly a matter of analogy of method, not of any analogy of (eminent) being.[9]

The concept of 'finite centres of experience' constitutes Bradley's analysis of the structure of which permanent feeling is the non-relational unity. That is to say, Bradley analogically analyses the structure of permanent feeling in terms of the

---

[8] There is no space here to deal with the tensions and ambivalences introduced into Bradley's thought by his treatment of non-relational feeling as at once a strong non-relational condition and an account of actual experience. On this, see my 'The Transcendental Turn in F. H. Bradley's Metaphysics of Feeling', in W. J. Mander (ed.), *Perspectives on the Logic and Metaphysics of F. H. Bradley* (Bristol: Thoemmes Press, 1996), pp. 39–60. As will emerge, there is no ambiguity of this kind in Whitehead.

[9] I take the use of analogy of method, as opposed to the analogy of being, to be characteristic of transcendental analysis from Kant onwards. See Gerd Buchdahl, *Metaphysics and the Philosophy of Science*, 2nd ed. (New York: University Presses of America, 1988); and *Kant and the Dynamics of Reason* (Oxford: Basil Blackwell, 1992).

difference between feeler and felt, between finite centre of experience and what is experienced. This difference of finite centre and experience is of course a difference of a special kind: it is a non-relational difference, in which the finite centre 'is the immediate experience of itself and the Universe in one' (*ETR* 410); or, as Bradley also puts it, it is the non-temporal 'presence' of all that is (*ETR* 410 and note 2).

Perhaps the first point to note here is that Bradley is quite explicit about the transcendental status of finite centres. He describes them as 'that which lies behind objects' – 'the basis on and from which the world of objects is made' (*ETR* 411) – which have the status of 'necessary ideas' (*ETR* 412). That is to say, finite centres are 'ideal constructions' (*ETR* 412) of a particular kind: they are not themselves given or presented but are the way in which the conditions of experience have to be conceived. Hence Bradley calls them 'special appearances' (*ETR* 412) in order to indicate their purely conceptual status as transcendental conditions in the strong sense.[10]

The second point that needs to be made is that a finite centre of experience is not to be understood as a cognitive self or subject nor as merely a condition of the cognitive self, but as a condition of any kind of difference whatsoever. That is to say, although in *Appearance and Reality* Bradley often talks of finite centres and selves in one breath, both in that work and even more clearly in *Essays on Truth and Reality* he defines finite centres as conditions of differentiation *simpliciter*, quite independently of the activity of ideal or cognitive differentiation (*AR* 464n., 468–9; *ETR* 350n.). It is of course tempting to describe Bradley's use of feeling here to move beyond the idealist view of differentiation as ideal or cognitive differentiation in terms of panpsychism. But he himself refuses to draw any such conclusion, for the obvious reason that the concept of finite centres of experience is an analogical and transcendental concept which, as prior to the distinction of subject and object, renders that distinction

---

[10] On the difficult question of what kind of distinction the concept of finite centres might be, and the relation of ideal distinction in general to Bradley's monistic concept of the Real, see my article cited in footnote 5 above.

relative – hence the point from which we elaborate their relativity is a matter of indifference.[11]

3. Besides being a theory of affirmative being with transcendental status, Bradley's non-relational feeling has a special and problematic connection to his concept of the complete real – a connection which allows him to employ feeling as the premise of his absolutism.

As initially introduced in *Ethical Studies*, Bradley's real is 'the unity of finite and infinite' where 'you can distinguish without dividing' (*ES* 77). But while he suggests there that such a familiar concept of the real must be established 'on a fresh basis' (*ES* 324n.) – a basis already hinted at by his claim that 'the felt contradiction [of moral experience] implies, and is only possible through, a unity above discord' (*ES* 324) – *Ethical Studies* is not a metaphysical work (*ES* 5, 60–61, 249) and he does not offer his account of the real as 'positive doctrine' (*ES* 249).[12] The same is true of *Principles of Logic*. Here, again, the real is the perfect infinite and, in tandem with a variety of accounts of feeling, that concept is appealed to throughout (cf. *PL* 46, 52, 71, 187ff.). But no direct defence of it is offered.

Appearance and Reality and *Essays on Truth and Reality* represent Bradley's attempt to develop a full-scale defence of the real understood as the supra-rational perfect infinite. In this respect, as has been indicated, non-relational feeling plays a crucial role: being in the nature of the case incomprehensible to relational thought, the non-relational unity of feeling means that intellectual satisfaction is to be found only in an absolute unity which includes both feeling and thought. Non-relational unity is thus the ground or foundation of Bradley's 'deduction' of the perfect infinite. As he says in repudiation of what he takes to be Hegel's dialectic (*ETR* 278; cf. *PL*

---

[11] See T. S. Eliot, *Knowledge and Experience in the Philosophy of F. H. Bradley* (London: Faber & Faber, 1964), p. 30.

[12] See my article in P. MacEwan (ed.), *Ethics, Metaphysics and Religion in the Thought of F. H. Bradley* (New York: Edwin Mellen Press, forthcoming).

515): 'I do not believe in any operation which falls out of the blue upon a mere object...the series of reflection is generated by and through the unity of immediate experience...the principle of the process therefore does not reside in pure thought, but on the contrary must be said to imply a mere conjunction [ie. it entails that mere conjunction is the character of thought; cf. *CE* 655].'

The question which Bradley obviously has to face here is whether or not the concept of feeling can carry the metaphysical weight he attaches to it. In this connection it is noteworthy that in *Appearance and Reality* he constantly reiterates that the non-relational unity of feeling is an 'imperfect appearance' or 'incomplete form' of the perfect unity of the real (*AR* 141, 156, 159, 199, 203, 215, 509). That is to say, the non-relational unity of feeling is throughout interpreted in terms of the concept of the perfect infinite. It is that concept which confers on feeling its special significance as 'substantial whole' for Bradley.

If, however, the concept of the real as perfect infinite were to be rejected, while much that Bradley says about non-relational feeling may well be cogent, it would not possess the metaphysically foundational importance he attaches to it. And that this is indeed the case is indicated not only by the obvious fact that Bradley's theory of feeling can be maintained as an adverbial analysis of perception quite independently of the concept of the perfect infinite, but also – as will emerge – by the account Whitehead offers of what Bradley calls non-relational unity. So while non-relational feeling certainly defines the nature of non-contradiction or intellectual satisfaction for Bradley, it does so only because it is viewed in the light of the concept of the perfect infinite. In providing Bradley with what he believes to be an anchor-point in actual experience for the concept of the perfect infinite, feeling takes on a momentous metaphysical significance it would not otherwise have. There would be no Bradleyan Absolute without the correlation of non-relational feeling and the concept of the perfect infinite.

4. In this connection, finally, it should be noted that Bradley's correlation of non-relational feeling and the perfect

infinite not only leads him to define the latter as suprarational, but also means that he deprives it of any productive relation to its appearances. To be sure, he retains the concept of limitation to define finite appearances. But limitation is not the limitation *qua* realization of a prior order of infinite possibility. Because no (relational) analysis can be given of how appearances appear, limitation for Bradley is in effect equivalent to difference or differentiation, ie. the real is no longer conceived as a causal or productive principle. However, it is but a short step from this to defining limitation wholly in terms of differentiation, ie. as nothing else than a matter of the self-differentiation of the finite without reference to the complete real. As will become evident, Bradley's abandonment of the real as a principle of production opens the door to a concept of the real quite different from his own.

IV

Perhaps the shortest route to understanding the relation of Whitehead to Bradley is to see Whitehead's metaphysics as the development and transformation of some of the central features of Bradley's theories of feeling and ideal construction. Whitehead is explicit about his debt to Bradley in both cases (*UA* chapter 1; *AI* chapter 15) – which allows his early concept of 'logical construction' to be seen as an elaboration of Bradleyan themes[13] – and he takes up both Bradley's affirmative account of feeling and his transcendentalism in order to elaborate a positive theory of being or existence. However, the primary motive for his redefinition of these theories is not difficult to see: he abandons the concept of the real as the

---

[13] On Whitehead's origination of the theory of logical construction, see Bertrand Russell, *Portraits from Memory* (London: George Allen & Unwin, 1956), p. 39; *Our Knowledge of the External World* (London: George Allen & Unwin; 2nd revised ed., 1926), pp. 7–8, 70ff. For Whitehead's own early version, see *UA* chapter 1, *AE* chapters 9, 10. For the purposes of this essay, the reader need only keep in mind the usual Russellian version of the theory.

perfect infinite (*AI* 330) – which he sees as the consequence of the subject-predicate model of analysis (cf. *PR* 157, 190; *AI* 133, 157) – and, taking the step Bradley's work invites, attempts an analysis of the real in terms of the principle of difference or differentiation, understood as a matter of the pluralistic self-differentiating or self-actualizing natures of things without reference to any principle of cause or production.

In this context, Whitehead's concept of self-actualizing 'occasions' can be seen as developing Bradley's concept of finite centres by universalizing the concept of construction. As Whitehead himself points out, because he understands all things as self-actualizing, construction becomes a concept of the real (*PR* 156), not primarily a concept of cognition as in Kant or Russell. To this end, he redefines construction in terms of 'process', ie. as the serial or, more precisely, vectorial (cf. *PR* 19, 164, 231, 237) connections or transitions between occasions of self-actualization. Indeed, it can be said that a great deal of the complexity of Whitehead's work arises from his attempt to undertake an exhaustive analysis of 'ideal' or 'logical' construction in terms of the 'genetic process' or vectorial connections of occasions. For this enterprise he appropriates Bradley's theory of the unity of feeling, but he redefines it as a matter of horizontal, vectorial connection.

In the present context only one aspect of Whitehead's detailed vectoral account of feeling needs to be considered: his concept of 'physical feelings', in particular 'simple physical feelings', defined as the 'initial data' in the process of becoming or 'concrescence' of an occasion out of antecedent occasions. A simple physical feeling is the relation between the objective datum – ie. the feeling of an antecedent occasion – and its feeling or 'prehension' by a subsequent, concrescing occasion (*PR* 236).

Now it will immediately be evident that Whitehead thinks of physical feelings in terms of an 'object-subject' relation (*AI* chapter 11). Here the object is the antecedent occasion and the subject is the concrescing occasion – or, as he also puts it, explicitly indicating his departure from Bradley, the object-occasion is the completed, antecedent 'reality', and the concrescent subject-occasion is 'appearance' (*AI* 269).

Despite the fundamental, vectorial difference, however, Whitehead agrees with Bradley that experience is not primarily a matter of the cognition of objects, insisting that 'the subject-object relation is the fundamental structural pattern of experience... but not in the sense in which subject-object is identified with knower-known' (*AI* 225). That is to say, the vectorial relation of object-subject in physical feeling is not for Whitehead a cognitive relation. Moreover, it cannot be said that there is in physical feeling any kind of distinct object-subject relation; for in genetic process the concrescent subject-occasion is not yet itself, but in process of becoming, ie. genetic process is (in a sense to be explained) an account of the conditions which make possible the differentiation of object and subject. Hence Whitehead regards physical feeling as the direct experience of antecedent occasions by subsequent occasions (cf. *PR* 55, 230, 237–8) – a position which Dorothy Emmet interprets as an adverbial theory of perception.[14] In this light, it may be said that, Whitehead's vectorial analysis of feeling perfectly preserves the unities of finite centre and experience, and of content and existence, which for Bradley constitute the non-relationality of feeling understood as an account of sensory awareness. Yet nothing alters the fact that Whitehead is engaged in what he calls 'a critique of pure feeling' (*PR* 113). In redefining the real as the becoming of occasions, the unity of feeler and felt no longer has for Whitehead the significance as criterion of the real it had for Bradley. Further, by analysing feeling as a matter of vector connection, Whitehead is able to combine the empiricist notion of the objective datum – of an object independent of the subject – with the idealist notion of constructive activity by placing them on a horizontal plane as different 'phases' or 'stages' in the becoming of occasions.

Something of the critical power of this transformation is indicated by what it allows Whitehead to do with the doctrine of internal relations. For Bradley, as for other idealists, the

---

[14] See Dorothy Emmet, *The Nature of Metaphysical Thinking*, 2nd ed. (London: Macmillan, 1966), pp. 46ff.

doctrine of internal relations is inseparable from some form of monism. For Russell, as for other empiricists, the asymmetry of serial relations destroys the doctrine of internal relations and any concomitant monism.[15] For Whitehead, however, the vector character of feeling means that any subsequent occasion is internally related to its antecedent occasions, but its antecedent occasions (as completed or 'perished') are not internally related to it. That is to say, the internal relations of occasions are serial or asymmetrical in character. In contrast to both Bradleyan idealism and Russellian empiricism, Whitehead's vector-analysis of feeling maintains the doctrine of internal relations in the context of a pluralist theory of serial or asymmetrical difference. His concept of the vectoral process of occasions is a concept of the nature of things as a matter of moving, interacting lines of force, which are rationally analysable as such.

V

For all the power of Whitehead's analysis, however, it obviously presents serious problems of interpretation.

Firstly, there is the obvious question as to whether or not Whitehead's theory of process, understood as universalizing the principle of self-actualization, constitutes a metaphysical realism which dogmatically assumes direct access to the real, blithely ignoring any critical analysis of the powers and limits of reasoning or language. This is certainly how many 'Whiteheadians' see him, even maintaining that his employment of the concept of feeling commits him to panpsychism.

Secondly, Whitehead is like Bradley in abjuring any principle of ground or production. But while (as has been noted) he analyses the real, not in terms of presence or the complete real, but in terms of the process of self-actualizing occasions, this is a strategy which presents as many diffi-

---

[15] See Bertrand Russell, *Principles of Mathematics* (Cambridge University Press, 1903), paras. 212–16; and 'The Monistic Theory of Truth', in *Philosophical Essays* (revised edition, 1966), pp. 131–46. See also Fred Wilson's essay in the present volume.

culties as does Bradley's monism. Just as Bradley faces the question of the relation of a plurality of appearances to the one real – a question which always threatens the status and possibility of his own analysis – Whitehead faces the difficulty as to whether or not the analysis of self-actualization is possible; ie. how can metaphysical reason analyse that which in the nature of the case is unique and unrepeatable or genuinely new? How is a *metaphysics* of the new possible (cf. *MT* 133)? It is surely no accident that other twentieth-century critics of the principle of ground have, in attempting to think the self-realizing new, taken their cue from the later Heidegger and announced the end of philosophy.

VI

In my view, Whitehead's response to these difficulties is best understood in terms of his elaboration of the concept of construction as that is self-referentially applied by philosophical analysis to itself. Here the full significance of his self-description as engaged in 'a critique of pure feeling' becomes evident. For apart from the obvious and direct influence of Kant,[16] Whitehead takes up and develops certain transcendental themes that characterize Bradley's analysis, and, under the inspiration of his own early concept of logical construction, transforms them into a philosophical method which he calls the 'intellectual construction' of a 'speculative scheme' of categories (cf. *PR* chapter 1).

In order to understand the nature and status of Whitehead's speculative scheme, it is essential to note that he makes a distinction between 'immediate experience' and 'feeling'. Feeling is a concept or category of the scheme; immediate experience, however, is his term for the 'topic' or subject-matter of the scheme – what he calls its 'empirical side' (*PR* 4). The significance of this designation cannot be underestimated.

---

[16] See Russell's remark in his *Autobiography*, one-volume edition (London: George Allen & Unwin, 1975), chapter 5, p. 129. See also my article, 'La cosmologie transcendentale de Whitehead', *Archives de philosophie*, vol. 56 (1993), pp. 3–228.

As he states at the beginning of *Process and Reality*, chapter 1, a speculative construction has for Whitehead two 'sides' – the 'rational side' and the 'empirical side' (*PR* 3). The rational side is constituted by the 'categorial scheme' (*PR* xi, 3–4). In contrast, the empirical side is defined as 'everything of which we are conscious as enjoyed, perceived, willed, or thought' (*PR* 3); or again as 'the ideas and problems which form the complex texture of civilised thought' (*PR* xi). That is to say, the subject-matter of a categorial scheme is immediate experience (*PR* 4), defined as the problematic welter of naturalistically conceived objects and past and present interpretations or beliefs. For clarity, in what follows I will refer to immediate experience so understood as the 'empirical world'.

Now clearly, in the first place, such a concept of the empirical world is not to be conflated with the indubitable sense-data of empiricists like Russell, nor with the immediate experience of the idealists, nor with the life-world of the phenomenologists (ie. it is not a complex of primitive meanings prior to any reflective or scientific conceptualization). Rather, the concept of the empirical world refers to everything of which we are conscious – doctrines and ditties as much as cabbages, sealing-wax, and physics. It is with 'assemblage' in this inclusive sense that philosophical construction begins (*MT* 2–3).

In the second place, understood as including our past and present beliefs, the concept of the empirical world is an historical concept, designating both the 'oceans of facts' and the 'evaluative interests' which are 'intrinsic within each historical period' (*MT* 25). What the philosopher works within, that is, is an historically-situated assemblage of interests, orientations, and attitudes characteristic of a given epoch. And what the philosopher seeks in respect of that assemblage is some 'thread of coordination' (*MT* 25) in order to 'coordinate the current expressions of human experience, in common speech, in social institutions, in actions, in the principles of the various special sciences, elucidating harmony and exposing discrepancies' (*AI* 286).

The coordinating generality of philosophy should not

however be confused with any kind of ahistorical neutrality or permanence. For, in the third place, if the empirical world is an historically-situated assemblage, so also is the categorial scheme which analyses it. That is to say, Whitehead sees the construction of a philosophical scheme of categories as an enterprise of 'imaginative generalisation', involving 'the utilization of specific notions, applying to a restricted group of facts, for the divination of the generic notions which apply to all facts' (PR 5; cf. 13). His point here is that the empirical world is historically related to the categorial scheme as a source of analogues for the definition of the nature of the real. In other words, when the main features of the empirical world are analysed or coordinated philosophically, this is done by means of the analogical employment of some one or other features of that world – features to which the strains and tensions, the discoveries and difficulties, of a specific historical period give an especial relevance or appropriateness. Hence our use of terms such as 'mind', 'matter', 'will', 'feeling', 'events', 'occasions', and so on. These terms do not refer to particular features of the world; rather, culturally-saturated and historically significant features of the world, representing routes of convergence in mathematics, art, politics, physics and technology, are generalized as analogues for the coordinating characterization of its main features. The construction of a categorial scheme, the creation of concepts (FR 15, 27), is primarily a matter of the construction of coordinating analogies out of the singularities of historical experience.

VI

Whitehead clearly shares with Bradley a recognition of the role of analogy in philosophical construction. But he also shares much more. For I would suggest that the purpose of Whitehead's rigorous distinction between the categorial and empirical sides of his analysis is to underline the *transcendental* status of his categorial scheme. The categorial scheme, that is to say, does not constitute a metaphysical realism but is an analysis of the conditions of possibility of the empirical world understood as conditions of self-actualization. So regarded, Whitehead's transcendental analysis has three key features.

Firstly, Whitehead's categories are transcendentals in the full, medieval sense that they refer, not only to the nature of cognitive representation, but to the nature of everything that is (*PR* 20). No transcendental subreption is involved here on account of the self-referentially inclusive character of the categories as historically-situated, analogical concepts. It is thus possible unproblematically to replace the transcendental concept of 'being' with the more inclusive concept of 'creativity' – something which, with his explicit references to the traditional medieval transcendentals, Whitehead quite clearly indicates to be his intention (*PR* 21–2).[17]

Secondly, however, the choice of creativity over being as the ultimate category indicates that the categories of the scheme are transcendentals in the Kant-derived sense that they are transcendental conditions. That is to say, transcendental analysis is here explicitly linked to the concept of construction, the categories of the scheme being given the status of principles of constructive activity (*PR* 156). Transcendental analysis is not now a matter of the basic properties of all things (*consequens omne ens*), but of the conditions of things and their properties (cf. Kant, *CPR* B114).

Thirdly, however, the categories of the scheme are conditions of the self-constructing natures of things. In contrast to medieval transcendentals, this means that the schematic categories are not structures of being (*ens*) but structures of the self-actualization of being (*esse*). In contrast to Kant, it means that the schematic categories are conditions, not of cognition, but of the natures of all things, understood as self-actualizing. As such, the schematic categories are not

---

[17] For a discussion of this point, see R. L. Fetz, 'Creativity: A New Transcendental?', in F. Rapp and R. Wiehl (eds.), *Whitehead's Metaphysics of Creativity* (Albany: State University of New York Press, 1990), pp. 189–208. I would further add that the concepts of 'beauty', 'adventure', and 'peace', developed by Whitehead towards the end of *AI*, represent perhaps the only significant developments in the analysis of transcendental properties since the medieval period. Whitehead can here be regarded as developing the concept of 'intelligible beauty' – on which see Umberto Eco, *Art and the Middle Ages*, trans. M. Carruthers (New Haven, Connecticut: Yale University Press, 1986).

metaphysically causal or productive principles; ie. they do not refer their empirical subject-matters away from themselves to something else as their ground, cognitive or otherwise. It can thus be said that whereas medieval transcendentalism thinks being in terms of its representable conditions, and Kantian transcendentalism thinks being in terms of the conditions of its representation, Whitehead's transcendentalism thinks being in terms of its immanent, vectorial conditions of self-actualization. In this context, it is hardly surprising that Whitehead disliked being called a panpsychist.[18]

VII

Even if a transcendental interpretation of Whitehead has some cogency, however,[19] the question as to how a transcendental analysis of self-actualization is possible remains to be answered. How can the transcendental structures of the categorial scheme be defined in such a way as to be 'structures' of the new?

Here, Whitehead exploits the character of his categories as analogical terms to the full. He defines what he calls the relation of 'application' that holds between the categories of the scheme and the empirical world as an analogical relation. Application is not a relation of analogical relation of attribution, however, but of proportionality; ie. it is a matter of the correspondence of relations (as a is to b, so c is to d), not of terms, as Whitehead indicates throughout (cf. *PR* 116, 117, 177, 212, 246; *MT* 231; *AI* 242). So understood, this 'substitutive' relation of scheme and world, as he also calls it (cf. *UA*, Introduction, *PR* 116), is a strictly equivalent or (so to speak) reflexive relation, such that the categories of the scheme are exhaustively translatable into their subject-matter

---

[18] See Victor Lowe, 'The Concept of Experience in Whitehead's Metaphysics', in G. Kline (ed.), *A. N. Whitehead: Essays on His Philosophy* (New Jersey: Prentice-Hall, 1963), pp. 124–33, especially p. 126.

[19] For an extended defence of such an interpretation of Whitehead, see my article 'Transcendentalism and Speculative Realism in Whitehead', *Process Studies*, vol. 23 (1994), pp. 140–72.

without any kind of etiological remainder. In Whitehead's hands, that is to say, the analogy of proportionality is nothing else than a particular principle of translation which allows the empirical subject-matter of the analysis to be translated into a set of categorial statements which say equivalent things, but not the same things, about their subject-matter as can be empirically stated. In contrast to the subject-predicate logic in which he sees Bradley as embroiled, Whitehead's model for the status of his categories is that of the propositional function (cf. *ESP* 127ff.). Being or existence can now be understood as having a positive nature of its own which is intelligible in terms of the vectoral structure of relations and is free of the noumenal content of Bradley's reality.

It should now be evident that on account of his elaboration and transformation of certain themes in Bradley, Whitehead can be accused neither of dogmatism, nor of ignoring the problems presented by the project of a metaphysics of the new. It is the status of the speculative scheme as a set of proportionally translatable categorial functions and their variables which makes possible a structural analysis of the unique and unrepeatable, ensuring that the transcendental conditions of self-actualization do not refer things away from themselves to anything else as their grounding principle. And so understood, Whitehead's categorial analysis does not represent a naive pre-Kantian metaphysical realism. The strong anti-idealist language of the philosophy of process is not the discourse of traditional metaphysical realism, but of a transcendental theory of self-actualization where, necessarily, conceptual analysis and empirical description disappear into each other in the reflexive relation of proportional translatability. Whitehead's analysis has always to be read with bifocals, as a simultaneous elaboration of transcendental meaning and empirical application (cf. *PR* xiii; cf. xi, xiv, *UA* 12).

Seen in this light, it can be said that the Bradley-Whitehead relation is one main strand in the movement from nineteenth to twentieth-century philosophy. It involves a complete transformation of metaphysics – but one carried out from within metaphysics and on behalf of metaphysics. Its significance resides in the fact that it represents the history of the anglo-american transition from a traditional metaphysics of presence to a metaphysics of the new, the different – a metaphysics of process. To forget Bradley's role in this transition is seriously to misunderstand what comes after him.

UNITY, THEORY AND PRACTICE:
F. H. BRADLEY AND PRAGMATISM[1]

Paul D. Forster

Periods of dramatic social upheaval are typically interconnected with ruminations on unity, that is, with the search for a framework within which to order and appease conflicting elements. In the nineteenth century, the industrial revolution and the Darwinian revolution conspired to produce a synthesis of philosophy, social theory and natural science that proved to offer a compelling moral vision.

For Herbert Spencer, the intellectual leader of this movement, the unity of Truth, Goodness and Beauty is viewed naturalistically as the relationship between Thought, Volition and Feeling. By insisting that each of these is a biological faculty contributing to the satisfaction of organisms, Spencer subsumes them under evolutionary laws. Practices, values and experiences that purport to transcend or enrich the natural world are shown to originate in, and to subserve, organic activity as part of a comprehensive natural order. The world of ultimate origins and ends, the world of the Divine, is, for Spencer, inaccessible and unknowable. It forms no part of the environmental pressures that determine and, thereby, give significance to, vital functions. Thus the transcendental has no explanatory role in the reality in which humans think, act and feel.

For Pragmatists and Bradley alike, Spencer's achievement is spurious. The *reduction* of humanity to biology, of culture to

---

[1] Comments by Margaret Morrison, James Wong, David Savan and participants in the symposium are gratefully acknowledged as is support by way of a Social Sciences and Humanities Research Council of Canada Post-doctoral Fellowship.

nature, does not *integrate* these conflicting elements, it simply denies reality to one component of the opposition. Spencer, in a sense, rejects the question of how the spiritual relates to the physical world since spirituality is nothing but a subjective manifestation of biological needs with no objects outside the natural environment. It is because this theory refutes the diversity of life, rather than reconciles its various aspects, that it is held by its critics to be suspect intellectually and unsatisfying morally.

Yet for both Bradley and the Pragmatists, Transcendental Idealism, in any of its myriad forms, does no better. The three strands of Kant's critical philosophy, for example, are united formally, but they are separate materially. For Kant, the objects constructed by our scientific interests are independent of those constructed for moral and aesthetic purposes; they are the products of distinct modes of objectification. The question of their relation, however, is left unresolved.

If we may call Spencer's strategy 'eliminative unification' and Kant's strategy 'methodological pluralism', then the Pragmatists' quest for a 'pluralistic universe' and Bradley's search for 'absolute unity in diversity' can be viewed as having a common goal, namely, the development of a conception of the unity of experience that involves neither reduction nor separation. The aim is to recognize the diversity of the domains of human experience while acknowledging the need to weave diverse ways of operating into a coherent life. The following discussion of Dewey and Bradley is intended to provide an outline of this project and to illustrate important differences in their respective approaches to it.

Bradley's Absolutism: Unity in Diversity
For Bradley, the question of the unity of diversity is ultimately the question of how Appearance stands to Absolute Reality. The Apparent is contingent, historical and mutable, the Absolute is necessary, timeless and permanent. What distinguishes them is their degree of perfection. Appearance is a self-contradictory plurality, Reality a self-consistent unity.

Despite their distinctness, the two realms are not ontologically separable. Appearance *is* the Absolute in its various manifestations and thus the Absolute is an active principle within the world of human endeavours (*AR* 128). Since it is immanent *in* every Appearance, the Absolute can never be wholly inaccessible to experience. Yet because it is neither exhausted by, nor reducible to, its various manifestations the Absolute maintains its status as a transcendent authority to which humanity, and the rest of existence, is ultimately subservient. The Absolute, though distinct from Appearance is, unlike Spencer's Unknowable or Kant's (alleged) noumena, immune from the objections of the global sceptic.[2] Bradley's Absolutism thus dissolves the opposition between empiricism and transcendental idealism by incorporating the fundamental motivations of each in a higher unifying framework (*AR* 128–9).

Recognizing the role of the Absolute as a mediator between the poles of dichotomies is crucial to understanding Bradley's relation to Pragmatism. For Bradley is every bit as dissatisfied as Dewey with such dualisms as subject and object, fact and value, theory and practice. Yet it is over how to construe the unity of such oppositions that they radically diverge.

A. *Bradley on Theory and Practice*

For Bradley, all modes of experience emerge out of immediate experience, or, Feeling. Feeling presents, if somewhat inadequately, the kind of fusion of diversity characteristic of the Absolute. It is both qualitatively variegated and yet whole. The complexity of its content is undistinguished (*ETR* 157n.), yet there is a many felt in one (*ETR* 174).

The shifting contents of Feeling give rise to tensions that render its unity precarious. These tensions make relational modes of experience, such as Theory and Practice, both necessary (since they are the development of Feeling's uneasiness) and possible (since Feeling is their inescapable ground).

Theory and Practice involve distinct relations between self and other (*CE* 515). But since any such distinction between

---

[2] Global scepticism is undercut out because Bradley rules out the possibility of an ultimate sundering of subject and object (*ETR* 160–61; *AR* 222–3).

subject and object arises *within* Feeling, it cannot mark a contrast *between* Feeling and some noumenal world.[3] Feeling cannot of itself yield unmediated *knowledge* of reality, but it does ground unmediated *interaction* between subjects and objects.[4] As a result, Theory and Practice, though distinct, involve relations within a single totality and cannot be assigned to separate ontological realms (*ETR* 128).

In Theory, Feeling is intellectualized by holding its obscurely felt diversities apart; that is, by individuating objects and attending to their distinctive traits. Thought confers ideal content on substantive existents through the development of discrete categories out of an integrated whole. Thought does not copy Feeling, it transforms, requalifies and thus objectifies felt tensions (*ETR* 473). Thus, the world of objects is an addition to Feeling, an intellectual construct, not an antecedent reality revealed when Feeling is stripped away.

Yet Thought does not *invent* its objects or *project* its forms onto experience (*AR* 424–5). Rather the real and the ideal emerge out of Feeling as part of a single developmental process involving the self-realization of an object within a subject. In Thought, the knower feels her unity with the object and thus cooperates in the ideal development of reality (*ETR* 119), yet reality is passively received as an *independent* 'other'. Objects, although not immediately given, are passively disclosed. Thus, for Bradley, judgements *do* mirror reality in the sense that their objects, although constructed, function as independent variables, that is, as limited, finite, self-subsistent realities that determine, but are not determined by, thought (*ETR* 117).[5]

---

[3] The question of whether Feeling is in itself public or private, inner or outer, real or unreal cannot arise since, in its immediate presentness, Feeling is prior to all such distinctions and relations (*ETR* 247).

[4] Judgements of truth and falsity involve relations between subjects and objects. Feeling taken in its immediacy is non-relational and therefore is non-cognitive (ie. it is neither true nor false). In other words, for Bradley, what is immediate is not cognitive and what is cognitive is not immediate. However, since thought is Feeling brought to a higher level of significance one cannot get outside Feeling and thus the Absolute is always in some sense given (*ETR* 175, 247).

[5] 'One or more elements are separated from the confused mass of feeling, and stand apparently by themselves and over against this. And the distinctive character of such

In Practice, by contrast, the subject does not function passively, but rather as an agent of change defined in opposition to present reality (*CE* 517).[6] In its practical attitude, the self, possessed of an ideal identity, struggles against a resisting world in order to make reality over in its own image.[7] Present reality is taken, not as material to be inquired into, but as an obstacle to be overcome, as a medium through which to realize unactualized possibilities of self-expression. In Practice, then, it is the ideal Will that functions as an independent variable: that which determines, yet is not determined by, concrete existence.

The difference between Theory and Practice renders each autonomous in its own domain and thus irreducible. Theory can subserve Practice by supplying knowledge of a determinate reality that can guide the realization of our Wills. But truth does not consist in successful action. Practical success presupposes but is not equivalent to intellectual success (*AR* 135). Ends constitute facts as means, and thus determine their instrumental value, but instrumental value does not determine cognitive merit; truth is independent of practical interests.

Similarly, in cases where we will to know, Practice subserves Theory. In the pursuit of truth agents act to change the course of events in order to qualify reality ideally, but the required modification is to the subject's existence as knower, not to the object known. Thus Theory, although it involves

---

an object is that it seems simply to be...the perceptional relation is supposed to fall wholly outside the essence of the object. It is in short disregarded, or else dismissed as something accidental and irrelevant' (*AR* 408). 'The object has been qualified ideally, and this, again is an event which has happened in me. My existence has, as existence, been changed...but the existence of the object itself, on the other hand, has not been altered at all. It has become qualified not in fact but, as we say, ideally; while the actual change which has taken place belongs, we say, only to me' (*CE* 479). See also *PL* 500–510; *CE* 412, 521, 547; *ETR* 105, 108.

[6] Where present reality is 'that actual series of events which is either (a) now and here, or is (b) continuous with my here and now' (*CE* 478). In some cases this reality will be inside an agent's person.

[7] 'It is will when an idea produces its existence. A feature in present existence, not in harmony with that and working apart from it, gives itself another existence in which it is realized and where it is both idea and fact' (*CE* 272).

activity, is practical only incidentally (*CE* 272).[8] The desire to know is a non-practical want; a good the pursuit of which need not benefit humans in their practical endeavours.

The relative independence of Theory and Practice keeps inquiry free from the meddlesome influences of morality, religion and politics (*ETR* 11–12; *AR* 136); influences which, from the point of view of knowledge, are subjective since they are 'irrelevant to its end' (*ETR* 328).[9] Similarly, it keeps morality and religion free from the reductive tendencies of Scientism. Furthermore, since both Theory and Practice are distinct from Feeling, neither can substitute for, or be reduced to, lived experience in its qualitative immediacy (*ETR* 176).

Thus, for Bradley, Theory, Practice and Feeling are not ontologically distinct. Their difference lies in our attitudes toward, and interests in, reality, not in the realms of being we inhabit. Yet they are separate and independent modes of experience. Each is equally an aspect of our humanity that claims to possess special rights of its own and thus neither is intrinsically subordinate to the other.[10]

B. *The Self-Transcendence of Theory, Practice and Feeling*
Despite appearances Bradley does not sever all ties between the moral, the intellectual, and the sentient, for the independence of Theory, Practice and Feeling is merely relative (*ETR* 329). Each presents an aspect of Reality that is ultimately 'incomplete and one-sided, and calls for assistance from without' (*AR* 405). Since neither Theory, Practice nor Feeling is capable of being a self-sufficient endeavour each is confined

---

[8] The alteration of existence is implied inseparably in the being of truth, but truth does not consist in this alteration (*ETR* 84–5). See also *AR* 134.

[9] 'If there is to be philosophy its proper business is to satisfy the intellect, and the other sides of our nature have, if so, no right to speak directly. They must make their appeal not only to, but also through, the intelligence. In life it is otherwise, but there is a difference between philosophy and life' (*ETR* 221). 'My will and my conscience can in short no more tell me how I ought to pursue the truth, than they can show me how to ride a horse or play a piano' (*ETR* 11).

[10] 'Our nature is complex, and on the other hand our nature has and ought to have a unity, but its unity it not to be found by setting up one element as absolute, and by turning all the rest into mere external means' (*ETR* 99).

to the domain of Appearance.

As noted above, discord in Feeling requires reconciliation through the ordering of its yet-to-be-distinguished elements (*ETR* 269–70). Feeling's demand for content yields mediate relations and qualities (*AR* 201). Thus Feeling contains the seeds of its own transcendence.[11]

Similarly, the aim of thought is the ideal expression of the universe, at once coherent and comprehensive.[12] However, this aim is at odds with the relational form of thought. Judgements involve selections that are always situated within, and thus conditioned by, a broader context of Feeling. Yet as representations of reality judgements are mediate and thereby incapable of capturing Feeling in its immediate wholeness. Thus Thought must always be less than all-inclusive.

In addition, each judgement professes to represent a reality that is both self-subsistent and independent of the knower. Yet the ideal realization of an object in a subject is conditioned in ways at odds with these requirements. The historical development of the subject, though contingent and irrelevant to the content of the judgement, is, in the end, an essential precondition of reality's becoming *known* (*ETR* 326). Similarly, the nature of the known object is dependent upon its relations with all the things outside it that make it what it is, as it is (*AR* 408). Since judgements are inevitably situated in, and determined by, conditions (both inside the knower and outside the particular object judged) that form no part of their content, they are doomed to be incomplete. Thus Theory is self-contradictory: it can take place only under conditions that preclude theoretical satisfaction. Thought,

---

[11] Although we find no contradictions manifest in immediate experience we do find features which warrant the suggestion, from the point of view of thought, that the self-transcendence of Feeling is due to its inherent contradictions. Thus the wholeness of Feeling is not absolute, its content is not wholly pent up. See Saxena (1967), pp. 91–4.

[12] Comprehensiveness demands the inclusion of everything that is in any sense given; coherence demands that it be included intelligibly. At bottom these are one and the same project.

therefore, also contains the seeds of its own transcendence (*ETR* 331).

Finally, Practice, as noted above, has its origin in the conflict of ideality and existence that typifies the Apparent (*AR* 410). The opposition is not *created* by the self's ideal, rather that opposition presupposes an existent that positively excludes, and is therefore independent of, the self (*ETR* 47). As a result, neither the practical Will nor the present reality that resists it can be all-inclusive.

In addition, in order to be *operative* in the development of reality, practical ideals must penetrate the course of events; their realization must be immanent in, and facilitated by, present existential conditions. Yet, in order to *govern* the unfolding of reality, they must transcend given conditions (*ETR* 31). Thus practical ideals must actively 'be' and yet 'not be'.

Finally, once an ideal realizes itself in existence, its opposition to the real disappears and its regulative function ceases. Thus even if the goal of self-realization were completable 'the relation between [the ideal and the existent] would have disappeared, and Will, as such, must have vanished' (*AR* 410). As a result, Practice takes place only under conditions that fail to realize its ultimate aim and therefore it too contains the seeds of its own transcendence (*ETR* 6).

Since neither Theory, Practice nor Feeling is self-sufficient each implies a broader reality, that makes them possible, and that includes and ultimately perfects them. What is more, the realities that ultimately perfect Theory, Practice and Feeling must be one and the same.

Since every aspect of being must express itself intellectually, theoretical interests will not be fully satisfied unless practical interests are accounted for as well. To theorize away moral experience is not only empirically unjustified (*ETR* 219 n. 1) but, since volition involves a struggle between the self and reality, there can be no theoretical satisfaction until all unrealized practical ideals have either been fulfilled (and thus confirmed as genuine possibilities) or rejected as utopian fantasies.[13] Since the perfection of the theoretical attitude requires the transcendence of the duality of subject and object and since this involves the realization of the ideal, theoretical perfection would simultaneously be absolutely Good.

Similarly, Practical perfection implies complete theoretical satisfaction. A theoretical framework that denies any hope of self-realization or fails to provide accurate means to its achievement would be *useless* as a guide to action and thus fail to satisfy practical interests. Furthermore, the complete realization of practical ideals would imply the identity of the real and the ideal constitutive of absolute Truth.

Finally, the satisfaction of both Theory and Practice involves the transcendence of their relational forms and the fusion of meaning and sentience. Thus their final perfection implies an ultimate, stable resolution of the qualitative tensions which give rise to them.

Recognizing the necessity of an Absolute in which Theory and Practice are unified with Feeling does not contradict or undermine their relative independence. While thought can disclose the need for a supra-relational Reality and can discern its general features, it cannot reveal its particular details.[14] The Absolute does not function as a standard outside experience against which perfection can be gauged. However unity appears it must appear through the concrete struggles of situated subjects (*ETR* 224). Thus ignorance of the precise connection of thought, volition and feeling preserves their relative freedom in concrete circumstances (*ETR* 130).

---

[13] As Bradley notes 'there cannot in the Absolute be unsatisfied desire or any practical unrest. For in these there is clearly an ideal element not concordant with presentation but struggling against it... Any such state is not compatible with theoretical harmony' (*AR* 137).

[14] Metaphysics does deal with Reality as opposed to Appearance but these are not separate ontological categories. Philosophy is transcendent only in the sense that it systematizes elements of experience, not in the sense that it deals with a separate ontological realm. Thus Metaphysics is prior to concrete knowledge, but also inseparable from it. Metaphysics deals with the most general features of reality in a timeless way, but because of its generality is in need of concrete content. Thus although everything is ultimately interconnected Bradley says 'I cannot believe that we can see this implication in detail, so as everywhere to use the consequence (whatever consequence it is) as a criterion' (*ETR* 123). See also *ETR* 10; *AR* 140–41.

For Bradley, then, errors result, not when Theory, Practice and Feeling are distinguished, but only when they are treated as ultimate metaphysical categories. To privilege Theory, for example, is to treat knowing as more human than doing, to ignore that we are passionate and active, as well as, intellectual beings. While this is acceptable, indeed mandatory, when the aim is knowledge, it is unacceptable as a blueprint for living.

Yet Bradley does more than give Practice and Feeling equal time with Theory since their separation is ultimately transcended. Not only do we have separate volitional, cognitive and sentient faculties, each with its distinctive needs, but the fulfilment of each contributes to, and is ultimately dependent upon, the fulfilment of one's entire being. The unity of the Absolute requires the integration of these diverse ways of being in the world in a single coherent life, and the further communion of that life with the rest of creation. What is seen from within each domain as a contingent connection between Theory, Practice and Feeling is, from the point of view of metaphysics, a necessary one.

Thus Bradley has it both ways: by restricting the separation of these faculties to the domain of Appearance he preserves all that the traditional distinction was designed to do, while at the same time recognizing its inadequacy for characterizing a complete human being (*ETR* 123). Thought, action and feeling remain distinct aspects of life but none is its ultimate end.

Bradley's Response to Pragmatism[15]

Bradley was confused about the degree to which he was a Pragmatist. He is far from unsympathetic for he agrees that thought emerges out of, is continuous with, and involves, activity. He accepts that traditional philosophical dichotomies must be reinterpreted. He holds that the truth of an idea is inseparable from its theoretical results and that enlightenment philosophy is wrong to claim that Theory gives

---

[15] The key text on this subject is *ETR* chaps. 4–5.

us knowledge of a reality independent of all human needs.

Thus central tenets of Pragmatism seem to find a place within Bradley's system. The doctrines that Bradley claims do not fit are ones he finds to be dangerously ambiguous. For example, Bradley views Dewey's suspicion of the Absolute as a threat to objectivity in thought and to the unity of experience. But, claims Bradley, that suspicion derives from Dewey's failure to realize that the Absolute is not a thing-in-itself. Secondly, Bradley fears that Dewey's attempt to make theory more relevant to social practice threatens the independence of fact and value. But that danger is avoided on Bradley's view since he accepts the ultimate unity of theory and practice while at the same time insisting on the relative distinctness of their aims. Thirdly, Bradley insists that conceiving of truth as a species of the good forces Dewey to deny inherent value to knowledge. However, Bradley thinks that view is based only on the unpromising argument that because activity is essential to knowing, the aim of knowledge must itself be practical. Finally, by applying his own account of Practice and its ultimate end to Dewey's views, Bradley argues that Dewey's view of Theory as a species of Practice implies that knowing subjects determine truth and that reality is *made* rather than *discovered*!

Having clarified Pragmatism, Bradley thinks he can capture its insights while avoiding its dangers. Alas, what Bradley claims to do for Pragmatism, Dewey claims to do for Absolutism. Rather than reject Bradley's views outright, Dewey reinterprets them in terms that are more concrete and, to his mind, less dangerous. Thus Dewey claims to remain sympathetic to Bradley's general aim while at the same time radically transforming its philosophical underpinnings.

Dewey's Response to Absolutism[16]
Dewey pursues two independent lines of criticism against

---

[16] Dewey's works are referred to using the following abbreviations: *LI – Logic: The Theory of Inquiry*; *HOC – Human Nature and Conduct*; *IDP – The Influence of Darwin on Philosophy*; *P&C – Philosophy and Civilization*; *QC – The Quest for Certainty*; *EEL – Essays in Experimental Logic*; *DAP – 'The Development of American Pragmatism'*. References to Morganbesser (1977) are abbreviated by *DC*. The abbreviations are followed by the page numbers.

Bradley's Absolutism. The first is to show that Bradley's position is flawed internally. The second is to show that, properly construed, naturalism can satisfy Bradley's demand for a conception of experience that does justice both to the diversity and unity of life while at the same time rendering Absolutism obsolete. The strategy is to displace, rather than refute Bradley's view, and to abandon, rather than solve, the questions to which it is addressed (*IDP* 19).

To begin with, Dewey argues that after claiming to have undermined intellectualism, Bradley nonetheless exploits intellectualist methods in demonstrating the existence and character of the Absolute. The result is an equivocation on the sense in which the principle of non-contradiction is ultimate. The fact that thinking requires consistency suffices to establish it as an absolute virtue *within* thought. But having argued that the domain of thought is Appearance, Dewey claims Bradley cannot then exploit an intellectual principle to characterize a Reality transcending thought (*IDP* 120–24). Of course, Bradley would agree that consistency is an absolute criterion only within metaphysics, however, he would argue, since metaphysics is an intellectual endeavour, exclusive reliance on theoretical standards and interests is not only justified but mandatory. But Dewey insists that it is the reliance on principles of thought in determining the nature of the Absolute that is called into question by Bradley's anti-intellectualism.[17] What is more, from Dewey's point of view, Bradley inverts the proper order of investigation. Rather than using thought as a basis for inferring the general character of reality Dewey insists that philosophical conceptions of the nature and function of thought be based on empirical investigation into the material circumstances of its concrete operations.[18]

[17] Dewey writes: '[g]rant the premises as to the character of thought, and the assertion of the final character of the theoretical standard within metaphysics – since metaphysics is a form of theory – is a warning against metaphysics. If the intellect involves self-contradiction, it is either impossible that it should be satisfied, or else self-contradiction is its satisfaction' (*IDP* 128).

[18] Here Dewey, in his effort to cast Bradley as an intellectualist, is insensitive to Bradley's repeated appeals to experience in defence of his view. Furthermore, he is presupposing naturalism rather than proving it and thus this point is effective only in conjunction with a detailed naturalist account of thought. This account is discussed below.

Dewey also argues that since the Absolute cannot function as a criterion in relation to which conflicts among theories, or between theoretical and practical ends, can be mediated, it is a wheel that plays no role in the mechanism of concrete, critical deliberation. The fact that the Absolute is said to be immanent in experience cannot help to end controversies, for the Absolute has no voice independent of the disputing parties. If standards cannot be measured against the Absolute, their authority must be otherwise explained. Since even the principle of contradiction is contingent, that is, it validly operates only within a certain domain under certain specialized circumstances, the conditions under which it, and other norms, emerge and become authoritative in the course of particular inquiries remains to be investigated.

More generally, Dewey intimates that there is an underlying link between Bradley's Absolutism and his intellectualism, for it is only after insisting that Theory, Practice and Feeling are essentially independent in function and outcome, that the Absolute becomes necessary as a device for reuniting them. But, for Dewey, the characterization of the function of thought in abstraction from other organic functions (and vice versa) is undermined by Darwinian naturalism. What is more, the success of both Darwinian biology and experimental science in disclosing the concrete conditions that generate ideas, objects and values, and that determine their consequences, further challenges the need for, and usefulness of, transcendental explanatory principles.[19] In fact, Dewey insists that despite the importance of immediate experience in Bradley's metaphysics, his separation of Theory and Practice and his subordination of the concrete and the particular to the universal and the abstract threatens to deprive intellectual inquiry, and philosophy in particular, of an active role in the reconstruction of practices and institutions. By encouraging the reification of contingent products of inquiry as necessary constraints and by directing attention away from the concrete

---

[19] Dewey would add that the existence of such principles is further undermined by the diversity of styles of thought in history and across cultures and by the failure of philosophy to develop convincing candidates for such principles (see *IDP*, especially chapter 1).

historical conditions in which disputes arise and are resolved, Bradley perpetuates the isolation of intellectuals from the rest of culture. The requisite remedy, for Dewey, is to characterize inquiry as dynamic, contextual and active.[20]

Dewey's Cultural Naturalism
A. The Theory of Inquiry

Dewey characterizes inquiry as the:

> controlled or directed transformation of an indeterminate situation into one that is so determinate in its constituent distinctions and relations as to convert the elements of the original situation into a unified whole. (*LI* 108)

An indeterminate situation arises through the collision of the habits and interests of an organism and its surroundings. The organism and surroundings are *in* the situation, not the other way around; they are interrelated and interdefined aspects of an 'environment'. Organisms not only live next to their surroundings, but they live by means of their surroundings. The nature of organic functions is dependent upon, and determined in interaction with, the extra-organic field in which they are embedded. Similarly, the character of the surroundings is determined by the organic functions by which they are appropriated. Since, the properties of each *qua* environment are characterizable only in relation to the other, neither the surroundings nor the organism functions as an independent variable; their relation is, what Dewey calls, transactional.[21]

---

[20] 'Better it is for philosophy to err in active participation in the living struggles and issues of its own age and times than to maintain an immune monastic impeccability, without relevancy and bearing in the generating ideas of its contemporary present' (*P&C* 54).

[21] For example, an apple is food only in relation to organic structures capable of extracting nutrients from it. Yet those organic structures are a digestive system only in relation to material capable of sustaining life. Although the apple is capable of existing independently of any organism, its nutritive properties are determined only in relation to, and in interaction with, systems that lie outside it (and vice versa). Hence 'the processes of living are enacted by the environment as truly as by the organism; for they are an integration' (*LI* 32).

A situation is indeterminate by virtue of a disruption of environmental unity, that is, in the integration of organic activity and surrounding pressures. It is not that there is an uncertain response to a determinate reality, rather the organism is confused *because* the surroundings are confusing in relation to it; and the surroundings are confusing *because* their impingement on the activities of the organism yields no verdict as to what the situation demands in the way of response.

Indeterminacy is manifested as a qualitative urgency, a shock that is pre-cognitive; one that is *felt* before it is known. A situation is intellectualized only when it occasions inquiry, that is, when the environment is examined with a view to determining which of the possible behavioural responses is appropriate.[22] The aim of concrete inquiries, for Dewey the *object* of knowledge, is not a passive representation of given reality but a transformation of situational elements into a definite means for achieving a unified environment. Activity is not deferred in inquiry, it is redirected towards the solution of the concrete problem that forms its immediate end-in-view.

Only in relation to a diagnosis can ideas and actions be evaluated as definite solutions and only in relation to the conditions that occasion inquiry can problems be made definite and the relevance of diagnoses be assessed. The aim of observation and hypothesis is not to include all of reality, but to *select* features *relevant* to the problem at hand. Thus observation and hypotheses are constructive and valuational: each is guided by the aim of the particular inquiry and in turn serves to render that end more definite. The products of each are evaluated in terms of their ability to *function* reliably in directing activity towards consummation.[23]

---

[22] Since anomalous experiences can arise only against a background of stable organic–environmental integrations, no situation is indeterminate in every respect.

[23] Only in relation to a theory is experience constituted as evidence, that is as signs that indicate appropriate reactions to future courses of events. Only in relation to concrete signs are theories evaluated as plausible solutions. Thus observation and hypothesis are transactional processes.

Although hypotheses originate in observation, as solutions they refer to unactualized conditions of a unified environment. They are projected meanings, or visionary ways of viewing a world in which current problems are overcome. Therefore they embody expectations about the outcomes of various courses of action that constitute testable consequences.

An experiment is an active intervention in the course of events that carries out a hypothetical plan of action. The conditions under which the hypothesis is claimed to effect its guiding function are brought about and the concrete changes that are thereby produced serve as a measure of its reliability. When inquiry is successful brute resistance is requalified as a set of signs with determinate meanings.[24] The significance of the result lies not merely in the presence of new ways of relating to the surroundings (a new environment) but in the fact that this resultant integration is the *product* of, and thus continuous with, deliberately directed *action*:

> The objective reality which tests the truth of the idea is not one which externally antecedes or temporally coexists with the idea, but one which succeeds it, being its fulfilment as intent and method: *its* success, in short. (*DC* 206)

Thus hypotheses are not verified against reality, rather it is reality-as-interpreted that is evaluated through the enactment of a unitary environment. Since meanings are transactional, determinacy is achieved in interaction with the surroundings. The distinction between the situations before and after successful inquiry, is not between an indeterminate subjective appearance and a determinate antecedently existing reality, it

---

[24] Thus, in judgement the real (the subject, that is, the antecedent conditions of inquiry) is (re)qualified by the ideal (the anticipatory interpretation of the meaning of the given elements), the copula of the judgement stands for the concrete organic act by which the connection is made between the fact and its signification. The object of the judgement is the original situation transformed, a situation which implies a change as well in the original subject as in the environment itself. 'The function of intelligence is therefore not that of copying the objects of the environment, but rather of taking account of the way in which more effective and more profitable relations with these objects may be established in the future' (*P&C* 30).

is between two distinct but continuous environments (*QC* 83–4).[25]

B. *Theory and Practice*

While Dewey insists that inquiry is a form of practical deliberation, he remains cognizant of the intuitions behind Bradley's distinction of Theory and Practice. But for Dewey the distinction is one of subject-matter rather than of logic, psychology, or ontology. The contrast is between scientific and common-sense contexts of inquiry.

Common-sense inquiries involve matters relating to the use, enjoyment and appreciation of objects in coordination with others and in ways that sustain subjects socially, personally, organically and even aesthetically (*LI* 66–8). They are self-consciously teleological since they treat objects in relation to the particular aims, desires and tastes of particular individuals or groups. These valuations form the conditions under which common-sense problems emerge, and are also elements out of which solutions to those problems are developed. Insofar as common-sense modes of practice guide stable environmental transactions, they constitute an objective finality for everyday life.

In science, however, common-sense solutions become problems to be solved, subject-matter to be inquired into and explained. Science relates to objects, not in abstraction from practical ends altogether, but from particular kinds of valuations, specifically those relating to the immediate use and enjoyment of objects by particular individuals and communities.[26] Science does not escape the common-sense world,

---

[25] Of course, each subsequent re-enactment of a verified idea presupposes its general reliability. Since no two situations are identical, there is no guarantee that ideas will be resilient to further interrogation. The conclusions of one inquiry form the contextual frame in which subsequent problems emerge, and thus provide part of the resources out of which novel solutions are constructed. Thus each idea is provisional and forever open to (re)development, (re)qualification and (re)validation through use.

[26] This does not mean that relations in the common-sense world among individuals and between individuals and objects cease to operate in science. Science itself is institutionally organized and is therefore implicated in economic, social and political relations. Similarly, the acts of scientists do not cease to have economic, social and political consequences. Acts of inquiry, like all other actions for Dewey, are complex and describable in a number of potentially conflicting ways.

rather it examines it with an eye to determining the conditions upon which common-sense values and experiences depend.

Science and common sense are distinct modes of objectification but the distinction is one of context, function, and subject-matter, rather than ontological status or epistemic authority. Because objects are constituted by their operational significance, that is, by their incorporation in purposeful activities, reality is plural to the degree that the practices through which meaningful integrations between organisms and surroundings are secured are plural. Yet these diverse practices are continuous. Just as common sense serves as a framework for scientific activity, scientific results transform common-sense concepts and practices. The two are inseparable and evolve in critical integration.[27]

But for Dewey the continuity of science and common sense is not a timeless metaphysical unity, it is a problem to be solved and re-solved in response to the concrete strains, tensions and conflicts that emerge within, and between, them as their respective contents evolve.

Dewey's Relation to Bradley

Affinities between Dewey and Bradley are not hard to find.[28] Both agree that thought and action emerge out of, are immersed in and bounded by immediate qualitative experience. Thus for both there can be no transcending experience, no ultimate sundering of subject and object, appearance and reality. Similarly both agree that meaning is

---

[27] Dewey thus preserves the autonomy of the operation of thought, 'yet so connects it with other activities as to give it a serious business, real purpose, and concrete responsibility and hence testability. From this point of view the theoretical activity is simply the form which certain practical activities take after colliding, as the most effective and fruitful way of securing their own harmonization. The collision is not theoretical; the issue in "peaceable unity" is not theoretical. But theory names the type of activity by which the transformation from war to peace is most amply and securely effected' (*IDP* 127).

[28] Dewey and Bradley themselves suggest that each is within a hair's breadth of agreement, yet each is equally adamant that, in this case, a miss is as good as a mile. Comparisons of the two can be found in Bradley (1984), Mack (1945) and Thayer (1981).

a product of the functional interaction of elements in broader organic totalities. Thus meaning involves the requalification and functional integration of experience, not merely the association of given atomistic sensa. Finally, for both, the paradigm of fulfilment is experience in which thought and volition are consummated in a pervasive, qualitative unity.

Nonetheless, as Dewey notes, it is Bradley's inability to break with the Spectator Theory of Knowledge that underlies his reading and rejection of Pragmatism. Despite his historicism and constructivism, Bradley insists that knowledge is a passive representation of a ready-made world and that practical reasoning is (relatively) independent of inquiry into how things are. What is more, Bradley's Absolute, although continuous with experience, remains an Archimedean point which is intended to underwrite and explain Theory and Practice by fixing the ends of humanity. Although the historical perspectives of knowers change, there remains an immutable end that absolutely determines the limits of the perfectibility of each point of view and thereby fixes the limits of pluralism. The result is a closed universe governed by principles intended to provide ahistorical conditions for any possible historical development. Contingency, history and activity thus remain subordinate to necessity, finality and determinacy.

Dewey's Pragmatism signals a radical transformation of Bradley's method and ontology. First, viewing thought, volition and feeling as intermediaries in the development by living organisms of responses to the environment adequate to their needs, focuses attention on the particular conditions under which concrete ends emerge, are projected and fulfilled. Thus rather than proceed by means of an abstract analysis of what Reality must be like in order to satisfy at large equally abstract human needs, Dewey investigates the conditions that satisfy particular people in particular situations. The generality of principles of thought and conduct does not derive from their relation to equally general and abstract ends. Rather, it is a matter of the relative insensitivity of the operational success of particular modes of response to variations in the concrete conditions under which they were originally developed.[29] So-called timeless truths and principles are, for Dewey, simply those that have proven themselves in a broad range of situations. Their worth is viewed not as dependent upon, nor explained by, their inherent perfection as manifestations of an Absolute, but as due to their ability to function practically in a variety of concrete, problematic contexts. The capacity of methods and principles to produce a unified environment is always a function of some limited set of contingent conditions. Thus they are to be viewed as rules of art, or habits, the value of which is constantly produced and reproduced through critical extension in new situations. To know when to extend, ignore or amend entrenched habits in the face of concrete recalcitrant experience is a creative and ineliminable part of life.

Secondly, Dewey's insistence that Theory is a mode of Practice, goes beyond Bradley's acknowledgement that knowing involves activity. For Dewey, action is not accidentally related to thought, for the development and control of action to secure a unified experience is the function of knowledge (*DC* 212); in abstraction from all practical interests there is no meaning at all.[30] Thus the instrumental is not to be contrasted with the cognitive for the authority of knowledge is *constituted*, not merely exemplified, by its active role in reconstructing problematic situations. The discovery of reliable ways of relating to the surroundings is not a fortuitous byproduct of successful inquiry, it is the *object* of successful inquiry.[31] Hence, Bradley's claim that ideas work

---

[29] For example, for Dewey, the aim of inquiry is never 'Truth, its object is never Reality at large, it is always the attainment of a resolution of a particular problem. Abstracted from concrete contexts of inquiry, Truth is devoid of content.

[30] Dewey writes, 'meanings in their logical quality are standpoints, attitudes, and methods of behaving toward acts and thus active experimentation is essential to verification' (*EEL* 332). Thus ideas and desires prove themselves to be real forces in the transformation of reality. 'Is it not rather true that the "knowledge" is instituted and framed in anticipation of the consequent issue, and, in degree in which it is wise and prudent, is held open to revision during it?' (*P&C* 42).

[31] Note that the end of thought is neither 'mere' activity; nor personal interest and profit. The methods of inquiry are 'pragmatic' because they are rules of art which are based on experience, are applicable to experience, and make reference to a definite human purpose (*DAP* 24). 'Practical' concerns the nature of knowing, not the nature of the consequences. Pragmatism requires that the final meaning and test of thought lies in its consequences but the consequences may be aesthetic, moral, political or religious; they need not be narrowly practical.

because they are True is, on Dewey's view, as empty as the claim that ideas are able to work because inquirers fashion ideas able to work. Yet inquiry, as means, is not externally related to its end-in-view, for the result has significance and cognitive authority only as the fulfilment of the conditions and processes out of which it developed and with which it is continuous. Thus, physical, biological and social conditions of thought do not merely facilitate judgements, they determine their significance.

Finally, Dewey surrenders the notion of a ready-made world. In inquiry situational elements (both the habits of the subject and the surroundings to which they are related) are inquired into in an effort to discern their meaning. But as meanings are transactional, the process of discovery is not a matter of uncovering a reality that is *under*determined by evidence, it is a matter of reconstructing a situation that is *in*determinate. Determinacy is a project to complete not a metaphysical principle or an antecedent unity to be disclosed. To modify our being-in-the-world in ways that carry forward current projects is to *make* reality significant by bringing about meaningful interaction with it. But such interactions are not timeless, they are produced in concrete situations by particular, historically-constituted agents and subject to readjustment in response to changing circumstances. Since reality functions significantly only as the product of an active determination, its meaning marks a creative achievement.[32] But the project of meaning is precarious. Growth and fulfilment are never assured, tragedy, stagnation, and even atrocity remain real possibilities.

For Dewey, then, authority and necessity are contingent, historical and active. Reality is not only emergent, but unfinished, open-ended, precarious and creative. The significance of existence is a project in which humans participate, rather

---

[32] 'Consequently reason, or thought, in its more general sense, has a real, though limited, function, a creative, constructive function. If we form general ideas and if we put them in action, consequences are produced which could not be produced otherwise. Under these conditions the world will be different from what it would have been had not thought intervened... It makes the world really more reasonable; it gives to it an intrinsic value' (*DAP* 33–4).

than a finished work to be passively contemplated or actively approximated, and it is in furthering particular creative projects that the source and measure of normative authority lies. While there is no end to Inquiry, Life, Culture or Humanity, there are ends in inquiries, lives, cultures and global populations. Such ends are historically conditioned and thus potentially problematic and conflictual, but they are not any less authoritative for being contingent. The fusion of perspectives Bradley seeks is, for Dewey, not to be sought through, or explained by, appeal to an Absolute framework, it is a problem to be solved through intelligent reconstruction of individual and social practices. The unity of experience is not a metaphysical principle, it is a pressing social and global concern, involving, in part the need to overcome the alienation of subjects (including family members, workers, students and citizens) from their surroundings by intelligent and deliberate means. Indeterminate and confused is what both we and our environment *are* but it is not what we or it are condemned to be.

The exchange between Dewey and Bradley, though confined to a relatively few pages, nonetheless marks a significant episode in the playing out of conflicts and tensions that emerge in the nineteenth century. Bradley and Dewey start from a shared desire to unify idealism and naturalism in an effort to find a place for value in a world of facts. Yet it is because their efforts end up in distinctive and opposed syntheses that each can lay claim to being a significant critical and formative influence on the other. Thus Bradley's charges of crude instrumentalism, and Dewey's counterSalvages of crude intellectualism, belie a debate considerably more subtle and broader in scope than either author represents.

The debate is also of significance for its similarity, in part, to contemporary debates about the nature of authority. Philosophers (metaphysical and 'internal' realists, for example) that situate *under*determined, *under*developed, and therefore, fallible subjects in a *determinate* universe share Bradley's desire, if not his specific view, for predetermined constraints that legitimate and explain beliefs, values and practices. On the other hand, contemporary friends of contingency (such as Rorty, Latour, and Hernstein Smith), follow

Dewey by situating *in*determinate, *open-ended*, *in*complete, and therefore, fallible subjects in an *indeterminate* universe. To the former, rejection of the transcendent seems like a nihilistic overreaction to the historical turn. To pragmatists, hankering after absolutes seems like wish-fulfilment; the reification of needs that are better abandoned. To this debate over how to reconcile the antinomy between the immanence and the transcendence of normative authority, the exchange between Dewey and Bradley can be seen as a significant precursor.

BIBLIOGRAPHY

Alexander, T. M. (1987). *John Dewey's Theory of Art, Experience and Nature: The Horizons of Feeling*, SUNY Series in Philosophy (Albany, New York: SUNY Press).

Bradley, J. (1984). 'F. H. Bradley's Metaphysics of Feeling and its Place in the History of Philosophy', in A. Manser and G. Stock (eds.), *The Philosophy of F. H. Bradley* (Oxford University Press).

Dewey, J. (1907). 'Reality and The Criterion for the Truth of Ideas', *Mind*, vol. 16, no. 63, pp. 317–42.

────── (1910). *The Influence of Darwin on Philosophy and Other Essays in Contemporary Thought* (New York: Henry Holt and Company).

────── (1916). *Essays in Experimental Logic* (University of Chicago Press).

────── (1922). *Human Nature and Conduct* (New York: Random House Inc.).

────── (1929). *The Quest for Certainty*, The Gifford Lectures (New York: Perigree Books).

────── (1930). 'From Absolutism to Experimentalism', in G. Adams and W. Montague (eds.), *Contemporary American Philosophy*, volume 2 (New York: Macmillan and Co.), pp. 13–27.

────── (1931). *Philosophy and Civilization* (New York: Minton, Birch and Co.).

―――― (1982). 'The Development of American Pragmatism', in H. S. Thayer (ed.), *Pragmatism: The Classic Writings* (Indianapolis: Hackett Publishing Company), pp. 23–40.

―――― (1986). *Logic: The Theory of Inquiry*, in J. Boydston (ed.), *John Dewey: The Later Works, 1925–53*, volume 12, 1938 (Carbondale, Illinois: Southern Illinois University Press).

Mack, R. (1945). *The Appeal to Immediate Experience: Philosophic Method in Bradley, Whitehead and Dewey* (Freeport, New York: Books for Libraries Press).

Morganbesser, S. (ed.) (1977). *Dewey and His Critics: Essays from the Journal of Philosophy* (New York: The Journal of Philosophy Inc.).

Saxena, S. (1967). *Studies in the Metaphysics of Bradley*, Muirhead Library of Philosophy (London: George Allen and Unwin Ltd).

Thayer, H. S. (1981). *Meaning and Action: A Critical History of Pragmatism* (Indianapolis: Hackett Publishing Company).

BRADLEY'S CONTRIBUTION TO THE DEVELOPMENT OF LOGIC

Nicholas Griffin

I

There are two widely held, diametrically opposed, views on Bradley's contributions to modern logic. The first is that he made none. Indeed, some go even further and say that Bradley was an important obstacle which had to be removed before modern logic could be developed. The second view, is that in many small ways Bradley did contribute to the development of modern logic. Neither view seems to me entirely satisfactory. Parts II and III of this paper will be concerned with two respects in which I think Bradley had an important influence on the development of logic. The first is his demolition of psychologism, or at least of a certain type of psychologism.[1] In this I think he was absolutely right, although nowadays, as moves are made to naturalize epistemology, we are in danger of forgetting the lessons he taught and of ignoring (what seems to me) the overwhelming force of the arguments he used. The second contribution I want to look at is his critique of Jevons's equational logic. In this we have learned his lessons so well that we have forgotten that he ever taught them.

This section of the paper, however, will be devoted to some of the issues raised by the second view: that Bradley contributed, but not much; that his contributions lay in matters of detail, local concerns rather than global ones. The

---

[1] This has been noted by Manser, 'Bradley and Frege', in A. Manser and G. Stock (eds.), *The Philosophy of F. H. Bradley* (Oxford: Clarendon Press, 1984) and by Richard Wollheim, *F. H. Bradley* (Harmondsworth: Penguin, 1969), pp. 24–8. See also the papers by Ferreira and Wilson in this volume.

evidence here is problematic. It comes mainly from two sources: a number of acknowledgements to Bradley from Russell[2] and a number of features in modern logic for which antecedents of some kind can be found in Bradley. To my knowledge, there is nothing in Bradley's entire corpus that was taken over without substantial modification into modern logic. But this, obviously, does not entail that he had no influence. The formerly dominant Whig history of logic portrayed its development as a gradual accumulation of doctrines towards the goal of classical logic (perhaps with modal embellishments) with a bivalent worlds semantics and a sharp object/meta distinction (the classical paradigm). Such an account makes for simple-minded views about who contributed and who did not: namely that an author contributed only if he added to the doctrines that make up the classical paradigm. But, first, there is more to logic than the classical paradigm; and, second, even those who contributed to the paradigm in decisive ways did not always do so by supplying one or more of its doctrines fully formed and ready for incorporation. The paradigm was built up through a process of adjustment and correction with the result that doctrines were rarely incorporated in exactly the form in which they were first proposed.

This makes the question of who contributed what, and the related but different question of influence, very much more complicated. This is certainly true in Bradley's case. For a number of Bradley's original doctrines find some echo (to put it as weakly as possible) in the classical paradigm, though none, as I've said, are actually part of that paradigm. Three such doctrines, in particular, have been discussed in the literature and I shall concentrate on them, before suggesting some further possible points of influence which, to my knowledge, have hitherto been overlooked. The most discussed of Bradley's possible contributions to logic is his analysis of

---

[2] The question of Bradley's influence on modern logic can be reduced very largely to the question of his influence on Russell. To my knowledge, Russell was the only modern logician of major significance on whose work Bradley was a direct and important influence.

universal (A-form) propositions. Bradley says that 'every such judgement is concerned with adjectivals', 'it does not assert the existence of the subject or predicate, but simply the connection between the two':

> In 'Equilateral triangles are equiangular' all I affirm is that with one set of qualities you will have the other set... The abstract universal, '*A* is *B*', means no more than 'given *A*, in that case *B*', or 'if *A*, then *B*'. In short, such judgements are always hypothetical and can never be categorical.
> (*PL* 82)

Wollheim says that 'This... is the view of universal propositions that was taken up by Russell, and through him had so powerful an influence on modern logic'.[3] But evidently it is not itself the view of universal propositions that is to be found in modern logic. One problem, indeed, is that it is difficult to be clear from the above passage just what position Bradley wants to defend – almost any view could find elements to commend in Bradley's account. He holds, first, that universal judgements assert a connection between a subject and a predicate – ordinary subject-predicate judgements do no less; then that they assert an implication between *A* and *B* where '*A*' and '*B*' are (perhaps) subject and predicate or (perhaps) qualities; and finally that they are not categorical but hypothetical. In fairness, a later passage is less ambiguous and (apparently) more modern: In the judgement 'Animals are mortal' we mean, Bradley tells us, '*Whatever is an animal will die*, but that is the same as *If* anything is an animal *then* it is mortal. The assertion is about mere hypothesis; it is not about fact' (*PL* 47). The first sentence of this passage requires only the addition of variables and an account of the quantifiers to yield the modern view.

And yet, when Bradley's account is placed within the wider context of his philosophy, its similarity to the modern account

---

[3] *op. cit.*, p. 48n. Wollheim's claim is taken up by H. B. Acton, in a review of Wollheim, *Philosophical Books*, vol. 1 (1960), p. 21; and by C. N. Keen, 'The Interaction of Russell and Bradley', *Russell: The Journal of the Bertrand Russell Archives*, vol. 3 (1971), pp. 7–11.

is not so great, as Scarrow has pointed out.[4] In the first place, Bradley's account of universal judgements quoted above is only a preliminary analysis, ultimately all judgements, for Bradley, have a different form and there is no clear distinction between hypothetical (universal) and categorical (singular) judgements. For the classical paradigm, however, the analysis is ultimate and the distinction between universal and singular propositions is final. Secondly, for Bradley all hypothetical judgements involve inference; whereas, the modern treatment of universal propositions construes them as universally quantified conditionals. Thirdly, Bradley goes on to say that on his preliminary analysis 'All animals are mortal' is categorical, not hypothetical, if by 'all animals' we mean 'each actual animal, or the real sum of existing animals' (*PL* 47; cf. also 82–3). On the classical paradigm, quantified variables range only over existing items, yet the proposition remains a universally quantified conditional.

Nonetheless, Wollheim's claim about Bradley's influence is not unfounded. It stems from a number of published remarks by Russell (confirmed apparently by Russell's reminiscences to Wollheim).[5] The first of Russell's published acknowledgements is in 'On Denoting':

> Consider next the proposition 'all men are mortal'. This proposition ['As has been ably argued in Mr. Bradley's *Logic*, Book I, Chap. II.', Russell adds in a footnote] is really hypothetical and states that *if* anything is a man, it is mortal. That is, it states that if x is a man, x is mortal, whatever x may be.[6]

---

[4] D. S. Scarrow, 'Bradley's Influence upon Modern Logic', *Philosophy and Phenomenological Research*, vol. 22 (1962), pp. 380–82. My first two arguments are taken from Scarrow, the third is not. Scarrow also gives three reasons, but two of his are so closely connected I have not distinguished them.

[5] Wollheim, *F. H. Bradley*, op. cit., p. 49n.

[6] 'On Denoting' (1905) in R. C. Marsh (ed.), *Logic and Knowledge* (London: Allen and Unwin, 1956), p. 43. Russell, who did distinguish between implication and inference (cf. *The Principles of Mathematics* (London: Allen and Unwin, 1964; 1st ed., 1903), pp. 34–5), presumably did not mean by 'hypothetical' quite what Bradley meant.

He writes at greater length in 'Mathematical Logic as based on the Theory of Types' where he criticizes the traditional subject-predicate analysis of A-form propositions:

> If this view were right, it would seem that 'all men are mortal' could not be true if there were no men. Yet, as Mr. Bradley has urged, 'Trespassers will be prosecuted' may be perfectly true even in no one trespasses; and hence, as he further argues, we are driven to interpret such propositions as hypothetical, meaning 'if anyone trespasses, he will be prosecuted'; ie., 'if x trespasses, x will be prosecuted', where the range of values which x may have, whatever it is, is certainly not confined to those who really trespass.[7]

Interestingly, in *Our Knowledge of the External World* Russell attributes to Frege and Peano the view that 'Socrates is mortal' and 'All men are mortal' are not of the same form.[8] This brought a pained letter from Bradley complaining that he had been overlooked, *not* as the originator of the modern analysis of universal propositions, but as having recognized that not all propositions were of subject-predicate form.[9] Russell's response has not survived, but he did not credit Bradley in subsequent writings, so far as I know. In *My Philosophical Development* he says he learnt that the two sentences were of different form from Peano and then discovered afterwards that Frege had anticipated them both.[10]

The question of the logical form of universal propositions is a relatively simple and circumscribed one, yet even it supplies startling possibilities for confusion and misunderstanding. If Russell got the idea from Peano, how could

---

[7] *Logic and Knowledge, op. cit.*, p. 70. A briefer passage to the same effect appears in 'The Philosophy of Logical Atomism', *ibid.*, p. 237 (*Collected Papers of Bertrand Russell*, vol. 8, *The Philosophy of Logical Atomism and Other Essays 1914–19*, ed. John G. Slater, London: Allen and Unwin, 1986, p. 208).

[8] *Our Knowledge of the External World* (London: Allen and Unwin, 1972; 1st ed., 1914), p. 50.

[9] F. H. Bradley to Bertrand Russell, 27 September 1914 (Russell Archives, McMaster University).

[10] Bertrand Russell, *My Philosophical Development* (London: Allen and Unwin, 1959), p. 66.

Bradley have been an influence? And if he wasn't an influence, why was it that Russell acknowledged him? The answers become a bit clearer when we consider Russell's earliest views. Russell first stated the view that universal propositions are not of subject-predicate form as his own in 1898 – before he had read Peano. In 1898 he treated universal propositions as implications holding between predicates; for example, 'all men are mortal' asserts 'human implies mortal'. Such judgements he called 'pure judgements of intension'.[11] Now this account is obviously very close to Bradley's view that universal judgements are 'concerned with adjectivals' and 'assert a connection between elements of content'.[12] Moreover, there is no reason to doubt that Russell's account in 1898 was indeed derived almost entirely from Bradley.

Russell's pure judgements of intension are quite different from subject-predicate judgements. It looks, therefore, as if Russell was just mistaken when he said he got the idea that the two judgements were of different types from Peano. But even this is too simple. For shortly afterwards, Russell retracted the account of pure judgements of intension he had given in 'An Analysis of Mathematical Reasoning'. In his book on Leibniz, also written before he'd read Peano, Russell treated A-form propositions as a variety of subject-predicate proposition, though not of exactly the same form as 'Socrates is mortal'. In 'All men are mortal' he held that a predicate was asserted of a concept (whereas in singular judgements the predicate was asserted of a thing).[13] This was certainly a retrograde move. On this theory 'all men are mortal' has the form 'human is mortal'. But this is an odd subject-predicate judgement by anyone's standards, for, if it has a subject, it is not the subject (viz. the concept 'human') to which the predicate applies. Russell was led to adopt it because the only

---

[11] 'An Analysis of Mathematical Reasoning' (1898), in Nicholas Griffin and Albert C. Lewis (eds.), *The Collected Papers of Bertrand Russell*, vol. 2, *Philosophical Papers: 1896–99* (London: Hyman Unwin, 1990), p. 172.

[12] PL 82. Bradley's term 'adjective', which Russell used frequently in earlier works, is replaced by 'predicate' or 'meaning' in Russell's writings from 1898 on.

[13] *A Critical Exposition of the Philosophy of Leibniz* (London: Allen and Unwin, 1975; 1st ed., 1900), pp. 17–18.

alternative he knew at the time was Bradley's view which required that predicates could occur as the terms of an implication relation. His study of Peano showed that a third view was possible.

Russell's study of Peano returned him to a position which was closer to the one he had had originally from Bradley, though with some crucial changes. The most important of these was the use of variables, of which there is no trace in Bradley but which are essential for the modern theory. Yet the theory he arrived at with Peano's help was not the modern theory either, for, as yet, Russell lacked the modern concept of the quantifier. A-form propositions were treated in *The Principles of Mathematics* (p. 6) by means of the concept of formal implication, in the way Russell explains in the passages quoted above from 'On Denoting' and 'Mathematical Logic'. There are a number of obscurities in Russell's account of formal implication. Scarrow (*op. cit.*, p. 381) treats it as a metalinguistic notion asserting that all implications of the form 'if x is a man then x is mortal' are true. From the point of view of the classical paradigm this has much to commend it, yet the point is anachronistic since the lack of a clear object/meta distinction is one of the cardinal features of the *Principles*. There Russell treats formal implication either as the assertion that all of a class of implications are true or as a relation holding between propositional functions.[14] What he does not suggest in the *Principles* is that they are implications holding between predicates or meanings, which had been his position in 1898. It was perhaps this divergence that led him not to acknowledge Bradley's influence in the *Principles*.

Though Bradley did not discover the modern analysis of A-form propositions, he did clearly influence Russell who, with some difficulty, did discover it.[15] Yet the influence was a

---

[14] The absence of an object/meta distinction in the *Principles* may well explain Russell's lack of concern that Bradley treats A-form propositions as hypothetical while the modern view treats them as universally quantified conditionals – a difference that Scarrow emphasizes. The concept of formal implication tends to blur this distinction.

[15] Or close enough. From the point of view of the classical paradigm, even the quantification theory of *Principia Mathematica* is a bit odd.

much more complex process than has been supposed. To begin with, Russell accepted that there could be true propositions asserting an implication relation between two predicates, and this allowed him a very Bradleyan account of A-form propositions. Later he came to reject the idea that predicates could truly imply one another and with it his earlier account of A-form propositions. Eventually, from Peano, he learnt how to avoid the implication of predicates by the introduction of variables and the correlative concept of a propositional function. And this enabled him to adopt an account of A-form propositions which is both very close to the modern one and at the same time rather closer to the Bradleyan position he had started from than was the position he had held in the interim in his *Leibniz*.

Bradley's analysis of A-form propositions commits him to another doctrine of importance for modern logic: the distinction between grammatical and logical form.[16] Evidently, the immediate constituent analysis of 'All men are mortal' will be of the form [NP] + [VP], which is clearly not the form Bradley would want to ascribe to it. Bradley does make the required distinction explicitly: he distinguishes, eg. between the grammatical subject of a judgement and its 'ultimate' subject (*PL* 22; cf. also 42). It is clear also that the distinction was very important in Russell's philosophy after 1905 when the discovery of logical forms was seen as a large part of the task of philosophy (or at least of the philosophy of logic).

It is important, however, not to overestimate Bradley's importance here. In the *Principles of Mathematics*, Russell thought that grammatical form and logical coincided much more frequently than Bradley supposed:

> The study of grammar...is capable of throwing far more light on philosophical questions than is commonly supposed by philosophers. Although a grammatical distinction cannot be uncritically assumed to correspond to a genuine

---

[16] Cf. Anthony Manser, *Bradley's Logic* (Oxford: Blackwell, 1983), p. 103.

philosophical difference, yet the one is prima facie evidence of the other. (p. 42)

This could be taken as a rebuke to Bradley, who had abandoned grammar as a guide to logical form in favour of metaphysics. It was Russell's discovery of the theory of incomplete symbols and the method of contextual definition that made the distinction between grammatical and logical form of real importance to Russell. Nor did Russell's views on logical form after 1905 coincide with Bradley's. In this case, it is not sufficient merely to point out that both philosophers held such a distinction. *Any* philosopher who applies a logic to natural language will require some such distinction. For the logic, if it is to serve any purpose, will obviously presuppose a certain amount of regimentation of natural language.[17] This would be as true for a traditional logician employing syllogistic as for a modern logician employing classical logic. The novelty in modern logic in this respect lies neither in the fact that it made the distinction between grammatical and logical form, nor in the extent of the discrepancies it found between them, but in the nature of those discrepancies.

On this last point, however, something can be said for Bradley's contributions. Unlike the traditional logician, who is obliged to recast all judgements in subject-predicate form, Bradley admits much greater diversity. Apart from universal judgements, Brenda Jubin[18] notes three types of judgement which Bradley thought were not of subject-predicate form: relational judgements, existential judgements, and judgements about non-existents. All three classes of judgement were of especial importance in the development of modern logic – certainly no less important than universal judgements – yet

---

[17] Even grammar requires some distinction along these lines, since it is not the task of a grammar (much less of a logic) merely to catalogue the utterances people actually make. Chomsky's distinction between competence and performance, is an initial step toward such a distinction; the common grammatical distinction between surface and deep structure takes us a good deal further.

[18] 'F. H. Bradley on Referring', *Southern Journal of Philosophy*, vol. 14 (1976), pp. 157–68.

when we look more closely at what Bradley has to say about them we find, once more, that his claims to modernity are ambiguous.

Consider, first, relational judgements. In 'most cases' of putatively relational judgements, he says, 'the ideal content, asserted or denied, will fall into the arrangement of a subject with adjectival qualities', though in other cases, 'the content takes the form of two or more subjects with adjectival relations existing between them' (*PL* 22). So far so good, in order to recognize the importance of relations it is not necessary to insist that every proposition which, in its grammatical form, contains a relation will also contain one when analysed into its logical form. But Bradley, even in the *Logic*, is less committed to relations than this suggests. He goes on to claim that a relational judgement may be 'tortured' into subject predicate form or into a form which makes the 'relation the subject, and [predicates] all the remainder as attribute' (*PL* 22). Relations, it seems, are not indispensable for Bradley; all he seems prepared to concede is that in 'most cases' a relational analysis of judgements like '*A* and *B* are simultaneous', and '*C* and *D* lies east and west' (*PL* 22) is more natural than some other analysis into which they may be 'tortured'. He can hardly be faulted over much for failing to give a general account of how and why this distinction between natural and tortured analyses is to be drawn, for the classical paradigm scarcely does better in motivating its own distinction between grammatical and logical form.[19] But on the specific topic of relations Bradley does offer less than the classical paradigm. For he nowhere recognizes that essential formal features of relational judgements are lost on a subject-predicate analysis – unless, that is, the predicate is regarded as syntactically and semantically complex (in which case the subject-predicate analysis ceases to be ultimate).

---

[19] The centrepiece of this distinction in the classical paradigm is Russell's theory of descriptions. But little is offered by way of a justification of the Russellian analysis of descriptions as an account of logical form, except (question-beggingly) in terms of the syntactical resources of classical first-order logic. It is rarely explained, for example, why Russell's analysis is preferred over a combinatory analysis which eliminates variables (cf. H. B. Curry and R. Feys, *Combinatory Logic* (Amsterdam: North-Holland, 1958), vol. 1, chaps. 3, 6). Defenses of Russellian logical form in terms of minimum vocabularies don't hold up against the combinatory alternative.

There are, however, still worse problems for Bradley's account of relations, for, as so often in his work on logic, the insights offered at one level are withdrawn at another. As noted above in the case of universal propositions, Bradley's analysis as so far considered is only a preliminary analysis. Ultimately any judgement, according to Bradley, will 'refer' an 'ideal content' to 'a reality' (*PL* 22). What has been discussed so far is the form of the ideal content rather than the form of the judgement. The latter, according to Bradley, is always 'Reality is such that...' where the ideal content fills the blank (*PL* 629). On this account, little importance is to be attached to the distinctions between the different types of ideal content. All judgements, ultimately, are of the same form, in which (on one plausible reading) the Absolute is subject and the ideal content predicate.[20]

On existential judgements there are further reasons for caution in interpreting Bradley, for much of what he says about them is said in reaction to other theories, rather than as a statement of his own position. When he discusses them in chapter 1 of the *Logic* (§ 16) he cites them as problems for the view that all judgements assert inclusions of the predicate in the subject. When negative existential judgements appear in chapter 2 (§ 2) he is concerned with them as possible counter-examples to the claim that *all* judgement involves reference to a reality. When he returns to existential judgements later in chapter 2 (§ 42) he uses them as counter-examples to the claim that all judgements consist in the relation of ideas.

---

[20] This line of thinking becomes much more evident in Bradley's later writings; cf. *AR* 144. The statement about the ultimate form of judgements quoted above comes from one of the Terminal Essays added to the second edition of the *Logic* in 1922. The claim about the unimportance of the distinctions between the different forms of ideal content is likewise added to the second edition (cf. 'Additional Notes' *PL* 10, n. 33). In the later writings, of course, the status of relations is further undermined by Bradley's well-known *reductio* arguments (in *AR*, chap. 3). It is worth noting, however, that 'substantive and adjective' are treated no more gently than relations in *Appearance and Reality*, chap. 2, though the *reductio* arguments used there have been less frequently noted. The fact is, of course, that in *AR* Bradley was dealing with 'first principles' while in the *PL* he was avoiding them. Relations and terms and subjects and predicates all belong to the preliminary levels of analysis, not to the level of first principles.

Jubin's case is strongest for negative existential judgements: as Bradley says, it is hard to give a subject-predicate reading to 'Nothing is here' (*PL* 22). It is even stronger for another class of cases she cites, judgements like 'There are two dogs in the yard' which ascribe numbers to collections. It is impossible to parse these in subject-predicate terms in such a way as to preserve their entailments. But, although Jubin's example sounds thoroughly Bradleyan, I have not been able to find it in Bradley, nor any discussion of judgements like it. This is a pity, since judgements which ascribe numbers to collections and relational judgements are Russell's two most important counter-examples to the claim that all judgements are of subject-predicate form.[21] Yet even if a discussion of such number-ascribing judgements could be found in Bradley, it would still seem doubtful whether they had a great deal of influence on Russell. Russell's interest in these judgements, and in relational judgements, arose from his work in the philosophy of mathematics rather than from his study of Bradley.[22] Moreover, Russell was always much more impressed by Bradley's final analysis of judgements – as the referring of an ideal content to a/the real – which he took to be a subject-predicate account.[23] What Russell is likely to have got from Bradley is a more general attitude towards the doctrine that all judgements were of subject-predicate form, rather than any specific arguments. Bradley was not impressed by this doctrine, and Russell, as a young man impressed by Bradley, very likely adopted the same attitude without much hesitation.

Bradley offers little discussion of the form of existential judgements in general, although he does say at one point that 'the idea of existence is never a true predicate' (*PL* 81). Bradley's main interest in existential judgements lies in the fact that they confirm his view that judgements do not consist in

---

[21] *A Critical Exposition of the Philosophy of Leibniz*, op. cit., p. 12.

[22] Cf. Nicholas Griffin, *Russell's Idealist Apprenticeship* (Oxford: Clarendon Press, 1991), chaps. 6, 8.

[23] 'An Analysis of Mathematical Reasoning' (1898), op. cit., p. 168.

the combination of ideas (*PL* 80–81):

> A judgement, we assume naturally, says something about some fact or reality. If we asserted or denied about anything else, our judgement would seem to be a frivolous pretence. We not only must say something, but it must be about something actual that we say it. (*PL* 41)

Since the judgement involves this reference to a reality beyond itself, it cannot consist merely of ideas in the mind of the creature doing the judging. From the point of view of Bradley's final analysis of the form of all judgements these passages claim that all judgements involve a reference to the Absolute. But it is clear that Bradley intends more than this. In the second Terminal Essay, Bradley emphasizes that, in each judgement, there is a reference to the Absolute and *also* a reference to 'something distinguished, ...a limited aspect and portion of the Universe, ...a selected reality' (*PL* 629). This is implicit also in his discussion of existential judgements in the first edition. The 'selected reality' is the subject of the ideal content which, in judgement, is predicated of the Absolute. I shall call this 'selected reality', 'the immediate subject' of the judgement, as distinct from the Absolute, which I shall call its 'ultimate subject'. Now the immediate subject of a judgement cannot always be identified with its grammatical subject, for the grammatical subject of some judgements is often an item which does not exist. Bradley mentions three examples (two of them drawn from Herbart): 'A four-cornered circle is an impossibility', 'There are no ghosts', and 'The wrath of the Homeric gods is fearful' (*PL* 42).

From the point of view of modern logic, Bradley's treatment of the first two examples is relatively conventional: he proposes to rewrite them as 'The nature of space excludes the connection of square and round' and 'The world is no place where ghosts exist', respectively. Though classical logicians would hardly want to accept Bradley's translations exactly as they stand, they would be in broad agreement with his approach. It is on the third example that they would demur, because Bradley proposes to treat the Homeric gods as 'existence of [a] different order' (*PL* 42), implying (when the resources of contemporary logic are added) a plurality of domains of quantification. In this, I think Bradley did better than the classical paradigm – though neither do quite well enough. What Bradley shares with the classical paradigm is what has been called 'the ontological assumption',[24] namely that all true judgements are about items that exist, an assumption for which very little evidence is (or can be) offered. Bradley does liberalize the assumption somewhat by admitting 'existences of different orders', but essentially he retains it. In the classical paradigm the ontological assumption is preserved from refutation (up to a point) by Russell's theory of descriptions. Russell defended it by appealing to his 'robust sense of reality' against the views of Meinong, the only thinker of the period who seriously rejected the assumption.[25]

Barring Bradley's different orders of existence (an idea which Russell characterized as 'a most pitiful and paltry evasion'),[26] it is tempting to suppose that Bradley's support for the ontological assumption was of some influence on Russell. This, however, would ignore, once again, the circuitous development of Russell's views. For Russell, before he discovered the theory of descriptions, went through a period in which he rejected the ontological assumption – or at least came close to doing so, for he compromised his rejection by ascribing being to all the items which did not exist. (Perhaps it was this that he later thought a 'pitiful and paltry evasion'.) The ontological status of Russell's realm of being is problematic at best. But for Russell in this period, from his rejection of neo-Hegelianism to the discovery of the theory of descriptions (1898–1905), the immediate subject of 'The wrath of the Homeric gods is fearful' would be the Homeric gods (or rather their wrath), items which did not exist but which

---

[24] Cf. Richard Routley, *Exploring Meinong's Jungle and Beyond* (Canberra: Australian National University, 1979), p. 16. Routley goes on to criticize the assumption severely, *ibid*., pp. 21–8.

[25] Bertrand Russell, *An Introduction to Mathematical Philosophy* (London: Allen and Unwin, 1965; 1st ed., 1919), pp. 169–70.

[26] *ibid*., p. 169. Russell did not specifically have Bradley in mind.

subsisted in Russell's realm of being.[27] Nor did Russell have Bradley in mind when he returned to the ontological assumption in 1905. Indeed, ontological considerations were not what led him to the theory of descriptions (despite received opinion about what he was up to). It was not Russell's robust sense of reality which led to the theory, but the theory which made it possible to have a robust sense of reality. In any case, Bradley was not alone in holding the ontological assumption: it's been a staple of Western philosophical thought since Parmenides. What makes Bradley seem relatively modern in his adoption of the assumption is his explicit rewriting of judgements so as to eliminate putative subjects which did not exist. Presumably the need for such rewriting was brought to his attention by Herbart (one of the rare thinkers who, like Meinong, rejected the ontological assumption). Bradley's distinction between the grammatical and the logical subject of a judgement was essential for the rewriting, though it was only with Russell's theory of descriptions that a clear prescription for carrying out the translation became available.

Another area in which Bradley has been thought to have made a contribution to modern logic is in his alleged anticipation of Frege's context principle, that a word has meaning only in the context of a proposition.[28] There is little reason to think that there was any direct link between Bradley and Frege, neither seems to have read the other;[29] though Manser

---

[27] Russell's position at this time was *similar* to Meinong's, though Meinong did not attribute being to those of his objects which did not exist. Whether Russell's ascription of being to them was really an ontological claim may be doubted. At all events being, for Russell, was quite different from existence.

[28] Frege, *The Foundations of Arithmetic*, trans. J. L. Austin (Oxford: Blackwell, 1950), p. x.

[29] It was Russell's *Principles of Mathematics* which introduced Frege's work to England. Bradley studied Russell's work in some detail, including the *Principles*, but his notes on the *Principles* don't get as far as Russell's appendix on Frege. (Cf. Bradley's 'Notebook' IB19, Merton College Library, Oxford.) Russell's work caused Bradley some difficulty: see his letter to Russell, 4 February 1904 (Russell Archives, McMaster University), and Russell's reply in *Selected Letters of Bertrand Russell*, ed. N. Griffin (London: Allen Lane, 1992), vol. 1, p. 274.

suggests there may have been an indirect link through Lotze, whom both read.[30] There is also some doubt whether the context principle should be included as part of modern logic, which in general tends either to dismiss meanings entirely[31] or to embrace the compositionality of meanings (ie. the view that the meaning of a proposition is a function of the meaning of its constituent words).

Manser has already made as strong a case as possible for thinking that Bradley anticipated Frege on the context principle and I shall not add anything to it.[32] Yet there are two reasons for thinking that Bradley did not really anticipate Frege's principle. In the first place, the context principle must have a different meaning for a holist such as Bradley than it could for a philosopher like Frege who thought that propositions were the fundamental unit of meaning and the bearers of truth-values – even if the two formulated the principle in exactly the same words. It is clear that for Bradley no single proposition could be considered entirely meaningful in itself or, at least, as entirely true or false in isolation. This general reason for doubting that Bradley could have affirmed quite Frege's context principle is supported by more specific evidence. If Bradley held Frege's context principle he would surely have to put the theory of judgement at the centre of his treatment of logic. Now, although he begins his treatment of logic with the theory of judgement, he explicitly denies that this order of proceeding is required by the nature of the subject (*PL* 1, 597). Inference, judgement or ideas could, he asserts, be equally well taken as the starting point. Such a view would hardly be open to someone who had embraced the context principle, and finding such views in Bradley must make us sceptical of Manser's claim.

---

[30] A. Manser, *Bradley's Logic*, op. cit., p. 61; 'Bradley and Frege', op. cit., pp. 305–307. See also Hans Sluga, 'Frege as a Rationalist', in Matthias Schirn (ed.), *Studien zu Frege* (Stuttgart: Fromman-Holzboorg, 1976), vol. 1, p. 37.

[31] Cf. James W. Allard, 'Bradley on the Validity of Inference', *Journal of the History of Philosophy*, vol. 27 (1989), pp. 267–84, who draws a sharp contrast between Bradley and the mainstream of modern logic on this point.

[32] A. Manser, *Bradley's Logic*, op. cit., pp. 60–63; 'Bradley and Frege', op. cit., pp. 307–309.

There is, however, one point that Bradley makes which gives him, not the context principle, but something else of significance. This is his claim that judgement does not require two ideas. He writes:

> We take an ideal context, a complex totality of qualities and relations, and we then introduce divisions and distinctions, and we call these products separate ideas with relations between them. And this is quite unobjectionable. But what is objectionable is our then proceeding to deny that the whole before our mind is a single idea. (*PL* 11)

This passage is not as unambiguous as we might desire, but one thing it surely suggests is that for Bradley propositions or judgements or ideal contents were not composed of ideas, nor of elements of some other kind, that they are perhaps simple items not analysable into constituents. I don't want to commend this view as an important truth that Bradley was on to, for it has some important problems. In particular it makes it difficult to explain the validity of arguments which depend *prima facie* upon identifying the constituents of propositions: it gives us propositional logic, but no predicate logic. Nor does the point about the simplicity of propositions or judgements yield Frege's context principle: it leaves entirely open the question of how words are to achieve a meaning. Yet at the same time Bradley's point does obviate certain difficulties (emphasized by Bradley) in accounts on which propositions are complex entities composed of constituents such as ideas or terms or concepts. For example, Russell's famous problems with analysis; namely, that a proposition consists exactly of its constituents, while analysing a proposition into its constituents destroys the original proposition yet preserves all the constituents, thus suggesting that the proposition is something over and above its constituents. Obviously, problems of this kind cannot arise if propositions are simple. Equally, Bradley's theory avoids the difficulty of specifying how many constituents a proposition has – a matter to which Russell devoted much inconclusive reflection.

So far I have considered only those aspects of Bradley's logic which may be thought to have in some way anticipated ideas which have become part of modern logic. At this level, the pickings are rather slim and typically turn out to be ambiguous when investigated. At this level, Bradley might have a walk-on part in a more than usually comprehensive history of logic, but little more. His real importance, however, lies on a different level. In the remainder of this paper I want to consider two respects in which he was, I believe, especially successful. In the first, his attack on psychologism, he helped create the philosophical climate in which modern logic could be developed; in the second, his attack on Jevons's equational logic, he may have helped to shape the way in which that development took place.

II

The centrepiece of Bradley's attack on psychologism is his critique of associationism, the dominant form of psychologism in the British empiricist tradition. There is no need to examine the arguments he used against it here, for that has been done by Ferreira elsewhere in this volume. Ferreira's estimate of the force of Bradley's arguments seems to me entirely just. They effectively put paid to associationism and have become (largely without acknowledgement) part of the stock-in-trade of philosophers who have to teach undergraduates what is wrong with the empiricist theory of mind from Locke to Mill.

But associationism is only one form of psychologism, and not the form most usually associated with the name. Originally the term was applied to some of the neo-Kantians, especially those of the Fries school, who came to prominence in Germany after the Hegelian tide had begun to ebb. Not all neo-Kantians accepted the label, some (eg. those of the Marburg school) thought that Kant's enterprise (suitably revised and updated) could be carried through without appeal to psychology. In Germany, therefore, psychologism had been eclipsed for a while by the rise of Hegel, and had then undergone a patchy revival with the 'Back to Kant' movement. In Britain, in the form of associationism, it had been strong continuously from the eighteenth century, until it was eclipsed by the rise of the British neo-Hegelians.

Although there was some British interest in Kant in the

early years of the nineteenth century, he was never so thoroughly established in Britain as he was on the Continent. Bradley, himself, so far as I know, never mentions him. Moreover, none of the arguments that Bradley uses against associationism is likely to be effective against Kantian psychologism. On the other hand, the theory of inference which Bradley develops at the end of *The Principles of Logic* is incompatible with all forms of psychologism, Kantian or otherwise. The same might be claimed of his theory of judgement on the grounds that he requires that all judgements involve a reference to an external reality: 'Judgement...refers an ideal content...to a reality beyond the act' (*PL* 10). But this, in itself, is insufficient to exclude psychologism in all its forms. It does not, for example, rule out the possibility that the external reality is partially constituted by the act of judgement. No such loopholes are left in Bradley's account of inference, however, and it is worthwhile to examine briefly what he has to say on the topic.

Bradley's theory of inference arises from a dilemma. An inference, it might be claimed, is a mental act which involves a transition from premises to conclusion. If the conclusion is exactly the same as the premises then there has been no transition and thus no inference. But if the conclusion differs at all from the premises, then the conclusion could not come from the premises but from the act of inference – 'we did not *draw* the consequence from the bowels of the premises, but inserted a product prepared by ourselves'. In this case, the inference is invalid (*PL* 552–3). This view is, of course, incompatible with any psychologistic account of inference. What makes an inference valid, for Bradley, is that the conclusion is already given in the premises.[33] If this is not the case, then the conclusion is (in part, at least) our own fabrication and the inference is invalid. To make it valid, we

---

[33] Quite how the two are related in Bradley's view is problematic. For, on his account, we cannot even assume the validity of inferences like, $A, B \vdash A \& B$ or $A \& B \vdash A$. For, if we have A and, separately, B what right do we have to assume that we have them both together? And, if we have them together, by what right do we assume that we can have each separately? (*PL*, pp. 553–4). There is no need, fortunately, to go into Bradley's discussion of these issues here.

would have to add to the premises a statement about the action of our minds (*PL* 553). This could stand as a classic statement of anti-psychologism.

Bradley, however, is left impaled on the other horn of his dilemma. If the premises give the conclusion in as tight a sense as Bradley seems to require, then the conclusion must be exactly the same as the premises, and no inference has taken place. Bradley gets out of the problem by as sharp a distinction as could be desired between the psychological process of inference and the objective validity of the inference itself:

> We have here nothing to do with the *real* validity of our reasoning process, but solely with its soundness as a logical transition. And hence at present we need to regard our reasoning as simply a change in our way of knowing... If, by altering *myself*, I so am able to perceive a connection which was before not visible, then my act conditions, not the consequence itself, but my knowledge of that consequence. It goes to make the consequence in my recognition, but stands wholly apart from this truth which I recognize. Though the function of concluding depends upon my intellect, the content concluded may be wholly unhelped, untouched, and self-developed. (*PL* 554–5)

The trouble with this approach, from Bradley's point of view, is that it is doubtfully consistent with his holism. It is doubtful, in view of his other philosophical commitments, whether Bradley can consistently accept the view that the conclusion is completely independent of, and 'untouched' by, the process of inference that enables us to know it.[34] But whether Bradley was entitled to his conclusion or not, there is no doubt that his account of the validity of inference at the

---

[34] It seems, in fact, that in his 'Additional Notes' Bradley came to reject the account just quoted (cf. notes 7, 8, 15; *PL* 573–5), excusing himself on the grounds that in *PL* he was not concerned with first principles. As a result he comes to the conclusion, when first principles *are* taken into account, that no inference is quite valid (cf. J. W. Allard, 'Bradley on the Validity of Inference', *op. cit.*). The later retraction (or qualification), which appeared in print in 1922, makes little difference, however, to Bradley's influence at the time when it counted; in particular, to his influence on Russell in the 1890s.

end of *The Principles of Logic* assumes (rather than argues for) a strongly anti-psychologistic account of validity. Indeed, Bradley draws exactly the distinction, between what is in fact the case and what we come to think is the case, that Moore, in his attack on Kant's psychologism, claimed Kant had overlooked.[35]

In this, Bradley's position had an important influence on Russell. For though Russell at the beginning of his career said little about inference, he did reject psychologism from the very beginning. The curious part of this is that Russell was very strongly influenced by Kant and hardly at all by Hegel. One might have expected, therefore, that he would revert to psychologism. But this was not the case. Russell, from the first, was insistent that his form of Kantianism would have nothing to do with psychology. He insists at the beginning of *An Essay on the Foundations of Geometry*,[36] his most thoroughly Kantian work, that the a priori principles on which he sought to base geometry were purely logical and completely untainted by psychology. In this Bradley was a paramount influence. While Frege had to fight his own battle against Continental psychologism (with some help from Lotze), Russell found British psychologism already vanquished by Bradley.

When Russell came to break from neo-Hegelianism he did not renege on his anti-psychologism. Indeed, he took it to further extremes, under the influence of G. E. Moore. Moore, in developing his own theory of judgement in his Fellowship Dissertation of 1898,[37] had taken Bradley's theory as his starting point but argued that Bradley, despite his good intentions, had not gone far enough in freeing his theory of judgement from psychologism. In place of Bradley's theory,

---

[35] G. E. Moore, 'Kant's Idealism' (1903), reprinted in G. E. Moore, *The Early Essays*, ed. T. Regan (Philadelphia: Temple University Press, 1986), pp. 233–46. This did not stop Moore from criticizing Bradley for some backsliding as far as anti-psychologism was concerned (see below).

[36] Cambridge University Press, 1897.

[37] The relevant chapter was subsequently published as 'The Nature of Judgement', *Mind*, vol. 8 (1899); reprinted in *The Early Essays, op. cit.*, pp. 59–80.

Moore proposed a theory in which judgements were objectively existing complexes composed of concepts which were entirely independent of the judging mind. This theory was one which Russell also embraced and developed rather more fully in unpublished writings around the same time.[38] Shortly afterwards Moore criticized Russell's own neo-Kantian philosophy, as presented in *An Essay on the Foundations of Geometry*, in a review[39] in which he argued that Russell, despite his good intentions, had failed to keep psychological concerns out of his a priori treatment of geometry and that his hope of founding geometry upon purely logical but synthetic a priori principles was doomed. Any such attempt would perforce reintroduce psychological concerns and thus would found geometry upon a branch of psychology; whatever resulted from such a procedure would be empirical and thus contingent. By the time the review was published Russell entirely agreed with Moore's criticisms. He had abandoned the Kantian method with the degree of scorn he generally reserved for errors that had once convinced him.

Bradley's attack on psychologism was, it seems to me, by far and away his most important contribution to modern logic. It is of course always dangerous to speculate what would have happened had things been different. But in this case there seems to me good reason for thinking that, without Bradley's guidance on this point, Russell would have fallen into some kind of psychologism (possibly associationism) and that, on this basis, his contributions to logic would have been impossible. Russell's contributions came from assimilating Cantorian set theory to logic and then applying the logic thus developed to the derivation of finite and transfinite cardinal and ordinal arithmetic. But anyone who thought mathematical propositions were true by virtue of the way the human mind worked could hardly take transfinite arithmetic seriously.

---

[38] Cf. *The Collected Papers of Bertrand Russell*, N. Griffin and A. C. Lewis (eds.), vol. 2, *Philosophical Papers 1896–9* (London: Unwin Hyman, 1990), pp. 167–79.

[39] *Mind*, vol. 8 ns (1899), pp. 397–405.

III

The other aspect of Bradley's legacy to modern logic that I want to deal with seems not to have been commented on at all by anyone. Right at the end of the first volume of Bradley's *Logic* is a chapter attacking Jevons's equational logic. So far as I know, no recent commentator has even noted its existence. Yet Bradley's critique seems likely to be a matter of some importance.

In the late 1860s W. S. Jevons developed a new system of formal logic, based on the logic of Boole,[40] in which propositions are represented as equations and inference was conducted through a single rule of substitution. It is not necessary here to give an elaborate account of the system, but it is sufficiently little known to make some explanation necessary. Jevons deals with class terms which he represents by upper case letters, *A*, *B*, *C*, etc. For negative class terms he uses the corresponding lower case letters: thus if *A* represents 'animals', *a* represents 'non-animals'. Unlike Boole, he has no universal class (but he keeps Boole's 'o' as the symbol for 'the impossible'). He uses '=' for identity and represents the Boolean meet and join operations by '*AB*' (or '*A . B*') and '*A• | •B*', respectively. Unlike Boole, he interprets '*A• | •B*' inclusively, which makes join the dual of meet, and gives him some algebraic elegances like *A• | •A* = *A*. We have, of course, *AA* = *A*.

A-form propositions (eg. 'all horses are mammals') are represented by means of identity as *H = HM*, ie. 'Horse = horse mammal'. I-form propositions (eg. 'some horses are wild') are dealt with similarly: *HW = W*, ie. (ignoring quantification of the predicate) 'wild horse = wild'.[41] Negative propo-

---

[40] The first statement of Jevons's new system occurs in his *The Substitution of Similars* (London: Macmillan, 1869). A more accessible account is to be found in his very popular textbook *The Principles of Science* (London: Macmillan, 1874; and many reprints). His *Elementary Lessons in Logic* (London: Macmillan, 1870; and many reprints) briefly outlines the basic idea in chap. 23.

[41] Jevons treats 'some' in a variety of ways – as a term (*S*) in its own right and as forming with 'horse' a new term (say '*H**') distinct from 'horse'. But neither *S* nor *H** can be terms strictly speaking, for neither *S = S* nor *H* = H** holds.

sitions (E-form and O-form propositions) do not have a logical form of their own but are expressed as positive propositions using negative classes: eg. 'No horses are mammals' becomes $H = Hm$, and 'Some horses are not wild' becomes '$Hw = w$'.

Jevons has a good deal more to say about all this (I've just summarized 50 pages of close type), but this brief survey is enough to show that with this apparatus the process of syllogistic inference can be carried out entirely by means of substitutions of identicals. Take the first figure in Barbara:

Socrates is a Greek
All Greeks are mortal
Socrates is mortal.

Jevons symbolizes the premises:

(1) $S = SG$
(2) $G = GM$

Now taking (1) and substituting for 'G' in it as permitted by (2) we get:

(3) $S = SGM$

This gives us 'Socrates = Socrates Greek mortal', a stronger conclusion than the usual one. Jevons now shows that the required conclusion, '$S = SM$' follows from (3) by the rule of substitution. By the law of identity we have

(4) $SS = SS$

and substituting from (3) in (4) gives us:

(5) $SS = SGM . SGM$

But since

(6) $SG . SG = SG$

we can substitute from (6) in (5), given commutativity rules which Jevons failed to state, to get

(7) $SS = SGM . M$

Now using the conclusion (3) that we've already drawn we can substitute in (7) to get

(8) $SS = SM$

whence, using $SS = S$, we get the desired result:

(9) $S = SM$

The derivation seems long and complex, but that is only because we've been working with the primitive substitution rule. Evidently, derived rules for the simplification of equations could be stated which would make the process simpler. Some non-syllogistic inferences can be handled by the system as well and Jevons was in high hopes of reducing the whole of deductive logic to a process of repeated substitutions.[42] With this calculus of equations reasoning could be mechanized and Jevons even devised a 'logical machine'[43] for this purpose.

I'm not concerned here with the adequacy or inadequacy of Jevons's equational logic. It is enough to say that Bradley didn't like it, although he was prepared to concede its simplicity and its adequacy in so far as syllogistic was concerned (*PL* 370, 377). Bradley objected to it as a philosophically acceptable account of logic. His criticisms fell into three groups: (1) those directed against the claim that all propositions are identities; (2) those directed against the claim that all inference is substitution; and (3) those directed against Jevons's method of indirect proof. There is a good deal of overlap between the first and second groups, for Bradley's arguments against substitution as the form of inference often depend on his arguments against identity as the form of propositions.

(1) *Arguments against the claim that all propositions are identities.* A good part of Bradley's dissatisfaction here is due to his general objections to identities stemming from his own theory of judgement. On Bradley's theory of judgement, all

---

[42] The inspiration for this project goes back to Leibniz. See his letter to Conring and the second letter to Clark, both in Leibniz, *Philosophical Papers and Letters*, ed. L. E. Loemker (Dordrecht: Reidel, 1976), pp. 187, 677, respectively.

[43] Jevons, 'On the Mechanical Performance of Logical Inference', *Proceedings of the Royal Society*, vol. 18 (1870), pp. 166–9.

propositions involve both identity and difference, as he reminds us in his attack on Jevons (*PL* 373–4). The case against identity propositions is the familiar one that an identity, if true, is trivial and if not trivial then false (*PL* 371–2). Moreover, for Bradley trivial propositions say nothing and are therefore 'unmeaning' (*PL* 141). On the other hand, he seems to think triviality is never quite reached, 'for even when we reach a tautologous statement we still have a difference in the position of the terms'. If we eliminate that, Bradley claims that we have, at least in the case where the terms are complex, the whole content of the proposition on one side, and that this side is 'what we really wanted to assert' (*PL* 372). The objection is puzzling, for '*AB*', to take a complex term in Jevons's notation, is not a proposition at all, but a complex class concept. It may or may not be what Bradley would regard as 'the content' of the proposition '*AB* = *AB*', but, if it is, the content of the proposition is not assertible.

Bradley's more specific criticisms seem to be based upon a misunderstanding of Jevons's theory. In asserting 'Caesar is sick', he says, we surely do not intend to assert an identity – he mischievously offers 'Although Caesar is sick he is still Caesar' as a ludicrous possibility (*PL* 371). Had he been more charitable, he might have remembered his own earlier distinction between an idea's 'universal meaning' and the 'occasional imagery' that accompanies it (*PL* 10) or his later one between the mental process of drawing an inference and the logical relations which make the inference valid. For Jevons has something similar in mind. Jevons is not offering his logic as an account of what we intend to say by uttering some proposition, but of how the logical features of that proposition can be perspicuously expressed for the purpose of drawing inferences from them. Bradley's argument here seems based on malicious misrepresentation.

His next argument, on the other hand, seems based on a rather startling ignorance of Jevons's theory:

> If $A = B$ and $B = BC$, and we can go from this to the conclusion $A = C$, then either B makes a difference to A or it makes no difference. In the one case the proposition

becomes quite false, and in the other it disappears, since B = 0. (*PL* 371)

It is difficult to be sure what Bradley's getting at here, because the argument he offers as an example is not a valid argument in Jevons's logic. If $A = B$ and $B = BC$ then we can obtain $A = BC$ (substituting the first in the second) and $A = AC$ (substituting the first in the third) but to get $A = C$ from this we need $C = AC$ and this we can't get from the premises offered, since none of them give us an identity with only C's on one side.

Nor is it any easier to see what his criticism amounts to as a criticism of the argument he offers. The criticism is a dilemma – 'either B makes a difference to A or it makes no difference' – if the former, then 'the proposition' (which proposition?) is false, if the latter then $B = 0$ and the proposition 'disappears'. Now the question of whether B makes a difference to A seems quite simply irrelevant to the premises Bradley offers, for the premises assert that the two are identical. It is tempting to suppose that there is a misprint[44] here, and that Bradley intended to say 'B makes a difference to C', and that his objection is to the premise $B = BC$. Then his objection makes sense *but only if he is assuming that Jevons's equations are the equations of ordinary arithmetical algebra*. If B does make a difference to C, then in ordinary algebra $B = BC$ is false, and if it doesn't make a difference then $B = 0$ and the proposition 'disappears' in the sense that it resolves to $0 = 0$. But it's hard to believe that Bradley thought Jevons's equations were to be understood as ordinary algebraic ones.[45] And even if he did, he still reads '*AB*' as both addition and multiplication. I can't claim to be happy with my understanding of Bradley's argument. No commentator can rest content with an interpretation which relies upon a misprint and an elementary blunder and, even then, does not really make sense.

---

[44] But, all things considered, it is unlikely, since the passage is unchanged from the first edition to the corrected (1928) impression of the second.

[45] Such a misinterpretation, however, would make sense of the complaint in his next sentence: 'How can it be true that *ABC* is the same as *A*?'.

A curiously different argument along the same lines occurs at the beginning of Bradley's *Logic* where he attacks the identity theory of subject-predicate propositions, in the particular form which requires what he calls 'specification of the predicate', as Jevons's theory does. On this view, 'iron is a metal' is construed as the identity 'iron = iron-metal' (a reading taken directly from Jevons). That A should be 'entirely identical' with AB is, he claims, a 'startling result'.

> If $A = A$, can it also be true that to *add B* on *one* side leaves the equation where it was? If B does not mean o, one would be inclined to think it must make some difference. But if it does make a difference, we can no longer believe that $A = AB$, and $AB = A$. (*PL* 25; first italics mine)

The argument here has the same dilemma form as the argument directed explicitly against Jevons. In this case the juxtaposition of terms is clearly construed as addition. For then, if the equation is true, $B = $ o. By contrast, in the later argument if $B = $ o, the proposition disappears, which is only possible if 'BC' represents multiplication.

(2) *Arguments against the claim that all inference is substitution.* Obviously, if propositions are not identities inference cannot proceed by substitution of identicals. Bradley points out, moreover, that mere similarity or equivalence will not be sufficient for substitution as employed by Jevons. For Jevons's logic requires unrestricted substitution and similarity or equivalence will give substitutivity under constraints which would have to be specified from case to case (*PL* 377–8).

Bradley's main complaint about substitution parallels his objection to identity statements (and his puzzle about inference). You can only substitute two terms which are the same, but if the terms are the same then there is no substitution: 'If your process does not give you a difference, it is no process. If it gives you a difference you have broken the identity' (*PL* 375). In inferences where substitution works, eg. in if $A = B$ and $B = C$ then $A = C$, what are really substituted are quantities and the quantities are really differences. The terms involved, Bradley tells us, are xA, xB and xC, where 'x' is some magnitude. If we substitute the x's we get no change and have not done anything. The only genuine substitution is to substitute xA for xB, but these two *quantities* are different, though of the same *magnitude*. In such cases, Bradley tells us, 'The real process of reasoning consists in connecting the differences A and C on the basis of their common identity x' (PL 375).

(3) *Arguments against Jevons's method of indirect proof.* Jevons took it to be one of the advantages of his equational method that it could handle various non-syllogistic inferences. The chief among these were indirect inferences by which, to be exact, he meant inferences which use either the law of non-contradiction, which can be stated in Jevons's notation as

(8) $Aa = 0$,

or the law of excluded middle,

(9) $A = AB \bullet | \bullet Ab$

(8) and (9), he points out, may be used for substitutions in any proof.[46]

Again Bradley's criticisms are often wide of the mark. Consider the following example in disjunctive syllogism that Jevons offers.[47] Suppose we have the disjunctive proposition

(10) $A = B \bullet | \bullet C \bullet | \bullet D$.

By disjunctive syllogism we can show that, if any disjunct can be excluded, at least one of the others must be the case. To show how this is achieved substitutionally, Jevons argues as follows: we can substitute from (10) in

(11) $Ab = Ab$,

to give

(12) $Ab = ABb \bullet | \bullet AbC \bullet | \bullet AbD$.

Of the three disjuncts in (12) the first is self-contradictory so we can 'strike it out', as Jevons says, to give:

(13) $Ab = AbC \bullet | \bullet AbD$

---

[46] *Principles of Science*, pp. 81–2.

[47] *Principles*, p. 77, quoted PL 379.

which is the result required.

Now Bradley's intention is supposedly to show that Jevons's indirect method 'can not possibly be reduced to substitution' (*PL* 378; also 381) and, indeed, his first comment on this example is that 'the operation of striking out one part and asserting the rest...is not even in appearance reduced to substitution' (*PL* 380). But then, curiously, he goes on to show that the argument can be stated entirely substitutionally. (Jevons doesn't make the substitutions explicit, and Bradley misses one that is important because he neglects the simplification principle (16) below.) We have, from the law of non-contradiction (8):

(14) $Bb = o$

and we have also the identities:

(15) $Ao = o$
(16) $A \bullet | \bullet o = A$.

Using these identities (or substitution instances of them) will give us (13) from (12) by substitution only. Since Bradley saw virtually all of this it is difficult to know why he thought the operation could not be expressed substitutionally. Maybe, since he missed (16), he didn't see how the o could be struck out.

His main criticism, however, is that Jevons's method only makes a simple matter complex. A doubting philosophical tradition notwithstanding, Bradley regards it as obvious that if *A* is *B* or *C* and it is not *B* then it must be *C* (*PL* 380). This might perhaps explain the sense in which he thinks the indirect method cannot be *reduced* to substitution: because he regards the indirect method as more basic than substitution. But this ignores the point of Jevons's logic, which is not to simplify all inferences, but to show how they can all be given a common pattern and worked by means of fully explicit rules.[48]

Bradley's final objection, that in so far as Jevons uses substi-

---

[48] Jevons did not quite satisfy this requirement since he never specified commutativity principles for . and • | •.

tution for indirect proofs, his use of it is not necessary, need not detain us. Bradley is quite right. But Jevons did not claim necessity for his method – merely sufficiency.

Taken all in all, Bradley's specific complaints about Jevons's logic are not very impressive. But, for all that, one cannot help thinking that there is something fundamentally correct about them: *Not* all propositions are identities; and *not* all inferences are substitutions. Now we might at this stage get bogged down in an unwieldy philosophical discussion of the nature of propositions or inferences in themselves, and Bradley seems only too anxious to encourage us in that direction. Indeed, if Jevons had shown that every proposition *could be represented* as an identity and every inference as a substitution, this might be the only way of attacking his logic. But Jevons has not shown this and, indeed, does not claim to have shown it. In fact, he admits that there are propositions and forms of inference that cannot be assimilated to the methods of his equational logic.

This limitation of equational logic is important and Bradley emphasizes it – and this, to my mind, is his most telling objection. Following a passage in Jevons's *Principles of Science* (pp. 22–3) closely, Bradley writes: 'the class of relations in time and space... are not amenable to the Method of Substitution' (*PL* 374). In fact, Jevons's equational logic as developed in his *Principles* cannot handle relations of any kind, and Jevons himself notes this as the chief shortcoming of his equational logic. Moreover, it would be impossible to extend his formalism so as to include them. Bradley states his objection no less than three times. On p. 377, he mentions relations of degree as well as relations in space and time as being beyond the capacity of Jevons's logic. He also notes that Jevons's logic 'is made too narrow because in its conclusions [and also, we might add, its premises] it is confined to the category of subject and attribute'. Finally, in a note added to the first edition but after the chapter on Jevons was written, he says that a mathematical logician who fails to treat such simple arguments as '*A* before *B* and *B* with *C* therefore *A* before *C*' 'has no strict right to demand a hearing' (*PL* 387).

Now Bradley's emphasizing Jevons's failure to provide a

logic of relations is extremely important. Contemporary logicians (notably De Morgan) were doing their best to remedy the defect, but doing so outside the confines of the equational logic. If Bradley's conclusion that a logician who doesn't offer a logic of relation has no right to demand a hearing is a bit draconian, his basic complaint is dead right and, I'm inclined to believe, of both direct and indirect importance for the future development of logic. When dealing with the influence of Bradley's critique of Jevons my evidence is bound to be impressionistic and my conclusions rather speculative. My first piece of evidence that Bradley's critique, despite its failings, was influential is a quite worthless old logic text, J. E. Creighton's *An Introductory Logic*.[49] Creighton was once – fortunately long ago – the Professor of Logic at Cornell, and the printing history of his useless little book makes depressing reading for anyone who's ever thought of writing a textbook. First published in 1898, it reached its fifth edition in 1932 for which it was overhauled by one of Creighton's colleagues, H. R. Smart who made 'major changes' and added 'new sections dealing with recent developments'.[50] The book reached its twentieth printing in 1950 – the date of my copy, which, from notes I found inside it, was still in use as a text at the end of 1954.

Now my reason for mentioning this curio is that it contains a short section (pp. 398–404) on Jevons's equational logic which is identified, quite erroneously, with symbolic logic in general. Creighton and Smart make no serious attempt to explain Jevons's system, but they do mention (none too accurately) its basic principles and then they run against it a number of objections – each of which comes from Bradley, though they don't acknowledge the source. The objections they use are from Bradley's first group – against the claim that all propositions are identities – and are generally pretty garbled. I do not wish to suggest that as logicians or philosophers we should take Creighton's book seriously. But, in view

---

[49] New York: Macmillan. My copy is the fifth, revised edition of 1932.

[50] H. R. Smart, 'Preface to the Fifth Edition', pp. vi, v. What in the entire volume he conceived to be a recent development I can't imagine.

of its printing history, we should do so as historians. Influence is not transmitted only by the famous and competent, and as regards Jevons's logic, Bradley criticisms seem to have been influential, even when they were not very good.

My second point about the influence of Bradley's critique of Jevons concerns Russell and is more serious. After he ceased to be a neo-Hegelian Russell spent two years working on logic before he discovered Peano. Among other things he was looking for a logic to use in the foundations of mathematics and the question quite naturally arises as to why, in that period, he seems never to have looked seriously at the main nineteenth-century English works of mathematical logic, in particular the work of Boole, De Morgan, and Jevons. We know that the psychologism implied by Boole's main title, *The Laws of Thought*, put him off and he got what he needed of Boolean algebra from Whitehead's *Universal Algebra*. He did make some acquaintance with De Morgan's work, though I'm not sure whether this was before or after his discovery of Peano. But Jevons he entirely ignores.

Yet he did know of Jevons's logical writings. He told Jevons's son that before he went up to Cambridge in 1890 he knew Jevons's *Elementary Lessons in Logic* (1870) 'by heart',[51] and the *Elementary Lessons* contains a brief account of the equational logic. Once at Cambridge, and especially when he started studying philosophy there in 1893, Russell came under the influence of the neo-Hegelians. He read Bradley's *Logic* in September 1893 and again in January 1898 and was extremely impressed. As a neo-Hegelian, he adopted what he thought was Bradley's identity-in-difference theory of judgement, though the theory he states is not exactly Bradley's.[52] The differences, however, are not important here, for the theory of judgement Russell adopts will yield the same objections to Jevons's logic as Bradley's theory.

[51] Russell to H. Stanley Jevons, 22 June 1955 (Russell Archives, McMaster University).

[52] See *An Essay on the Foundations of Geometry*, p. 184. For the differences between Russell's 1897 theory of judgement and the theory Bradley actually held, see N. Griffin, *Russell's Idealist Apprenticeship* (Oxford: Clarendon Press, 1991), pp. 167–8.

There is no evidence to show whether or not Russell accepted all Bradley's arguments against Jevons, including the mistaken ones. But as a neo-Hegelian he would certainly have accepted those which stemmed from the doctrine that all judgements involve identity-in-difference. Moreover, Bradley's complaint that the equational logic could not handle relational arguments would have weighed heavily with Russell both as a neo-Hegelian and afterwards. As a neo-Hegelian one of Russell's main concerns was precisely the treatment of spatial and temporal relations, and Bradley's correct assertion that the equational logic could not cope with these relations in particular would no doubt have served to convince Russell that there was nothing to be learnt from Jevons. As Russell came to abandon neo-Hegelianism, moreover, relations came to have greater importance for him as one of the requirements for any theory of mathematics.

The inferences that Bradley complained that Jevons could not deal with (such as 'A before B and B with C, therefore A before C') were exactly the sort of relations (viz. ordering relations) which were giving Russell most trouble. It was the inability of the idealist logicians like Bradley to cope with these inferences themselves that led Russell to abandon his idealist theory of relations and, with it, neo-Hegelianism. That Jevons could do no better with them would have convinced him, once again, that nothing was to be gained from studying Jevons. In the next two years Russell, largely in isolation, developed his own rudimentary theory of relations, though he could not connect it to other parts of logic (nor develop it fully) until he discovered Peano. It was certainly useful to Russell that he did not pursue Jevons's equational logic, for it could not offer what he was looking for. The equational logic, despite its attractions, was essentially a dead-end and one from which Russell was saved from exploring by Bradley.[53] It is ironical that Bradley, a

---

[53] In a letter to Couturat (17 January 1901), written shortly after his discovery of Peano's logic, Russell complained that 'from the point of view of logic, I think we have insisted too much on equations, which have hardly any importance' (*Selected Letters of Bertrand Russell*, ed. Nicholas Griffin (London: Allen Lane, 1992), vol. 1, p. 211).

philosopher best known for his arguments against relations, should have made one of his most important contributions to the development of logic by emphasizing their importance in logic.

To end on a more speculative note, Bradley's rejection of Jevons's logic may have had wider implications as well. Jevons's work was part of an algebraic tradition in the development of logic going back to developments in the theory of differential operators and functional equations at the beginning of the nineteenth century. Through the nineteenth century this algebraic tradition ran parallel to another logical tradition arising from Cauchy's work in mathematical analysis, through Cantorean set theory, to Peano's mathematical logic.[54] During the middle years of the nineteenth century, from the 1820s to the 1870s, British logic was dominated by the algebraic tradition. Boolean algebra took some of its inspiration from the earlier theory of differential operations and De Morgan's treatment of relations from the theory of functional equations. Yet it is notable that when mathematical logic emerged in British philosophy at the beginning of the twentieth century, the (roughly indigenous) algebraic tradition had been eclipsed by the analytic one largely imported from the Continent. This change was pretty much Russell's doing.[55] Even where logicians in the algebraic tradition had gone further towards solving those problems that dominated Russell's early thinking on logic, as De Morgan and Peirce had done with their theories of relations, Russell largely ignored their work, preferring to improve the Continental tradition by adding a new theory of relations to Peano's logic. Now Jevons's equational logic belonged firmly

---

[54] The two traditions are outlined in I. Grattan-Guinness's excellent survey 'Living together and living apart. On the interactions between mathematics and logics from the French Revolution to the First World War', *South African Journal Of Philosophy*, vol. 7 (1988), pp. 73–82.

[55] Whitehead's *Universal Algebra* (1898) was in the British algebraic tradition and provided much of Russell's early knowledge of Boole and De Morgan. Despite the enthusiasm with which he greeted Whitehead's book, he was unable to make progress with the (largely philosophical) problems that concerned him on the basis of Whitehead's work. It was Russell who persuaded Whitehead that Peano's system, which forms the basis of *Principia Mathematica*, was preferable.

in the algebraic tradition and it may be that Bradley's attack on the equational logic helped convince Russell that little was to be gained from the algebraic tradition as a whole, which he made little effort to master. Russell's researches in logic were driven largely by philosophical, rather than purely mathematical, concerns and Bradley's objections to Jevons's theory as a philosophically perspicuous account of propositions and inference may have made him suspicious of the philosophical utility of a logic stemming from largely algebraic concerns. If this is the case, then the shape of logic as it emerged in British philosophy departments this century owes, indirectly, much more to Bradley than has previously been supposed.[56]

---

[56] Thanks to Alison Miculan for her help with this paper. Research supported by the Social Sciences and Humanities Research Council of Canada.

BRADLEY ON TRUTH AND JUDGEMENT

Walter Creery

The customary and standard interpretation of Bradley's *Principles of Logic* seems to assume that Bradley is a precursor to the type of logical theory underlying *Principia Mathematica*. This assumption takes it to be the case that one can find, in the Bradleyan texts solid evidence for this interpretation, and, on the surface, it's easy to find passages which strongly suggest some of the logical theses and theories later developed by Russell and Whitehead, and which was the basis for the classical propositional and predicate calculus. The thesis that universal categoricals must be analysed in terms of hypotheticals is one such well-known claim. This, and numerous other theses, suggest and support the interpretative thesis that the classical predicate calculus might well be a reliable model for the interpretation of Bradley's logic. It is not supposed in the following that this is an erroneous view, but there is an alternative interpretation of the *Principles of Logic*, and according to this interpretation, whatever similarities there are are purely accidental. On the proposed interpretation Bradley should be seen as, not only a critic of classical empiricism and the traditional logical theory but primarily as undertaking a phenomenological analysis of experience, and in particular that type or aspect of experience identifiable as the act of judgement. It is not claimed that Bradley was a precursor to Husserl. Nor is it claimed that there is an historical antecedence between the *Principles of Logic* and the *Logical Investigations* of Husserl, but there is, according to this interpretation, a coincidence of method, analysis and argument. The major consequence of this interpretation is that the more or less standard view of what Bradley means by 'logic' should be revised and that, above all, this type or theory of logic must not be supposed to be computational.

Bradley's initial characterization of judgement proper is '...the act which refers an ideal content (recognized as such) to a reality beyond the act'.[1] In the revised 1922 edition, a number of qualifications are added: first, the term 'act' in the original definition raises a number of questions which are of importance in psychology and metaphysics, but these questions need not arise, Bradley holds, so far as the issues are strictly logical; secondly, the expression 'recognized as such' is unnecessary and were it a requirement for the investigation of logic, only those judgements occurring with conscious awareness of the act would count as judgements, and this would be far too restrictive; thirdly, 'beyond the act' again raises several questions of a metaphysical nature which need not occur within the confines of logical theory. The first and third qualifications, however, raise several questions. When the act of referring is considered only as an intentional act, apart from either the content of the judgement itself or the 'object' of reference and solely as a condition for judgement to occur at all, there can, perhaps, be no reason to disagree. There is, however, the content of the judgement and the reality to which the ideal content is referred, and both of these terms in the definition require considerable clarification. Bradley was well aware that referring is something one does, and it can be done successfully, unsuccessfully, ineptly and so on. The nature of Reality, or the realities, to which the ideal content is referred is clearly, in some sense, internal to the analysis of truth and judgement.[2] No act of referring would be possible if there was not, in Bradley's term, some *idea* of

---

[1] Bradley's formula 'Reality is such that S-P', discussed below, should not be taken as purely formal, and above all should not be interpreted as something closely analogous to the Fregean assertion sign. Abstracting the act from the content in the case of judgement, or the referent in the case of judgements, cannot be supposed to be more than a matter of convenience for the sake of clarity.

[2] Nicholas Griffin, 'What's Wrong with Bradley's Theory of Judgement?', *Idealistic Studies*, vol. 13 (1983), pp. 199–224.

the object of reference. How the object of reference and the content of the act of reference are to be distinguished is a point on which Bradley is obscure, and yet, clearly, if truth and falsity is to emerge in, or from, the act of judgement, these must be identified and distinguished.

The content of a judgement is an ideal content referred beyond the act, but the preliminary, and perplexing question is: What *does* Bradley mean by the term 'ideal content' or 'idea'? Nicholas Griffin notes that 'For Bradley a subject-predicate judgement refers an ideal content (or predicate) to reality (*PL* 10). But the ideal content, which Bradley refers to (somewhat misleadingly) as an idea, is an abstract universal and does not exist.'[3] Griffin notes that 'idea' is not to be confused with the ideas of the associationists, and goes on to add, somewhat confusingly, that 'the ideal content is rather what such ideas mean'. But since Bradley states that ideal contents as universals do not exist, it must then follow that meanings do not exist either, and one is then left acutely puzzled as to what these 'ideal contents' are, and above all, what Bradley supposes he is talking about. Furthermore, while there is no question that Bradley implies that these 'ideal contents' are predicates,[4] the model of a predicate clearly is not to be derived from the meaning and function of 'predicate' in the natural language of English. Bradley not only does not make any such claim, but he has practically nothing to say about the natural language at all, and this in itself should arouse a suspicion that Bradley's meaning of 'predicate' is different from the contemporary usage of the term. Furthermore, even if Bradley does hold the view that many of these predicates of a natural language have ideal contents 'associated' with them, these ideal contents, on

---

[3] Bradley not only implies, but in many places uses the expression itself. But it is the sense or *intelligible meaning-content* that Bradley is concerned with.

[4] Propositions as entities should, therefore, become nonsensical and the term empty of any meaning whatsoever. Those who opt for using the classical predicate calculus should, therefore, opt for substitutional quantification rather than objectual quantification. Cf. Susan Haack, *Philosophy of Logics* (Cambridge University Press, 1978), pp. 50ff.

Griffin's account, do not exist. Therefore, the predicates can be nothing more than the grammatical predicates of some natural language, and the theory of judgement will collapse into a descriptive survey of sentences only, which completely trivializes any such a theory. Similar remarks will apply to the interpretation that makes use of the notions of 'proposition' and 'propositional function' as these are often used in the standard calculus, and where these are taken to be 'abstract entities'.[5]

I suggest, then, that an examination of Bradley's use of this term 'ideal content' is in order before any attempt is made to determine the significance of the terms 'truth' and 'judgement'. Truth and falsity is, as Bradley is well aware, a function of the relation of ideas to reality, and no judgement can occur at all unless there are ideas, and, in the act of judgement, ideas are used as ideas (PL 2). Ideas, as Bradley indicates in several places, are meanings, but this is equally obscure, since it is apparent that Bradley does *not* understand the term 'meaning' in the more common contemporary senses. One can, however, approach Bradley's sense, and from this will emerge the sense of the term 'ideal content', by considering his criticism of the earlier empiricists, particularly Berkeley and Hume. Berkeley held that ideas are particulars and in the strict sense ideas are the only fundamental existents.[6] Such existents occur only in minds and are, strictly, mental entities (on the act/object interpretation) or mental events (on the adverbial type of analysis). Ideas are not, however, independently existing entities, but rather are dependent on function and operations of some mind or other; in the case of one's own ideas, they are products of the acts

---

[5] 'But it is a universally received maxim, that every thing which exists is particular', *The Works of George Berkeley*, ed. A. A. Luce and T. E. Jessop, vol. 2, p. 192. Bradley makes an important distinction between 'particularity' and 'individuality'. Every particular is an individual, but it is mistaken to claim, on his view, that the converse also holds true.

[6] Berkeley does not explicitly say this, but it is clearly implied by his doctrine that physical objects are collections of ideas. Since the physical object includes both the tangible and the visible, and these are type-distinct (heterogeneous), it is apparent that Berkeley considered the physical object to be collections of collections of ideas.

of remembering or imagining; in the case of sensible ideas they are the products of a deity or Absolute mind. Physical objects are ordered *sets of sets* of sensible particulars: there is the set of visual ideas, the set of tactual ideas, the set of auditory ideas, and so on. In the case of the set of visual ideas, each of these sets is a perspective and in the case of the visual modality, the physical object is an ordered set of sets of such perspectives. In some manner (not explained either by Berkeley or Hume) the ideas of the imagination are derived from the sensible ideas; they are perhaps produced by them, and the physical object, as this appears and reappears in memory and the imagination, resembles the complex sensible particular. As they occur in memory, there is a very high degree of what might be called structural resemblance, but at the same time the content of the remembered idea lacks the vividness of the initial or recurrent sensible particulars. In the imagination, however, the structural features of the imagined are open to individual voluntary manipulation and change; as a consequence, the structural features as well as the content of the imagined can be changed and varied.[7] But it is a feature of both Berkeley's and Hume's account of the mind that these ideas of the imagination, however they may be manipulated, varied, and modified relative to the sensible 'originals', nevertheless they are existent particulars. Berkeley (and Hume as well) seems to have thought that this was all there was to the experienced, perceived, objects – along with the multitude of relations holding between the many existent ideas. There are colours, in their many shades and hues, sounds with their multitude of qualitative differences, and these are particular existent entities. They are, to use a contemporary idiom, variables out of which are constituted the physical objects whether this is a sensibly perceived object, a remembered object, or an imagined object. This irreducible

---

[7] Berkeley insists that the voluntary operations within the imagination is the paradigm case of the mind as active. Cf. *Principles*, p. 28. This passage is strongly in support of the act-object interpretation of ideas.

datum, sometimes misleadingly called a sense-datum, must be present as an item or datum within consciousness or there can be no objects and no world. Later, Husserl will identify this component of the perceptible as the *hyle* of the object – roughly, the 'matter' out of which (in part) the object is constituted.

The central and core difficulty of the Berkeleyan account is the lack of any generality. On the Berkeleyan (and Humean) account of perception the occurrence of a particular object, such as the ash tree in the yard, is a distinct, complex, particular on each occasion when it should be perceived. But the ash tree is experienced and recognized as the identically same tree. It was assumed, of course, that the grounds for this recognition were the *similarity* of shape, configuration, colours, and so on, which, in turn must be a matter of the similarity of the particular ideas. It is whether there are any grounds or bases for the similarity that creates the difficulty. The act of recognition itself is not sufficient, since this at most would be a single capacity. Each sensible complex idea is also a single particular, but these are transient and fleeting entities with nothing that might even give sense to the evident generality as a fact of experience. Bradley refers to these particulars as the psychic fact. With respect to 'idea' in the sense of Berkeley and Hume, Bradley writes:

> Each we know exists as a physical fact, and with particular qualities and relations. It has its speciality as an event in my mind. It is a hard individual, so unique that it not only differs from all the others, but even from itself at subsequent moments. And this character it must bear when confined to the two aspects of existence and content. (*PL* 5)

The particulars of Berkeley (as physical, mental, existents), and less clearly in Hume, are atomic particulars. They have no generality about them at all, nor could they still remain particulars. Taking this view to its extreme form, every occurrence of a physical object, whether the sensible object, the remembered object, or the imagined object, will be a radically different individual, a consequence contrary to immediate experience and surely false to the point of absurdity. Neither Berkeley or Hume seem to have been aware of this consequence, and especially Berkeley when he toyed with the theory that the 'physical object' might be construed as complex (ordered) sets of *minima sensibilia*.[8] It is patently obvious that there is *similarity* from one presentation to the next, and the question the classical empiricists did not answer was the source or ground of this similarity. To suppose that the ground of similarity is in the reproduction by memory or imagination is clearly to beg the question, since the very possibility of recognition of 'this' as similar to 'that' assumes and presupposes some ground from the claim. To suppose that it is the form or structure that is the ground for similarity is quite obviously to suppose a universal property. Similar remarks will apply to all of the associationist theories.

It might be argued that at least Berkeley assumes a universal element, and this may be the case. If so, Berkeley is certainly not explicit and the only reference to some kind of universality in the early works is the oblique remark in the Introduction to the *Principles of Human Knowledge*: 'Now, if we annex a meaning to our words, and speak only of what we can conceive, I believe we shall acknowledge that an idea which, considered in itself, is particular, becomes general by being made to represent or stand for all other particulars of the same sort' (sect. 12). What Berkeley does not seem to have realized, or to have done so only obliquely and obscurely, is that the possibility of the very act of generalizing requires something more *in the perceptible* than the mere act of using one idea to stand for or signify a diverse set of other perceptibles.

This is the point at which Bradley initiates what is, in effect, a refutation of classical empiricism. Bradley's crucial and central insight is that every psychic content has a 'meaning-complex' intrinsic to it, and it is this 'meaning-complex', or ideal content, that makes logical investigations possible.

---

[8] It is significant that Berkeley makes no further use of the doctrine of *minima sensibilia* after the *Essay Towards a New Theory of Vision*.

> I have the 'idea' of a horse, and this is a fact in my mind, existing in relation with the congeries of sensations and emotions and feelings, which make my momentary state. It has again particular traits of its own, which may be difficult to seize, but which, we are bound to suppose, are present. It is doubtless unique, the same with no other, nor yet with itself, but alone in the world of its fleeting moment. But for logic, and in the matter of truth and falsehood, the case is quite changed. The 'idea' has here become an universal, since everything else is subordinate to the meaning. (PL 5)

The 'what' of the idea is the ideal content, and it is this which makes judgement possible at all. This ideal content has been identified as the 'concept of X', so the 'concept of "horse"'. This seems plausible, and in certain respects it is in accord with the texts. If, however, the 'concept of X' is understood, as it often is in contemporary terms, as the meaning of the linguistic expression, and with the usual assumption that the linguistic expression is a necessary condition for the occurrence of meaning, then Bradley will be seriously misunderstood. There are several reasons for this, but the primary consideration arises from the fact that Bradley has almost nothing to say about natural language, but a great deal to say about meaning. Bradley's theory of mind requires one to assume that a natural language is a system of visible marks or audible sounds, and as such are also psychical facts. These psychical facts are no doubt associated with ideal contents or meanings, but the latter are quite independent of the former. Whatever might be the objections against this view, for Bradley, as for the British empiricists generally, the relation between meanings (and this is construed in different ways by Berkeley, Hume, Hartley, Mill, and others) are *contingently* related to the psychical facts of linguistic tokens. Meanings or ideal contents can not only be distinguished, they have a reality independent of whatever psychic factuality may be associated with them.

The status of the ideal contents or meanings becomes somewhat confused when Bradley writes: 'But an idea, if we use idea of the meaning, is neither given nor presented but is taken. It can not as such exist' (*PL* 7).[9] This statement appears to have misled some commentators. But the immediately following sentence makes clear what Bradley intends by this statement: 'It can not ever be an event, with a place in the series of time or space.' Existence applies to that which is given, whether in the sensible, memory or the imagination; it refers to the psychical fact, or hyletic content and not to the ideal contents. Ideal contents do not, therefore, exist; but it simply does not follow that Bradley thinks they are nothing at all. They are intelligibles, but not perceptibles. They are to be compared with what Frege later will call 'thoughts' and what Husserl will identify as *noemata*. It is apparent that if the term 'exist' applies to the given psychical or hyletic content then Bradley has no term left to describe the intelligible aspect or feature of conscious experience. Here Bradley could have used a term of Brentano's, namely 'intentional inexistence'. Brentano used this term with respect to the intentional object, even though Brentano's account of such objects is ambiguous with respect to what Bradley calls the 'psychical fact' and the meaning (or ideal content). Every act has a 'directness' to it, but it also must have, according to Brentano, an object. This required Brentano to accept that imaginary objects such as centaurs, unicorns, the Present-King-of-France, and so on, are real, having intentional inexistence. It also required the admission that the objects of ordinary veridical perception are not the real objects either. Both of these consequences are, in different ways, contrary to ordinary intuitions. Husserl revises Brentano's conception by insisting that there are (at least) three distinct components in the intentional act; there is, first, the intentional fact itself; secondly, the intentional or noetic content of the act, and then, in some cases but not in all, there is an object towards which the act is directed. To think of a unicorn there is the intentional act – that to which one refers – the form or structure of the act, which is the intel-

---

[9] Bradley does not discuss the nature or status of the universal element in the *Principles of Logic*. He assumes there are such, and his manner of statement suggests that he thinks of these as entities. This text supports this interpretation, and since they 'are taken' it also supports the interpretation that these universals are, in some undefined sense, *before the mind* as individual (although not as particulars).

ligible idea of a unicorn, but there is no object, since there are no unicorns. Here the temptation, of course, is to suppose that the specific image of a unicorn, which one might have or, to be more exact, any one of the multitude of images one might have, constitute the object of the intentional act. This, however, would be to confuse the particular hyletic content with the object, or in Bradley's terms, to confuse the psychic fact with the object of reference.

It is useful to recall that the term 'noema' has the sense in Plato of 'thought', and a companion term 'noesis' is the name of the upper level of the divided line analogy. The noetic is the intelligible; it is not the perceptible. It will also be useful, for purposes of comparison, to note several of the theses Dagfinn Follesdall has proposed for an interpretation of Husserl's notion of *noema*.[10] Of these the most important for the present purposes are, *first*, that the noema is an intentional entity and is a generalization of the notion of meaning. *Secondly*, the noema has two distinct components, namely '(1) one which is common to all acts that have the same object, with exactly the same properties, oriented in the same way, etc., regardless of their "thetic" character of the act – that is whether it be perceiving, remembering, imagining, etc., and (2) one which is different in acts with different thetic characters'. *Thirdly*, the noematic meaning is that in virtue of which consciousness is related to the object. *Fourth*, the noema of an act is not the object of the act but the 'meaning-condition' whereby the act is possible. *Fifth*, there corresponds one and only one object to one specific noema, but (*sixth*) there may correspond several distinct noemata to one and the same object. *Seventhly*, each act has one and only one noema. Finally, noemata are to be described as abstract entities, and noemata are not perceived through the senses. They are known or apprehended through phenomenological reflection.

---

[10] Dagfinn Follesdall, 'Husserl's Notion of Noema', in Hubert L. Dreyfus (ed.), *Husserl, Intentionality and Cognitive Science* (Cambridge, Mass.: MIT Press, 1982), pp. 73–80. Follesdall gives twelve theses. Not all of these are of immediate relevance here.

Bradley's use of the term 'ideal content' and his discussion of these entities, corresponds very closely with Husserl's theory of noemata. First, ideal contents are explicitly identified with meanings, and there is every reason to think that the ideal content, as a theoretical term, is a generalization on the notion of 'meaning'. ('The idea in judgement is the universal meaning; it is not even the occasional imagery, and still less can it be the whole psychic event', *PL* 10.) Furthermore, ideal contents are intensions. ('If in considering an idea you attend to its content, you have its intension or comprehension', *PL* 168.)[11] Secondly, ideal contents are explicitly described as universals, and, while Bradley is not at all explicit about the nature of universals, since ideal contents are universals, they are clearly common to a number of instances – specifically, to an indefinite number of psychic particulars. The ideal contents are, however, abstract entities; but they are clearly not intended to be thought of as having no reality whatsoever. Ideal contents are the product of a process or act of abstraction. In a note to p. 8, Bradley writes: 'I may point out that, even in this sense, the idea is a product of abstraction. Its individuality is conferred upon it by an act of thought.'[12] It is, perhaps, useful to state this point in terms of a contrast between 'invention' and 'discovery'. There is no evidence that Bradley ever thought that ideal contents considered as universals are inventions of the mind. (Were this the case, Bradley's idealism would amount to nothing at all!) There are numerous passages where Bradley speaks of the ideal content as being 'cut off' from the psychical fact. 'That connection of attributes we recognize as horse, is one part of the content of the unique horse-image...'. 'But an idea...by itself is an adjective diversed, a parasite cut

---

[11] It would be instructive to compare C. I. Lewis's use of the term 'intension' with Bradley's use as well as the traditional theory Bradley is opposed to (ie. the inverse relation between denotation and intension). This, however, cannot be attempted here. Cf. C. I. Lewis, *An Analysis of Knowledge and Valuation* (La Salle: Open Court, 1946), pp. 38–47.

[12] That abstraction means (minimally) an intentional distinction between the psychic contents and the intelligible ideal content is clear. A necessary, but not sufficient, condition for this act to occur is an intentional act of selective attention. Whether Bradley thought there is more to the abstractive process is less than clear.

loose, a spirit, without a body seeing rest in another...' (p. 8). Just how this separation is possible, or what 'mechanism' might be supposed to make the act more intelligible, is not explained. Nor is there an explanation of how these ideal contents can be used or manipulated. It is possible that these questions need not be the concern of logical inventions as such, belonging to the larger issues of metaphysics, and on this point Bradley may be right. Nevertheless, there remain intriguing questions. Some of these puzzles Bradley considers in the essay, 'Of Floating Ideas and the Imaginary'.[13]

'Judgement proper is the act which refers an ideal content to a reality beyond the act' (*PL* 10). A judgement says something, by way of the ideal content, about a fact or reality. 'If we asserted or denied about anything else, our judgement would seem to be a frivolous pretence. We not only must say something, but it must also be about something actual that we say it' (*PL* 41). Bradley then goes on to insist that a judgement must be true or false, and its truth or falsity cannot be a function of itself, and hence what would normally be called analytic statements are excluded from this characterization. Bradley necessarily has to revise this account, but as a general characterization of an important type of judgement, it provides a starting point. The immediate question now becomes the sense and significance to be attached to the term 'reality'. If there is to be any intelligible account of truth, there must clearly be some sort of 'relation' between the ideal content, and the reality to which the act refers the ideal content.

It would appear that Bradley does not have an account of *factual* truth at all. Indeed, one may well wonder whether there is *any* theory of truth anywhere in the works. As Manser notes, Bradley is obsessed with the problem of what it is for judgements to be true or false. That some judgements are sometimes true and some are false is a given datum. Yet, because reality never seems to be specifiable, except partially or generally, it would appear then that at least there is no

---

[13] It might be noted here that Bradley's discussion of 'floating ideas' suggests an interpretation in terms of possible worlds theory.

specific theory of truth, and if as Manser claims the reference to reality is that which 'lies outside the mind', truth and falsity must surely be transcendental; but because there is no distinction for us within the transcendent reality, save those which we find pragmatically satisfiable, *that* conception of truth would clearly appear to be quite empty.

Both Manser and Stock claim that Bradley's statement, appearing in the Terminal Essays, 'Reality is such that S is P' should be understood something like the Fregean assertion sign '[—'. It seems, however, that the logical form of this, if the analogy with Frege is to be retained, provides very little more than a 'semantic marker', and Manser is aware of this. The assertion sign functions as a single predicate, and therefore the term 'reality' must be taken to be in the predicative position, and if the analogy is continued, it is the common predicate for all judgements. Frege and Bradley, indeed, appear much closer than might at first appear. 'We can imagine a language in which the proposition, "Archimedes perished at the conquest of Syracuse", would be expressed in the following way: "The violent death of Archimedes at the conquest of Syracuse is a fact." Even here, if one wishes, he can distinguish between subject and predicate; *but the subject contains the whole content, and the predicate serves only to present this as a judgement.*'[14]

This interpretation, however, does not provide a theory of truth. Manser suggests, in this respect, that Bradley does not need such, since his concern is solely with the logical form of judgements:

> In any case, it is not clear that a 'theory of truth', in the sense in which correspondence and coherence are alternative candidates, is needed by Bradley. His point is that what is required by logic is to establish the logical form of judgements, and this is 'Reality is such that S-P'. Both true and false judgements have the same form, and it is not in general the task of logic to establish whether a particular judgement is true or false. Logic can say that of two contra-

---

[14] T. W. Bynum (Oxford, 1972), p. 113. Italics have been added.

dictory judgements one at least must be false; inference can produce new truths from ones already accepted. It is not in the same business as the special sciences, which may well be concerned with details of verification of particular types of judgements. To say this is to say that reality or truth are for logic undefined and indefinable notions.[15]

But it would then appear that Bradley's 'obsession' with the truth of judgements is merely mistaken, and it is to be doubted whether Bradley could have ever accepted such a view. All judgements will then have precisely the same form, and it is difficult to understand how there could possibly be any difference at all between conditional, counterfactual, or (above all) negative judgements. This view is only plausible if it is supposed that judgement is nothing more than a mental act of referring. What Bradley says, of course, is that it is the act that refers an *ideal content* to something else. Here a consequence of Frege's distinction between sense and reference must apply; it is not possible to refer to anything unless this reference is mediated by a sense. Manser seems to be aware of this when he notes:

> To have reached the conclusion that the logical form of all judgements is 'reality is such that S-P' is not to have solved all problems, for it certainly seems that judgements can refer to 'reality' in a variety of ways, make different kinds of truth-claims. There is a substantial difference between 'This is white' and 'If anything is a metal, then it conducts electricity'.[16]

The term 'truth-claim' suggests immediately that Manser is aware that there is indeed more to the act of judgement than merely a reference to 'reality as such'. Specification of the sense of the term 'truth-claim' requires an immediate distinction between the grounds for the claim, and whether

---

[15] Anthony Manser, *Bradley's Logic* (Oxford: Basil Blackwell, 1983), p. 106.
[16] *ibid.*, p. 107.

the claim is correct or holds. Following the contemporary idiom here, we should capture this more accurately by distinguishing between 'truth-conditions' and 'satisfaction of the truth-conditions'. Again, in a contemporary idiom that derives (in part) from Frege, truth-conditions are quite simply the conditions under which the judgement *would* be true, and it will be, is, or was true if those conditions, or some conventionally specified set of those conditions, are 'in fact' satisfied.[17] It is here that the proposed interpretation of Bradley's term 'ideal content' is important and effective. For a large class of judgements, the truth conditions just are those which the ideal contents contain, and on the proposed interpretation these ideal contents make the act of reference, and therefore the act of judgement, possible. Ideal contents, meanings (or much less accurately, universals) are *not* the psychic contents. Sensible psychic contents, or roughly sense data, but this term, if it is to be roughly the same in meaning as psychic fact is not the perceived object or even the perceived colour, since these – as Bradley makes clear in numerous places – are already structured with meanings.

This immediately suggests that a Tarskian account of truth might be appropriate – that is, the 'T-formula'[18]

(T)   X is true iff p

As I shall show, given the account of judgement so far, there are some very good reasons for supposing that the Tarskian account does capture Bradley's intention, at least for a large class of judgements, and this is so even if the multitude of remarks about the term 'true' do not always readily lend themselves to this interpretation. However, because the

---

[17] Warranted assertibility is very different from the conditions which might (or might not) make such assertibility intelligible. The truth-conditions (or meaning-conditions) must be kept clearly distinct from the *satisfaction* of those conditions. Warranted assertibility, as distinct from assertibility, refers to the latter and not to the former.

[18] Alfred Tarski, 'The Semantic Conception of Truth', *Philosophy and Phenomenological Research*, vol. 4, 1944. (Page references in the following are to the reprint of the original article in Feigl and Sellars (eds.), *Readings in Philosophical Analysis*, New York: Century-Crofts, 1949.)

Tarskian formula for material adequacy is frequently misunderstood, partly owing to the misleading character of its popular form,

'Snow is white' is true iff Snow is white.

Tarski has, however, been systematically and seriously misunderstood. There is thought to be an ambiguity present in this formula that renders the account of truth utterly trivial. On the left-hand side of the equivalence is the name of the sentence, a token of which appears on the right hand side. Both of these are, of course, expressions within the natural language of English, and it has therefore been thought by some that 'truth' has been defined internal to a language. C. G. Prado has claimed, for example, that

> Tarski offered what Donald Davidson and Rorty assume he offered: namely, a way of understanding how 'a natural language [is] a learnable, recursive structure...'. Tarski did not propose a way of articulating how language 'hooks on' to the world. His formulation captures what it means to say *within language*, that a declarative sentence is true. The sentence 'snow is white' is juxtaposed not to the brute whiteness of snow, whatever that may be, but to what speakers of English consider to be the truth conditions for the sentence.[19]

This is either completely mistaken or at least a serious distortion of Tarski. The question is whether the truth-conditions are merely linguistic items or whether they are separate from the linguistic tokens altogether. At one point in the paper, Tarski makes use of the medieval distinction between *suppositio formalis* and *suppositio materialis*: 'Employing the medieval terminology we could also say that on the right side the words "*snow is white*" occur in *suppositio formalis*, and on the left in *suppositio materialis*.' Tarski clearly means the term *suppositio formalis* to be understood as the medievals understood it, namely 'when the *thing signified* is

---

[19] C. G. Prado, *The Limits of Pragmatism* (Humanities Press International, 1987), p. 13. There is a common tendency to read Tarski as providing only an empty formalism. This is an utter mistake, and supposes that Tarski was unaware that sentences are merely instances of visible marks or audible sounds. Tarski assumes, as patently obvious, that the sentences are themselves meaning units.

under consideration'. The right-hand sentence, *qua* sentence, is not under consideration at all. With respect to this Tarski writes replying to the objection that his account commits one to an uncritical realism:

> For these words convey the impression that the semantic conception of truth is intended to establish the conditions under which we are warranted in asserting any given sentence, and in particular any particular sentence. However, a moment's reflection shows that this impression is merely an illusion....
>
> In fact, the semantic definition of truth implies nothing regarding the conditions under which a sentence like (1):
>
> (1) snow is white
>
> can be asserted. It implies only that, whenever we assert or reject this sentence, we must be ready to assert or reject the correlated sentence (2):
>
> (2) the sentence 'snow is white' is true.
>
> Thus we may accept the semantic conception of truth without giving up any epistemological attitude we may have had; we may be naive realists, critical realists or idealists, empiricists or metaphysicians – whatever we were before. The semantic conception is completely neutral towards all these issues.[20]

Asserting a sentence is one sort of activity; entertaining whether the sentence may or may not be true, whether the truth-conditions or meaning-conditions may be satisfied is a distinct and quite different sort of activity. The truth-conditions, or meaning-conditions, of the sentence named by 'snow is white' are just exactly those which the *user* of the English sentence *assigns* to the sentence, and these are distinct from the sentence as a sequence of linguistic marks or sounds. Tarski assumes that the sentence is meaningful, and the meaning – so far as this is a matter of truth-conditions is what one understands or intends, namely such meanings as white

---

[20] Tarski, *op. cit.*, p. 71.

powdery stuff, cold to touch, and which turns to water when heated, that which comes down on cold winter days, and so on. To use another term which Bradley himself uses, these are (a part of) the intensionality of snow. Whether there are sensible or empirical states of affairs in which these intensions are instantiated is a separate and distinct matter.

The truth-conditions, or alternatively the intension of the term, form an indefinitely large set. In Bradley's terms, we might also say that the ideal contents analyse into an indefinitely large number of 'universals'. Tarski is not concerned with this matter, nor is he concerned with the question: 'Which truth-conditions, or which set of truth-conditions needs to be satisfied in order for the sentence (on Bradley's terms, the judgement) to be satisfied?' This is a matter for the particular discipline, empirical or otherwise, to decide. There is, however, a little-noted feature of the Tarskian account which must be emphasized. So far as the intension of the terms is concerned, there is a large number of selections from the indefinite number of truth-conditions, any one of which will constitute satisfaction of the sentence – or in Bradley's terms, the judgement. The whiteness of snow has a relatively wide range of that particular colour such that the 'sensible instantiation' would still be called 'white', and similarly, snow comes in a relatively large number of different types and kinds, but all of these would still be called snow. What constitutes the satisfaction of this type of sentence, or judgements, is a conventional matter, or, perhaps, a matter of convenience, and in the case of discourse, a question of contextual considerations. Tarski is not concerned with this issue for, again, such is presumably a matter for the individual sciences or disciplines. The significant point here, however, is the necessity of conventions, when it is a matter of public agreement. For the individual entertaining the sentence, 'snow is white', any subset of the conditions will constitute satisfaction of the sentence.

Given that the above analysis of what Bradley can be taken to mean by judgement is correct, it is not too surprising that he does not specify exactly what would be the satisfaction of judgements. It has been claimed that the ideal contents (for the relevant empirical-type of judgement) are the truth-conditions. These are to be distinguished from the 'psychic facts' as Bradley calls the transient mental contents. Bradley is, in fact, much more acutely aware of the open-ended character of verification than might appear to be the case. The difficulties which Bradley finds with the analytic judgements of sense are evidence of this. This aspect of judgements is not, in general, a consideration for the investigations of logic, and Bradley should not be expected to provide satisfaction-conditions for judgements. Furthermore, it is doubtful whether he could do so without introducing the notion of 'convention', and in this respect it is not at all clear what theory of convention would be consistent with his theory of mind.

BRADLEY'S IMPACT ON EMPIRICISM

Fred Wilson

Bradley, late in his career, had occasion to respond to criticisms that Russell had made of his idealism.[1] On Bradley's view, Russell had returned to the atomism of Hume and Mill, a view that he (Bradley) believed that he had long ago refuted.[2] In effect Bradley is arguing that his own work has had no real or lasting impact on British philosophy. Interestingly enough, this view seems to be shared by David Pears who, in his relatively recent book on Russell, argues that Russell restores the Humean empiricism that had been forced underground by several decades of idealism: 'what [Russell] did was to take over and strengthen the type of empiricism whose most distinguished exponent had been David Hume.'[3] To be sure, Russell did respond to Bradley,[4] but the empiricism that Russell defends is essentially that of Hume. Pears thus seems to share Bradley's view that Bradley existed but had no lasting impact.

This view is quite wrong. It is certainly true that the Russell that emerged in the first two decades of the century was thoroughly empiricist, and that this empiricism has strong roots in the earlier empiricism of Hume and the Mills. But it certainly was not the same empiricism. Russell made important contributions that enabled empiricism to overcome defects that were present in its earlier versions. Those defects

---

[1] F. H. Bradley, 'Relations', in CE 628–76.

[2] 'Relations', CE 656ff.

[3] D. F. Pears, *Bertrand Russell and the British Tradition in Philosophy* (London: Collins, 1967), p. 11.

[4] *ibid.*, pp. 165ff.

had also been noticed by Bradley. Bradley, too, had offered solutions to those problems. Those solutions were, however, idealist rather than empiricist. Russell's contribution consisted, on the one hand, of responding on behalf of empiricism to the criticisms of Bradley while, on the other hand, criticizing Bradley's idealist response to the empiricism of Hume and the Mills.[5]

I. *The Earlier Empiricism*
There are two aspects of the empiricism of Hume and the Mills to which Bradley attended. One was the doctrine of relations, the other the doctrines of associationism. We shall be concentrating on the former.[6] After examining this earlier empiricist ontology of relations, we turn to the argument developed by the empiricists against necessary connections. For Bradley also replied to this argument.

(a) Relations
The empiricists took over the nominalistic account of relations that had dominated philosophy since Aristotle and before.[7] Consider the relational statement that

(@) a is R to b

or, in symbols that Russell has made familiar to us,

$R(a,b)$

On the nominalist account, such a statement has a two-fold analysis. On the one hand, there are the *objective truth conditions*, the objective facts concerning a and b which determine whether the statement is (objectively) true or false. On the other hand, there is the *subjective mental state* that the *use* of the relational statement *expresses*. As for the former, the objective facts represented by (@) are *non-relational*:

---

[5] This is not the only point where Russell can be seen as responding to Bradley; see the essay by N. Griffen, 'F. H. Bradley's Contribution to the Development of Logic', this volume.

[6] For the latter, see P. Ferreira, 'F. H. Bradley's Attack on Associationism', this volume.

[7] See J. Weinberg, 'Relation', in his *Abstraction, Relation and Induction* (Madison, Wisc.: University of Wisconsin Press, 1965).

(#) a is r_1 and b is r_2

or, in symbols,

$r_1(a)$ & $r_2(b)$

The non-relational properties r_1 and r_2 are the (objective) *foundations* of the relation. As for the subjective state that the use of (@) *expresses*, this is a *judgement of comparison*.

Notice that, upon this account of relations, if one of the relata, say b, ceases to exist, so will the relation – objectively, together of course with the possibility of comparison – but this happens with no change in the other relatum: b's ceasing to exist, or ceasing to be r_2, is compatible with a continuing unchanged, and in particular with a remaining r_1. This account of relations was explicitly stated by Locke,[8] and is the view that Russell was later to call the 'monadistic' account of relations,[9] making reference to Leibniz's adoption of the same position. The position is adopted by Hume, who considers relations as at once philosophical, that is, objectively, or as natural, that is, subjectively.[10] The same monadistic account

---

[8] This account of relations is stated explicitly by Locke in his *Essay concerning the Human Understanding*, ed. P. H. Nidditch (Oxford: Clarendon Press, 1975):

> The nature therefore of Relation, consists in the referring, or comparing two things, one to another; from which comparison, one or both comes to be denominated. And if either of those things be removed, or cease to be, the Relation ceases, and the Denomination consequent to it, though the other receive in it self no alteration at all, v.g. Cajus, whom I consider to say as a Father, ceases to be so to morrow, only by the death of his Son, without any alteration made in himself.
> (Bk II, chap. xxv, sect. 5, p. 321)

A little later Locke adds that:
> there can be no Relation, but betwixt two Things, considered as two Things. There must always be in relation two Ideas, or Things, either in themselves really separate, or considered as distinct, and then a ground or occasion for their comparison. (Bk II, chap. xxv, sect. 6, p. 321)

[9] B. Russell, *Principles of Mathematics*, 2nd ed. (London: Allen and Unwin, 1937; 1st ed., 1903), pp. 221f.

[10] Thus, 'The word Relation is commonly used in two senses considerably different from each other. Either for that quality, by which two ideas are connected together in the imagination, and the one naturally introduces the other ...; or for that particular circumstance, in which, even upon the arbitrary union of two ideas in the fancy, we may think proper to compare them', David Hume, *Treatise concerning Human Nature*,

of relations was also adopted by James Mill[11] and John Stuart Mill.[12] Prior to Bradley, it is safe to say, the empiricists explicitly adopted the monadistic account of relations.

This account was applied to all relations. Thus, for example, it was applied to *resemblance*. If Peter and Paul resemble each other in respect of being red, then the relation of resemblance is analysed objectively into two non-relational facts, that of Peter being red and that of Paul being red, and subjectively into the comparison of Peter and Paul in respect of colour.[13] It was also applied to *causation*. Hume argued in detail that the judgement that *A*'s cause *B*'s is to be analysed *objectively*, that is, in Hume's terms, as a relation considered philosophically, into a regularity, a mere conjunction if you wish, between *A* and *B*, and *subjectively*, or, in Hume's terms, as a relation considered naturally, into an association between (the impression or the idea of) *A* and (the idea of) *B*.[14] The Mills adopt the same view of

---

ed. L. A. Selby-Bigge (Oxford University Press, 1888), bk I, pt i, sect. V, p. 13). These two sides of relational statements, the objective and the subjective, are reflected in the two definitions of 'cause' that Hume offers, *Treatise*, p. 172; see F. Wilson, 'Hume's Theory of Mental Activity', *McGill Hume Studies*, ed. D. F. Norton et al. (San Diego: Austin Hill Press, 1979).

[11] James Mill, in the section of the *Analysis of the Phaenomena of the Human Mind* (1st ed., London, 1825; reprinted ed. J. S. Mill, with notes by J. S. Mill, A. Bain, et al., London: Longmans, Green, Reader, and Dyer, 1869; page references are to the latter) devoted to 'Relative Terms', states that 'If it is asked, why we give names in pairs? The general answer immediately suggests itself; it is because the things named present themselves in pairs; that is, are joined by association' (vol. 2, p. 7; see also vol. 1, p. 185).

[12] John Stuart Mill draws our attention in his notes to his father's *Analysis* to the 'set of facts, which is connected by both the correlative terms' that constitute the *fundamentum relationis*; and goes on to remark that 'objects are said to be related, when there is any fact, simple or complex, either apprehended by the senses or otherwise, in which they both figure. Any objects, whether physical or mental, are related, or are in relation, to one another, in virtue of any complex state of consciousness into which they both enter; even if it be a no more complex state of consciousness than that of merely thinking them together' ('Notes', to James Mill, *Analysis of the Phaenomena of the Human Mind*, 1869, vol. 2, pp. 9–10).

[13] Cf. Hume, *Treatise*, p. 14.

[14] *Treatise*, bk I, pt iii; the conclusion occurs on pp. 169ff. See Wilson, 'Hume's Theory of Mental Activity', and also 'Hume's Defence of Causal Inference', *Dialogue*, vol. 22 (1963), pp. 661–94. For an extended defence of the Humean account of causation see F. Wilson, *Laws and Other Worlds* (Dordrecht, Holland: Kluwer, 1989).

causation.[15] But Hume applies it to all sorts of relations, including spatial and those of degree, eg. of hot and cold.[16] Again he is followed in this by the Mills.[17]

(b) The Argument Against Necessary Connections
A is necessarily connected to *B* just in case that it is impossible for the one to exist and the other not. The empiricist claims that there are no necessary connections among matters of fact, things that can be known through ordinary sense experience. The empiricist argument against necessary connections among things was first fully developed by Hume. There are two threads to this argument and, it is important to note, these are not carefully distinguished by Hume.

The first thread of the argument is this. If we take the idea of some cause and the idea of its effect, then there is no contradiction in supposing the former to exist and the latter not: 'the actual separation of these objects is so far possible, that it implies no contradiction nor absurdity; and is therefore incapable of being refuted by any reasoning from mere ideas; without which 'tis impossible to demonstrate the necessity of a cause' (*Treatise*, p. 80). There is no contradiction in separating the ideas because these ideas derive from perceptions and in perception there is no necessary connection that is presented to us: 'as all our ideas are deriv'd from impressions, or some precedent *perceptions,* 'tis impossible we can have any idea of power and efficacy, unless some instances can be produc'd, wherein this power *is perceiv'd* to exert itself... [But] these instances can never be discover'd in any body...' (*Treatise*, p. 160; Hume's italics).

Hume's appeal here is to the empiricist Principle of

---

[15] James Mill, *Analysis*, vol. 1, pp. 362–74, 389–91; John Stuart Mill's 'Notes' to his father's *Analysis*, vol. 1, pp. 412, 437–8; and John Stuart Mill, *System of Logic*, vols. 7 and 8 of *The Collected Works of J. S. Mill*, ed. J. Robson (University of Toronto Press, 1974), pp. 338ff.

[16] *Treatise*, pp. 14–15.

[17] James Mill, *Analysis*, vol. 2, p. 7, vol. 1, p. 185; J. S. Mill, 'Notes' to his father's *Analysis*, vol. 2, pp. 7–8.

Acquaintance (PA).[18] Among the entities that are given to us in our ordinary sensory experience we discover no connections such that one of these entities cannot exist unless another of these entities exists. In identifying the property that characterizes the cause we do not have to refer as a matter of necessity to the property that characterizes the cause, one to which it is necessarily tied; the properties are presented as logically self-contained rather than as necessarily tied to one another. We are, in other words, acquainted with no such entity as a necessary connection in ordinary experience, and there is therefore no necessary connection among the ideas that we use to describe whatever is given to us in experience.

This argument from acquaintance derives from Locke. Locke considers the regular activities of external substances. These include the production of the ideas of the secondary qualities, the simple ideas of red, sweet, etc. For these activities to be explained as those who defend necessary connections require, there must be necessary connections between red, sweet, etc., and the natures or real essences of the substances that cause these qualities to appear. These necessary connections must be both ontological, in the entities themselves, and epistemological, giving us, when in the mind, scientific knowledge of those entities. But, Locke argues, we grasp no such connections.

> 'Tis evident that the bulk, figure, and motion of several Bodies about us, produce in use several Sensations, as of Colours, Sounds, Tastes, Smells, Pleasure and Pain, etc. These mechanical Affections of Bodies, having no affinity at all with those *Ideas*, they produce in us, (there being no conceivable connexion between any impulse of any sort of

---

[18] For a discussion of this principle see F. Wilson, 'Acquaintance, Ontology and Knowledge', *The New Scholasticism*, vol. 54 (1970), pp. 1–48; 'Effability, Ontology and Method', *Philosophy Research Archives*, vol. 9 (1983), pp. 419–70; 'The Role of a Principle of Acquaintance in Ontology', *The Modern Schoolman*, vol. 47 (1969), pp. 37–56; and also 'The Lockean Revolution in the Theory of Science', in S. Tweyman and G. Moyal (eds.), *Early Modern Philosophy: Epistemology, Metaphysics and Politics* (New York: Caravan Press), pp. 65–97.

Body, and any perception of a Colour, or Smell, which we find in our Minds) we can have no distinct knowledge of such Operations beyond our Experience; and can reason no otherwise about them, than as effects produced by the appointment of an infinitely Wise Agent, which perfectly surpasses our Comprehension.

(*Essay*, bk IV, chap. iii, sect. 28, pp. 558–9)

Locke's appeal to a Principle of Acquaintance is clear. Properties are presented as logically self-contained; there is nothing about them as presented that requires us when we are identifying them to refer as a matter of necessity to other properties, those to which they are necessarily tied. We are, in other words, not presented with necessary connections, and we can therefore, by PA, not admit them into our ontology.

But there is a second strand in Hume's argument against necessary connections. It is this. There is no necessary connection between cause and effect for the reason that

> as all distinct ideas are separable from each other, and as the ideas of cause and effect are evidently distinct, 'twill be easy for us to conceive any object to be non-existent this moment, and existent the next, without conjoining to it the distinct idea of a cause or productive principle.
>
> (*Treatise*, p. 79)

This is not mere logical separability. It is, rather, the stronger claim that the effect can exist as it *is*, that is, *unchanged*, were the cause to exist or not. To be sure, the latter claim entails the former. But the converse does not hold. It is one thing to hold that there is nothing about Caius minor *qua* effect that entails that Caius major *qua* cause *must* exist. In that case it would be contradictory to suppose that Caius minor *qua* effect exists while Caius major *qua* cause does not. But this does not entail that Caius minor would have all the same properties, that is, remain unchanged, if Caius major did not exist. This is what Hume is now claiming: the effect and the cause can exist independently, and unchanged, even if the other does not exist, or were to cease to exist. This latter is a stronger claim than the former. If a being F causes b to be G, then the first argument claims that it is not self-contradictory to assert both that *a* is not *F* and that *b* is *G*. This does not entail the *b* would be *unchanged* were *a* to cease to exist. But this latter is what is asserted by the second thread of the argument.

The first strand of the argument against necessary connections proceeded on the basis of an appeal to the empiricist's PA. The second strand has a different basis. Quite clearly it is rooted in the monadistic account of relations that Hume had inherited from the tradition. Hume is clearly assuming that all relational statements can be analysed into non-relational statements about foundations. For, on that account, one of a pair of relata could cease to exist while the other remains unchanged.

Hume notes that his opponents – he considers the Cartesians to be the most significant among those who hold that there are necessary connections – admit that necessary connections are not given in ordinary sensory experience.

> The small success, which has been met with in all attempts to fix this power, has at last oblig'd philosophers to conclude, that the ultimate force and efficacy of nature is perfectly unknown to us, and that 'tis in vain we search for it in all the known qualities of matter.
> (*Treatise*, bk I, part iii, sect. XIV, p. 159)

The entity thus *transcends* ordinary experience. This implies that it must be located ontologically outside ordinary experience and, epistemologically, that we must know it by some means other than ordinary experience. How this will be done will depend upon one's specific views. The Cartesians locate the necessary connections in the activities of the Deity, and as a means of knowing these invent the mechanism of innate ideas.

> 'tis impossible we can have any idea of power and efficacy, unless some instances can be produc'd, wherein this power *is perceiv'd* to exert itself. Now as these instances can never be discover'd in body, the *Cartesians*, proceeding upon their principle of innate ideas, have had recourse to a supreme spirit or deity, whom they consider as the only active being in the universe, and as the immediate cause of

every alteration in matter. (*Treatise*, p. 160; Hume's italics) Others, such as the Aristotelians, locate real powers and necessary connections in finite substances, and invent special abstract ideas as ways of knowing these powers. In general, '...since we can never distinctly conceive how any particular power can possibly reside in any particular object, we deceive ourselves imagining we can form any such general idea' (*Treatise*, p. 162).

The result of this analysis of the thesis that there are necessary connections is the conclusion that upon that view we end up in a state of complete scepticism with respect to causation: '...when we speak of a necessary connection betwixt objects, and suppose, that this connexion depends upon an efficacy or energy, with which any of these objects are endow'd; in all these expressions, *so apply'd*, we have really no distinct meaning, and make use only of common words, without any clear and determinate ideas' (*Treatise*, p. 162; Hume's italics). In contrast, with Hume's own account of causation, conforming to the empiricist's PA, there is no similar impossibility of knowing causal relations. To be sure, since causal judgements are judgements of general regularity about a population that go beyond the limited sample to which we, as finite human beings, are inevitably restricted, they cannot be known infallibly. But at least they can be known fallibly, which is rather more than is possible on the view that causation is a matter of necessary connections. *The introduction of transcendent entities inevitably leads to scepticism; conforming one's ontology to the empiricist's Principle of Acquaintance permits one to avoid such radically sceptical conclusions.*[19]

II. *Bradley's Critique of Empiricism*
Bradley criticized the monadistic account of relations that Hume and the Mills had adopted.[20] In the context of criti-

---

[19] Hume thus spots a problem that is general to any non-empiricist metaphysics that attempts to solve philosophical problems by introducing transcendent entities. Cf. Wilson, 'Acquaintance, Ontology and Knowledge'.

[20] This was the foundation of other of his criticisms of empiricism as he knew it, eg. the associationism of Hume, the Mills, and Spencer. But we cannot go into these other issues here.

cizing the account of relations he proposes his own alternative account. This account is that which Russell was later to call the 'monistic' account.[21]

(a) Relations
Bradley's contention is that the monadistic account of relations in effect eliminates everything that makes a relation relational, and he concludes that since clearly there are facts which are essentially relational the monadistic account of the empiricists simply will not do.

Consider again the relational statement that

(@) a is R to b

or, in symbols,

$R(a,b)$

The monadistic account proposes to reduce this to

(#) a is r_1 and b is r_2

or, in symbols,

$r_1(a)$ & $r_2(b)$

On this view, the objects a and b are *independent* in the sense that *if the one ceased to exist the other would continue to exist unchanged*. Bradley argues that there are relational wholes in which the relata are *not* in this way independent.

He proposes that genuine relations are incompatible with the independence that is a consequence of the monadistic view. '...a mode of togetherness such as we can verify in feeling', he tells us, 'destroys the independence of our reals' (*AR* 125). Conversely, if we do make the relata independent or absolute, then we destroy their relatedness: 'Relations are unmeaning except within and on the basis of a substantial whole, and related terms, if made absolute, are forthwith destroyed' (*AR* 125).

Bradley's point is that, if (@) is genuinely relational, then what is predicated of a is the property 'R to b':

[21] *Principles of Mathematics*, p. 222.

(@')   *a* is (*R* to *b*)

and what is predicated of *b* is the property '*R*-ed by *a*':

(@")   *b* is (*R*-ed by *a*)

This being so, if *a* ceases to exist, then perforce *b* ceases to have the property of being '*R*-ed by *a*'. That is, if *a* ceases to exist then, when one has genuine relations, it is *not* the case that *b* remains unchanged. In this sense, genuine relations always affect the being of things. As Bradley puts it, 'If the relations in which the reals somehow stand are viewed as essential, that, as soon as we understand it, involves at once the internal relativity of the reals. And any attempt to maintain the relations as merely external must fail' (*AR* 125).

Nor is this simply a matter of trying to turn relations into properties, that is, non-relational properties, as Pears naively suggests.[22] This is what the monadistic view attempts, and it is precisely this that Bradley is arguing against. Pears tells us that Bradley

> would argue that, if two people are married, the relation must make some difference to them. If this contention is interpreted in the ordinary way, nobody would deny it. But he means that the two people must each possess a property which makes the relationship intelligible. If this were interpreted to mean that they must possess traits of character which would explain the marriage, it would seldom be denied. But he means something very different. He means that the relation can be understood only if it is taken to be *identical with* certain properties of the individuals.[23]

But, of course, allowing for definitional shorthand that allows the rewriting of (@) as (@') and as (@"), the latter two *non-relational predications* ARE *identical with* the *relational predication* (@). The relation simply is identical to certain non-

---

[22] David Pears, *Bertrand Russell and the British Tradition in Philosophy*, p. 165.
[23] *ibid.*; his italics.

relational predications of the relata. In fact, the monadistic account agrees with this. What is crucial about Bradley's argument is that where the relation is genuine, the relation *makes a difference to the being* of the relata in this way: if one of the relata ceased to exist the being of the other would change, in the sense that something previously predicated of it could no longer be predicated of it. That is, if one of the relata ceased to exist, then one of the ways in which the other relatum *is*, one aspect of its *being*, would cease to be a way in which that thing is, cease to be an aspect of its being. Bradley is not here attempting to turn relations into properties; to the contrary, he is arguing against the monadistic attempt to do that. He is simply insisting that, where the relation is genuine, the being of one relatum, that is, the way in which the relatum *is* or may be said to be, is not separable from the being of the other relatum, the way in which that other relatum is or may be said to be.

John Stuart Mill argued that 'The only difference between relative names and any others consists in their being given in pairs; and the reason of their being given in pairs is not the existence between two things, of a mystical bond called a Relation, and supposed to have a kind of abstract reality' ('Notes', vol. 2, pp. 7–8). In asserting this, Mill is simply restating the monadistic account of relations. But he also holds that at least some relations are presented to us in experience:

> A rudimentary conception [of extension, that is, of structure] must be allowed, for it is evident that even without moving the eye we are capable of having two successive sensations of colour at once, and that the boundary which separates the colours must give some specific affection of sight, otherwise we should have no discriminative impressions capable afterwards of becoming, by association, representative of cognitions of lines and figures which we owe to the factual and muscular sense.[24]

---

[24] J. S. Mill, *Examination of Sir William Hamilton's Philosophy*, vol. 9 of *The Collected Works of John Stuart Mill*, ed. J. Robson (University of Toronto Press, 1979), p. 230.

Now, the relation is experienced, so, by PA, we must admit it into our ontology. But the monadistic account of relations will require that we treat it, not as tying the two relata into a unity, but as somehow a further thing alongside the two relata. But this simply won't do: we have lost, according to Bradley, the essential feature of a relation, namely, that where there is a relation things form unified wholes, not parts lying as it were side by side.

> Let us abstain from making the relation an attribute of the related, and let us make it more or less independent. 'There is a relation C, in which A and B stand; and it appears with both of them.' But here again we have made no progress. The relation C has been admitted different from A and B, and no longer predicated of them. Something, however, seems to be said of this relation C, and, again, of A and B. But this something is not to be the ascription of one to the other. If so, it would appear to be another relation, D, in which C, on one side, and, on the other side, A and B, stand. (AR 17–18)

The infinite regress is clear. So is its vicious nature. One aims to capture the relational fact that is presented to one, but every time one does that the monadistic analysis eliminates the relational feature. Thus, even where the empiricists are prepared on the basis of their PA to admit relations into their ontology, the monadistic account immediately eliminates those relations.[25]

What Bradley is insisting upon is that where the relations are genuine the relata are not independent in ways in which they must be if the monadistic account is correct. Thus, if (@) is genuinely relational then *a* and *b* are *not* independent as required by the monadistic account of relations. Nor will it do for the empiricist to suggest that she does insist upon there being a connection between the relata, save that it is subjective rather than objective. What is needed is an *objective* relation. As Bradley puts this point,

[25] Standard discussions of Bradley's case generally fail to note that it is perfectly sound against the monadistic account; cf. B. Blanshard, 'Bradley on Relations', in A. Manser and G. Stock (eds.), *The Philosophy of F. H. Bradley* (Oxford University Press, 1984), pp. 215f.

> to understand a complex AB, I must begin with A or B. And beginning, say, with A, if I then *find* B, I have either lost A or I have got beside A something else, and in neither case have I understood. For my intellect cannot simply unite a diversity, nor has it in itself any form or way of togetherness, and you gain nothing if beside A and B you offer me their conjunction in fact. (*AR* 509)

So much the worse, then, for the monadistic account of relations: since the empiricist account of relations makes it unintelligible how any two things can be genuinely related, that position is just wrong.

(b) Bradley's Alternative

What Bradley proposes is an alternative account of relations which can, unlike the monadistic, allow that there are relations that are genuine in the sense that their relata are not independent, or, equivalently, in the sense that the being of one relatum is not separable from the being of the other relatum.

> If it [a relation] is to be real, it must be so at the expense of the terms, or, at least, must be something which appears in them or to which they belong. A relation between A and B implies really a substantial foundation within them. This foundation, if we say that A is like to B, is the identity X which holds these differences together. And so with space and time – everywhere there must be a whole embracing what is related, or there would be no differences and no relation. It seems as if a reality possessed differences A and B, incompatible with one another and also with itself. And so in order, without contradiction, to retain its various properties, this whole consents to wear the form of relations between them. (*AR* 18)

Bradley concludes against the monadistic account that 'there must be a whole embracing what is related'. From this he infers his own account of the nature of this whole. The relata A and B are different things within a whole (A, B). This whole then 'consents to wear the form of a relation'; thus, if

A and B stand in the relation R, then the correct representation of this fact consists in attributing a property corresponding to R, say r, to (A, B). Thus, according to Bradley's account, the correct way to represent the fact reported by

(@)   a is R to b

is given by

(*)   (a, b) is r

or,

r(a, b)

The whole (a, b) is itself a particular thing (cf. CE 635–6), of which the two terms a and b are but aspects, and where the arrangement r characterizes the whole. But this whole consists of the relata as parts. Thus, the relation holds of the relata, not separately as in the monadistic account, but jointly (CE 636): 'where the whole, relaxing its unity, takes the form of an arrangement, there is co-existence with concord' (AR 19).

Bradley applies this account to all relations. He mentions something being *like* something else, which is to say, he applies it to resemblance. He applies it to space and time. He applies it to quality orders (AR 19), and to causation (AR 46ff). He applies it to contrariety among qualities, so that the general facts of the sort

(!) $(x)[Fx \longrightarrow \sim Gx]$

which record such contrariety become relational facts among qualities (AR 19). He applies the account to all predication (AR 16–17). At each stage newer, and more embracing unities appear to support the relations that structure the world. In the end all the apparently separable particulars, and all the apparently separable qualities or properties of things that we are aware of in ordinary experience disappear into one all-embracing unity. The ultimately real thing is one substantiality (AR 124–6). This is the Absolute (AR 151).

Thus, Russell's characterization of Bradley's account of relations as 'monistic' is quite apt. Not only do relations characterize unities, but in the end it requires all reality to be a unity of seamlessly inseparable parts.

We should also note that Bradley's account of relations introduces particulars that are not given in ordinary experience. In experiencing, say, a being to the left of b, we experience two particular things, a and b. We also experience the unity of a being to the left of b, the sort of unity represented by (@). But Bradley asserts that there is a further entity, a further particular thing, present in the situation. That is the whole (a, b) that is the subject of the arrangement. This further whole is not given in ordinary experience. It is rather, something discovered by the faculty that Bradley calls 'thought'. The object of thought is not something given in sense experience: 'That is [the object of thought] is not mere sense-experience should be a commonplace' (*CE* 208). Rather, 'judgement, on our view, transcends and must transcend that immediate unity of feeling upon which it cannot cease to depend' (*ETR* 231). Thought 'grows from, and still it consists in, processes not dependent on itself. And the result may be summed up thus; certainly all relations are ideal, and as certainly not all relations are the product of thinking' (*AR* 426). And since relations are in effect not known by sense experience our knowledge of them is a priori; and since they are all ideal, transcending the entities of sense experience, they hold necessarily.

In short, Bradley's monistic account of relations requires the introduction of transcendent entities and the creation of a species of cognition through which we are supposed to be aware of these entities. And since these entities are necessary and are known a priori, they in effect reintroduce the necessary connections against which Hume and the empiricists argued. But Bradley's case for necessary connections goes beyond dogmatism: it is based on his account of relations which responds to real difficulties in the monadistic account that was accepted by the empiricists.

III. *Russell's Reply to Bradley*

Bradley's case against empiricism rests on the monistic account of relations; remove that, and the case disappears. The monistic account of relations is offered as a solution to certain problems about relations that are insoluble upon the monadistic account of relations that the associationists had adopted. Russell accepted Bradley's criticism of the monadistic account of relations. But he rejected Bradley's own monistic account. Rather, he proposed a still different, third account of relations. This third account of relations is not subject to the criticisms that Bradley advanced against the monadistic account; it thus fulfils the same needs that the monistic account aims to fulfil. Yet it is also perfectly compatible with the associationist account of thought; adopting it, one has no need to abandon associationism. Nor is one required to abandon empiricism and introduce transcendent entities; in other words, it is also compatible with the empiricist's PA. Russell's account of relations does accept that one must abandon the monadistic account of relations that earlier empiricists had taken over from the tradition, but it also shows that that account is not essential to empiricism. Conversely, it shows that one can acknowledge the reality of genuine relations while rejecting Bradley's claim that to do so requires one to accept the monistic account of relations and the consequent abandoning of empiricism.

In effect, Bradley's critique of empiricism depends upon two things. The first is the need to account for genuinely relational facts. The second is the assumption that the only way to satisfy the first need is by accepting the monistic account of relations. Russell accepts the first, while rejecting the second. He rejects the second by finding a third alternative that Bradley has not considered.

(a) Russell's Account of Relations

Russell's ontology of relations has become the commonplace. It does not therefore require much development.

Consider once again the relational statement that

(@) a is R to b

or, in symbols,

$R(a, b)$

Russell rejects both the monadistic account in which (@) is to be analysed into

(#)   a is r_1 and b is r_2

or, in symbols,

$r_1(a)$ & $r_2(b)$

and also the monistic account in which (@) is to be analysed into

(*)   (a, b) is r

or,

r(a, b)

where the whole *(a, b)* is taken itself to be a particular thing. Both the monadistic and the monistic accounts of relations assume that predication always involves only one term. This is the 'common opinion...that all propositions, ultimately, consist of a subject and a predicate' (*Principles*, p. 221). Russell rejects this common assumption.

Russell's account of relations takes the grammatical form of (@) to perspicuously represent its logical form. The objective fact represented by (@) does not dissolve into a pair of facts about individuals – (#) – as on the monadistic account. Rather, as on the monistic account, *a* and *b* are located in a genuine unity such that, if one of *a* or *b* were not to exist, that unity could not exist. But on the other hand, this unity is not a whole of which the relation is predicated, as on the monistic account. Rather, the relation is predicated of the terms jointly. It is *a* and *b* being related that is the unified whole, rather than *a* and *b* being constituted into a whole of which the relation is then predicated.

(b) Russell's Criticisms of Bradley

Russell offers three sorts of objection to the monistic account of relations. In the first place, there are certain relations for which the theory can provide no satisfactory account; it therefore fails as an ontology of relations. (Russell directs the same criticism at the monadistic view of relations.) Secondly, the account leads to a radical scepticism in which in the end nothing can be known. And thirdly, it introduces entities that violate the empiricist's Principle of Acquaintance.

First: On the monistic view, relational states of affairs

consist of a relational property *r* being predicated of a complex individual whole (*a*, *b*). The relation of *a* to the whole (*a*, *b*) is the same as the relation of *b* to that whole. That is, the role of *a* in that whole is symmetrical with the role of *b*. Thus,

(*)   *r(a, b)*

represents indifferently both the fact that

(@)   *a* is R to *b*

and its converse, the fact that

(@$_c$)   *b* is R to *a*

Where R is a symmetrical relation, one for which we have

$(x)(y)[R(x,y) \longrightarrow R(y,x)]$

then we have no problem: if (@) obtains so does (@$_c$), and (*) can represent the two indifferently. But the same does not hold for asymmetrical relations (*Principles*, p. 221). Where R is asymmetrical, we have

(+) $(x)(y)[R(x,y) \longrightarrow \sim R(y,x)]$

In this case (@) obtains while (@$_c$) does not. In the case of an asymmetrical relation, there is a difference – an ontological difference – between a relational fact and its converse that is not captured in any account, like the monistic, that requires both facts to be represented indifferently by the same notation. But the monistic account was introduced to solve the problem of relations. Since it cannot do that, it must be rejected.[26]

To this objection, Bradley replies (*CE* 672), that the incompatibility between a relation and its converse, that is, the law (+), if it is to be more than a matter of chance, must be the expression of a real relation that obtains between a relational fact constituted by R and the converse of that fact. It will,

---

[26] For a more recent discussion of the problem of order, see E. B. Allaire, 'Relations: Recreational Remarks', *Philosophical Studies*, vol. 34 (1978), pp. 81–9.

therefore, be a necessary fact about R, part of the meaning of R, that its obtaining excludes its converse obtaining. Now, this may well be the case, given the monistic account of relations. It does not, however, adequately reply to Russell. For, even if it is somehow a necessary truth that the obtaining of a relation excludes the obtaining of its converse, that is, if it is somehow a necessary truth that a relation is asymmetrical, it still does not follow that one has provided an account of relations that adequately captures the difference between a relation and its converse. The point remains that (*) represents both (@) and (@$_c$) indifferently, and this because a and b occur symmetrically in (a, b). There is therefore nothing that accounts for the difference between (@) and (@$_c$). Bradley looks at the contrariety between (@) and (@$_c$) rather than the difference between them that is presupposed by the contrariety.[27]

Second: As we saw, upon the monistic account of relations, all relational statements are ultimately about a single individual whole, the Absolute, that contains all reality within it. Hence, in order to know any truth, one must grasp this individual totality, the Absolute itself. But we are finite; it is impossible for us to fully grasp this one subject of predication. It follows that we, that is, we as we in fact are in our ordinary experience, finite beings, cannot know any relational truth. In short, a radical scepticism about relational facts results from the monistic account of relations, even though that theory was introduced precisely to account for certain truths about relations that the empiricists had neglected.

It is worse than this, however. Bradley applies his account of relations to predication itself. The judgement that c is H, ie. that c is qualified by H, becomes a judgement in which the property of 'qualifying' is now predicated of the whole (c, H). But this leads to an infinite regress, one which is vicious in the sense that in order to make one judgement one must make an infinite number of further judgements. To avoid such a

---

[27] In fact the difference is there also in the case of symmetrical relations, and is equally overlooked in such cases also. But in those cases it is open to the monists to dismiss the difference as ontologically irrelevant. In the case of asymmetrical relations, such dismissal is not possible.

regress, one must insist in the end that one arrives at a whole in which the difference between it and its predicates disappears.

Bradley accepts this conclusion: '...to reach a mode of apprehension, which is quite identical with reality, surely predicate and subject, and subject and object, and in short the whole relational form, must be merged' (*AR* 151–2). But any judgement, any proposition, involves a distinction between subject(s) and predicate. So, on Bradley's view, no judgement about the Absolute can ever be wholly true. In fact, any judgement must be self-contradictory. For, on the one hand, it purports to be true. On the other hand, it purports to ultimately be about reality, that is, the Absolute since it is the only reality, and this reality is such that it must be false. Any judgement must therefore claim of itself to be both true and false. This, moreover, must be equally true of the judgement that no statement about the Absolute is ever fully true: this statement of Bradley's view is itself contradictory upon that view. This, surely, is to condemn it. As Russell puts it,

> we find monists driven to the view that the only true whole, the Absolute, has no parts at all, and that no propositions in regard to it or anything else are quite true – a view which, in the mere statement, unavoidably contradicts itself. And surely an opinion which holds all propositions to be in the end self-contradictory is sufficiently condemned by the fact that, if it be accepted, it also must be self-contradictory. (*Principles*, p. 226)[28]

Oddly enough, Bradley himself accepts this conclusion. In primitive feeling, instinct, we are aware of the world and of ourselves in it as a simple indivisible unity. But we are led to develop arguments to lead to this conclusion. Unfortunately, since these arguments involve judgements, they must all be unsound. Hence, as Bradley says, 'Metaphysics is the finding of bad reasons for what we believe upon instinct...' (*AR* x).

---

[28] Russell elaborates this case in detail in his essay on 'The Monistic Theory of Truth', in his *Philosophical Essays*. Russell was not the only one to advance this sort of criticism; see the discussion of C. A. Campbell, in Lorne Maclachlan, 'F. H. Bradley and C. A. Campbell', this volume.

In all his sturdy Victorian manliness, Bradley accepts all the consequences of his account of relations, however absurd they may be. For the rest of us, these consequences condemn it, if not as silly, then as philosophically unacceptable: any view that, in attempting to solve philosophical problems, leads to a radical scepticism must be rejected.

Third: We noted above that Hume discovered a radical scepticism implicit in the rationalist doctrine that there are necessary connections. This radical scepticism derived from the fact that the rationalists introduced transcendent entities into their ontology. We now see that Bradley's monistic account of relations similarly introduces transcendent entities, and similarly leads to a radical scepticism. It is the introduction of transcendent entities that generates the scepticism. One can eliminate the scepticism by eliminating the transcendent entities upon which it is parasitic. Hume achieved this elimination by appeal to the empiricist's PA. Russell does the same.

If Bradley is correct, then one can identify a quality of a thing only if one goes beyond that quality and relates it to other qualities. For, qualities of things stand in the relation of contrariety one to another, that is, for qualities we have laws of the sort

(!) $\quad (x)[Fx \longrightarrow \sim Gx]$

If this regularity is to be more than a matter of chance, it must be the expression of a real relation, or, what amounts to the same, a necessary connection, that obtains between the qualities F and G. Thus, in order to identify the quality of a thing as F, one must also refer as a matter of necessity to the property G, to which it is necessarily tied.

Russell argues to the contrary that the identification of a property is a matter of that property alone; identifying it as what it is does not require that we also identify what it is not. Russell (*Principles*, p. 448) refers to G. E. Moore's essay on 'The Nature of Judgement'.[29] Moore makes the point that we

---

[29] *Mind*, vol. 8 ns (1899), pp. 176–93.

have seen Russell make, that Bradley's view of relations requires us to ascend to the Absolute before we can make any true judgement at all:[30] it requires 'the completion of an infinite number of psychological judgements before any judgement can be made at all' (Moore, p. 178). The problem is Bradley's theory of relations. This account

> presupposes that I may have two ideas, that have a part of their content in common; but...at the same time compel[s] us to describe this common part of content as part of the content of some third idea. (Moore, p. 178)

That is, Bradley's account of relations requires the introduction of a third particular, the Whole, over and above the two particulars that stand in relation to each other. This relation is such that the one quality cannot be identified independently of its necessary connections to other qualities. But in fact qualities can be identified as themselves without reference to the relations in which they stand to other qualities and other things. Moore makes the point with specific reference to the relation between qualities and the mind that knows them:

> It is indifferent to their nature whether anybody thinks them or not. They are incapable of change; and the relation in to which they enter with the knowing subject implies no action or reaction. (Moore, p. 179)

But Moore implies it in full generality, and Russell says just that:

> To say that two terms which are different if they were not related, is to say something perfectly barren; for if they were different, they would be other, and it would not be the terms in question, but a different pair, that would be unrelated. The notion that a term can be modified arises from neglect to observe the eternal self-identity of all terms and all logical concepts, which alone form the constituents

---

[30] Moore does not add the further point that Russell makes, that *even then* we cannot make a true *judgement*.

of propositions [here Russell refers to Moore's essay]. What is called modification consists merely in having at one time, but not at another, some specific relation to some specific term; but the term which sometimes has and sometimes has not the relation in question must be unchanged, otherwise it would not be that term which has ceased to have the relation. (*Principles*, p. 449)

Note that here Russell is allowing Bradley's point against the monadistic account of relations. On the latter, the predications of one term of a relation would not change if the other relatum ceased to exist. Russell accepts this. What he is denying is the implication of the monistic account of relations that there is something about properties or qualities as presented that requires us when we are identifying them to refer as a matter of necessity to other properties, those to which they are necessarily tied. Russell is holding that properties are presented to us as logically self-contained rather than as necessarily tied to one another; he concludes that there are no such necessary connections. But such connections are required by the monistic account of relations. The falsity of the latter view follows. Russell's rejection of Bradley's monistic account of relations in the basis of an appeal to the empiricist's Principle of Acquaintance is clear.

Russell's general position against Bradley thus accepts the latter's criticism of the monadistic account of relations that had been adopted by the earlier empiricists. Yet Russell also attacked Bradley's own positive account of relations on the basis of an appeal to the empiricist's PA. Russell was thus, under the impact of Bradley, rejecting part of traditional empiricism, while at the same time appealing to the central empiricist principle of Locke, Hume and the Mills, that is, PA, to reject Bradley's monistic relations. How much of empiricism survived?

(c) Empiricism and Necessary Connections Once Again
Bradley's monistic account of relations reintroduced the necessary connections against which Hume had argued. Hume's argument against those connections had two strands. The second of these was based on an appeal to the monadistic

account of relations. Bradley made a compelling case against the latter, a case that Russell accepted. So this part of the argument against necessary connections is eliminated.

What of the first strand? This argued that there is no necessary connection between cause and effect because it is not self-contradictory to affirm the existence of the effect while denying the existence of the cause. Among the entities that are given to us in our ordinary sensory experience we discover no connections such that one of these entities cannot exist unless another of these entities exists. In identifying the property that characterizes the cause we do not have to refer as a matter of necessity to the property that characterizes the cause, one to which it is necessarily tied; the properties are presented as logically self-contained rather than as necessarily tied to one another. We are, in other words, acquainted with no such entity as a necessary connection in ordinary experience, and there is therefore no necessary connection among the ideas that we use to describe whatever is given to us in experience. The appeal is to PA to establish that presented properties are logically self-contained. But we have seen that Russell adopts this very same appeal to PA to argue against Bradley's necessary connections. So the first strand of the empiricist's case against necessary connections stands.

Bradley attacked the Humean account of causation and of laws. This case was based on the alleged need to adopt the monistic account of relations. But Russell showed that that argument was unsound by introducing his third alternative to the monadistic and monistic accounts. And he showed that in any case the monistic account was untenable, on precisely the same ground that Hume used to argue against necessary connections. So the empiricist account of causation and laws emerges saved by Russell from Bradley's critique.

Russell thus ensures not only that empiricism in its central tenets survives Bradley's critique, but also that it emerges strengthened, with a new account of relations that is at once compatible with PA and meets the objections that Bradley had raised against the monadistic account that earlier empiricists had taken over uncritically from the previous tradition.

IV. Bradley vs. Russell

Bradley argues that relations understood as holding between their terms generate a vicious infinite regress. We have seen above that this is so if one adopts the monadistic view of relations. Russell argues that the same is not true of his account of relations. To be sure, if we have the relational fact

$R(a, b)$

then one can define the propositional function

$R(r, x, y)$

and assert that

$R(R, a, b)$

Clearly, this process can be repeated indefinitely. We thus have an infinite regress. But Russell notes that it is an infinite regress of implied propositions, and is no more vicious than the regress p, $\sim\sim p$, $\sim\sim\sim\sim p$,... of implied propositions following upon the law of double negation. 'The endless regress is undeniable, if relational propositions are taken to be ultimate, but it is very doubtful whether it forms any logical difficulty' (*Principles*, p. 99; cf. p. 51).

Against this, Bradley was simply to restate his point that a relation taken joining two terms can never achieve a genuine unity.[31] In an experienced relational whole, 'You can have the terms, without which you cannot have the relation, only so far as (in order to have the relation) you abstract from the...unity, on which (to keep your relation, which requires some unity) you are forced vitally to depend' (*CE* 637). But this is merely to reassert his own monistic account of relations, rather than a reply to Russell's point that the empiricist can simply take relational unities to be 'ultimate'.

This ultimacy of relational facts means in part that such wholes cannot be analysed as Bradley requires if he is to get

---

[31] For more recent discussions of Bradley's regress, see E. B. Allaire, 'Wolterstorff and Bradley on Ontology', *Journal of Philosophy*, vol. 89 (1968); Kenneth Barber, 'A Note on the Paradox of Analysis', *Philosophical Studies*, vol. 19 (1968); and Richard Gull, 'Bradley's Argument against Relations', *The New Scholasticism*, vol. 45 (1971).

his regress off the ground. If we have the relational fact that

(a) $R(a, b)$

then this can be analysed into three parts:

(b) a, b, R

But the fact *(a)* cannot be reconstructed from the list of parts *(b)*. For that list is compatible with another, quite different fact:

(c) $R(b, a)$

In this sense the crucial unity of the fact that is created by the relation always escapes analysis. As Russell once put it, 'I do not admit that, in any strict sense, unities are incapable of analysis; on the contrary, I hold that they are the only objects that can be analysed. What I admit is that no enumeration of their constituents will reconstitute them, since any such enumeration gives a plurality, not a unity.'[32] Bradley holds that if we are to discern three entities in *(a)* as Russell does, then we need yet another entity to achieve the unity of the fact. 'The relation...has been admitted different from [its terms], and is no longer predicated of them. Something, however, seems to be said of this relation..., and said, again of [its terms]...it would seem to be another relation...in which [the first relation], on the one side, and, on the other side, [its terms] stand' (*AR* 18). What Russell does, on his account of relations, is insist that the relation is indeed to be admitted as different from its terms and that it is predicated of them.

> What is called analysis consists in the discovery of the constituents of a complex. A complex differs from the mere aggregate of its constituents, since it is one, not many, and the relation which is one of its constituents enters into as an actually relating relation, and not merely as one member of an aggregate. I confess I am at a loss to see how this is inconsistent with [Russell's own] account of relations,

---

[32] B. Russell, 'Some Explanations in Reply to Mr. Bradley', *Mind*, vol. 19 ns (1910), p. 373.

and I suspect that the meaning which I attach to the word 'external' is different from Mr. Bradley's meaning; in fact he seems to mean by an 'external' relation a relation which does not relate.[33]

As Russell's last remark indicates, Bradley's argument works against the monadistic account but not against Russell's which denies one of its crucial premises. But in denying that crucial premise Russell's account requires that one distinguish the relational fact from the set of its constituents. In this sense, any relational fact is more than the sum of its constituents.

Since the fact cannot be reconstructed from the analysis, Bradley rejects the claim that one can distinguish by analysis three constituents in the relational fact *(a)*. 'Since what I start with in fact is this, and what analysis leaves to me instead is that – I therefore can not but reject, at least in part, the result of analysis' (*PL* 693). Elsewhere he characterizes Russell's position in this way:

> On the one side I am led to think that [Russell] defends a strict pluralism, for which nothing is admissible beyond simple terms and external relations. On the other side, Mr. Russell seems to assert emphatically, and to use throughout, ideas which such a pluralism surely must repudiate. He throughout stands upon unities which are complex and which cannot be analysed into terms and relations. These two positions to my mind are irreconcilable, since the second, as I understand it, contradicts the first flatly. (*ETR* 281)

But this is simply to deny Russell's account of relations; it is not to argue against it.

In fact this is all that Bradley ever does in reply to Russell. Thus, once again, Bradley, writing in response to Russell's insistence that there is a distinction between a fact and the set or aggregate of its constituents,

> Is there anything... in a unity besides its 'constituents', ie. the terms and the relation, and, if there is anything more,

---

[33] Russell, 'Some Explanations in Reply to Mr. Bradley', p. 374.

in which does this 'more' consist? Mr. Russell tells us that we have not got merely an enumeration or merely an aggregate. Even with merely so much I should still have to ask now even so much is possible. But, since we seem to have something beyond either, the puzzle grows worse.
(*ETR* 288–9)

Bradley is here doing nothing more than assert that that which yields the unity of the fact must appear in the analysis. If it does not, then one has not captured the unity. He concludes that any attempt like Russell's to distinguish among the constituents of a relational fact will not do. Rather, one needs an account of relational unities such that one does not lose the unity. What this means is that one in effect achieves unity while losing the diversity of the parts. This is, of course, precisely what the monistic account of relations ultimately implies. 'For me', Bradley asserts, 'immediate experience gives us a unity and unities of one and many, which unities are not completely analysable or intelligible, and which unities are self-contradictory unless you take them as subject to an unknown condition. Such a form of unity seems to me to be in principle the refutation of pluralism...' (*ETR* 281). But all this is simply to beg the question against Russell. Bradley is denying precisely what is central to Russell's account of relations, that the unity of a relational fact is something ultimate and does not appear among the constituents of the fact. But he merely denies. When it came to Bradley's monistic account of relations, Russell provided an extended argument against it. In contrast, when it comes to Russell's account of relations, Bradley is content simple to deny, recognizing no need to make a case. Naturally, we are not convinced. Russell's account of relations emerges unscathed.[34]

---

[34] For another perspective on the disagreement between Bradley and Russell on the possibility of analysis, see P. Dwyer, 'Bradley, Russell, and Analysis', this volume.

V. Conclusion

For many years Bradley was taken to be a prime example of a metaphysician gone mad, and *Appearance and Reality* was read for no other reason than that of finding 'metaphysical' statements that could be held up for ridicule as metaphysical 'nonsense'. Thus, A. J. Ayer, in *Language, Truth and Logic*, uses a quotation 'taken at random' from *Appearance and Reality* to show the way in which metaphysicians are inclined to make statements which 'have no literal significance, even for themselves'.[35] The assumption was that the whole business had been radically mistaken.

That philosophers could arrive at that opinion was due in no small part to Russell's critique of Bradley. But if the opinion was in a way justified by that critique, it was nonetheless radically mistaken. That Bradley required a sustained critique was itself the measure of the philosophical significance of his views.

Moreover, a good part of Bradley's critique of earlier empiricism survived in Russell. Russell recognized the force of Bradley's critique of the monadistic account of relations that earlier empiricists had adopted. Russell recognized that if empiricism was to be defended it required an account of relations that was at once compatible with PA and met the objections of Bradley to the doctrine accepted by Hume and the Mills. It was Bradley's prodding and Bradley's challenge that moved Russell to develop a doctrine of relations and a version of empiricism that was free from the problems of its earlier versions. Bradley, in short, has had a significant impact on British empiricism. If Russell re-established empiricism after a long bout of idealism, this empiricism was no longer merely that of Hume, but something more defensible. That it was more defensible was due in no small part to Bradley.

If empiricists have come to be able to look back from a defensible empiricism to Bradley as a metaphysician gone mad, it is only because Bradley was not that but rather a searching and careful philosopher whose effective criticisms

---

[35] London, 1950, p. 36.

of empiricism and defence of rationalism moved Russell to create an empiricism that could in fact be reckoned as defensible. Even where we disagree with Bradley, we must, like Russell, give him his due.

BRADLEY'S ATTACK ON ASSOCIATIONISM

Phillip Ferreira

With the appearance of F. H. Bradley's *Principles of Logic* nineteenth-century empiricism came under heavy attack. Although there were a number of writers who persisted in the face of his arguments, Bradley's denunciation of the theory of 'the association of ideas' provided the basis of what was to become for many years the new orthodoxy in English speaking philosophy.[1] Indeed, even with the 'revolution' that the writings of Russell and Moore set in motion, Bradley's anti-psychologistic views on inference continued to exert an influence. It was only when the rationalist tendencies of the early analysts gave way to the more positivistic elements within the movement that associationism began to regain its lost respectability.

The precise nature of Bradley's attack has, however, long been lost to the common philosophical understanding which inhabits the English-speaking journals. Even though many of us have read of Bradley's influence in this area few can say precisely what his arguments were and why they were seen as important by figures as diverse as Russell, Alexander and

---

[1] Persistent proponents of associationism at this time included Croom Robertson (the editor of *Mind*) and Alexander Bain. I would point out, though, that after Bradley originally made these arguments in the 1883 edition of the *Principles of Logic* there was not an immediate effort to defend the theory. Although only one of the figures whom he directly criticized was capable of providing a response, it wasn't until 1887 that Bain countered Bradley's arguments. The essence of Bain's 'defence' essentially centred around the claim that no one ever really held the position as described in the *Principles of Logic*. According to Bain, Bradley not only attributed to the associationists a conception of particularity that they did not hold, he also exaggerated the degree to which the bonds developed between contiguous particulars characterized the position (see *Mind*, vol. 46 os, pp. 170–73). Bradley was, however, not moved by Bain's response. See 'Association and Thought' in *CE*.

283

Dewey.[2] Hence, what I would like to do in this paper is briefly review Bradley's position, providing at the end an estimate as to its significance for contemporary philosophy. It will be my claim that Bradley's views – although ignored – have hardly been refuted. And, I shall suggest, they still stand as a significant challenge to much of today's theorizing.

I

I think it not at all unfair to say (and Bradley himself certainly believed) that *the* empiricist theory of inference is to be found in what is called the theory of the 'association of ideas' – or more simply – 'associationism'. Given its first complete statement by Hume, it underwent development at the hands of a number of writers including: David Hartley, Jeremy Bentham, James and J. S. Mill and, in Bradley's own day, Alexander Bain.[3] It was (and still is today) considered by many to be the philosophical ally of 'scientific' theories of reasoning in that it does not postulate the existence of doubtful non-material 'ideas' or problematic substances such as 'universals'.[4] Although proponents of the theory have

---

[2] For an account of Bradley's influence on Russell see (in this volume) N. Griffin's 'Bradley's Contribution to the Development of Logic'. The reader might consult the index (esp. p. 431) of Alexander's *Space Time and Deity* (New York, 1920) for an idea of the extent to which Bradley's views were considered significant. One might begin to get a sense of Bradley's relation to Dewey by reading Forster's 'Unity, Theory and Practice: F. H. Bradley and Pragmatism' (also in this volume). However, a more sympathetic account of the relation between Bradley and Dewey can be found in Bosanquet's *Logic or the Morphology of Knowledge* (2nd ed., Oxford, 1911). See book 2, chapter 9, 'Truth and Coherence' (pp. 263–94).

[3] Certainly in the writings of Hobbes and Locke there are intimations of the theory. And, although his account was wholly inadequate, the Revd John Gay is often acknowledged as providing the first explicit statement of 'associationism'. While he published his *Preliminary Dissertation* (1731) some nine years before Hume's *Treatise*, it appears that Hume was unaware of Gay's work. See Albee's *History of English Utilitarianism*, pp. 69–113 on this point. Also of value is D. B. Klein's *A History of Scientific Psychology* (New York, 1970), pp. 638–759.

[4] That associationism is not dead is evidenced by the recent appearance of Fred Wilson's *Psychological Analysis and the Philosophy of John Stuart Mill* (Toronto, 1990). Wilson provides a spirited (if unconvincing) defence of Mill's theory. See also (in this volume) Wilson's 'Bradley's Impact on Empiricism' where it is argued that Russell overcame whatever defects Mill's version of empiricism contained.

admitted that its truth could be fully ascertained through an act introspection, in treating thought as consisting in nothing other than factual 'psychical states' it believed itself to be keeping the study of inference on a basis which was – if not rigorously experimental – at least devoid of 'armchair metaphysics'.[5]

However, the idea that a meaningful thought could be reduced to a factual, psychical state is precisely what Bradley found objectionable. That the fundamental 'furniture of the mind' might consist in nothing more than disconnected, discrete sensa and a set of psychological habits developed out of them, Bradley was unwilling to accept. Whether they are called 'impressions' or 'ideas' the belief that *psychical states* (which have some sort of existence in time and which are the possession of an isolated perceiving subject) could be the essential constituents of significant thought was to him an anathema. What was the doctrine of associationism that both Bradley and empiricism saw as the logical development of such an understanding of ideas?

We may briefly describe associationism as the account of inference that sees ideas (psychical states) as establishing psychical 'bonds' or dispositional 'connections' with one another on the basis of the 'contiguous relations' in which they appear. And for associationism the inferential process should be seen as one that unfolds essentially on the basis of these contiguously established psychical bonds. One of the most succinct statements of the theory's principles has been supplied by J. S. Mill who briefly states the 'laws of associationism' as follows:

(i) Similar phenomena tend to be thought of together. (ii) Phenomena which have either been experienced or conceived in close contiguity to one another, tend to be thought of together. The contiguity is of two kinds; simultaneity, and immediate succession. (iii) Associations produced by contiguity become more certain and rapid by

---

[5] See E. G. Boring, *A History of Experimental Psychology* (New York, 1950), esp. pp. 219–46 and 459–501 for an account of this development.

repetition. When two phenomena have been very often experienced in conjunction, and have not, in any single instance, occurred separately either in experience or in thought, there is produced between them what has been called Inseparable, or less correctly, Indissoluble Association... (iv) When an association has acquired this character of inseparability – when the bond between the two ideas has been thus firmly riveted, not only does the idea called up by association become, in our consciousness, inseparable from the idea which suggested it, but the facts or phenomena answering to those ideas, come at last to seem inseparable in existence.[6]

Let us examine the mechanism that Mill describes more closely. It appears that condition A (which first comes to us as a sensuous impression) will become associated with condition B – also directly sensed – through the repeated experience of their simultaneous or successive conjunction. Somehow, through this repeated contiguity, a 'mental bond' will develop between the preserved impressions (which in their 'less lively' and preserved form have usually been called 'ideas'). Indeed, the theory tells us that it is only through this repeated contiguous experience of conditions A and B – let us say 'fire' and 'heat' – that we have formed in us any mental habit or disposition to see these terms as belonging together at all. The strength of any association which so develops is entirely dependent, Mill tells us, upon the frequency and regularity of their prior contiguous appearance.

Hence (because of the previous regularity of their conjunction in my experience), whenever I think of 'fire' I shall also think of 'heat'. But, what is of great significance here is that when I am presented with the isolated impression of 'fire' this impression will 'trigger' or 're-stimulate' or cause to 'associate' the *idea* of 'heat' even though there is no *impression* of 'heat' presently given to sense, and even though there is nothing in the content of the experienced impression

---

[6] *Examination of the Philosophy of Sir William Hamilton* (London, 1865, 6th ed., 1889), chap. 11, pp. 190–91.

'fire' which itself implies (or in any way necessitates) that of 'heat'. It is solely on the basis of the psychic bond which has been established through their prior conjunctive regularity (and not because of any intrinsic connection of content) that what Mill calls their 'inseparable' or 'indissoluble' association comes about.

We find, however, that there is a further condition which is required for the theory of associationism to work. Although we must have first developed through the repeated contiguity of conditions a dispositional 'psychic bond', we must also have before us the relation of *resemblance* or *similarity* (I treat them as synonymous here) between a present impression (or idea) and a previous one. We must not forget that the theory of the association of ideas is supposed to be a theory that explains how it is we can *reason* given that the fundamental nature of an idea is to be a psychical image or mental fact. And it is only through the doctrine of resemblance that one idea (or impression) is said to bring before the mind another which can then bring forth a further idea on the basis of the dispositional bond existing between contents. But let us develop this central notion by considering an example.

I am presently smelling cod liver oil; this is the impression which is before my mind. And according to the associationist, it is the result of the relation of resemblance (similarity) which exists between my present impression of cod liver oil and previous impressions (now, less lively 'ideas') that sets the inferential process in motion. I smell cod liver oil and I think of orange juice. Why? Because (let us suppose) invariably in my youth when my mother forced me to take cod liver oil she also insisted that I wash it down with a glass of orange juice. And, since *every* time I smelled cod liver oil I experienced the taste of orange juice immediately thereafter, the appropriate bond developed between the two conditions.

So, the present impression of cod liver oil 'calls up' the idea (the preserved, less lively impression) of cod liver oil which in turn is attached to the idea of orange juice. We have first, a relationship of resemblance or similarity between the present impression of cod liver oil and a previous one, and we have next an associative bond (approaching indissoluble association) between cod liver oil and orange juice based upon their prior contiguous relation. Of course, the idea of orange juice could itself call up a further idea (either through resemblance or prior conjunctive regularity) which could in turn call up yet another. For example, it could be the case that after my present impression of cod liver oil calls up the idea of orange juice, it calls up the idea of grapefruit which – since I always ate grapefruit on the porch of my beach-front summer cottage – brings to mind the smell of the sea and salt air.

There is, of course, virtually no limit to the associative connections that could develop, and to give further examples would be redundant. But, always at work is this two-fold mechanism of contiguous relation and resemblance. Although both the psychical ideas and the associative bonds that develop between them may become quite complex, reduced to its essentials we are left with only these mechanisms. In the end, virtually all of our thinking can, according to the associationist, be understood to follow this pattern.

II

As mentioned above, Bradley saw the theory of associationism as the logical consequence of empiricism's greatest sin – the reduction of significant ideas to psychical states. I would mention at the outset, though, that in criticizing empiricist associationism Bradley did *not* deny that our ideas do associate or that the thinking of one idea somehow 'calls up' or 'brings to mind' further ideas which are similar. Bradley was completely willing to grant to the empiricist – indeed, insist along with him – that presented with one idea another with a similar content would develop out of it. What Bradley did object to, however, was the *theory* used by empiricism to explain this phenomenon (cf. *PL* 300). It is what Bradley saw as the shortcomings of the associationist's explanation that we must next examine.

Although he believed that the theory fails for more general reasons, Bradley does draw our attention to two immediate difficulties entailed by associationism – both of which, he thinks, should arouse our suspicion. Firstly, he claims that, although the theory demands that our ideas be somehow *preserved* – that they exist in a 'storehouse' of such ideas in order that they might be called up by a present impression or idea – no intelligible account can be provided of how this might occur. Secondly, he tells us, the theory rests upon a problematic account of the relation of similarity.

As for the first claim, Bradley argues that the 'School of Experience' (his mocking term for empiricism) could provide absolutely no evidence that its idea-qua-image could – after its first occurrence – preserve itself so that it can be called up again at a later date. He maintains that not only was there no empirical evidence of such a collection of stored image-ideas, but that the very notion fails to appreciate the nature of determinate existence which must characterize these psychical particulars. Although Bradley admits that psychical images can (and often do) succeed one another in our consciousness as the inferential process develops, he utterly rejects the claim that the image which is before the mind at any time is one that has somehow been 'revived' – that it is in any way the *same* (albeit weaker) image as the one originally experienced:[7]

...the particular fact is made particular by an elaborate context and a detailed content. And this is *not* the context or content which comes back. What is recalled has not only got different relations; itself is different. It has lost some features, and some clothing of its qualities, and it has acquired some new ones. If then there is a resurrection assuredly what rises must be the ghost and not the individual. (PL 306)

According to Bradley, any imaged content which comes before the mind as a result of the inferential process *always* reflects its new circumstances and the development of experience since its original appearance. Try as I may to

---

[7] I say 'often' here – but not always. See PL chapter 1, note 8 (p. 38). In the second edition of the *Logic* Bradley claimed that, although there must always be a 'psychical event' which accompanies our having a significant idea (and the event is not the idea), this psychical event can not always be characterized as an *image*.

recover the same sensuous impression of (for example) my first taste of vanilla ice cream I cannot. My present image, we are told, must necessarily contain both more and less than the original. Although I may be able to bring before my mind the idealized conception of my first taste of vanilla ice cream, the present image (which accompanies this conception) is entirely new and it cannot fully recover the intense nature of the varied data of sense as they originally occurred; nor can it divest itself of the awareness of subsequent experiences. No matter how hard I try I shall be unable when thinking about my first taste of vanilla ice cream to fully suppress the fact that when I had my second taste it was covered with chocolate topping. And this new development, Bradley claims, will always manage to infiltrate any subsequent image or idea I might possess (*PL* 588).

If Bradley is right about this, and if an image is not capable of being recalled in its original particularity, the traditional theory of associationism fails. It fails because one if its central tenets is that *what* is associated just *is* the prior impression (now an idea). Should this be shown to be impossible, the theory betrays itself as incoherent.[8]

Of course, one could charge Bradley with begging the question here. It could be argued that it is only on the assumption that the particularity which accrues to psychical images is relational that there is any force to this claim. And, indeed, Bradley's justification of this point is to be found only within the discussion of his fuller metaphysical views – views which we cannot enter into at present. However, this is certainly the least important of his criticisms.[9] We can say that even if it be granted that there is some

---

[8] It should be noted that on most interpretations 'impressions' turned into 'ideas' along with present impressions (part of which is the felt dispositional bond between present impression and preserved idea) is all that the theory sees as belonging to our thinking experience.

[9] In commenting on this paper Nicholas Griffin has (correctly) pointed out that the source of an idea's particularity is – at least when establishing the existence of universals – ultimately unimportant. The collapse of the associationist's argument would require only the admission that what is numerically distinct has 'recurred.' This is because (i) to admit that a numerically distinct idea has recurred is already to admit the existence of a universal (or a bond of identity between similars); or (ii) if not a 'universal' (as ordinarily understood), the item before the mind must be the sort of

storehouse of psychical images which somehow preserves each and every impression in its original particularity we are still confronted with the second – and more serious – problem mentioned above.

The empiricist doctrine of resemblance (or similarity) as it is employed within the theory of associationism is, Bradley tells us – although essential to the theory – ultimately incoherent. And, simply put, the problem is that one of the resembling psychical particulars must, on this account, be both present *and* absent at the same time in order to do the work required of it. But, let us consider this point in greater detail.

Bradley claims that for there to be any relation of similarity both terms which stand in this relationship must be *simultaneously* before the mind. But, then he asks if it makes any sense to say that a *present* and existing impression stands in the relation of resemblance or similarity to an absent – *yet to be associated* – idea? Let us consider Bradley's own words here:

> Similarity [we are told] is a relation. But it is a relation which, strictly speaking, does not exist unless both terms are before the mind. Things may perhaps be the *same* in certain points although no one sees them; but they can not properly *resemble* one another, unless they convey the impression of resemblance; and they can not convey it unless they are both before the mind. (*PL* 320)

---

thing, knowledge of which could arise only as a result of the associative process. (This is the aspect of Bradley's argument which I emphasize in the text.) The associationist defence against this first point is, of course, to claim that when a psychical fact 'recurs' via the associative process, the recurring idea possesses precisely the same particularity as the original because it is the same idea (albeit now obscured by other contiguous psychical facts). This move denies that there really is a 'numerical distinction' between the original idea and that which is revived through associationism. But with this move the associationist is (once more) obliged to answer (a) how it is that a 'past' idea can persist if ideas are understood to be mere psychical particulars; and (b) how these persisting images are connected to the new psychical facts which somehow 'call them up' from their state of slumber. (See also footnote 14 below on why Bradley's positive theory must reject the non-relational model of particularity.)

It would appear, Bradley tells us, that the associationist has an insoluble problem here. If two ideas are said to resemble one another (or be similar) then they must both be before the mind at once in order to stand in this relation (*PL* 320–21). But, if they are both before the mind how is it that the relation of similarity (or resemblance) can 'call up' an absent idea via resemblance? It would seem that the idea – in order to resemble – must *already* be present as an aspect of the existing impression. Yet, if it is already present, the relationship of resemblance cannot explain how it is that one idea 'calls up' or 're-stimulates' the next. Hence, besides conjuring up the non-existent past particular and placing it alongside the present impression, Bradley claims that the theory presupposes the very fact it was developed to explain; in the end, it is 'utterly bankrupt' as an explanation of the inferential process (*PL* 321).

But (and this really takes us to the heart of Bradley's opposition to the theory), even if both of these objections were met, Bradley believes that associationism should still be rejected as an accurate account of the inferential process. And this, we are told, is because it results in a vicious sceptical subjectivism which must ultimately appeal to the *arbitrary frequency of conjunction* between psychic particulars as that which effects the associative bonds between ideas. Even if it be granted that there exists a 'natural affinity' between certain ideas due to their resembling content, that one idea might come into contact with another so as to let this natural 'chemistry' work is, for associationism, a wholly contingent matter which could in no way preclude radically different word-world associations between judging subjects.[10]

> Association [Bradley tells us] implies chance; that is, it depends on circumstances external to that which is conjoined. And so, when we use the term, we must be taken to suggest that, if A and B had not been associated,

---

[10] It should be noted that on *some* statements of the theory even this 'natural affinity' was the result of contiguous (and wholly contingent) relations between particulars that were themselves entirely distinct and which had no content in common with another.

they would nevertheless have been A and B. For the conditions, which happened to bring them together, do not follow in fact, nor are deducible in idea, from the existence or character of mere A and B. (*PL* 300–301)

The point here is, I think, the simple one that the train of association which is set in motion by the relations of resemblance and contiguity is one which ultimately contains no necessity – no intrinsic connection – between the phenomena themselves; and, this account (if true) describes a process of 'reasoning' which reflects only the idiosyncrasies of the individual's own experience (*PL* 302).

For the associationist, it is entirely possible that when I smell cod liver oil *I* immediately think of orange juice as its necessary accompaniment; but when Smith smells cod liver oil *he* has called up before his mind the taste of mashed potatoes; and when Jones is exposed to this same fishy aroma *he* becomes overwhelmed with grief. And, since it is the frequency of previously experienced conjunctions between conditions that determines the *force* of this associative bond, it is all but impossible that when I smell or taste cod liver oil I should ever think of fish before orange juice. (Given that I have experienced few if any contiguous relations between the odour of cod liver oil and the image of a fish.)

But this, according to Bradley, is just the problem. Since these ideas-qua-images are seen as intrinsically disconnected there is nothing about the *content* of the one which would demand the *content* of the other; and neither for associationism can there exist any real criterion which would make the thought of gilled creatures swimming in the ocean a more rational, a more appropriate inference from the smell of fish oil than the taste of mashed potatoes or orange juice. Although the real universe may ultimately falsify my associative bonds, it would be (on this theory) not only impossible, but also *irrational* to think of fish as being more intrinsically connected to the aroma of cod liver oil than the taste of orange juice if my own experience did not *already* have developed within it the appropriate psychical bond between these elements. Hence, rationality just *is* what our arbitrarily established associative habits dictate. And there can thus be as many 'rationalities' as there are diverse, idiosyncratic experiences of the universe. For Bradley, though, such a result is unacceptable.

III

What was Bradley's proposed alternative? Although I can provide here only the suggestion of his positive views, we may note at least the following differences between empiricist-associationism and Bradley's conception of inference.

First, Bradley entirely rejects the psychical atomism of empiricist associationism. His own theory of knowledge (which stands in direct opposition to this view) claims that it is the necessary presupposition of any experience that Reality exist as a unified though diverse whole (cf. AR 464–5; also ETR 326–7). However, I would quickly add that he does not see this 'presupposition' as taking place at the level of conscious awareness. It is forced upon us, Bradley claims, in what he calls the 'feeling base' of experience. Although the perceptually discrete sensa which empiricist associationism describes may, indeed, be found at the level of 'relational' experience, to view these disconnected sensa as the primitive constituents of all experience is, Bradley believes, mistaken.[11] Experience *must* begin with a felt unity-in-diversity, we are told, and this unified though diverse content must be understood as not only preceding but also as continuing behind every perception and thought we might have.[12]

What is Bradley's proof of such a claim? Although the details of his rejection of atomistic theories is beyond the scope of this paper we may note that Bradley continually

---

[11] It must not be forgotten that perception is, for Bradley, 'relational'. And by this he means that it is already permeated by the process of thought. To identify 'feeling' with mere perception is, then, to make a serious (albeit common) error in the interpretation of his philosophy.

[12] Although the unities we encounter at the level of relational experience may be 'learned' the connections of content which feeling imposes on us are not. They are *given* (in the sense of being primitive) and as such they constitute the truly a priori aspect of our experience. I would emphasize here, though, that when Bradley tells us something is 'given' he does *not* mean that it is 'non-conceptual' or a 'naked' fact.

opposes such views by a series of reductio arguments. Bradley asks us to see where our theory would stand if we assume for a moment that our most primitive experience did *not* contain an intrinsic unity as he describes it. As a result of this thought experiment Bradley hopes that we shall understand that should there not exist a primitive unity of content within experience then every judgement we make – about both fact and value – would be groundless (*AR* 129, 221–2). This would follow, he believes, because if the connections of experienced content are postulated as belonging – not to the objects themselves – but rather to the finite and individuated minds of perceiving subjects, any sustainable notion of objectivity has been abandoned. When these connections of content have been reduced to merely personal 'dispositions' and 'habits' to associate imaged contents it is not the object that dictates the course of inference; rather it is the *arbitrary mental state* of a finite knower. But, Bradley tells us, if this theory were true then there would exist no non-arbitrary basis upon which inference could proceed; *radically* diverse conceptual schemes become logically possible and the doors to scepticism are opened wide (*AR* 134–6).

In opposition to such an account Bradley claimed that it is just the bringing into conscious awareness the 'sinew and joints' of Reality (which first come to us in the feeling base) that constitutes the act of judgement. And, to infer, for him, was to take one judgement and – based upon the clues which Reality provides at the level of feeling – develop this conscious, assertive apprehension into differing and expanding contexts through what he calls 'redintegration' (*ETR* 316–17; *CE* 212–14). Again, although any fuller description of this doctrine cannot be pursued here we should be clear on at least these points.

Through this process of 'redintegration' (which is at other times the 'ideal re-construction') of what is perceptually before us, Bradley believes that we can inferentially develop the object according to its *own* lines of universal content; and this he claims we can do in a manner which is not rigidly dictated by the mere conjunctive regularities of our prior perceptual experience (*PL* 466–77, 507–508). Even though I may have always tasted orange juice immediately after smelling cod liver oil, I can – if I attend to the object itself – eventually become aware that there is no intrinsic, no necessary connection between the odour of fish and the citric bitterness of orange juice. I shall through this 'ideal development' of the perceptual object begin to unravel *its* true structure in a manner which is not determined in advance by the merely contingent character of my previous idiosyncratic associations, but rather by the presupposed nexus of universals which together make up the given, felt Reality out of which all judgement and inference develop (PL 436–9).

We should pay particular attention to Bradley's claim that the feeling base – which he sees as including and *exceeding* the bounds of our momentary conscious perception – contains 'suggestions' as to how we might proceed to think about the object which is at hand (ETR 159, 195, 225–6). According to Bradley, even though I may never have experienced the smell or taste of cod liver oil without that of orange juice following in rapid succession, there is, nevertheless, something about the given experience of cod liver oil that will 'reverberate' through my feeling-based world and which will bring to mind thoughts and images for which the theory of inseparable association can provide no account (those of 'fish', for example). For Bradley, it is entirely possible – indeed, it is a common occurrence – for me to override the arbitrary associations of my previous (idiosyncratic) experience and allow the felt universal content of what is before me – in both thought and perception – to determine the direction in which its inferential reconstruction must be taken. All of this, he would emphasize, may occur *without* repeated exposure to new sensuous impressions which establish new associations (CE 222–31).

According to Bradley, the universal bonds of content which extend beyond my immediate apprehension of cod liver oil will progressively begin to link up with the 'ideal' (ie. universal) connections which reach out from my larger experience of fish. And I shall find at some point that I have rearranged my intellectual universe so that the relation between thoughts of cod liver oil and those of orange juice stand at a further remove from one another than thoughts of cod liver oil and cod. Through the synthetic analysis of perceptions *already* received I may reorder my conscious experience so as to overcome the arbitrary associations which characterized my previous awareness and replace them by an order which is both natural and necessary.[13] I may think to myself 'This is the smell of cod liver oil', and although for a time I might be inclined to follow this judgement by 'so there must be orange juice near by', after a while the collective force of my larger experienced Universe will begin to break down this 'indissoluble association'. And, it will begin to break down this association – *not* because I have replaced the old bonds with new ones – but because the synthetic analysis of the given, infinitely complex content has revealed the structure of reality to me (*CE* 212).

Bradley believes that a fuller examination of our experience will provide an awareness of a unity and wholeness that has been *made* by none of us (cf. especially *PL* 493–4). The unity of our experienced world is not for him a mere psychological super-addition placed upon 'bare percepts' – a reality that has resulted from our contingent and capricious exposure to the 'naked' and 'disconnected' facts. But rather, this given unity – even if incapable of being fully brought into view – is not only that which all experience presupposes, it is the ground of every inference we make (*ETR* 336–42).

IV

Although many of Bradley's readers have viewed such claims with suspicion, even his harshest critics have acknowledged that his objections to associationism are not without force. Hence, we must now ask: just how strong is Bradley's attack?

As already mentioned, Bradley's first objection seems to revolve around a notion of particularity which is wholly contextual. Indeed, much (if not all) of its force grows out of the claim that since it is always the context of a fact that

---

[13] Bradley believed that all judgements were both analytic and synthetic – hence the phrase 'synthetic analysis'. See *PL* 476–86.

makes that fact uniquely itself, then certainly given the ever-changing context within which psychical facts occur, none could (in principle) recur in its original form. We must ask here if the empiricist should concede this point.

Certainly the empiricist who is committed to the notion that the particularity of anything is inherent to that thing in a manner which is externally and indifferently related to all else will not be moved by Bradley's claim. And, certainly only a great deal of metaphysical argument could begin to persuade most readers otherwise. Of course, Bradley spent much of his philosophical career defending the claim that the contextual model of particularity was the only one which could begin to do justice to our experience.[14] But, unless it can be shown that the empiricist's conception of externally related psychical facts involve one in incoherencies there seems to be little reason to pursue Bradley's rather extreme doctrine.

We might also notice that the committed empiricist is unlikely to be moved by the demand that the storehouse of psychical particulars be given a complete explanation. Certainly it could be claimed that Bradley's own 'timeless nexus of universals' which possesses 'precise relations of content' is *at least* as problematic as the position of the associationist. Indeed, we might easily imagine the empiricist associationist to claim that the belief in particular mental facts which are somehow preserved is far less a strain on our credulity than is Bradley's 'Absolute' (which functions as *his* 'storehouse of ideas'). It could be that these ideas are preserved in potential form; and when the appropriate condi-

---

[14] We might at this point briefly consider why Bradley is so committed to a relational notion of particularity. Bradley felt that we must understand particulars as relational because to concede the existence of non-relational particulars would, on his theory, simultaneously be to reduce one's 'universals' to entities which (in the end) do no work. A universal – that is, a 'concrete' universal – is a content which 'binds together' or 'runs through' diverse contents within our experience. A concrete universal may also function as a (concrete) particular when it is seen as something which falls under a broader, more encompassing organizational principle. Hence Bradley sees all particulars (which also function as universals) as comprising a hierarchical network of experiential contents, the precise relations of which constitute the 'threads' along which inference proceeds. He believes that to concede the existence of either the non-relational 'universal' or 'particular' is to start down the road to insoluble difficulties, in that such a strategy would break apart the very system (that is, the hierarchical identities of content) upon which all actual reasoning is built.

tions are realized these potentials are actualized as present impressions.[15] Just because a complete explanation of the mechanism has not yet been provided does not mean that one is incapable of (eventually) being produced. If such stringent demands on theory were consistently applied then the advances of empirical science would never have taken place.

As for the problem of resemblance, much the same response might be made. 'Is it really that implausible', it might be asked, 'that within my present impression of, let us say, "orange juice", there might exist some sort of capacity to attract or perhaps regenerate those previously experienced images which have a similar content?'. We observe similar phenomena regularly in our experience of the external world. Just as the magnet attracts iron filings across the distance of space, so too might a present impression attract a previous impression (across the distance of time) which has been preserved in a potential form; and this attraction itself would be what essentially constitutes resemblance or similarity. 'There is', it might be claimed, 'nothing at all unreasonable about this – even if we may not yet have a complete understanding of the scientific laws which are involved.[16] In the end, this is all that the theory of associationism really asserts. That there *are* laws of thought which *can* be studied. Although we leave it up to the experimental psychologist to determine the physiological and behavioural aspects, associationism attempts only to supply a description of our experience from a more philosophical perspective; but, what makes our philosophical theory superior to most is that it is entirely consistent with the results of these sciences; indeed, it even seems to be demanded by them.'

Certainly, there is an air of plausibility which we must grant to this response. But as for the charge that associationism allows for 'arbitrariness' in our inferences, something

---

[15] This is, in essence, the reading of Mill's psychology which Wilson wants to maintain.

[16] There is something of this flavour to the interpretation of Mill's 'potentiality' in Fred Wilson's *Psychological Analysis and the Philosophy of John Stuart Mill*. See pp. 107–18. Also see Mill's *A System of Logic* (London, 1843, 8th ed., 1972), bk vi, chap. iv, sect. 3.

more, I think, must be said. Although I do not have space in this paper for an extended defence on this point, I think that something like the following is likely.

It might easily be suggested that we are not creatures possessed by omniscience; and that our thinking processes reflect the idiosyncrasies of our experience is only natural. Indeed, it could be claimed that what would be truly *un*natural is a process of thought which did not reflect our individual experience. Might we not see it as a positive thing that – since my own experience of cod liver oil was closely bound up with orange juice – *my* thinking processes reflect this? Surely (one could argue) it is perverse to hope that our inferences to the facts might be such as to ignore the radically individual nature of our experience. Our direct perceptual experience (so the associationist might tell us) is all that we have of the universe about which our inferences are made. To claim that this perceptual experience should be 'short-circuited' by some sort of appeal to the 'hidden universal contents' which 'timelessly subsist' is for the empiricist associationist to search for something which is neither possible nor desirable.

'We must not forget', our hypothetical associationist might continue, 'that whatever associative bonds and mental dispositions *I* possess are the result of the experience of the *same* universe as has brought about *your* associative bonds. And, although we may not see eye-to-eye in the beginning, the continued perception of this real universe will gradually bring about associative bonds that are in harmony with its structure – that reflect its reality. Indeed, it is this progressive duplication in thought of the nature of reality that is the hallmark of science. And, what distinguishes our theory (associationism) from yours (Bradley's) is that ours *never goes beyond the bounds of perception* in order to come to its results. However, yours is not only guilty of this sin, it openly advocates it as a method by which "truth" may be realized. By claiming that we may grasp the "intrinsic connections of content" which reality possesses without first having explicitly experienced them in explicit perception is a commitment to the most objectionable sort of a priori metaphysics which has ever been made.'

V

I think that there is much force in this hypothetical reply, and much here that any critic of associationism must take into account. An intelligible discussion of inference which proceeds upon bases other than that provided by associationism has, it must be admitted, formidable obstacles to overcome. And, to take on a theory of thought which seems so easily conformable to the presuppositions of common sense and working science must only be done if there prove to be insuperable problems within that theory. And certainly the metaphysics behind Bradley's attack lead us into difficulties with which we might be unable to deal.

However, Bradley's positive account is not our concern here. And when we move beyond the spheres of common sense and workaday science there are some theoretical problems which cannot be avoided through an appeal to philosophical complexity or experimental success. We must always remember that Bradley was entirely willing to grant the legitimacy of 'associationism' within these narrow confines. His concern was with the intelligibility of associationism as a *philosophical* theory. And considered from this perspective we are still haunted by enormous difficulties.

To consider the problem of resemblance first: although it may be granted that a 'capacity' does exist between resembling contents (one of which is only 'potential') this does not solve the problem that on any theory which views thought as consisting in factual states (call them 'psychical' states or 'brain' states or whatever) the relational activity of resembling demands that both terms of the relation be present at once. But (as already noticed), if more than one term is present then it is certainly not through resemblance or similarity that a present impression calls up a previous one. Even if one attempts to avoid the difficulty by claiming that the preserved mental particular is merely 'potential' until associated (at which point it becomes 'actual') the following difficulty remains.

Either the past (merely potential) state is a factual existent or it is not. If it is not then associationism has been cast aside in favour of something else. If the past particular *is* a factual psychical state then the postulation of 'potentiality' seems to have accomplished nothing (cf. PL 209–11, AR 339–43). We must not forget that resemblance is a two term relation; and, neither must we forget that this relation is said to appear in an impression – a concrete psychical state. Hence, to say that one of the terms in the *actually* existing (and wholly concrete) impression of resemblance is 'actual' while the other is merely 'potential' is to say that something is both 'actual' and 'potential' at once. But, on most interpretations of these words this amounts to contradiction.[17]

There is yet another problem with the defence we have considered. I think that, for Bradley, the claim that resemblance might be interpreted as a law-like 'capacity' to attract other psychical states would require some clarification. Although I suspect that he would not find it objectionable that such capacities exist, he would, I believe, take issue with the claim that a capacity could be 'self-contained' or that these capacities were consistent with the idea of 'indissoluble association'.

The problem here is that to claim that psychical facts are (a) law-like in their resembling relations; and yet (b) capable of 'indissoluble' or 'inseparable' association seems to involve an inconsistency. According to Bradley it is quite perverse to argue for the existence of natural and law-like relations between particulars in the one case while denying them in the other because, if we are to say that impressions have the capacity to call up other similar impressions (or ideas) via resemblance we are implicitly claiming that there is a natural *attraction* for what is like and a *repulsion* for what is unlike (PL 598). Yet if such a natural repulsion exists, how is it that 'indissoluble' bonds can form between ideas which do not resemble one another at all? While the 'natural' and 'objective' basis of resemblance is put forth as a defence against the

---

[17] What the theory of 'potentiality' is driving at (but is unable to coherently state) is that there *is* a connection of content between what exists 'now' and what 'was'. However, for Bradley, only a theory which sees these contents as *universals* (and not psychical particulars) can consistently state how this can obtain.

claim that associationism leads to 'arbitrary' inferences, in order to save the theory of indissoluble association these natural affinities are (whenever required) conveniently set aside. If there *are* natural affinities at the basis of resemblance then certainly these *same* affinities should be admitted as effecting what sorts of ideas can and cannot form associative bonds. But that aspect of the theory which sees contiguous relation as the *sole basis* of indissoluble association openly denies that such forces are at work.

The uncritical metaphysic behind associationism has, it would appear, a further result. If we take seriously the claim that indissoluble associations form as described by the theory (that is, in a manner which is indifferent to their content) then it is with the associationist's claims to a 'regularity of reference' that Bradley also takes issue. Upon what possible basis, Bradley asks, can the associationist justify his claim that his own inferentially constructed 'world' and those of others are in harmony or that they constitute an accurate representation of the external reality? Bradley's answer (which is in complete agreement with Hume) is that there can be no guarantee because wherever the principle of indissoluble association is allowed, a completely subjective world-view could develop. By making the content of an experienced fact wholly internal to itself (as does the theory of indissoluble association through contiguous relation) we are left with the real possibility that the way our respective visions of reality develop may not at all coincide.[18]

It would seem that if the associationist is to avoid a sceptical result he must acknowledge the existence of objective and law-like forces at work within the reasoning process.[19]

This he usually achieves by claiming that a certain 'natural' affinity – a capacity to attract – exists between psychical

---

[18] Our respective visions of reality may not coincide since there is nothing which could guarantee that they do. That is, since there are no structural relations between discrete contents which are other than the internal states of perceiving subjects any combination is, in principle, possible.

[19] It should be noted that Bradley (along with all post-Kantian idealists) took the problem of scepticism far more seriously than his twentieth-century empiricist successors.

particulars. But, Bradley asks just what could such a capacity mean if not the existence of a 'universal'. Indeed, it is Bradley's claim that any 'capacity' within psychical particulars (to effect or be effected) must be understood as something which can*not* be wholly internal to these mental facts. And if it be admitted at all that *something* extends beyond the boundaries of these individuated psychical elements, then we are left with precisely what Bradley means when he talks of 'universals' and 'identities of content'.[20]

VI

Although few today openly espouse associationism, Bradley's attack still stands, I think, as a challenge to much of contemporary philosophy.[21] To the modern empiricist and the advocate of 'naturalized epistemologies' his arguments point out the problematic nature of any theory which attempts to reduce human thought to psychical or physicalistic states of the subject. And perhaps what should be taken most seriously is his claim that any appeal to law-like behaviour on the part of psychical states is one which cannot be consistently maintained alongside the view that these states are essentially discrete, isolated and capable of 'inseparable associations' as postulated by the older theory. Although we may attempt to deflect Bradley's criticism by claiming that 'law-like' behaviour consists only in observed conjunctive regularity, with this move the problems of Hume are with us once more. If our grasp of a law consists in nothing more than the observation that an isolated Y has regularly followed an isolated X, then this 'law' is subject to not just modification and correction, but radical falsification by future experience. However, such a view of laws is – despite the persisting

---

[20] Of course, if one admits that there is something 'in' a particular psychical state that is simultaneously 'beyond' it as well, then certainly one is no longer entitled to view these psychical states as 'self-contained' or 'discrete'. But, if no longer seen in this atomistic fashion the heart of empiricist associationism disappears.

[21] Of course, one may dismiss the objections by claiming that associationism is an anachronistic 'subjectivist' account of inference which modern 'physicalistic' theories need not consider. However, in making such a move one has also dismissed the very idea of a philosophical theory of reasoning or inference.

positivist tradition which provides it with a veneer of respectability – both counter-intuitive and logically incapable of defending itself.

Equally problematic from the Bradleyan perspective, however, is the theory which – although it admits the existence of universals as the condition of inference – still claims that these universals are abstract, isolated and externally related. To see universals in this fashion is, Bradley believes, to see them wrongly. And as long as we fail to view the relations between universals as precise, hierarchical and the same for everyone we shall, he tells us, be confronted by the same problems that confront the associationist. If we sever the bonds of content between universals then we are at a loss to say both why one form of reasoning is more correct than another or why one moral course is to be preferred.[22]

We may conclude, then, that it is against atomism of any sort that Bradley protests; and this because to accept the atomistic pluralism that characterizes empiricist associationism is to open the door to, if not a thoroughgoing scepticism, then at least to a radical relativism that cannot adjudicate between 'higher' and 'lower' or 'better' and 'worse'. By viewing the contents of our experience as essentially discrete and disconnected we have reduced our individual knowledge of the world to little more than 'interpretations' with one being as good as the next. Indeed, if this exploded view of the contents of experience is an accurate one then the canons of rationality themselves would (as some have recently suggested) be subject to a thorough and complete 'deconstruction'.

I would end by pointing out that, although Bradley is the first to acknowledge that one may intellectually espouse a position which levels down all truths (of both fact and value), no one, he insists, can actually *live* according to this belief. And, despite the fact that his metaphysics sometimes demand

---

[22] Since, according to Bradley, all such normative claims presuppose that we knowingly participate in the same Reality.

more of us than we feel we can give, perhaps it is through a careful consideration of *this* point that contemporary philosophy can find in Bradley's thought something which is both immediately relevant and of lasting value.

JUSTIFICATION AND THE FOUNDATIONS OF EMPIRICAL KNOWLEDGE

David J. Crossley

This paper is concerned with certain aspects of F. H. Bradley's views on empirical knowledge. Beginning with a standard problem for a coherence theory of justification I present a number of interrelated issues, ultimately leading to a difficulty which is central to both Bradley's account of empirical justification and his doctrine of immediate experience.

That the discussion is about empirical justification locates all issues within what Bradley sometimes calls a 'sphere' of inquiry. In any such sphere we are free to operate with certain concepts and assumptions (or working hypotheses), and to seek explanations of the phenomena we encounter there, so long as we remember that we are not doing metaphysics, at which level all the provisional concepts and assumptions of a specific inquiry are subjected to scrutiny and to an ultimate test of their intelligibility. Given this, I stay clear of Bradley's metaphysics as much as possible.

I. *The Input (Isolation) Problem*
Bradley accepts a correspondence view of the nature of empirical truth.[1] He thinks that, despite their disagreements, the foundationalist, the coherence theorist and the sceptic all begin from a realist assumption: all assume both 'a real world

---

[1] There has recently been a recognition that Bradley's account of the *nature* of truth is not coherentist, and this is correct. Whether it is, then, a correspondence view depends on what that is taken to mean. Steward Candlish, in 'The Truth About F. H. Bradley', *Mind*, vol. 98 (1989), pp. 331–48, and Thomas Baldwin, in 'The Identity Theory of Truth', *Mind*, vol. 100 (1991), pp. 35–52, argue for an identity rather than a correspondence theory of truth in Bradley. It seems clear, however, that Bradley holds that within the restricted sphere of empirical knowledge we can and do employ correspondence as our definition of truth.

in space and time' and that putative sensory 'facts' are erroneous or imaginary when they do not represent this real world. Bradley further stresses the importance of sensory experience: we return to the sense-world 'not only to gain new material but to confirm and maintain the old' (*ETR* 209; cf. 203).

But does dependence on the 'sense-world' mean that my system of beliefs is built upon foundations? There are no foundations as advocated by traditional foundationalism: that perceptual beliefs or reports of phenomenological states express infallible facts which do not themselves need justification and which are the termini of justifications of other beliefs. If, on the one hand, the foundationalist's basic 'facts' are judgements then they are fallible, for they will involve mental operations, such as conceptualization, and rely on memory. Moreover, if the foundationalist thesis is that these judgements are of *particular* facts, Bradley's question is how sentences necessarily employing terms such as 'I' and 'here' and 'now' can be about particulars. And here he appeals to the familiar Idealist point that these terms are all universals and so cannot designate particulars. This point can be made by noting that the example Bradley is working with (*ETR* 205–206) is a token-reflexive expression. If such an expression depends on its context for its meaning, leave alone its truth, then my justification for accepting it depends on establishing the relationship between its utterance and other factors which I believe to be true of the utterance-context. Whatever else this might show, it at least defeats the foundationalist claim that this sort of item stands on its own.

On the other hand, if the foundationalist's basic experiences occur 'below' the level of judgement, how, Bradley asks, could they be *used*; how could they be or express facts (*ETR* 204)? This is similar to BonJour's worry about how non-cognitive[2] mental states lacking propositional content could ever justify other beliefs in one's belief system, and thereby

---

[2] I employ 'cognitive' and 'non-cognitive' in BonJour's senses. Roughly, 'cognitive' indicates any access to one's belief system which is judgemental (cf. BonJour, *The Structure of Empirical Knowledge*, pp. 69, 76). Thus, a cognitive mental state is, for BonJour, always a propositional attitude with a propositional object.

presents one horn of the anti-foundationalist dilemma. The previous point expresses the other horn.

However, Bradley does admit a foundation. The beliefs justifiably accepted at any given time are used in evaluating further candidate-beliefs, and must be provisionally taken to be true if the epistemic enterprise is to get off the ground. This is Bradley's version of BonJour's 'doxastic presumption'.[3]

There is, moreover, another sense in which Bradley allows a foundation of empirical justification. Immediate experience (immediate feeling) is a condition 'with which knowledge begins' and it 'remains throughout as the present foundation of my known world' (*ETR* 159–60). But, unless this is simply restating the doxastic presumption, how are these experiences foundational in any other sense than that intended by epistemic foundationalism?[4]

While empirical truth is understood in terms of correspondence, the criterion of justification is coherence. We only take 'facts' to be justified if they 'contribute to the order of experience' (*ETR* 210; cf. *ES* 74) – ie. if they cohere with our system of beliefs. This demands not merely that a system of beliefs be consistent, but that it be comprehensive as well. This is perhaps Bradley's way of stating that a system must be *maximally* coherent, that one cannot obtain the desired result by arbitrarily reducing the number of endorsed beliefs. And

---

[3] BonJour, pp. 101–106; Bradley, *ETR* 209 and 212. A similar point is entailed in Lehrer's views about our 'acceptance system'. See Keith Lehrer, *Theory of Knowledge* (Boulder: Westview Press, 1990), pp. 114–15 and *passim*.

[4] It may just restate the doxastic presumption from a more psychological perspective; see *AR* 198; *ETR* 46. However, as I shall suggest later, there is textual evidence for a third sense of 'foundation' (and which sounds close to the first sense, attributable to epistemic foundationalism).

Part of the problem is Bradley's tendency to talk of the 'beginning' and of the 'foundation' of knowledge almost as though they were the same thing (eg. *ETR* 209). He would agree that the psychological point of entry (the beginning) need not be the ultimate epistemic ground (the foundation), and he is marking this sort of distinction when he warns the reader to 'carefully distinguish' the 'cause in psychology and the ground in logic' (*PL* 546). (This is part of the case made by the Oxford Idealists against the psychologism of the 'new way of ideas'.) Perhaps he is led to the more careless way of talking when he is claiming that immediate experience is both beginning and foundation. But then the issue is what the latter means.

this point about comprehensiveness is the basis of his response to the alternate coherent systems objection (*ETR* 214).[5]

But this raises one of the standard concerns about a coherence theory of empirical justification. Have we any assurance that a maximally coherent set of beliefs is not isolated from the empirical world? Is there any characteristic of any of our experiences which suggests that we are receiving input from the external extra-theoretic world?

Bradley claims there are certain experiences which do have a distinctive character; namely, the given experiences of feeling, which have special significance because they are compulsory. This is a familiar argument in the history of the subject. Both Locke and Berkeley held that it is our inability to produce and banish ideas of sensation which suggests their external aetiology. These ideas are involuntary in the sense that we can detect no inferences being made and no mental processes operating in a productive capacity when they occur. Similarly, BonJour's 'cognitively spontaneous beliefs' have a special place because they are not the products of inferences (BonJour, pp. 117, 129).[6]

Hence, the immediacy of involuntary experiences – that they are not mediated products of mental processes – suggests they are not mere fancies of our mind. That they are *forced* upon us makes them the putative locus of input from the external world. These experiences are characterized by Bradley as 'feelings',[7] which purportedly are non-cognitive,

---

[5] The 'alternate coherent systems' objection is related to the isolation problem, for both require the realist assumption that there is one world which it is the goal of our beliefs to represent. Given this assumption multiple coherent systems, if they really were significantly different, could hardly be thought of as *each* being truth-conducive in the sense of accurately representing the one empirical world.

[6] For BonJour, 'spontaneity' is a feature of beliefs. Bradley would reject this and make spontaneity a function of presentational non-cognitive sensory states.

[7] There is an important ambiguity that attaches to 'immediate experience' and 'feeling' (cf. *AR* 198 and 405ff.). It can refer to the primordial unified situation that is logically presupposed by certain activities, such as judgement, but which at the same time is never fully or finally transcended. In this sense it likely reflects a doctrine of substance. But when used in the plural – 'immediate experiences' or 'feelings' – the reference seems to be to individual non-cognitive acts of sensing or apprehension of a finite centre. The latter will then allow for singular expressions to refer to one of these. It is this second sense which is important in the discussion which follows, and it probably marks the site of a connection with views of sensation found in classical empiricism.

non-conceptual sensory mental states. This raises the questions of their nature and status. (It also raises the question of how we establish, if we can, that they represent the real world. I do not discuss this here.)

Moreover, Bradley must explain how feelings can be presentational, and thereby candidates for input from the external world and putative checks on our system of empirical beliefs, without abandoning a coherence theory of justification. A pure coherence criterion should give them no special status. Therefore truth – as correspondence between our system of beliefs and the real world – ought not to be achievable at the level of these 'foundational' experiences, whatever their nature turns out to be, but only after some form of elimination, or best explanation, argument at a metajustificatory level. Yet, that feelings are said to provide the 'foundation' of knowledge (*ETR* 159–60) suggests they do have special epistemic authority.

II. *Bradley's Solution*

The main outline of Bradley's solution to the isolation problem appears in the first pages of the paper, 'On Our Knowledge of Immediate Experience' (*ETR* chap. 6). He begins by asserting that not all experience is cognitive in the sense of entailing a propositional attitude or a propositional object. 'The experienced will not all fall under the head of an object for a subject.' First, pain and pleasure seem obvious counter-examples and, secondly, '[i]n my general feeling at any moment there is more than the objects before me...' (*ETR* 159).[8] These non-cognitive experiences are immediate in the sense of being a 'direct sense of my momentary contents and being'; they are experiences 'in which there is no distinction

---

(For a discussion of this link see James Bradley's 'F. H. Bradley's Metaphysics of Feeling and its Place in the History of Philosophy', in A. Manser and G. Stock (eds.), *The Philosophy of F. H. Bradley* (Oxford: Clarendon Press, 1984.) There are also contexts in which Bradley uses 'feeling' in a third and more ordinary sense to refer to an emotion as opposed to a thought or a volition (eg. *AR* 463).

[8] A useful way to view this is provided by Candlish's analysis of Dretske's distinction between digital and analogue forms of information carriers. See Steward Candlish, 'The Truth About F. H. Bradley', *Mind*, vol. 98 (1989), pp. 347–8.

between my awareness and that of which it is aware' (*ETR* 159–60). (Here we seem to have the key elements required for a foundational theory of empirical justification and thus face the basic problem noted in the previous section. If the criterion of justification is coherence, then the non-cognitive experiences of feeling should have no epistemic authority or priority. Yet if they really are both the beginning and the foundation of our knowledge, these experiences must have special epistemic status and authority; and if they do, are they not then foundational experiences which not only provide central clues about the empirical world, especially since they are not products of our mental processes, but are also experiences which must ground other beliefs and against which these other beliefs must be adjudicated?)

Clearly, these remarks raise crucial questions. Stout, for one, suggested that in order to know anything about an immediate experience, or to speak about it, it must be an object for us and thereby loses its immediacy (cf. *ETR* 160). Moreover, if such knowledge requires an awareness or attending to the experience there is no guarantee that the activity of attention has not altered the experience, resulting in failure to grasp what the feeling was in and of itself.

A further difficulty lies in Bradley's claim that these non-cognitive experiences have contents. Even as unprocessed via conceptualizations or judgements, feelings must have content if they are to mark sites of empirical input and are to be connectable to beliefs and other cognitive states. Bradley himself acknowledges the problem of determining the role such non-cognitive items could possibly play in justification when he asks how the alleged 'facts' of a foundationalist theory could ever be 'used' if they are construed as occurring 'below' the level of perception and memory (*ETR* 204–205). Moreover, do we not have to be aware of, or attend to, these contents, which thereby makes them *objects* of immediate experiences? Yet, immediate experience is supposedly non-cognitive and without objects.

In response to this, Bradley notes that we can, on some occasions, 'become aware of sensations which previously we did not notice'. Given this, there then 'may be a doubt whether they were actually there before, or have on the other

Justification and Empirical Knowledge 313

hand been made by our attending' (*ETR* 161–2). The questions to be asked here are: (1) what is the nature of the experiences of unattended-to sensations or immediate feelings, and; (2) once brought to the level of attention, can we compare the sensation, as attended to, to the immediate felt sensation, in order to judge that the object of attention accurately represents the felt sensation?

There seems no disagreement about the nature of attention. As a focusing on, or a noticing of, something it is a cognitive activity beyond the level of immediate experience. This is for two reasons. First, there is already a distinction between the self which is attending and the sensation which is being attended to. Secondly, attention is clearly a voluntary intentional mental state with a *propositional* object, for in attending to my bitten finger I am aware *that* my finger has a certain felt quality or *that* my finger has been affected by something.

Yet Bradley believes there are sometimes more primitive experiences to which the act of attention is attracted, and which are direct apprehensions which neither require propositional attitudes in order to exist nor require attention, or any other propositional attitude, in order for one to experience them as having at least some very general determinate character. Bradley further holds that there is evidence that they are not altered by attention when they are noticed or attended to. If attention is an activity requiring time and if the sensation appears to us 'as soon as we attend, the sensation must have preceded' (*ETR* 162). I assume an example might be that I can suddenly notice the pressure of the chair on my leg when someone asks whether I am comfortable. While not conclusive, Bradley thinks this is the source of our common-sense belief that the sensation was there to be noticed and not created by the act of attending.

The key is that 'apart from any attention we can experience a change in our condition' (*ETR* 163).[9] Suppose that

---

[9] There are some assumptions and further details to this solution (*ETR* 163ff.) which I am omitting here.

I feel a change, and that something has happened to my finger. On attending I find that it has been bitten by an insect. Of the previous sensation I have possibly enough remaining or reproducible to enable me to know that before the change my finger felt much like the others. ...I now attend to my other fingers, but they do not, on this, become bitten. (*ETR* 164)

Even if attention produces a felt change, it does not produce the previous feeling which attracted my attention in the first place. Here Bradley repeats the point about involuntariness: the initial felt change triggering the act of attending is spontaneously produced and so is not the product of attention.

But are we certain that attention, although not producing the feeling, has not altered it? There are two points to consider here. First, Bradley introduces the notion of felt agreement or disagreement (felt contradictions). Having 'translated' my feelings into objects, there remains something of the original feeling and these 'persisting feelings can be felt to jar or to accord with the general result of observation' (*ETR* 167–8). Secondly, another example, from introspective attention, suggests a test. Suppose I feel despondent or angry (presumably without having *judged* that I am in such an emotional state). In such cases 'a man can feel that a description of such states is right or wrong, though he may be unable to compare this description with another object' (*ETR* 168).

Where has all this got us? First, that some experiences are involuntary and spontaneous shows that we are being affected by something outside ourselves. That there are sometimes unnoticed feelings which we can come to be aware of and to attend to confirms this view. Second, since these feelings have content we can determine – again at the level of felt harmonies or felt contradictions – that judgements about these feelings either cohere or fail to cohere with them. That is, the felt non-cognitive states can provide support for beliefs and be used in confirming or disconfirming those beliefs. Third, in so far as the feelings tend to develop themselves or are developed into observation statements they provide putative input from the empirical world. Thus, there is reason to hold that our system of beliefs is not isolated from the external, empirical world.

However, this is not good enough as it stands. First, it is not yet clear how to describe non-cognitive immediate experiences possessing content. The content of a belief is a proposition but what exactly is the content of a non-cognitive mental state? Further, how can these non-cognitive apprehensions be related to cognitive items, such as beliefs and perceptual judgements? A belief can be consistent with another belief in virtue of the logical relations obtaining between the propositions constituting the contents of the beliefs, but can a non-cognitive sensory state lacking propositional content be said to be consistent or inconsistent with a belief in any meaningful sense? Bradley's answer to this hinges on the unique doctrine of felt harmonies and felt contradictions – usually presented in metaphorical terms such 'jarring' or 'uneasiness'. Experiencing these jarrings or harmonies provides a type of coherence test across the cognitive/non-cognitive boundary.[10] But these metaphors need to be cashed out. (I will not attempt this here.)[11]

III. *The Antifoundationalist Dilemma*
In *The Structure of Empirical Knowledge* BonJour suggests that foundationalism faces a dilemma in explaining the given of sensory experience. One horn is this: if the immediately given is a direct awareness which is cognitive or 'judgemental' then, while these intentional states can serve to justify other beliefs in virtue of their propositional content, they will themselves require justification. Thus, they cannot then be the basic epistemic items the foundationalist seeks. The second horn is this: if the immediately given apprehensions are non-cognitive or non-judgemental, then, even if they thereby

---

[10] These may only be quasi- or pseudo- coherence tests bearing, at best, some analogy to full-blooded consistencies and contradictions, which hold only of propositions. Note Bradley's remarks at *ETR* 270 and *CE* 660.

[11] I suspect the notion of 'satisfaction' is crucial in this context. For a discussion of that notion see James Bradley's 'From Presence to Process: Bradley and Whitehead', in this volume.

require no justification themselves, they cannot serve to justify other beliefs.[12] Bradley himself employs a variant of this dilemma in On Truth and Coherence (ETR 204–205).

BonJour's second horn raises, among others, the question: Why are non-cognitive states not able to justify cognitive states?

This question is crucial for the foundationalist who believes in epistemic intuitions for if one cannot cross the non-cognitive/cognitive boundary, it becomes difficult to see how these intuitions could generate belief claims or be employed in empirical tests to confirm or disconfirm beliefs. This question is also important for Bradley's programme, for if BonJour is right, the feelings of immediate experience could not fulfil the roles Bradley assigns them, of being the 'present foundation of my known world' (ETR 160) and, presumably, of being the point of contact with the sense-world from which we 'not only gain new material but...confirm and maintain the old' (ETR 209). Interestingly, both Bradley and the epistemic foundationalists – at least any committed to the phenomenologically given – appear to be impaled on the second horn of BonJour's dilemma.

Why does BonJour hold that non-cognitive states cannot bear justificatory relations to cognitive states? I think the basic reason is that he holds that justification requires providing *reasons* and providing reasons requires linking the target belief to the supporting items (other beliefs or whatever) by the sorts of links provided by inferences and explanations. What these share is that the linking is always accomplished via the logical or nomological relations between the propositions which are the objects or contents of the mental states involved.[13] Given this, all justification must be routed, as it

---

[12] BonJour, pp. 69, 76. Wilfred Sellars proposed this dilemma in 'Epistemic Principles', in H. N. Castenada (ed.), *Action, Knowledge, and Reality: Critical Studies in Honour of Wilfred Sellars* (Indianapolis: Bobbs-Merrill, 1975). Also see Ernest Sosa, 'The Raft and the Pyramid: Coherence versus Foundations in the Theory of Knowledge', in P. French et al. (eds.), *Midwest Studies in Philosophy*, vol. 5, *Studies in Epistemology* (Minneapolis: University of Minnesota Press, 1980).

[13] Here BonJour appears to assume what Sosa calls 'the Intellectualist Model of Justification'. See 'The Raft and the Pyramid', pp. 312–13.

were, through cognitive states since only these have propositional content. Non-cognitive states cannot be terms in these linking or supporting relations because they lack propositional objects. Also, BonJour apparently holds that non-cognitive mental states, even if they have non-propositional content of some sort, could not be *used* in epistemic justification without our awareness of these contents, which awareness would automatically convert them to propositional objects of propositional attitudes.[14] (Given his query about how items 'below' the level of judgement can be used (*ETR* 204), Bradley should accept this last point. But then how does such a conversion proceed? This question takes us to the problem of the 'contents' of immediacy, discussed in section V below.)

Bradley confronts Bonjour on this issue at two points. First, Bradley claims there are non-cognitive states which have content and apprehension of these states does not automatically translate them into cognitive states with propositional objects or, indeed, into states having *any* objects. Secondly, Bradley holds that the non-cognitive *can* link to the cognitive via 'felt contradictions' or 'felt harmonies'. (It is important to note that both these claims depend on a successful explication of the concept of the 'contents' of immediate feelings.)

The previously mentioned example of the bitten finger is relevant here. Bradley's analysis of this experience discloses two distinct stages: I feel a change, located in my finger, and; I attend to this feeling, which entails a second and distinct felt

---

[14] That the cognitively spontaneous items in BonJour's theory are cognitively spontaneous *beliefs* need not entail that there are no non-cognitive mental states. For BonJour, what one spontaneously *has* in a case of observation is the direct (non-inferential) belief that, for example, 'the blue book is on the table before me', not an awareness of qualia. Still, he could hold that an analysis of such beliefs reveals qualia or sensory intuitions, while maintaining that these cannot play a role in epistemic justification since this is reserved for cognitive states for the reasons suggested in the text.

It might be that an externalist account could assign a role to non-cognitive mental states which we are not aware of, at least in the sense of not being conscious of these states or of what they are states of; but BonJour would reject this since his internalist account insists that all items employable in justification be available to the knower. And here I believe Bradley would agree. (In fact, Idealists and Phenomenalist might hold that we are all internalists of necessity.)

change. The second has not produced the first, because attending to my other fingers does not produce either a 'recall' of a previous felt change or an effect (a sensation in my attended-to finger). While operative in producing the second level feeling, attention has not produced the initial first-order felt change, which 'special feelings therefore, I infer, have come to me otherwise' (*ETR* 164). The initial felt change is a distinct event which precedes my attending to it. Consider attending to a hurt finger and deciding that it had been stung by a bee. There might be visual clues, such as a small puncture of the skin or redness and swelling which make me think I was stung by a bee. Now I might believe this in part because the context allows for no serious competing explanation. I am in the woods, not at my work bench, so it is not likely that I have pricked my finger with a sharp nail or an awl. Yet, my belief that it is a bee-sting also depends on my knowing that a bee sting 'feels like this'. Granted, this may require semantic information and previous experience but I count this as a bee sting not simply because I have reasoned that a bee's stinging me is the best explanation of this sensory event, but because it actually feels right. It is a painful stinging sensation, not a feeling of sudden cold or of diffused pressure. If I felt the change, and did not see the bee, but my companion saw the bee strike and said, 'You were stung by a bee', I can corroborate this judgement, at least in that I can recognize that the feeling was of the right sort, that the description offered is likely correct. This example thereby supports two claims which are relevant here. First, I can apprehend a felt change – come to be in a certain mental state – before I attend to this experience and conceptualize it or make judgements about it or its cause. Second, I can compare this feeling with a description of it provided by my companion or with the propositional object of my own later attention to it, which suggests that I can use this experience in justifying my belief that I was stung by a bee.

IV. *Direct Apprehensions of Objectless Content*
Since Bradley insists that we not analyse these first-order sensory apprehensions in terms of sensible *objects* before an attending mind, but as experiences of an immediate, fused act

of apprehension, it seems he is endorsing an adverbial theory of sensing.[15] One current version of an adverbial theory, which seems very like Bradley's, is available in Paul Moser's *Empirical Justification*. Moser takes 'immediate apprehension as an objectless event of sensing' (Moser, p. 162). There are two types of apprehending: I might, for example, hear a loud sound or hear a trumpet; or I might smell a smell or smell a rose. While the former in each pair of alternatives is a phenomenological experience which may not be related to any physical stimulus object, the latter of each pair of apprehensions, so long as they are veridical, involve three elements: the sensory experience, a physical stimulus-object, and events at a physiological level, such as the excitation of sense organs, neural firings, etc. By contrast, the first sort of apprehending does not have an object but is, for visual experiences for example, identical with the visual experience. The sensing of blue, thereby, does not present an object to me, not even a phenomenological object; rather, it is a species or kind of visual experience. As it is often expressed, although Moser does not himself use these terms, it is a *manner* or *mode* of sensing. To have a sensation of blue is to 'sense bluely'. Blue is, on this account, 'a quality or a content, but not a property or an object, of my current sensing event' (Moser, p. 163). A proper analysis of sentences about such sensing reveals their adverbial logic.

We seem to have just such a position, albeit not *called* an *adverbial* theory, indicated by Bradley's claim that a felt non-cognitive experience, which is a 'direct sense of my momentary contents and being', is one 'in which there is no distinction between my awareness and that of which it is aware' (*ETR* 159–60). Unfortunately, we apparently have to argue indirectly for an adverbial interpretation of felt sensations in Bradley: if the contents of immediate feelings are not adjectives or substances, even if the felt states of which they

---

[15] In the current literature, this is taken as largely deriving from the work of Chisholm and Sellars. Its present defenders include Michael Tye and Romane Clark, with one of its chief opponents being Frank Jackson.

are the contents are 'individuals' or 'substantial' in some sense, then the elements or contents of immediate feeling must be species or manners or modes of feeling – ie. they must be interpreted adverbially. This reading gets support from texts such as the one just quoted and others, such as that claiming that the content of felt pleasures and pains 'is not always taken apart from their existence, and applied to the thing as one of its adjectives' (*PL* 441).

In passing, it must be noted that there is reason to think that an adverbial account of immediate sensory and other felt mental states may initially have been taken to be what Bradley was trying to formulate. Moser traces his adverbial account back to Ducasse, but Ducasse's target is Moore's 'Refutation of Idealism',[16] which in turn is attacking Bradley at key points.[17] Soon after Moore's article was published, C. A. Strong – who was a disciple of Bradley to the extent that he believed Bradley was correct about the nature and role of immediate experience[18] – in essence came to the defence of Bradleyan objectless immediate experiences. And in Strong's paper we get what is probably the first statement of an adverbial theory of feeling – at any rate, one which sounds familiar to modern ears.[19]

---

[16] Moser cites Ducasse's *Nature, Mind, and Death* (La Salle: Open Court, 1951), pp. 253–90 and his *Truth, Knowledge, and Causation* (London: Routledge and Kegan Paul, 1968), pp. 90–131. Ducasse's original discussions occurred in 'Introspection, Mental Acts, and Sensa', *Mind*, vol. 45 (1936) and in 'Moore's 'Refutation of Idealism', in Paul Schlipp (ed.), *The Philosophy of G. E. Moore* (La Salle: Open Court, 1942).

[17] G. E. Moore, 'The Refutation of Idealism', *Mind*, vol. 12 ns (1903); reprinted in G. E. Moore, *Philosophical Studies* (London: Routledge and Kegan Paul, 1922), pp. 1–30.

[18] See his *A Theory of Knowledge* (New York: Macmillan, 1923).

[19] The early history of the adverbial theory and whether it represents Bradley's view of immediate feelings need fuller exploration. I am presently preparing a paper on this topic, provisionally entitled, 'Adverbial Sensing and Moore's "Refutation of Idealism"'. Whether we can extend the history of this theory back even further is an open question. T. H. Green quotes, with guarded approval, Fraser's interpretation of 'visible experience' in Berkeley as 'coloured experience in sense' and of 'tangible experience' as 'resistant experience in sense' (*Works*, vol. 1, sect. 177). But whether these are precursors of an adverbial thesis is hard to decide.

Strong first notes, as others did,[20] that Moore's main claim – that 'esse is percipi' is false – fails to take into account non-cognitive mental states such as pain, for which the 'esse is percipi' principle *is* true and which states do not entail objects for a subject. (Bradley himself had taken pain and pleasure to be counter-examples to the claim that all experience entails an object, *ETR* 159.) In applying this lesson to a colour sensation Strong gives us an adverbial reading of that experience: 'our intuitive sense recognizes blue to be a *mode* of experience or consciousness' (Strong, p. 182, my emphasis). He even anticipates modern syntactic ways of representing this: 'in the case of blue, you have only to insert a hyphen, and make it a 'blue-feeling' or a 'blue-sensation', for all difficulties to be miraculously removed' (*loc. cit.*). And earlier: 'In simple sensation or feeling, the quality is the concrete description of the *nature* of the awareness, as the awareness is the *mode of existence* of the quality' (p. 181, my emphases). Also compare his use of 'mode of feeling' (p. 177). He concludes that, 'in the simple experience of blue, there is no ground whatever for opposing the blue to the experience and considering the former to be the object of the latter' (p. 181).[21] Clearly, these passages offer evidence that something akin to what we would now identify as an adverbial theory may have been taken, at least as early as 1905, as representing Bradley's view of the logic of immediate feelings.

Returning to the main discussion, Moser holds that a person can 'immediately apprehend the phenomenological content of his current sensing events' (Moser, p. 165). What Moser claims about such apprehensions exactly fits Bradley's account of an immediate felt change in the example of the insect bite:

---

[20] Eg. J. S. Mackenzie, 'The New Realism and the Old Idealism', *Mind*, vol. 15 ns (1906), pp. 308–28. Mackenzie also claims Moore is wrong about Berkeley in that the key really is that esse is *intelligi* (*ibid.*, p. 319). This point was earlier made by T. H. Green (*Works*, vol. 1, sect. 183).

[21] Strong expresses a legitimate worry about using 'content' in describing these immediate experiences (p. 181) and this may be a comment about not only Moore's but also Bradley's use of that term. Of course, Moore probably used it because Bradley had.

it is not inferential; it is logically independent of judgement and thus of conceptualization; it is not equivalent to focusing attention; but *does* involve 'attention-attraction'.[22]

There are two related questions about this account which are relevant to Bradley's thesis. First, do these apprehensions, in so far as they entail 'attention-attraction', presuppose individuation? Bradley's insect bite example suggests that they may, for we not only have *a* feeling or *a* felt change, but one which has a fairly specific character and is *locatable* as a felt change in the state of my finger. Moreover, the contents of such immediate apprehensions will have to be separated from the remaining felt background.[23] If the immediate apprehensions are not individuated, it is unclear how Bradley can continue to insist that immediate feelings can be used in adjudicating beliefs or other cognitive states. (It is important to remember that Bradley distinguishes immediate experience, taken as the undifferentiated unified backdrop of higher order experiences, from immediate experiences or feelings, which I am interpreting as immediate objectless apprehensions which require an adverbial analysis. The latter are distinct events in someone's mental history – or at least occurrences for a finite centre – and as such seem to require individuation (here, *event*-individuation). This poses a problem, for if individuation requires, for example, designation, then these feelings cannot be immediate.)

The second question is about the determinateness of the contents of immediate apprehensions. Moser recognizes that we have not got much if the immediate apprehensions reduce to mere sensory stimulation. Indeed, at such a level both Moser and Bradley himself would face Bradley's warning that if one descends too far below judgements one ends with nothing one can use in the justificatory process (*ETR* 204). Moser's response is that in so far as one can talk of 'attention-

---

[22] Moser discusses these points on pp. 166–7. For present purposes I am ignoring the details of his discussion.

[23] If there really are contents then Bradley has to face the 'many property objection' to adverbial theories. For a discussion of this see Frank Jackson's *Perception* (Cambridge University Press, 1977), pp. 63ff.

attraction' one is already beyond mere sensory stimulation, and here Bradley would surely agree. Some sensory stimulation is so weak that it is seldom noticed. The constant contact with our clothes might afford one example. And I will never have occasion to formulate any beliefs or make any judgements, such as 'My sweater feels rough', until such time as my attention is first attracted or directed to some aspect of my current felt state. The immediate apprehension pre-dates and is not equivalent, in Moser's view, to *focusing* one's attention. This is because focusing of attention is voluntary (Moser, p. 167) and here Bradley is in agreement again for the immediate feelings in question are, as we saw, compulsory rather than the result of voluntary acts of the perceiver. Moreover, focusing attention 'necessarily involves a primitive form of conceptualization, since it necessarily involves a psychological act of individuating' (Moser, p. 167). In contrast, immediate apprehension purportedly does not involve conceptualization or individuation. But how can this be if the adverbial contents of these apprehensions are fairly specific and determinate?

V. *The Contents of Immediate Feelings*
The problem is really about how we are to understand the concept of 'content' as applied to immediate experiences. If experiencing this content presupposes conceptualization or individuation it would fail to be immediate and direct; and its role as the *given* foundation of sensible experience becomes obscure. Yet, without these operations can the content of immediate experiences be determinate enough to ground, say, perceptual judgements?[24]

This topic is addressed in *Appearance and Reality* in a number of places. In chapter 26, 'The Absolute and Its

---

[24] Moser anticipates a similar problem for his form of epistemic foundationalism. Expressing this in terms Bradley would find familiar, Moser expects the critic to object that an immediate apprehension, since it is non-conceptual, 'relates a perceiver at most to a mere homogenous *this*, and not to determinate perceptual content having definite ostensible empirical properties' (Moser, p. 169).

Appearances' (*AR* 405ff.), Bradley states that 'feeling' has two senses. 'It is first the general state of the total soul not yet at all differentiated into any of the preceding special aspects [sc. perception, thought, will, desire, pleasure and pain]. And again it is any particular state so far as internally that has undistinguished unity' (*AR* 405). Presumably Bradley would claim that although the latter makes reference to *particular* states these are not, at the level of immediate apprehension, individuated. Nevertheless, it would seem that they must be individuat*able* if they are *presented*, and can ground judgements. What makes them individuatable, one assumes, is their content.

But here we meet a problem, for although a feeling has a content this 'finite content is irreconcilable with the immediacy of its existence'. The 'finite content is necessarily determined from the outside; its external relations... penetrate its essence, and so carry that beyond its own being'. The '"what" of all feeling is discordant with its "that"' (*AR* 407). A feeling has content which apparently makes it already more than a mere 'this'. The evidence that feeling does pass beyond itself, as it were, is evidenced by 'the hard fact of change' (*loc. cit.*). Again we have the 'felt change' encountered in the insect bite example. It is a hard fact presumably because it is forced upon us. Moreover, while feeling is a 'foundation of further developments' (*loc. cit.*) which means in this context that knowledge begins from the total occurrent psychical state of a finite centre – it is a foundation which has its essential nature destroyed by later developments. Thus, judgements or beliefs are not descriptions of, or reports on, these foundations; which is what Bradley means by saying that these products are not its 'adjectives' (*loc. cit.*). Nevertheless, this passage confesses that a feeling has content, has a 'what', which implies it has a determinate character. The critic will then want to know why these are not really adjectives, the experiencing of which presupposes mental operations, or, at least, relations.

The basic dilemma arises in other places in *Appearance*.[25]

---

[25] Bradley acknowledges problems, for he continually comments on consistencies which keep arising (eg. *AR* 203, 206).

Justification and Empirical Knowledge 325

On the one hand, to remain *immediate* and direct there must be no *object* of a feeling. It has thereby to be an objectless apprehension, the contents or characteristics of which are to be construed adverbially, as indicating types of immediate experiences in a finite centre. On the other hand, the content as a character – as a 'what' distinct from a 'this' – must be something both apart from the experience and something set against a felt background. Since we are supposedly below the level of cognitive experiences this must somehow be 'done', as it were, by the given itself, by the content rather than by the finite centre. But this is to construe the contents of immediate experiences as at least analogous to adjectives which qualify reality. And no advantage seems gained by interpreting these contents as sensory *events* rather than *objects* of sensing.

Bradley cannot, the critic will say, have it both ways. The adverbial thesis about the intuitive apprehensions of objectless contents seems required if we are to get any grip on what is meant by the 'fused' nature of immediate feelings. But the 'content' of an immediate experience, taken as a 'what' or a character necessary for generating perceptual beliefs, for example, makes these contents into adjectives of immediacy. Thus, the doctrine of immediate contents is incoherent.

Nor is this charge averted by the later confession that taking a content *as* a content involves ideal operations; for the contents of immediate feelings must somehow be determinate and separate if their negative element is to *introduce* the external relations necessary for getting us beyond immediate experience. Determinate contents are also required if there is truly to be something *presented* in immediate experience and if we are to retain the possibility of experiencing felt contradictions and felt harmonies across the cognitive/non-cognitive boundary.

One might hope for some help on this from Terminal Essay V of *Principles of Logic*, which was written after *Appearance and Reality*. Here Bradley says that the given, as felt, has a content or a character and it is upon this that we build our 'ordered Universe' (*PL* 661). At last we have a clear statement of what I called, near the beginning of this paper, the third sense of 'foundation' employed by Bradley: the contents of immediate felt states are the basic epistemic building blocks. And the note to this Essay refers the reader back to a place in the text of the *Logic* where Bradley says that 'we can not have the given either as simple being or as a sensuous felt mass without character or feature' (*PL* 477). But we still do not know what view to take of these characters or contents. That this note speaks of 'the character of that which is felt and given' (*PL* 661n.) suggests we are to view the character as a separate object of consciousness. But Bradley's official doctrine presumably is that *as* felt there is no separation (which reaffirms the adverbial thesis about immediate apprehensions) even though there must be a separation of 'that' from 'what' for the ideal construction of the world to begin. If these contents are not separate but need only be separable, we then need to know what accounts for this possibility.

How is this possibility to be explained? If the knower does the work of separating the 'this' into distinct characters or contents there is then no clear sense in which the character or content of immediate feeling is really *given* or *presented*. Yet, if the felt experience already comes with determinate and distinct contents – which is clearly implied by Bradley's talk of the 'this' having 'elements' which are 'conjoined' albeit not 'connected' – or if the felt experience somehow divides itself, with the contents in some sense emerging from the felt totality, then they must already be something very like objects which appear to a mind (finite centre). If they are to be the foundations (in Sense Three) of empirical knowledge the content must emerge on the side of the *presentation* rather than on the side of the experiencer (finite centre) of that experience. But then the problem is not just that it suggests that immediate feelings are not really unities, but that it is inconsistent with the adverbial account which, I have argued, is offered via examples such as that of the insect bite or the experiencing of an as yet unnoticed emotional state. Yet, immediate experiences must have what might be called an 'adjectival' nature if they are to be both presentational and usable. Since the account is, among other things, to deal with the presentational aspect or the given element of a veridical perception, it cannot be that the knower is responsible for this feature (and here we might have to substitute 'finite centre' for 'knower', provided this would make any sense). Rather, the presented contents must carry their determinate content with them as it were, independent of any cognitive operations of the knower.[26]

There is a related issue which must also be faced by Bradley; namely, whether an immediate feeling (experience) should be *a* feeling or some *set* of feeling*s*. That there are content*s* indicates the latter – or at least suggests that the unified experience of a finite centre as felt is somehow composed of parts or contents which can become the objects of knowledge at a later and logically anterior stage of experience. (Again, Bradley does say that the 'this' has 'elements' which are 'conjoined' (*AR* 199; cf *ETR* 174) which apparently indicates that the felt 'this' is actually a feeling-*set*.) One thing this points to is that Bradley's doctrine of immediacy is up against, and does not offer a solution to, Jackson's 'many property problem' for adverbial theories of sensing.[27] More interestingly, perhaps, it would seem Bradley faces a dilemma similar to that Green posed for Berkeley. Green's claim against Berkeley turned on the question whether visible extension – a 'coloured experience of sense' – was 'complete in a single feeling or consists in a succession of feelings'. If the former, 'it is clearly not extension as a relation between parts'; if the latter, it requires 'a synthetic principle, which is not one of the feelings, but equally present to each of them' (*Works*, vol. 1, sect. 177). A similar dilemma occurs when we take feeling in a synchronic rather than a diachronic reading. On the one hand, if there is but one felt state at one moment, and thus one 'feeling', then this state cannot have elements or various presented contents. Moreover, there would thereby seem to be nothing constraining the mind as it carves this up in its

---

[26] The text of *CE* 660, seemingly suggests that the 'many' contents of the one experience are just presented to the passive mind. But how, then, is this felt state a unity? That the relations of the given datum (and here Bradley uses the singular) are explicitly present in immediate experience is confessed at *PL* 482, accompanied by the puzzling view that immediate experience is an 'activity' of a pseudo-intellectual sort.

[27] In a way Green's dilemma, which follows, is expressing the sort of difficulty posed by the Many Property Problem.

judgements – ie. there is no way immediate experience can be a 'given' which is 'transcended' to become the experience of a world of perceivable objects. Indeed, there just would not really be anything for the mind to 'carve up' via its conceptual and judgemental operations. (Bradley acknowledges this at times: cf. *AR* 24; *CE* 659.) We thus have no clue how empirical knowledge can arise out of immediacy and no possibility of input, as we would normally conceive of it, from that world. On the other hand, if there are contents of, and hence a number of feelings within, any felt state at one time, the immediate felt state has already broken into at least two sets of relations: those holding between the feelings 'contained' in the felt state (the feeling-set), and those holding between the feelings and the finite centre whose experience holds the various felt contents (feelings) together as units of the one felt state (feeling-set). There seems no clear way for Bradley to avoid being impaled on one of these horns.[28]

One final point should be noted. On page 203 of *Appearance and Reality* Bradley presents a puzzle: (1) as a 'what' distinct from a 'that', content is 'absent from the "this"'; yet, (2) as 'what' without distinction from the 'this', 'the "this" is not anything but content' (*AR* 203; cf. 206). Bradley goes on to talk of the 'features' which can be made qualities, and of 'aspects' which can be 'separated by distinction and analysis' (*AR* 203). Here our critic will still want to ask whether these aspects and features are in some sense *there* in the given or not. Bradley's answer is that since the given is *experience* then of course they are there in the given. To fail to see this is to fail to understand the adverbial theory of sensing.

But are these features there as *distinct, determinate* events of sensing? It seems that knowledge requires that we get from an initial stage of immediacy, where content is absent, to a second stage of immediacy, where content has somehow appeared. If we are to take seriously Bradley's claim that in

---

[28] Whether Bradley can be saved from this charge of incoherence can only be determined after full analyses of the adverbial theory of sensing and of Bradley's understanding of the 'elements' and 'contents' of immediate feelings. I cannot offer these here and must remain content, for present purposes, with having sketched the problem.

the latter the 'what' is present 'without distinction from the 'this', then either the 'whats' are all somehow contained *within* immediate experience – Bradley often talks of them being 'conjoined' but not 'connected' – or else the second stage is already beyond pure immediacy. I take it the latter is the case. But then how do we get from the first to the second stage? The main problem we have been facing once again reappears. And at this point we may, in Bradley's view, be up against the great ineffable fact, that 'experience should take place in finite centres, and should wear the form of finite "thisness"' (*AR* 200).[29]

In conclusion, the problem I am suggesting centres on the apparent admission that relations are already at work at the level of immediacy even on the adverbial interpretation. At best, that theory has merely moved from a position requiring relations among phenomenal *objects* to a position entailing relations among *events* of adverbial sensing. Thus, there is reason to hold that there is an incoherence in Bradley's account of immediate experiences (feelings). This will also occasion the collapse of his attempt to bridge the cognitive/non-cognitive boundary via 'felt contradictions' and 'felt harmonies' for this depends on being able to make sense of the claim that felt states, although unities, nevertheless have contents. And because of the central place of feelings in Bradley's solution to the input problem this incoherence obscures his theory of empirical justification.

---

[29] We may also be at the point at which Bradley would simply remind us that the fact that contradictions and incoherences have arisen in the account of empirical justification merely signals our necessary entrapment in the realm of appearance. Indeed, he might very well have felt that an adverbial theory of sensations is not much more help than an 'adjectival' one, since the reality we seek must be 'substantial and individual' (*PL* 46; cf. 487).

BRADLEY, RUSSELL AND ANALYSIS

Philip Dwyer

Bradley's relation to analytic philosophy is, for most analytic philosophers, largely vague and impressionistic. The vagueness goes primarily to saying what constitutes analytic philosophy, while the impressionistic sense of Bradley is pretty much ignorance. Apart from Ayer's throwaway remark on the Absolute and verifiability in *Language, Truth and Logic*,[1] I suspect that most of what many people know on this score comes almost entirely from biographical or autobiographical accounts of Russell, and though or because what we then have comes from the horse's mouth, the story tends to remain at the level of impression and legend. At its most impressionistic and legendary we seem to hear that Russell and Moore, the ungrateful sons of Bradley, slew him with the weapon of 'analysis' and thence ruled the philosophy harem. This weapon was simply picked up one day, after contact with the mysteries of mathematics, much as the apes in Kubrick's *2001* pick up the bones as weapons after contact with the mysterious monolith. From that day things were never the same.

This kind of genesis story is now, a century later, beginning to break down or break up. There is a scholarly surge in early Russell, seeking out the 'historical' Russell as one might seek out the historical Jesus.[2] And too, many of those yuppie

[1] A. J. Ayer, *Language, Truth and Logic* (New York: Dover Books, 1952): 'On the other hand, such a metaphysical pseudo-proposition as "the Absolute enters into, but is itself incapable of, evolution and progress", is not even in principle verifiable' (p. 36). In a note Ayer says that the remark is taken at random from *Appearance and Reality*. Bradley in fact addresses, briefly, the issue of the Absolute and verifiability at *ETR* 249.

[2] See, for example, Peter Hylton, *Russell, Idealism, and the Emergence of Analytic Philosophy* (Oxford: Clarendon Press, 1990), and Nicholas Griffin, *Russell's Idealist Apprenticeship* (Oxford: Clarendon Press, 1991).

analytic philosophers seem to be suffering Alex Haley syndrome – they yearn to know their roots. And these roots appear ever more to be precisely idealistic.[3] I propose to jump on this revisionary bandwagon in pressing the following claim: Russell's primary concept of 'analysis' is taken directly from Bradley himself. Thus if anthologies of twentieth-century philosophy bear titles like *The Analytic Tradition* or *The Age of Analysis* because of what Russell practised under the name of 'analysis', this in turn is because of, not in spite of, what he learned from Bradley.

In his article 'The Nature of the Proposition and the Revolt against Idealism',[4] Peter Hylton, discussing Russell's theory of 'terms' and 'propositions' in *The Principles of Mathematics*,[5] makes the following parenthetical remark: 'The validity of this process of decomposition, or analysis, as a philosophical method is a central claim of the new philosophy of Moore and Russell, and a point of sharp disagreement with their idealist precursors' (p. 376). Hylton does not follow up on the nature of this 'sharp disagreement' about 'the validity of analysis' in this article, but he does deal with it briefly in his book *Russell, Idealism, and the Emergence of Analytic Philosophy* (see footnote 2). There, writing of Moore's early views, Hylton says:

---

[3] I would cite here Hans Sluga's *Frege* (London: Routledge and Kegan Paul, 1980), and in connection with this Anthony Manser's paper 'Bradley and Frege', in A. Manser and G. Stock (eds.), *The Philosophy of F. H. Bradley* (Oxford: Clarendon Press, 1984). The idealist roots and downright idealist doctrines of Wittgenstein's *Tractatus* have long been known.

Regarding the opening of Walter Creery's contribution to this volume, 'Bradley on Truth and Judgement', whether Bradley's *Principles of Logic* is a precursor of the type of theory underlying *Principia Mathematica* I should not like to say, but the claim that this is a 'customary and standard assumption' certainly conflicts with my second-level impression of the customary and standard impression of the relations between Bradley and Russell. In any case, more on the positive influence of Bradley on Russell can be found in Nicholas Griffin's 'Bradley's Contribution to the Development of Logic', this volume.

[4] In R. Rorty, J. B. Schneewind and Q. Skinner (eds.), *Philosophy in History* (Cambridge University Press, 1984).

[5] Bertrand Russell, *The Principles of Mathematics*, 2nd ed., 1938, 1st ed., 1903 (New York: W. W. Norton and Co.).

The question of the legitimacy of analysis as a philosophical method is directly connected with the issue of internal relations. The method of analysis is an attempt to understand a complex whole by seeing what parts compose it, and by gaining knowledge of each of those parts by considering it in isolation, abstracted from the whole. If the parts are internally related to the whole, each partially constituted by its position within the whole, then the abstraction of each part from the whole will not leave it unchanged. The parts, each of which we consider in isolation, will not suffice to reconstitute the whole that we wish to understand. For the Idealists, therefore, analysis would not have been acceptable as a method in philosophy. They could admit the legitimacy of analysis in areas of human knowledge which are, and must be, content with partial truth – the whole of science, for example. But in metaphysics, where our aim is complete and ultimate truth, they would reject analysis. (p. 143)

Unlike the previous quotation, however, the subjunctive mood of this quotation tends to leave intact, if not reinforce, the prevailing impression that 'analysis' is some kind of method for doing philosophy and discovering truth which the idealists, and especially Bradley, were simply unapprised of until Moore and Russell invented it out of whole cloth. Hylton's book admirably demonstrates how various idealist doctrines inform the views of Russell and Moore even as they are rebelling against idealism, but the picture of 'analysis' as one thing *they* knew about but Bradley didn't, remains.[6]

Apart from Hylton's 1984 article, I have come across only two other indications in recent scholarship (both very brief, and rather oblique) that this picture is misleading. The one

---

[6] Much perhaps in the way we are given to think that we now know about non-Euclidean geometry, but (poor) Kant didn't. This too, evidently, is a questionable view. See Nicholas Griffin, *Russell's Idealist Apprenticeship*, pp. 104–106.

I shall cite presently is a note by John Slater in the critical apparatus attached to 'The Philosophy of Logical Atomism' in Russell's *Collected Papers*.[7] At the beginning of 'The Philosophy of Logical Atomism', having just referred to 'the monistic logic of the people who more or less follow Hegel' (p. 160), Russell says: 'One is often told that the process of analysis is falsification, that when you analyse any given concrete whole you falsify it and that the results of analysis are not true. I do not think that this is a right view' (p. 160). Slater's note for this passage says: 'see, e.g. Bradley, 1883, 95, where he writes: "It is a very common and most ruinous superstition to suppose that analysis is not alteration, and that, whenever we distinguish, we have at once to do with divisible existence." He goes on to call the method of analysis "this cardinal principle of error and delusion"' (p. 348).

These are quotations from Bradley's *Principles of Logic*, and indeed from that work in 1883 until his very last work (the unfinished 'Relations' essay of 1924, in *CE*), Bradley inveighed against what he called 'analysis', primarily on the grounds cited, viz., that analysis is falsification.

It is not then merely that the idealists, that is to say, Bradley, *would* reject analysis, but that he *did* reject analysis. Moreover, he not only actively rejected analysis as practised by Russell, but, as the above quote shows, his later attacks on Russell and analysis were polemical business as usual: Bradley was attacking 'analysis' when Russell was primarily concerned with balls and jacks. In its defects, 'the new philosophy of Moore and Russell' was, for Bradley, nothing very new. This of course raises the question whether Bradley meant by 'analysis' what Moore and Russell meant by 'analysis', but the answer, I believe, must be, by and large, yes. Certainly when Bradley and Russell are directly tussling with each other about 'analysis' they mean the same thing, and it

---

[7] Bertrand Russell, *Collected Papers*, vol. 8, ed. John Slater (London: Allen and Unwin, 1986). The other indication is in D. Lackey, 'Russell's Map of the Mind', in P. A. French, T. E. Uehling Jr. and H. K. Wettstein (eds.), *Midwest Studies in Philosophy VI, The Foundations of Analytic Philosophy* (Minneapolis: University of Minnesota Press, 1981), p. 136. The relevant quote from Lackey is given and discussed in footnote 25 below.

is clear that Bradley employs a univocal sense of 'analysis' throughout his career, including that part of it (his heyday) which precedes Russell. On the other hand, for all the accretion Russell's concept of analysis is subject to in his long career, if any thread remains constant it is the issue of whether analysis entails falsification and distortion. But let me proceed to some of the details of the story.

In *The Principles of Logic* Bradley has a single, but multilayered concept of 'analysis'. It is first of all a label for a certain psycho-cognitive-intellectual process which we engage in whenever we infer, reason or judge. This same process pursued, as it were, in the other direction, he calls 'synthesis',[8] but these processes are, in any case, such as to render all judgement defective (see chapter 6, 'The Final Essence of Reasoning', *PL* 470–73, 486–9). This implicit exercise of analysis in all judgement[9] may, however, be exercised explicitly and self-consciously as a method: 'If this is true when we apply the principle unconsciously, it continues to be true at a later stage. We may deliberately adopt the so-called Analytic or Synthetic Method, and there is of course a real difference between them. But the result is always a two-sided product' (*PL* 473). Understandably, much of what Bradley says about analysis applies indifferently to the process implicit in all judgement as well as to the explicit method, in particular that analysis always involves some falsification of what is analysed. But in either case analysis is understood

---

[8] Corresponding somewhat roughly to this distinction of processes are what Bradley calls 'analytic' and 'synthetic' judgements. The potential for confusion raised by such terminology is, of course, immense, though Bradley explicitly marks the difference from Kantian usage. More interesting is the similarity of Bradley's distinction between 'analytic' and 'synthetic' judgements, and Russell's later distinction between 'knowledge by acquaintance' and 'knowledge by description'. See *PL* 49, and subsequent index entries under 'Analytic Judgement'.

[9] Cf. 'When we analyse (and to think we must analyse), the immediate bond of union, with its unknown condition, is perforce more or less discarded' (*ETR* 270); and 'Synthesis and analysis are each alike, begin as psychical growths; each precedes and then is specialized and organized into thinking' (*AR* 425). Also see 'Association and Thought', *CE* 231–6.

entirely formally; whether as an aspect of all judgement or as a method, its object or content may be anything which is a whole, a totality, a unity.[10]

Finally, however, there is a third sense of analysis, and this *is* tied to a particular object or content. Bradley uses the term 'analysis' for a doctrine of experience, a doctrine employing analysis as a method. He attributes this doctrine to Hume and J. S. Mill, the ringleaders of what he variously calls 'The English School' (*PL* 475), 'The Philosophy of Experience' (*PL* 34, 95, 300–302, 560), 'Psychological Atomism' (*PL* 302) and 'The Analytical School' (*PL* 302). Bradley thinks such atomistic analysis is phenomenologically defective in its account of experience and logically defective in its account of inference. This latter point, on the logic of analysis, has to do with the nature of wholes, parts and 'abstraction', abstraction – 'Where we separate ideally one element from the whole...' (*PL* 560) – being, for Bradley, in many contexts, essentially a synonym for 'analysis'.[11] He writes:

> For how shall we tell, and what justifies our confidence, that our element remains when the rest is removed? We strike out the mass of accompanying detail, and treat the residue as belonging to the real. But who goes surety that the roots

---

[10] 'The essence of analysis consists in the division of a given totality, and in the predication of either whole or part of the discrete result... When reality first appears as a whole and then as a number of divided units, something certainly is gained but something else is eliminated. For the aspect of continuity or unity is left out...' (*PL* 451–2). The passage goes on to discern analysis as operating in 'Abstraction' (going from 'We are burnt' to 'Fire burns'), arithmetical subtraction, and 'Distinction', where 'A totality is divided by a function of analysis, and ignored in the product by an act of elimination' (*PL* 452).

[11] See footnote 2 above, as well as the index entry for 'Abstraction'. In *The Philosophy of Leibniz* (London: Allen and Unwin, 1900), Russell mentions in passing 'The essentially Hegelian view that abstraction is falsification' (p. 110). Beginning at least with the Leibniz book, 'Hegelianism' becomes a Russellian euphemism for 'Bradley', both as a way of dismissing Bradley's views as guilty by association, but also, I think, out of respect for Bradley when it was necessary to speak of his views with disrespect. See above and below for instances of 'Hegelianism' as a whipping-boy. So, too, Russell is never a direct target of Bradley's notoriously withering polemic, though there is reason to think that Bradley was as much cowed by Russell's mathematical ability as he was impressed by his philosophical ability.

are not twisted, that, in cutting between the reality and its detail, we have not severed some fibres of the selected element? If we find that a–b is true *within x*, on what ground do we rest for our desperate leap to the assertion that a–b is true without condition? It is one thing specially to notice a member. It is one thing to say that this member at any rate is certainly here. It is quite another thing to take that member apart, and to assume that, by itself, it remains what it was when it lived in the whole. This fatal confusion between theory and fact, this blind assumption that our intellect's work must always present us with the nature of things, is a special trait of the 'Philosophy of Experience'. Bad metaphysic supports it against logic and the cry of facts. (*PL* 560)

Further on he writes: 'In dividing the wholes, if we could divide them, we should modify the parts; and in summing these parts we should not regain the wholes. We are here as powerless to construct the facts *a priori*, as we are to dissect them by ideal analysis' (*PL* 562). So much presently for Bradley's initial notion of analysis, though we shall return to his critique of the Analytical School.

In his 1924 essay 'Logical Atomism', Russell recalls that 'At Cambridge I read Kant and Hegel, as well as Mr. Bradley's *Logic*, which influenced me profoundly'.[12] But by 1899 Russell no longer subscribed to a metaphysics of Absolute Idealism, nor, evidently, did Bradley ever subscribe to a Platonic metaphysics of 'propositions' and 'terms', but this did not affect their shared conception of analysis which was wholly formal or logical, and almost always highly abstract in its presentation. However, to anticipate, the difference between Russell and Bradley as to the primary objects of or material for analysis – for Russell it is 'propositions', for Bradley, 'experience' – will be crucial in their ultimate dispute as to the efficacy and value of analysis, that is to say, crucial to their dispute about analysis being falsification.

---

[12] *Collected Papers*, vol. 9, ed. John Slater with the assistance of Bernd Frohmann (London: Unwin Hyman, 1988), p. 162.

338   Philosophy After F. H. Bradley

Nevertheless, except for what Russell takes to be the basic objects of analysis, his initial notion of analysis is Bradleyan[13] in two senses: 1) it is essentially a matter of the relations of wholes and parts,[14] and 2) analysis is falsification. In an unfinished work of 1899 called *The Fundamental Ideas and Axioms of Mathematics*, Russell writes in the chapter entitled 'Plurality':

> It may be observed that analysis is, strictly speaking, *only* possible in the case of such a combination as 'A is B'. Wherever there is a relation, wherever, that is, we have truth and falsehood, analysis is more or less destructive... That something is lost by analysis appears from the fact that the whole is true or false, while the parts are neither...

---

[13] I am arguing, of course, only for Bradley's being the immediate source of Russell's concept of analysis. A generic decompositional sense of analysis certainly precedes Bradley – the 'Analytical School' of Hume being one of his chief targets – and is of course prominent in Leibniz, as well as Descartes and Locke. On the latter, see Peter Schouls, *The Imposition of Method* (Oxford: Clarendon Press, 1980).

[14] In discussing Russell's 1898 views on geometry, Nicholas Griffin writes: 'It [the part/whole relation] was, in fact, for a brief period, a key concept in Russell's semantics, underlying his new notion of philosophical analysis, of implication, and of order in general' (*op. cit.*, p. 358). I demur at his use of 'new', not only because this concept of analysis would not have been new to Bradley, but also because, because of that, it was not even new to Russell as someone who had been 'profoundly influenced by Mr. Bradley's *Logic*' (see the quote above from 'Logical Atomism'). Further, though the part/whole idiom is found only in the semantics of *Principles of Mathematics* and earlier writings, its successor idiom of complex/constituent is used for years to come.

Moore's initial notions of analysis and definition are also essentially a matter of the relation of wholes and parts. See the quote above from Hylton, *op. cit.*, as well as pp. 143–5. Hylton's text contains the notoriously strange 'definition' from *Principia Ethica* (Cambridge University Press, 1903), not of 'horse' but of *horse*: 'We might think just as clearly about a horse, if we thought of all its parts and their arrangement instead of thinking of the whole...' (p. 8). As with horses, so with propositions: they are non-linguistic wholes composed of parts for both Moore and Russell at this stage. I suspect that, as with Russell, Moore's early concept of analysis up to at least *Principia Ethica* is taken straight from Bradley; that it is a holdover from 1896–7 when he could write: 'It is to Mr. Bradley that I chiefly owe my conception of the fundamental problems of metaphysics' (cited in Hylton, *op. cit.*, p. 44). Further, what Russell didn't take directly from Bradley on the score of analysis, he may have taken indirectly through Moore: the Preface to *The Principles of Mathematics* tells us that 'On the fundamental questions of philosophy, my position, in all its chief features, is derived from G. Moore' (p. xviii). This of course too, even as Russell is some way from the time in 1894 when he 'read Bradley... with avidity, and admired him more than any other recent philosopher' (*The Philosophy of Bertrand Russell*, ed. P. A. Schilpp, La Salle: Open Court, 1944, p. 10).

Thus wherever we have relations which actually relate, i.e., which are not used as terms, there analysis is not wholly legitimate.[15]

Russell's next work, *The Principles of Mathematics*, was completed, published (in 1903, composition begun in 1899), and really put him on the philosophical map. The chapter entitled 'Whole and Part' begins: 'For the comprehension of analysis, it is necessary to investigate the notion of whole and part, a notion which has been wrapped in obscurity – though not without certain more or less valid logical reasons – by the writers who may be roughly called Hegelian' (p. 137). 'Hegelian' is, of course, code for 'Bradley'. Russell goes on to distinguish three kinds of 'wholes'. There are firstly what he calls 'aggregates', and secondly 'aggregates of aggregates'.

But there is another kind of whole, which may be called a *unity*. Such a whole is always a proposition, though it need not be an *asserted* proposition. For example, 'A differs from B', or 'A's difference from B', is a complex of which the parts are A and B and difference; but this sense of whole and part is different from the previous senses, since 'A differs from B' is not an aggregate, and has no parts at all in the first two senses of parts. It is parts in this third sense that are chiefly considered by philosophers, while the first two senses are those usually relevant in symbolic logic and mathematics. This third sense of *part* is the sense which corresponds to analysis: it appears to be indefinable, like the first sense – i.e., I know no way of defining it. (p. 139)

I am strongly inclined to believe that first among the 'philosophers' Russell has in mind here is Bradley, and that the analysis which corresponds with this third sense of *part*, 'chiefly considered by philosophers', is analysis as Bradley conceived and discussed it.

Further on in the chapter Russell refers back to his opening remarks:

---

[15] Bertrand Russell, *Collected Papers*, vol. 2, ed. Nicholas Griffin and Albert C. Lewis (London: Unwin Hyman, 1990), pp. 299–300.

I have already touched on a very important logical doctrine, which the theory of whole and part brings into prominence – I mean the doctrine that analysis is falsification. Whatever can be analysed is a whole, and we have already seen that analysis of wholes is in some measure falsification. But it is important to realize the very narrow limits of this doctrine. We cannot conclude that the parts of a whole are not really its parts, nor that the parts are not presupposed in the whole in a sense in which the whole is not presupposed in the parts, nor yet that the logically prior is not usually simpler than the logically subsequent. In short, though analysis gives us the truth, and nothing but the truth, yet it can never give us the whole truth. This is the only sense in which the doctrine is to be accepted. In any wider sense, it becomes merely a cloak for laziness, by giving an excuse to those who dislike the labour of analysis. (p. 141)

The ambivalence of this passage – the combination of Calvinist finger-wagging together with the concession that analysis is falsification is 'a very important logical doctrine' – as well as the grudging opening remarks of the chapter, suggest that the *Principles* is not the decisive break with 'Hegelianism' that it is usually presented as being. Certainly Bradley's concept of analysis and his view that it entails falsification has been retained. And much later on in the *Principles*, in the chapter on Matter, Russell again makes concessive, almost contrite remarks:

It is also said that analysis is falsification, that the complex is not equivalent to the sum of its constituents and is changed when analysed into these. In this doctrine, as we saw in Parts I and II, there is a measure of truth, when what is to be analysed is a unity. A proposition has a certain indefinable unity, in virtue of which it is an assertion; and this is so completely lost by analysis that no enumeration of constituents will restore it, even though itself be mentioned as a constituent. There is, it must be confessed, a grave logical difficulty in this fact, for it is difficult not to believe that a whole must be constituted by its constituents.

(pp. 466–7)

However, in this very section a certain cat noses its way out of the bag, revealing a deeper doctrinal difference between Russell and Bradley which will open the way to Russell relinquishing even his last tie to 'Hegelianism' – the doctrine that analysis is falsification – leaving only, but importantly, a shared concept of analysis.

In this section (p. 439) of the *Principles*, in making a distinction between 'conceptual' versus 'real' complexity, Russell asserts: 'All complexity is conceptual in the sense that it is due to a whole capable of logical analysis; but is real in the sense that it has no dependence upon the mind, but only upon the nature of the object. Where the mind can distinguish elements, there must *be* elements to distinguish; though, alas! there are often different elements which the mind does not distinguish' (p. 466). Now for reasons wholly other than Hume's, and so likely quite unwittingly, Russell has here revived the Humean doctrine which was poison to Bradley. In *Principles of Logic* Bradley paraphrases Hume – 'All our distinct perceptions are distinct existences, and the mind never perceives any real connexion among distinct existences'[16] – and goes on to say tersely: 'The philosophy of experience is psychological atomism' (*PL* 301–302).

In an above quote from *Principles of Logic* we have already seen Bradley execrate 'this blind assumption that our intellect's work must always present us with the nature of things', and the point was also made in the quotation cited

---

[16] David Hume, *A Treatise of Human Nature* (Oxford: Clarendon Press, 1888) p. 636. For other statements of the principle that whatever is distinguishable is separable, see the *Treatise*, pp. 10, 18–19, 24, 36, 79, 634. Russell's reasons for holding this view are not only wholly other than Hume's, they are wholly opposite to Hume's. Hume stated reasons for the doctrine I find unclear, but I suspect that his basic thought is that since all we are given are perceptions, and they are *phenomenal*, what you see (any distinction) is what you get (a separable thing). Russell's propositions are anything but phenomenal; they are perfectly objective and mind-independent. His belief that where the mind can distinguish elements, there must *be* elements to distinguish, seems to rest on verbs like 'distinguish', 'discover', and ultimately 'analyse', being 'success words' (à la Ryle): 'What can be discovered by a operation must exist apart from that operation: America existed before Christopher Columbus, and two quantities of the same kind must *be* equal or unequal before measurement' ('The Axioms of Geometry' (1899) in *Collected Papers*, vol. 2, p. 396).

above by John Slater in connection with Russell's 'The Philosophy of Logical Atomism'.[17] I should like to reproduce this latter passage at some length, both to elaborate Bradley's complaint, and because it contains some of his most delightfully purple anathematizing:

> It is a very common and most ruinous superstition to suppose that analysis is no alteration, and that, whenever we distinguish, we have at once to do with divisible existence. It is an immense assumption to conclude, when a fact comes to us as a whole, that some parts of it may exist without any sort of regard for the rest. Such naive assurance of the outward reality of all mental distinctions, such touching confidence in the crudest identity of thought and existence, is worthy of the school which so loudly appeals to the name of Experience. Boldly stated by Hume (cf. Book II. II. chap. I. 5), this cardinal principle of error and delusion has passed into the traditional practice of the school, and is believed too deeply to be discussed or now recognized. The protestations of fidelity to fact have been somewhat obtrusive, but self-righteous innocence and blatant virtue have served once more here to cover the commission of the decried offence in its deadliest form. If it is true in any sense (and I will not deny it) that thought in the end is the measure of things, yet at least this is false, that the divisions we make within a whole all answer to elements whose existence does *not* depend on the rest. It is wholly unjustifiable to take up a complex, to do any work we please upon it by analysis, and then simply predicate as an adjective of the given these results of our abstraction. These products were never there as such, and in saying, as we do, that as such they are there, we falsify the fact. You

---

[17] Cf. also 'If the Philosophy of Experience is content with the result, then surely the product of the analysis must be a fact' (*PL* 302); and in the same paragraph the equally sarcastic, 'And, since that analysis has been firmly established, it is clear that its basis cannot be unreal' (*PL* 303); and also, 'For not all of us follow the "School of Experience"; we are not all equipped with an a priori principle, which tells us that to every distinction of the mind a division corresponds in the actual world' (*PL* 563). Evidently the antipathy to Hume does not extend back to include Bradley's earliest writings on historical knowledge; see Lionel Rubinoff's contribution to this volume.

can not always apply in actual experience that coarse notion of the whole as the sum of its parts into which the school of 'experience' so delights to torture phenomena. (*PL* 95) The idea that the very fact of analysis as an activity shows that reality must *be* analysable, such that analysis *can't fail* to get things right, was the fundamental monstrosity Bradley saw in analysis throughout his career. Chapter 10 of *Essays on Truth and Reality* (1914) is entitled 'A Discussion of Some Problems in Connexion with Mr. Russell's Doctrine'. Most of the article deals with Russell's 1910–12 views on judgement and relations, but there is a section of the article called 'On analysis – its nature', and here Bradley takes Russell to task for his neo-Humean principle: 'The principle here involved leads to results which, so far as I can see, are wholly ruinous. It will follow that without any exception every distinction which I can make anywhere, exists bare and by itself' (*ETR* 299–300). In 1912 appeared a then widely discussed volume of philosophy from America entitled *The New Realism*.[18] Bradley is an implicit target of this school as a whole,[19] and an explicit target of one of the essays entitled 'A Defense of Analysis', by Edward Gleason Spaulding.[20] Spaulding is, to some degree, a Russell surrogate, his essay being peppered with allusions to Russell as guiding light,[21]

[18] E. B. Holt, W. T. Marvin, W. P. Montague, R. B. Perry, W. B. Pitkin and E. G. Spaulding, *The New Realism* (New York: Macmillan Co., 1912).

[19] See the Introduction to *The New Realism*: 'It cannot, then, be proper to assert that such a procedure [analysis] destroys its object' (p. 24); and in the Appendix, the 'Program and Platform of Six Realists' (pp. 471ff.).

[20] Spaulding subsequently produced a full-length presentation of his philosophy in *The New Rationalism, the development of a constructive realism upon the basis of modern logic and science, and through the criticism of opposed systems* (New York: Henry Holt and Co., 1918). This tome contains passing negative references to Bradley and positive references to Russell, and several discussions of 'analysis'.

[21] Russell's own relations to 'New Realism' is unclear, partly because there were, according to Charles W. Morris, English, German and American versions of the movement. See *Six Theories of Mind* (University of Chicago Press, 1932) p. 110, note 1. Russell took 'the technique of analysis' to be the distinctive method characteristic of 'the so-called "new realists"', including in the school, 'insofar as there can be said to be a school', the Britons, Alexander, Whitehead and Broad. See his article 'Philosophic Idealism at Bay' (1922) in *Collected Papers*, vol. 9, pp. 410–13, a review of May Sinclair, *The New Idealism*. In an earlier review (1917) of an earlier Sinclair book (*A Defense of Idealism: Some Questions and Conclusions*), Russell says of himself, regarding the New Realism,

and he goes after Bradley for attacking 'analysis' in *Appearance and Reality*, and in general for propounding the doctrine that analysis is falsification (*The New Realism*, p. 164). Bradley responded to Spaulding in one of the so-called 'Terminal Essays' appended to the second edition of *The Principles of Logic*. In this essay, 'A Note on Analysis', Bradley's basic riposte is again 'a question which is, I presume, both familiar and fundamental. Is every result of distinction to be taken as an independent reality or not?' (p. 691). Finally, in his last writing of 1924, Bradley laments that in *The Analysis of Mind*,[22] 'Mr. Russell does not even raise the question whether anything distinguishable has, in and by itself, reality' (*CE* 656).

For Russell's part, after *Principles of Mathematics*, attacking the view that analysis is falsification becomes a perennial concern. In the uncompleted *Theory of Knowledge* of 1913, the defense of analysis against the charge of falsification is rather oblique, but the context of the defense is explicitly Bradleyan: part 2, chapter 2, entitled, 'Analysis and Synthesis'.[23] Though Russell wishes to apply these notions to

'It is, of course, impossible to achieve a complete absence of bias in regard to a system which one has oneself advocated...' (*Collected Papers*, vol. 8, p. 113). Morris's tracing of the origin of New Realism to Hume would certainly be found plausible by Bradley (see Morris, *op. cit.*, pp. 102–105). So too, Bradley would likely have found David Pears' genealogical account of Russell vis-à-vis Hume only too plausible, though Pears, who devotes a chapter to Bradley and Russell, makes no mention of the Humean doctrine in Russell which so annoyed Bradley. See David Pears, *Bertrand Russell and the British Tradition in Philosophy* (New York: Random House, 1967); for more on Pears, see Fred Wilson's contribution to this volume.

[22] Bertrand Russell, *The Analysis of Mind* (London: George Allen and Unwin, 1921).

[23] Bertrand Russell, *Theory of Knowledge, The 1913 Manuscript*, in *Collected Papers*, vol. 7, ed. E. R. Eames in collaboration with Kenneth Blackwell (London: George Allen and Unwin, 1984). Russell begins his discussion of 'Analysis and Synthesis' autobiographically, and with not a little sarcasm: 'Most of us have been told in youth that analysis is easy and base, whereas synthesis is glorious and difficult. Some of us may have felt inclined to reverse that judgement; but however that may be, it is only by analysis that we can hope to discover what analysis and synthesis are, and therefore only the humble analyst can know in what the glories of synthesis consist' (p. 119). A few pages on he states that 'The usual arguments of philosophers who dislike analysis are largely drawn from such examples as the experience of a visible motion' (p. 122). Though Bradley is not mentioned by name in the chapter, the reference, in the first quote, to what Russell had been told in his youth points in the direction of Bradley, while the latter quote may be a reference to chapter 5 of *Appearance and Reality*, 'Motion and Change and Its Perception', where Bradley writes, eg. of the problem that, with motion, time seems to be both one and many:

propositions as he then conceived them, his definitions of analysis and synthesis replicate Bradley's, and, in Bradleyan fashion, he explicates the notions by way of their application to experiences. The following year, *Our Knowledge of the External World*[24] takes an explicit swipe at 'the general doctrine' that 'analysis always falsifies' (p. 119). I have already cited the opening remarks from 'The Philosophy of Logical Atomism' (1918). Even in *My Philosophical Development*[25] at the end of the chapter 'Revolt into Pluralism' we read: 'Although I have changed my opinion on various matters since those early days, I have not changed on points which, then as now, seemed of most importance. I still hold to the doctrine of external relations and to pluralism, which is bound up with it. I still hold that an isolated truth may be quite true. I still hold that analysis is not falsification' (p. 63).

Thus, while Russell's concept of analysis undergoes development throughout his career, it retains enough constancy for him to sustain a dispute with Bradley, over decades, as to what it is which does or does not falsify, viz., analysis. Along with sharing the same formal concept of analysis on the model of decomposing a whole into its parts (though Russell will increasingly prefer the terminology of 'complex and constituent'), Russell and Bradley shared the same formal concept of the nature of these wholes, which they called 'unities'. However, for Russell, the platonist, these are,

---

'A common "explanation" is to divide both space and time into discrete units, taken literally ad libitem... But as a theoretical solution this device is childish' (*AR* 37). Thus I follow Douglas Lackey in citing Bradley as the obvious source of the problematic in Russell's chapter. Lackey writes: 'The chapter on "Analysis and Synthesis" has a slightly archaic ring; the topics discussed are the topics of F. H. Bradley, who is less a figure of current interest than is Russell or Wittgenstein... The analysis of complexes and propositions that contain asymmetrical relations presents special problems. If *A precedes B* cannot be analysed wholly into A, precedence, and B, it appears that analysis destroys the sense of the proposition, and the Bradlean view that analysis is destructive will carry the day' ('Russell's 1913 Map of the Mind', in *Midwest Studies in Philosophy VI*, p. 132).

[24] Bertrand Russell, *Our Knowledge of the External World* (New York: Mentor Books, 1960).

[25] Bertrand Russell, *My Philosophical Development* (London: George Allen and Unwin, 1959).

initially, propositions – objective, mind-independent entities – while for Bradley, the idealist, they are experiences. The unity of a Russellian proposition is such that an analysis of it falsifies it, for a laundry list of the proposition's constituents does not equal a unified proposition. But the unity of the proposition is intrinsic to the proposition and quite independent of us. The unity of a Bradleyan 'whole' or 'totality' or 'complex phenomenon' or 'reality' is a function of its always being given in experience, or simply of its *being* experience. Once Russell gives up the thoroughly Platonist model of a proposition for a 'multiple-relations' theory of judgement, as he does after 1906, analysis then targets the whole judging situation, and he can, finally, in accord with his neo-Humean intuitions, relinquish the view that analysis ever falsifies.[26] Still, through this change in Russell's view, he and Bradley, both always more than willing to argue at the highest levels of abstraction, manage to sustain for two more decades a debate on the nature of 'unities', correlative to their long-running dispute about analysis. The dispute about unities is complicated and difficult and so, mercifully, beyond the scope and space available for this paper,[27] but together with the

[26] I draw here on Peter Hylton's 'The Nature of the Proposition and the Revolt Against Idealism', in R. Rorty et al. (eds.), *Philosophy in History*, which gives a most interesting account of Russell's struggle with the unity of the proposition and the idealist antecedents of this, though (strangely) not of Bradley. In *Theory of Knowledge* (1913), having moved away from the thoroughly Platonist view of propositions in *Principles of Mathematics*, Russell does take experiences to be equally as good, or even better, material for analysis as propositions. See *Collected Papers*, vol. 7, p. 121.

[27] While mixed with other issues, the dispute on unities carries on from Russell's *Principles of Mathematics* through at least the following: first Bradley in 'On Appearance, Error and Contradiction', especially Supplementary Note 2, *Mind*, April 1910, pp. 153–85 (*ETR* chapter 9); Russell replied to this in 'Some Explanations in Reply to Mr. Bradley', *Mind*, July 1910, pp. 373–8; Bradley replied to this in 'Reply to Mr.Russell's Explanations', *Mind*, January 1911 (*ETR* chapter 9, Supplementary Note 3), and carried on the discussion in 'A Discussion of Some Problems in Connexion with Mr. Russell's Doctrine' (*ETR* chapter 10); Russell replied to the *ETR* discussion of unities in 'Logical Atomism' (1924), in *Collected Papers*, vol. 9, pp. 172–4. By 1910 Russell's propositions had become less Platonic and more in the nature of facts, but they were still composed of 'constituents' (see, eg. 'Knowledge by Acquaintance and by Description', *Proceedings of the Aristotelian Society*, 1910–11, p. 117). Ultimately, for Russell any think-about-able, and for Bradley any 'experience' is a unity – which means just about *anything* is a possible object of analysis. I will mention in passing that I find Morris Weitz's sixty-four page 'Analysis and the Unity of Russell's Philosophy', and Russell's blithe two-page reply, oddly unilluminating about *analysis* (in P. A. Schilpp, ed., *op. cit.*).

dispute about analysis they constitute a fascinating but neglected episode in early analytic philosophy, distinct from, if internally related to, their more celebrated dispute about internal relations.[28] These close-up historical points to one side, my wide-view historical point is that it was Bradley who put the *analysis* in 'analytic philosophy'. Analytic philosophy, so-called, would be different in many ways if there had been no Bradley to beget Russell. One particular way analytic philosophy would differ is that it would not be so-called.

---

[28] A further distinct but related component in the controversy about analysis and unities is the issue of 'bare relations'. This goes back to Russell's *Principles of Mathematics* discussion of analysis and the unities in the chapter on wholes and parts, which proceeds to the view that 'a relation is one thing when it relates, and another when it is merely enumerated as a term in a collection' (p. 140), this being, as he had earlier put it, 'the difference between a relation in itself and a relation actually relating' (p. 49). For Bradley this is a prime example of original sin: the belief in a relation in itself ('a bare relation') is the belief that whatever is distinguishable is separable and has independent reality (see especially *ETR* 302). For more on the connection between the disputes on relations and analysis, see Fred Wilson's contribution to this volume.

BRADLEY AND MACINTYRE:
A COMPARISON

Don MacNiven

The Dark Age of the Enlightenment
In *After Virtue*, Alasdair MacIntyre unleashed a blistering and to my mind devastating attack on orthodox contemporary moral philosophy.[1] Whether in its English-speaking version, espousing various forms of analytic ethics, utilitarianism, or emotivism or in its continental version, espousing various forms of neo-Kantianism or existentialism, it is morally and intellectually bankrupt and totally incapable of recognizing or coping with the contemporary crisis in morality. He argues that a radically new philosophical approach is required if we are to escape a complete cultural catastrophe. He suggests that only a modern revival of Idealism, based on the historical method, will allow us to discover the cause and the cure of our contemporary moral malaise. MacIntyre is consciously working in the tradition of the English Hegelians and the purpose of this paper is to compare his work with his idealist predecessors, in particular, with F. H. Bradley.

MacIntyre notes in *After Virtue* that a prominent feature of modern social life is the interminability of its moral debates. He says:

> The most striking feature of contemporary moral utterance is that so much of it is used to express disagreements; and the most striking feature of the debates in which those disagreements are expressed is their interminable character. I do not mean by this just that such debates go on and on

---

[1] Alasdair MacIntyre, *After Virtue*, 2nd ed. (Notre Dame Press, 1984), chaps. 1–9.

and on – although they do – but also that they can find no terminus. There seems to be no rational way of securing moral agreement in our culture.[2]

No matter what we debate, nuclear war, abortion, or economic justice, we are unable to resolve our moral dilemmas. We appear to have no rational way of settling moral arguments and hence for securing moral agreement. The explanation for this unsettling phenomena is, according to MacIntyre, that each opposing answer starts from normative premises which appear to be logically incommensurate. Each is put forward as the rationally best answer, based on objective standards which are derived from the best ethical theory. The trouble is that there is no rational way to choose between the theories they are based on:

> Every one of the arguments is logically valid or can be easily expanded so as to be made so; the conclusions do indeed follow from the premises. But the rival premises are such that we possess no rational way of weighing the claims of one as against another. For each premise employs some quite different normative or evaluative concept from the others, so that the claims made upon us are of quite different kinds.[3]

The chaos of moral reasoning which pervades our current culture is reflected at the philosophical level. Most strongly in the emotive theory of ethics, which MacIntyre argues is the paradigm of modern ethical theory, at least in the English-speaking world.[4] Emotivism holds that moral language is essentially emotive rather than cognitive. To make a moral judgement is to give expression to our personal preferences, not to put forward a claim that can be rationally defended. Moral claims, unlike factual or scientific claims, are not capable of verification or falsification. There is no moral

---

[2] *After Virtue*, p. 6.

[3] *After Virtue*, p. 8.

[4] *After Virtue*, pp. 11–22. Some forms of utilitarianism could be selected for this honour, although utilitarianism has the same empiricist roots which tend to make subjectivism of some sort inevitable.

crisis because incommensurability is to be expected in the subjective world of morality. On the emotivist view the incommensurability of contemporary moral debates is not a contingent feature of our society but a reflection of the basic irrationality of morality. The assumption that moral debate is rational masks the fact that morality is really about the individual's desire for power. In an emotive society, moral relationships, in which persons are treated as ends in themselves, are replaced by power relationships, in which people are used merely as means to further selfish interests. Because it is emotivist, modern society is essentially manipulative:

> What is the key to the social content of emotivism? It is the fact that emotivism entails the obliteration of any genuine distinction between manipulative and non-manipulative social relations.[5]

We now deal with each other in terms of power rather than morality. We have not just substituted one morality for another but substituted one form of life 'morality' for another, 'power politics', even if we behave as if this is not the case. Emotivism is not just one ethical theory among many developed by Western moral philosophers, it is the negation of all ethical theory. It expresses the complete breakdown of the moral order which the Western world is now experiencing, a moral order which informed and sustained Western culture from classical Greece to the Enlightenment.

It was the Enlightenment and its philosophy which led to the unravelling of the moral world. For MacIntyre the Enlightenment was really the beginning of the moral dark ages which now completely envelope us like some deadly spiritual smog. According to MacIntyre, the Enlightenment was marked by several characteristics:

1. It was essentially a product of northern European, Protestant Christian cultures.
2. Its great philosophical project in moral philosophy was to create a science of ethics. All of the great moral philoso-

[5] *After Virtue*, p. 23.

phers of the period, Hume and Kant included, were foundationalists who were seeking a secure rational basis for morality which was logically independent of any cultural or historical context.

3. It created the idea of radical individualism, ie. the individual is ontologically and morally independent of the social groups and institutions to which they belong, and the cognate idea that social institutions are ontological fictions.

4. It defended the principles of equality and individual liberty and a system of human rights.

5. It attempted to provide a rational foundation for liberal democracy.

It was these doctrines which eventually led to the rise of general moral scepticism. A doctrine which has rendered modern moral philosophy intellectually impotent, and which sowed the seeds of moral anarchy which now typifies our social environment. In particular, it was the failure of foundationalism which was responsible for the catastrophe. By the end of the nineteenth century and the beginning of the twentieth, the failure was already apparent. Kantian rationalism had spawned Kierkegaardian existentialism, in which ultimate moral decisions become matters of faith not reason. Hobbesian and Humean empiricism discovered the fact/value dichotomy and spawned emotivism. Hume's Law, the 'no ought from is' rule showed by general logical analysis that no set of non-moral premises can entail a moral conclusion. Once G. E. Moore had articulated the 'Naturalistic Fallacy', his version of Hume's Law, it became clear that there was no valid way of deriving morality from theories of human nature.[6] Foundationalism was dead and with it the moral life.

In all these observations MacIntyre is surely correct. His description of the origins and the general philosophical outlook of the Enlightenment are both illuminating and accurate. There is no doubt that foundationalism, radical individualism, the principles of individual liberty and equality,

---

[6] G. E. Moore, *Principia Ethica* (Cambridge, 1903), chap. 1. MacIntyre argues that within an idealist framework facts do entail values, but Bradley is sceptical of this derivation. See my discussion of Bradley on the naturalistic fallacy, *Bradley's Moral Psychology* (New York: Mellen Press, 1987), chap. 1.

liberal democracy, and the fact/value dichotomy are historically interrelated. Their simultaneous historical occurrence is not surprising because they have natural intellectual affinities with each other. Adopting one tends to lead to the adoption of the others. This is made abundantly clear by MacIntyre, as it had been by his Idealistic predecessors in Britain, like F. H. Bradley in *Ethical Studies*. What is less clear is whether these theses mutually entail each other, so that if one is rejected all the others must be rejected. MacIntyre, in *After Virtue*, leaves the distinct impression that this is the case. To escape from the dark ages of the Enlightenment we must jettison the whole package, foundationalism, radical individualism, the principles of individual liberty and equality, natural rights, liberal democracy, and the fact/value dichotomy. All must go! However if these theses do not mutually entail each other, which I hold to be the case, then it is possible to mix and match them, so to speak.

It might then be possible to reject foundationalism, radical individualism, and the fact/value dichotomy, yet retain the principle of individual liberty, equality, and defend democracy. A commitment to Idealism does not then imply the wholesale rejection of the Enlightenment.

Bradley on the Enlightenment
F. H. Bradley appears to be doing this sort of mix and match in *Ethical Studies*. Speaking, perhaps unkindly, about the utilitarians, he says:

> The Utilitarian believes on psychological grounds that pleasure is the sole desirable: he believes on the strength of his natural and moral instincts that he must live for others: he puts the two together, and concludes that the pleasure of others is what he has to live for. This is not a good theoretical deduction, but it is the generation of the Utilitarian monster, and of that we may say that its heart is in the right place, but the brain is wanting. (*ES* 114–15)

Many of the moral positions adopted by the philosophers of the Enlightenment were acceptable to Bradley. It was the theoretical basis which he found unacceptable. He believed in moral progress, hence he could not take such a dark view of the Enlightenment as MacIntyre does. Bradley, like MacIntyre, rejected foundationalism, the attempt to provide an abstract rational basis for morality. Foundationalism was certainly the great philosophical project of the Enlightenment, and its failure is a serious blow to modern philosophy. Foundationalism has its roots in Descartes' 'method of doubt'. Descartes set out to systematically question every belief he thought was true. He discarded every belief he could not be absolutely certain of, whose truth he could doubt. He doubted the truth of his common-sense beliefs about the existence of material objects, like tables and chairs, as well as his most sophisticated and complex mathematical and scientific beliefs, until he arrived at his famous cogito. The proposition 'I think therefore I am', he thought could not be doubted without self-contradiction. This was the absolutely certain truth on whose foundation he would reconstruct the house of knowledge which his method of doubt had destroyed.[7]

As it turned out Descartes was wrong about the absolute certainty of his basic necessary truth, as the empiricists, like Locke, Berkeley and Hume, were quick to demonstrate. They showed that even our knowledge of the self, which was presupposed in the cogito, was insecure and could be doubted.

Although they rejected necessary truth, the empiricists did not abandon foundationalism, the search for absolute certainty on which to build our knowledge and to confound the sceptic. In fact they thought that they had discovered absolute certainty, in simple judgements of perception, like, 'I see this patch of colour!'. These were propositions which could not be sensibly doubted and which possessed the absolute certainty which provided the rock on which we could construct our scientific and moral knowledge.[8] It was soon realized that the empiricists were also chasing epistemological rainbows, because they could not show that sense

---

[7] See Rene Descartes, *Discourse On Method and The Meditations* (Penguin Books, 1968).

[8] See L. J. Bennet, *Locke, Berkeley, and Hume* (Oxford, 1971).

data were uninterpreted. Foundationalism floundered and the sceptic triumphed. The failure of the foundationalist program in ethics became painfully clear with the discovery that there was no valid way to get from theories of human nature to morality. The dream of scientific ethics vanished and was replaced by the current theoretical and practical anarchy in morals. Hume's law, which gave formal expression to the unbridgeable gap between fact and value, is a sign of the bankruptcy of ethical foundationalism, rather than the crowning achievement of modern moral philosophy.

The failure of foundationalism in ethics would come as no surprise for Bradley, as he had shown that general moral scepticism was both theoretically and practically incoherent.[9] It is practically incoherent because to deny morality is to assert it. The sceptic wants to be an amoralist and avoid making moral judgements, but amoralism is existentially impossible. Choosing to be an amoralist is choosing to be a person of a certain kind, to realize oneself in a specific way, hence it is a moral choice. R. M. Hare has argued that it is logically possible to be an amoralist, someone who simply refuses to make moral judgements.[10] However they pay a price for their moral indifference. The amoralist must withdraw from the moral arena, and abjure from any benefits which morality might provide. The price of consistent amoralism is probably too high for most people to pay. Pure amoralists are likely to be few and far between. In any case, Hare thinks that this possibility is not a shortcoming for an ethical theory.

If someone opts out of the moral game there is nothing any theorist can do about it. He says:

> Just as one cannot win a game of chess against an opponent who will not make any moves – and just as one cannot argue mathematically with a person who will not commit

---

[9] Cf. my 'Metaphysics and Ethics in Bradley's Idealism', in Philip MacEwan (ed.), *Ethics, Metaphysics and Religion in the Thought of F. H. Bradley* (Mellen Press, 1993), p. 193.

[10] R. M. Hare, *Freedom and Reason* (Oxford, 1963), pp. 100–102.

himself to any mathematical statements – so moral argument is impossible with a man who will make no moral judgements at all, or – which for practical purposes comes to the same thing – makes only judgements of indifference.[11]

Turning one's theoretical back on the amoralist as Hare does, will not really solve the problem. It is really an admission that the sceptic has won. General scepticism always defeats foundationalism no matter how sophisticated its form. For Bradley the amoralist is at best deceiving himself if he thinks he can opt out of morality. Morality is not a game like chess in which we can shed morality, like a snake sheds its skin, because we are not interested. It is an intrinsic part of our humanity. We cannot avoid making ourselves into a person of a certain kind. To a certain extent we choose our virtues and vices. The amoralist chooses to be a person who buries his head in the self-deceptive quick sand of moral indifference. That certainly is more his problem than ours but this does not make a moral ostrich less irrational. In *Ethical Studies* Bradley argued that morality and self-realization are co-extensive:

> It is a moral duty to realize everywhere the best self, which for us in this sphere is an ideal self; and, asking what morality is, we so far must answer, it is coextensive with the self-realization of the ideal self in and by us. (*ES* 219)

For Bradley the duty of self-perfection is all pervasive, but this does not mean that all of our choices are moral choices. Some of our choices, such as which shoes we are going to wear, are morally indifferent. Bradley recognizes a sphere of moral indifference in life, but this only makes sense within the wider context of the moral universe.

We cannot treat the sphere as whole with moral indifference. There is no way to avoid making fundamental moral choices, so we cannot avoid morality, and general scepticism is shown to be practically incoherent.[12]

---

[11] R. M. Hare, *Freedom And Reason*, p. 101.

[12] See my *Bradley's Moral Psychology*, pp. 217–21.

Moral scepticism is also theoretically incoherent. If we deny that moral judgements have any truth value we are implying that we know enough about the moral universe to be able to say so. To deny that something has value presupposes that you have a standard for judging the value of things. For Bradley all negative judgements presuppose a positive ground, so all forms of general scepticism are theoretically incoherent (PL 125). Foundationalism was bound to fail because it starts by taking the general moral sceptic too seriously. For the foundationalist, only necessary moral truth or the undeniable feeling of pleasure and pain can defeat the moral sceptic. Only these indubitable moral absolutes would do. Bradley, however, like all idealists, holds that it is the project of foundationalism, the search for moral absolutes which is wrong, and not simply the answers which Kantians or utilitarians have provided. Because Bradley is a coherentist in epistemology the whole problem of moral scepticism has to be redefined. The problem of scepticism becomes that of particular moral scepticism which makes sense only within the context of a developing moral tradition. This is a healthy scepticism which stimulates moral growth, not the pathological kind which leads to the destruction of the moral life.

Bradley, like MacIntyre, also rejects radical individualism, the view that individuals are ontologically and morally independent of the social groups to which they belong. The theory implies that society and morality are not natural to man. They are artificial constructs imposed on the individual, which restrict and diminish our natural freedoms and rights. Indeed some of Bradley's most vitriolic criticisms are directed against this theory. He says:

> In short, man is a social animal; he is real only because he is social, and can realize himself only because it is as social that he realizes himself. The mere individual is a delusion of theory; and the attempt to realize it in practice is the starvation and mutilation of human nature, with total sterility or the creation of monsters. (ES 174).

Nowhere did he express this hostility more intensely than in his 1894 article 'Some Remarks on Punishment' (CE 149–64).

Here Bradley is equally antagonistic towards the theory of individual rights, the view that:

> The individual may be taken, as such, to have positive and negative rights not derived from another world, but still inhering in him independent of his place in the community.
>
> (CE 157)

The view that the individual has rights which are absolute universal and natural, belonging to the individual simply because they are human beings, and independent of some community is, Bradley thinks, ontologically false, intellectually incoherent and contrary to fact. It is ontologically false because rights only exist in communities. To say 'X has a right to Y' only makes sense if it means, 'X has a right to Y in community A'. In the current debate over the right to abortion in Canada, people who defend the pro-life/anti-abortion position, often base their criticisms of the pro-choice/pro-abortion position on the ground that the foetus has a right to life which abortion denies.

But this argument is clearly invalid because to claim that a human foetus has a right to life simply because it is human cannot be defended. To say: 'A human foetus has a right to life' only makes sense if it means something like, 'A human foetus has a right to life in community A', eg. 'A human foetus has a right to life in Canada'. In Canada a human foetus in fact does not have a right to life hence the claim to a right to life, if made in a Canadian context, is false.[13] According to Bradley, to claim that a foetus has right to life simply because it is human, is not just false but nonsense, because no such rights exist:

> But both the individual and his rights, in this sense, certainly do not belong to the human world, and hence, unless they exist in some other world, they are existent nowhere.
>
> (CE 158)

---

[13] See, for example, *You and the Law*, 3rd ed. (Canada: Reader's Digest Association, 1984), pp. 464–5.

The theory of individual rights is also incoherent because absolute rights must surely conflict and the theory is incapable of providing a way of arbitrating between these opposing claims:

> But the rights of these supposed individuals, once placed in a community, must necessarily collide, and all attempts to avoid this collision are idle. And to find a rational ground on which mutual interference is here legitimate, and there unlawful, is once more impossible. (CE 158)

For example, should the rights of the mother take precedence over the rights of the foetus with respect to abortion in situations where her life is also threatened? If both rights are absolute, as the theory of individual rights maintains, how can we choose between them? One might make appeals to the principle of double effect, as some defenders of natural rights do. If saving the mother involves the doctor directly killing the foetus, whereas saving the foetus does not involve the doctor directly killing the mother, then the doctor should save the foetus, and let the mother die. The death of the mother then would be a foreseeable but unintended consequence of the doctors actions in saving the foetus, hence he is not violating the rights of the mother.[14] This solution however is clearly ad hoc and its recommendations arbitrary. They imply that moral agents are not morally responsible for the unintended consequences of their actions. But if this were true we could not make sense of the concepts like that of criminal negligence, in which doctors are held responsible for the unintended consequences of their actions.

The theory is also contrary to fact because in practice, as Bradley points out, the community frequently and justifiably overrides individual rights for the welfare of the community as a whole:

> The welfare of the community is the end and is the ultimate standard. And over its members the right of the moral organism is absolute. Its duty and its right is to dispose of these members as it seems to it best. (CE 158)

---

[14] See Alan Donagan's useful discussion of the doctrine of double effect in *The Theory of Morality* (Chicago, 1979), chap. 5.

Neither the person, nor the property of the individual, are sacred. In the name of the general welfare the state confiscates private property, it limits individual freedom, it conscripts citizens into the military, and it punishes the innocent as well as the guilty. We incarcerate the criminally insane indefinitely in hospitals. With the process of civil commitment, we incarcerate people, thought to be mentally unstable, to prevent them from harming others or themselves:

> To remove the innocent is unjust, but it is not, perhaps, therefore in all cases wrong. Their removal, on the contrary, will be right if the general welfare demands it.
>
> (CE 155)

The recognition that in certain cases punishing the innocent can be justified for the general welfare is a radical modification of the theory of punishment Bradley developed in *Ethical Studies*.[15] There he argued for a synthesis of Kantian retributive and utilitarian social utility theories, with certain axioms of retributivism being elemental.

Bradley maintained that an adequate theory of punishment required acceptance of the common-sense notion of the necessary connection between guilt and punishment. The two fundamental moral axioms of the retributive theory: only the guilty ought to be punished, and never punish the innocent, must be retained. For Bradley we have no right to punish anyone unless they have done something wrong. Guilt is a necessary condition of punishment. But he did not think that guilt was a sufficient condition of punishment, as traditional retributivism held. Utilitarian considerations could legitimately enter the picture when deciding the nature of the punishment or whether to carry it out or not. Utilitarian theories which argued that punishment could only be justified by appeal to the public good, ie. deterred others from committing similar crimes or reformed criminals so that they ceased to be public menaces, could not be basic.

---

[15] ES 26–33. See also my discussions of Bradley's theory of punishment, *Bradley's Moral Psychology*, pp. 61–4.

Utilitarianism, Bradley argued, turned punishment into treatment, used persons as mere means to the good of others, and perhaps most importantly, allowed the punishment of the innocent in theory, if not in practice. Consideration of the general good could enter the picture once guilt had established the right to punish but could never override the basic retributive axioms.

In his later view Bradley says that he is modifying the retributive basis of his earlier theory but that he is not abandoning it (*CE* 153). He will retain as elemental the first or positive axiom: only the guilty ought to be punished.

This remains a necessary but not a sufficient condition for punishment. But he will cease to treat the second or negative axiom: never punish the innocent, as absolute. In certain cases this axiom can be overridden by appeal to the general good. This is necessary, he believes, because of the practical difficulties in establishing responsibility. It may appear that by making concessions to the notions of diminished responsibility and civil commitment Bradley has more or less abandoned retributivism. Perhaps the two axioms of the original theory are such that they mutually imply each other, so that you cannot assent to one without assenting to the other. To be innocent surely means not to have done anything wrong. So, if we punish the innocent surely we are punishing people who are not guilty? This analysis of the concept of innocence however appears to be too narrow, for we often say of someone that they did something wrong but are not responsible. Perhaps they are guilty by reason of insanity.

How we justify ascriptions of responsible is a complex and difficult question, the answer to which is not clear. It is just this complexity that led Bradley to correctly modify his earlier theory of punishment, rather than abandon it completely. He is concerned about cases in which people do harm to others or who are a clear threat to others but who are not clearly responsible for what they do and so are innocent in this sense. Do we kill the insane sniper who is gunning down the innocents in a shopping mall? Bradley would suggest that after we tried everything else perhaps this is what we ought to do.

However, in spite of his savage assault on the theory of individual rights, it would be wrong to infer that Bradley is against individual rights, that he thinks that the individual has no valid claims against the community. Bradley is primarily arguing against a methodology for establishing rights, and the ontological doctrines about individuals and the community it presupposes, not against the notion of individual rights as such. In the first place, for Bradley, the community does not exist apart from its members, hence the welfare of the community can only be realized in its members. The welfare of the community is the same as the self-realization of its members, the happiness and perfection of the individuals who compose it. Self-realization requires individual rights:

> The welfare of this whole exists, of course, nowhere outside the individuals, and the individuals have rights and duties as members in the whole. (CE 150)

A system of individual rights will only make sense if it is developed in the context of this organic conception of community welfare. Individual rights are limited by welfare in this sense. In the second place some rights are ideal as well as real. A real right, for Bradley, is one which is recognized by a particular community. An ideal right is one which ought to be recognized in any community:

> Wherever in the world you have law you also have right and rights. These may be real or ideal. The first are the will of the state or society, the second the will of the social-ideal or the non-social ideal. (ES 208)

For example, all Canadians have a legal right to equality, not to be discriminated against on the grounds of race, colour, creed or sex, but they do not have a legal right to achieve equality by reverse discrimination against others. Canadians also have a legal right to refuse life-saving medical treatment if they so incline, but they have no legal right to aid suicide, nor to request others, including their doctors, to aid their suicide.[16] Some reformers believe that we ought to have these

---

[16] See, for example, *You and the Law*, p. 814.

rights. They are ideal rights which ought to be made real.[17] Ideal or moral rights, unlike real rights cannot be justified by an appeal to existing legislation, they must be given rational defence. Within idealist theory they can only be established by appeal to the principle of self-realization or individual perfection. The appeal to self-realization is the ultimate criterion. It is the basis on which we can establish individual rights, like the so-called right to die. It is also the basis on which we can disestablish real rights, individual or communal, which ought not to exist, like the practice of capital punishment perhaps.

The debate over ideal rights represents a higher level of moral thought for Bradley and it takes logical precedence over discussions concerning real rights. Ideal rights override real rights. Moral rights override legal rights.[18]

Bradley's views on which rights ought to exist and which ought not are perhaps more conservative than many of us would currently accept. For example, Bradley defended the state's right to use capital punishment, although he did so partly because he thought it less barbarous that life imprisonment in a nineteenth-century British prison. He certainly seemed unsympathetic to the rights of criminals and the insane. He appeared to support selective human breeding of some sort, and entertained the idea of placing limits on the right of the individual to procreate:

> I am oppressed by the ineffectual cruelty of our imprisonments. I am disgusted by the inviolable sanctity of the noxious lunatic. The right of the individual to spawn without restriction his diseased offspring on the community, the duty of the state to rear wholesale and without limit an unselected progeny – such duties and rights are to my mind a sheer outrage on Providence. A society that can endure such things will merit the degeneracy it courts. (*CE* 163–4)

These reflections will not sit well with those of us who occupy the liberal left of the political spectrum but we should

---

[17] See for example Derek Humphry, *Final Exit* (The Hemlock Society, 1991).

[18] See my *Bradley's Moral Psychology*, pp. 221–34.

remember that Bradley was a man of his time. Even John Stuart Mill defended capital punishment.[19] We also need to remind ourselves that properly balancing the rights of the individual and the community is not an easy task.

Think of the following hypothetical examples which reflect recent cases in Canada. A serial child molester and killer is paroled after serving only a minimum of his prison term and shortly after molests and kills two more children before he is recaptured and brought to justice. A rapist is released to a halfway house where he can come and go with relative ease, to facilitate his reintegration into society. Shortly after he rapes and kills a young women who lived in an apartment near the halfway house. A woman repeatedly appears in court for abusing her offspring and is suspected in the death of two of them. She is pregnant in her latest appearance. The judge is so horrified with the case that he suggests the state perhaps should limit the right to procreate in certain cases.

It was the abuse of individual rights rather than the rights themselves which abhorred Bradley. Rights in these situations appear to be privileges rather than absolute claims than can never be revoked. In any case it is not Bradley's practical proposals which are important here but his theory of rights. Bradley did not think very highly of practical ethics. He certainly did not believe that moral philosophers had a privileged position in moral affairs. And he did not think much of himself as a moral reformer:

> I'm sceptical as to the value of such a purpose of any moral philosophy, and I'm sure that my small energies would not be decently expended in the field of practical reform.
>
> (CE 163)

It might be worthwhile to take Bradley at face value here and accept that his reflections on moral methodologies are to be taken more seriously than his moral opinions. Certainly his theory of rights when understood as new theory of individual, as well as, communal rights designed to replace radical

---

[19] See J. S. Mill, 'Parliamentary Addresses', *Collected Works* (University of Toronto Press).

individualism, is worth taking very seriously. It certainly should be taken seriously by all idealists because idealism will not be acceptable if it cannot make its peace with the principle of individual liberty.

It is here that we may find the greatest divergence between Bradley and MacIntyre. For MacIntyre has not fully achieved this synthesis of liberty and idealism, either at the theoretical or practical level, although there are indications in his latest book on justice that he is moving in that direction.[20] Bradley, on the other hand, has achieved that synthesis at the theoretical level, if not fully at the practical.

---

[20] Alasdair MacIntyre, *Whose Justice? Which Rationality?* (Notre Dame, 1988), especially chaps. 1, 18, 19 and 20.

LIST OF CONTRIBUTORS

Leslie Armour, Professor of Philosophy, University of Ottawa, Ontario.

James Bradley, Associate Professor of Philosophy, Memorial University of Newfoundland.

Walter Creery, Professor of Philosophy, York University, Toronto, Ontario.

David Crossley, Associate Professor of Philosophy, University of Saskatchewan, Saskatoon, Saskatchewan.

Philip Dwyer, Associate Professor of Philosophy, University of Saskatchewan, Saskatoon, Saskatchewan.

Phillip Ferreira, Assistant Professor of Philosophy, Kutztown University, Pennsylvania.

Paul D. Forster, Assistant Professor of Philosophy, University of Ottawa, Ontario.

Nicholas Griffin, Professor of Philosophy, McMaster University, Hamilton, Ontario.

Lorne Maclachlan, Professor of Philosophy, Queen's University, Kingston, Ontario.

Don MacNiven, Professor of Philosophy, York University, Toronto, Ontario.

Lionel Rubinoff, Professor of Philosophy, Trent University, Peterborough, Ontario.

Notes on Contributors

William Sweet, Associate Professor of Philosophy, St Francis Xavier University, Antigonish, Nova Scotia.

Elizabeth Trott, Associate Professor of Philosophy, Ryerson Polytechnical University, Toronto, Ontario.

Michael Walsh, 114 St. Leonard's Avenue, Toronto, Ontario.

Fred Wilson, Professor of Philosophy, University of Toronto, Ontario.